Geopolitics and Energy Security Policies in the Caspian Region

Geopolitics and International Relations

Series Editor

David Criekemans (*University of Antwerp*)

VOLUME 5

The titles published in this series are listed at *brill.com/geop*

Geopolitics and Energy Security Policies in the Caspian Region

By

Justyna Misiągiewicz

BRILL | NIJHOFF

LEIDEN | BOSTON

Originally published in hardback in 2024.

Cover illustration: Provinciarum persicarum Kilaniae nempe Chirvaniae Dagestaniae aliarumque vicinarum regionum partium (1728) by Johann Christoph Homann. Public Domain, retrieved from Wikimedia. https://commons.m.wikimedia.org/wiki/File:Provinciarum_persicarum_Kilaniae_nempe _Chirvaniae_Dagestaniae_aliarumque_vicinarum_regionum_partium.jpg

The Library of Congress Cataloging-in-Publication Data is available online at https://catalog.loc.gov
LC record of the hardback edition available at https://lccn.loc.gov/2024012174

Typeface for the Latin, Greek, and Cyrillic scripts: "Brill". See and download: brill.com/brill-typeface.

ISSN 2666-6669
ISBN 978-90-04-73834-8 (paperback, 2025)
ISBN 978-90-04-69760-7 (hardback)
ISBN 978-90-04-69761-4 (e-book)
DOI 10.1163/9789004697614

This book is printed on acid-free paper and produced in a sustainable manner.

Contents

List of Figures and Tables   VII
List of Maps   X
Abbreviations   XI

Introduction   1

1   **Specificity of Energy Security Policy**   15
    1   Energy Security Policy Actors   16
        1.1   *States*   16
        1.2   *Non-state Actors*   21
    2   The Object of the Energy Security Policy   28
        2.1   *Energy Security as an Area of International Security
            Research*   28
        2.2   *The Essence and Dimensions of Energy Security*   42
        2.3   *Threats to Energy Security*   50
    3   Conclusion   68

2   **The Caspian Region as a Space for Energy Security Policies**   70
    1   Criteria for Distinguishing the Caspian Region   71
    2   Legal Status of the Caspian Basin Region   77
        2.1   *Joint Use*   79
        2.2   *International Sea*   79
        2.3   *Internal Lake*   80
    3   The Geopolitical and Geoeconomic Position of the Caspian
        Region   91
    4   Energy Potential of the Caspian Region   106
    5   International Conflicts in the Caspian Region   114
    6   Conclusion   130

3   **Energy Security Policy Actors in the Caspian Region**   132
    1   Energy Security Policies of the Caspian Region States   133
        1.1   *Republic of Azerbaijan*   133
        1.2   *Republic of Kazakhstan*   145
        1.3   *Turkmenistan*   153
        1.4   *Russian Federation*   160
        1.5   *Islamic Republic of Iran*   169

2   The Caspian Region in the Energy Security Policies of External
     Actors   176
     2.1   *People's Republic of China*   176
     2.2   *Republic of Turkey*   184
     2.3   *European Union*   192
3   Conclusion   204

4   **Geopolitical Routes and Policies to Transport Fossil Fuels as a
     Reflection of Energy Interdependence**   209
     1   The Northern Route of Fossil Fuel Exports from the Caspian
          Region   212
     2   The Western Route of Fossil Fuel Exports from the Caspian
          Region   221
     3   The Southern Route of Fossil Fuel Exports from the Caspian
          Region   231
     4   The Eastern Route of Fossil Fuel Exports from the Caspian
          Region   237
     5   Conclusion   246

5   **Perspectives for Energy Security Policies in the Caspian Region**   249
     1   New Challenges of the International Energy Market   250
     2   The Importance of the Caspian Region in the Context of Future
          Challenges to the Global Energy Market   262
     3   Conclusion   271

Conclusions   273

References   281
Index   313

Figures and Tables

Figures

1.1   Relations between energy security actors   17
1.2   Objectives of the national energy policy   18
1.3   Securitization of energy security   31
1.4   Risk factors in the Caspian energy market   42
1.5   Relationships between different dimensions of energy security   45
1.6   Consumption of energy resources, 1971 and 2018   52
1.7   Change in energy demand, 2020   53
1.8   Energy demand by region, 2018   53
1.9   Electricity production in OECD countries   54
1.10   Production of energy resources   56
1.11   Change in global hydrocarbon production   57
1.12   Global energy production (%)   58
1.13   Major energy producers in OECD countries   59
1.14   Changes in energy demand, 1900–2020   66
1.15 CO_2 emissions from energy sector activities, 1900–2020   68
3.1   Energy consumption in Azerbaijan   137
3.2   Pillars of the energy policy strategy of Kazakhstan   147
3.3   Energy policy objectives of Kazakhstan   147
3.4   Energy mix in Kazakhstan   153
3.5   Energy consumption in China   179
3.6   Turkey's energy policy priorities   187
3.7   Strategy of the Ministry of Energy and Natural Resources   188
3.8   Scenario of competitive transit through Turkey   191
3.9   EU's position in the global energy consumption   193
3.10   Consumption of energy resources in the EU   194
3.11   Main gas importers into the EU, 2017   196
3.12   Main oil importers into the EU, 2017   196
3.13   Main coal importers into the EU, 2017   197

Tables

1.1   Market position and financial resources of the largest energy corporations
       (USD billions)   25
1.2   Methodology of energy security research study—the MOSES model   34
1.3   Methodology of energy security research study—the ERIA model   35

1.4   The main debates and theses present in the literature concerning energy
        security   40
1.5   Main threats of energy security   51
2.1   The stages of introducing regulations on the status of the Caspian Sea   88
2.2   Steps in the implementation of the CEP and the Tehran Convention   89
2.3   Energy potential of the Caspian region countries   110
2.4   Actors involved in the Caspian energy market   111
3.1   Azerbaijan oil production (barrels per day)   137
3.2   Natural gas production in Azerbaijan (billions m³)   137
3.3   Export directions for gas from Azerbaijan (billions m3)   144
3.4   Kazakhstan oil reserves (billions barrels)   147
3.5   Kazakhstan gas reserves (billions m3)   148
3.6   Oil production in Kazakhstan (bbl/day)   148
3.7   Natural gas production in Kazakhstan (billions m3)   148
3.8   Challenges of energy security policy in Kazakhstan   149
3.9   Major foreign business involved in the Kazakhstan energy sector   150
3.10   Kazakhstan oil exports (billion barrels per day)   152
3.11   Kazakhstan gas reserves (billions m3)   152
3.12   Turkmenistan gas reserves (billions m3)   154
3.13   Turkmenistan oil reserves (millions barrels)   155
3.14   Oil production in Turkmenistan (bbl/day)   155
3.15   Gas production in Turkmenistan (billions m3)   157
3.16   Turkmenistan gas exports (billions m3)   157
3.17   Oil reserves in Russia (billions barrels)   163
3.18   Natural gas reserves in Russia (billions m3)   163
3.19   Oil production in Russia (barrels per day)   164
3.20   Gas production in Russia (billions m3)   165
3.21   Russia's oil exports (billions barrels)   166
3.22   Gas exports by Russia (billions m3)   167
3.23   Production and consumption of oil in China   178
3.24   Production and consumption of gas in China   178
3.25   Oil import sources in China (%)   179
3.26   Gas import sources in China (%)   180
3.27   Consumption of energy resources in Turkey (million tonnes of oil
        equivalent - mtoe)   185
3.28   Gas Consumption in Turkey (billions m3)   185
3.29   Gas imports in Turkey (billions m3)   186
3.30   Turkey's oil imports (billion barrels per day)   186
3.31   Turkey's energy policy goals   188
3.32   Energy savings in Turkey (in tonnes of oil equivalent—toe)   189
3.33   EU's reliance on imports of energy   195

3.34   EU Energy Security Strategy   199
3.35   EU energy objectives   199
3.36   Pillars of the energy union strategy   200
4.1   States and companies participating in the production and transit of
        Caspian oil   210
5.1   Environmental impact of individual energy sources   256

Maps

1.1   "Bottlenecks" in the transport of energy resources   62
2.1   The Caspian region: between Central Asia and the Caucasus   73
2.2   The division of the Caspian Basin by the center line   81
2.3   The division of the Caspian Sea according to the 2018 Caspian Sea
        Convention   85
2.4   The Nagorno-Karabakh conflict area   119
2.5   The Nagorno-Karabakh conflict area after the entry into force of the truce of
        November 10, 2020   128
3.1   Oil and gas fields in Azerbaijan   138
4.1   Caspian Pipeline Consortium   217
4.2   Baku–Supsa pipeline   223
4.3   Southern Gas Corridor   227
4.4   Trans-Caspian Pipeline project   230

Abbreviations

ACG	Azeri, Chirag, Gunashli
AIOC	Azerbaijan International Operating Company
AKP	Adalet ve Kalkınma Partisi (Justice and Development Party)
BOTAŞ	Boru Hatları İle Petrol Taşıma Anonim Şirketi (Oil and Gas Corporation in Turkey)
BP	British Petroleum
BRUA	Bulgarian–Romanian–Hungarian–Austrian pipeline
BSEC	Black Sea Economic Cooperation
BTC	Baku–Tbilisi–Ceyhan pipeline
BTE	Baku–Tbilisi–Erzurum pipeline
CAC	Central Asia–Center pipeline
CACO	Central Asia Cooperation Organization
CAREC	Central Asia Regional Economic Cooperation Program
CEP	Caspian Environmental Program
CGE	Computable General Equilibrium
CIPCO	Caspian International Petroleum Company
CIS	Commonwealth of Independent States
CNODC	China National Oil & Gas Exploration & Development Corp.
CNOOC	China National Offshore Oil Corporation
CNPC	China National Petroleum Corporation
COPRI	Copenhagen Peace Research Institute
CPC	Caspian Pipeline Consortium
CROS	Caspian Sea Republic's Oil SWAP
CSIS	Center for Strategic and International Studies
CSRK	Committee of Statistics of the Republic of Kazakhstan
DCFTA	Deep and Comprehensive Free Trade Areas
EAPC	Euro-Atlantic Partnership Council
EAPI	Energy Architecture Performance Index
EBRD	European Bank for Reconstruction and Development
ECO	Economic Cooperation Organization
ECOTA	Economic Cooperation Organization Trade Agreement
EDB	Eurasian Development Bank
EEZ	Exclusive Economic Zone
EGF	European Geopolitical Forum
EIA	United States Energy Information Administration
EITI	Extractive Industries Transparency Initiative
EIU	Economist Intelligence Unit
ENP	European Neighbourhood Policy

EPCA	Enhanced Partnership and Cooperation Agreements
ERIA	Economic Research Institute for ASEAN and East Asia
ESI	Energy Sustainable Index
ESIA	Environmental and Social Impact Assessment
EurAsEC	Eurasian Economic Community
FTA	Free Trade Agreement
GKOA	Nagorno-Karabagh Autonomous Oblast
GUAM	Organization for Democracy and Economic Development
IEA	International Energy Agency
IEP	International Energy Programme
IFC	International Finance Corporation
IMF	International Monetary Fund
IMU	Uzbekistani Islamist Movement
INOGATE	International Oil and Gas Transport to Europe
IOC	International Oil Companies
IPAP	Individual Partnership Action Plan
KCBC	Kazakhstan-China Business Council
KCO	Kazakhstan Operating Company
KEGOC	Kazakhstan Electricity Grid Operating Company
KMG	KazMunaiGaz
MLG	Multi-Level-Governance
MOSES	Model of Short-Term Energy Security
NACC	North Atlantic Cooperation Council
NATO	North Atlantic Treaty Organization
NCOC	North Caspian Operating Company
NDRC	National Development and Reform Commission
NEA	National Energy Administration
NIGC	National Iranian Gas Company
NIOC	National Iranian Oil Company
NRF	NATO Response Force
OCST	Collective Security Treaty Organization
OECD	Organisation for Economic Co-operation and Development
OEF	Operation Enduring Freedom
OKIOC	Offshore Kazakhstan International Operating Company
OOC	Oman Oil Company
OPEC	Organization of the Petroleum Exporting Countries
OSCE	Organization for Security and Co-operation in Europe
OSW	Centre for Eastern Studies
PCA	Partnership and Cooperation Agreements
PDVSA	Petroleum of Venezuela
PfP	Partnership for Peace

PISM	Polish Institute of International Affairs
PSA	Production Sharing Agreements
RGK	Nagorno-Karabakh Republic
RSC	Regional Security Complex
RSSC SG	Regional Stability in the South Caucasus Study Group
SASAC	State Commission for the Supervision of Property and Administration
SCO	Shanghai Cooperation Organization
SLEGM	Single Liberalized Electricity and Gas Market
SOCAR	State Oil Company of the Republic of Azerbaijan
SPCIB	State Petroleum and Chemical Industry Bureau
SPECA	United Nations Special Economic Program for Central Asia
TACIST	Technical Assistance to the Commonwealth of Independent States
TANAP	Trans-Anatolian Pipeline
TAP	Trans-Adriatic Pipeline
TAPI	Turkmenistan–Afghanistan–Pakistan–India pipeline
TASIM	Trans-Eurasian Information Super Highway
TPAO	Turkish Petroleum Corporation
TPES	Total Primary Energy Supply
TRACECA	Transport Corridor Europe–Caucasus–Central Asia
UNCTAD	United Nations Conference on Trade and Development
UNDP	United Nations Development Programme
UNEP	United Nations Environment Programme
UNFCCC	United Nations Framework Convention on Climate Change
USDoE	US Department of Energy
WEC	World Energy Council

Introduction

In contemporary international relations, the problem of energy security is becoming a key issue. Access to energy resources is the existential need of every country, conditioning economic and social development. In such a situation, states try to construct long-term energy security policies aimed at ensuring a smooth supply of energy resources or—in the case of producers—diversifying export routes and making the greatest possible profits from the sale of energy carriers. Energy interdependence is a key determinant of contemporary international relations, where not only states but also non-state actors are involved. Under these conditions, a dialogue between energy-resource producers, consumers, and states whose geopolitical location allows to play a transit role, is necessary. Serious threats to energy security include technological and economic barriers in the mining industry and the slow but inevitable process of nonrenewable resources depletion. As global demand for energy commodities increases, producers are forced to invest more in exploration, while consumers are seeking to pursue a policy of supply diversification.

The research question analyzed by this book is the analysis of energy security policies of states in the specific geoenergetic and geostrategic aspects of the Caspian region, considering the variability of its security environment. In terms of the actors, the analysis includes the energy security policies of the Caspian region states and external actors. In terms of the object, it includes the Caspian region's energy resources and activities in the development of its energy infrastructure.

Energy security is the basic analytical category for the study and research carried out for the book. From the authorial viewpoint, and considering the context of the Caspian region, this category defines the scope and specific character of research carried out for the book and its relation to security studies. It is an important element of the epistemic layer of the conducted research of the book. On the other hand, in terms of social reality and ontology, energy security is a foreign policy objective, an international value, and a dynamic process. There are various types of actors involved—from individuals to large social groups, institutions, states, nations, and international systems—and this impacts their needs. Therefore, the energy security policy aims to protect the state and society against numerous threats, the multitude of actors involved, unpredictability, and complexity that result from the polyarchic international environment. Threats to energy security are dynamic, changing, and evolving. However, there is a threat of interruption of the supply of energy carriers

© JUSTYNA MISIĄGIEWICZ, 2024 | DOI:10.1163/9789004697614_002

(resulting in the destruction of social life at the political, economic, social, and environmental levels).

Capturing the specificity of energy security is very difficult due to the complexity of the global energy market and the fact that it is a relatively new concept in international relations. Energy security policy results not only from objective economic premises but also from the balance of political power. The variety of definitions of this concept makes it difficult to determine clear boundaries of the meaning of energy security, both in theoretical and practical dimensions.

The analysis of energy security policies in the Caspian region is a challenging research task. This is because of the specific development of international relations in this region and the evolution of its importance in the context of the functioning of the global energy market. Due to its special geopolitical location in Central Eurasia and at the junction at the world's largest trading routes, the region is gaining in importance, both politically and economically in contemporary international relations, and becoming a place where of actors involved also satisfy the need for energy security.

The Caspian region has been exploited for energy since the mid-19th century. From that time, it has been one of the richest areas in energy resources. About half of the world's oil resources has been extracted in the Baku area in Azerbaijan. This impressive level of production was possible due to the investments of the brothers Robert, Ludvig and Alfred Nobel and Royal Dutch Shell. They enabled Russia to exploit the Caspian deposits. Caspian oil had a strategic value during both world wars. In the 1950s, Russia shifted its energy investments from the Caspian region after oil resources were discovered in the Urals and Siberia. Such a policy limited mining in the area.

The Caspian region opened up to global energy markets only as a result of geopolitical transformations after the end of the Cold War in 1990. In the second half of the 1990s, the international community became aware of the energy potential of the Caspian region states. It was estimated at the time that the world's largest potential oil and gas resources were located here. After the fall of the Soviet Union, the newly established states of Central Asia and the Caucasus opened up to foreign investment and became significant players in the global energy markets. Given the political instability in the Middle East, as well as the shift of global energy production from north to south of the world, Caspian resources played an increasingly important role in the diversification of global energy supplies. The increase in energy investments contributed to the political stability and economic development of the emerging Caspian states on the ruins of the Soviet Union.

According to the British Petroleum Statistical Review of World Energy, oil and gas resources in the Caspian region (excluding Russia and Iran) account for approximately 3% of the global resources (BP, 2020). All of this makes the Caspian region increasingly attractive for foreign actors, especially because this market has not yet been fully penetrated by investors.

The terminological difficulties and various definitions of the word "region" used in the literature make it necessary to specify the meaning of this term along with its spatial range. A region can be defined as a certain compact area, homogeneous in terms of certain criteria. This means that, theoretically, there is an infinite number of regions, depending on the adopted criteria. Furthermore, each of the systems of separating space seems to be legitimate and debatable at the same time. The Caspian region can be distinguished by conditions that suggest certain common elements, characteristic of its constituent actors. The value of the Caspian reservoir and its energy resources unite the interests of the states that have a coastline here. So, the Caspian region should include Russia, Azerbaijan, Iran, Turkmenistan, and Kazakhstan. The region is surrounded by nuclear powers: China, India, Pakistan, and NATO member Turkey. Having taken into account the political and economic instability that emerged in Central Asia and the Caucasus after the fall of the Soviet Union, Zbigniew Brzeziński referred to the region as the "Eurasian Balkans" (Brzeziński, 1999, p. 125). The functioning of regional cooperation in economic, political, and cultural dimensions existing between actors is a key issue here. This dominant approach to defining regions and regionalisms is, however, useful for analyzing the center of regions that share values, institutions, and integrative processes. Nonetheless, the integration potential of regionalization processes is weakening in the peripheral area of the region in proportion to the distance from the center, where the regionalization process was initiated, promoted, and monitored. The existence of border regions requires a new approach, and their specificity is difficult to grasp. In contrast to the center of the region, the "intermediaries" or border regions can be referred to as "peak" or "on the edge" (Altunisik & Tanrisever, 2018, p. 260). The conceptualization of border regions as "peak regions" enables the study of simultaneity, complementarity, and conflicting regionalization processes in the Caspian region.

The Caspian Sea is an area characterized by numerous geopolitical, legal, economic and environmental challenges related to the exploitation of energy resources. The area has been affected by conflicts between coastal states over access to resource deposits and the division of the seabed. It is also a closed reservoir with no access to the ocean, so a fundamental problem and the object of energy security policies is the transit of energy resources to global markets overland via pipelines. Many transport routes now operate have the chance to become even more important in the future. Iran could play the role of the main transit state for Caspian energy, but such an option is unacceptable to the United States due to sanctions related to the nuclear program that the Iranian government established. The expansion of the pipeline infrastructure across the territory of Russia will increase the country's superpower role in the region of Central Asia and the Caucasus, making the concept of "near abroad" a reality. China is currently becoming the largest global importer of energy resources and is looking for suppliers in the Caspian region. Therefore, the Eastern route of oil and gas transit is becoming a key challenge, both for the states of the Caspian region and for international energy companies. An important development is the expansion of the Western transit route for Caspian fossil fuels to European markets, bypassing Russia. Today, the European Union (EU), as a key global importer of energy resources, is looking for new oil and gas suppliers in the region.

Oil and gas extraction and transport in the Caspian region is currently a field of geopolitical competition between states and international companies. Thus, the Caspian region plays an increasingly important role in contemporary international relations in the economic, as well as political and cultural dimensions.

Given the growing consumption of energy resources on a global scale, the "Great Game" in the Caspian region will likely gain momentum. At the same time, the emerging prospect of changing the structure of consumption of energy towards the exploitation of renewable sources could reduce the geopolitical importance of the region.

The study of energy security policies in the Caspian region may therefore make a significant contribution, both to the understanding of the specificity of this area and to the explanation and understanding of its importance in the evolution of the contemporary energy market.

The main research objective of the monograph is to analyze, in accordance with selected theoretical and methodological assumptions, the energy security policies of the states, both inside and outside the Caspian region, in the context of its geopolitical importance in contemporary international relations. The following specific study objectives have also been distinguished:

1. analysis of the essence and specificity of energy security policy;
2. analysis of energy security policies of the Caspian region;
3. analysis of the geo-energetic and geostrategic space of the Caspian region;
4. identification of prospects for the implementation of energy infrastructure projects in the Caspian region; and
5. analysis of the interdependencies between actors who define the shape and future energy market functioning in the Caspian region.

The issues outlined above provide a premise for undertaking research aimed at solving the problem and answering the main questions of: how, and under what conditions, do energy security policies evolve in the Caspian region in the context of its growing geopolitical position? To solve the research problem, several detailed questions were also posed:

1. What is the character of the security environment in the Caspian region?
2. What are the interdependencies of energy security policies in the Caspian region?
3. What is the prospect of developing energy security policies in the Caspian region?
4. What determines the evolution of energy security policies in the Caspian region?

The monograph has verified four research hypotheses. First, the geo-energetic position of the Caspian region, conditioned by political, economic, and social instability makes it largely susceptible to the influence of external players. The weakness of states undergoing transformation, experiencing international conflicts, and threats posed by the instability of the international environment are not conducive to intraregional integration.

Second, the evolution of energy security policies in the Caspian region and the prospect of their development largely results from the relationships in the global energy market. Nowadays, it is very turbulent and uncertain mainly because of the escalation of the Russian war in Ukraine. It is still unclear what the new energy deal will be and the role of the Caspian region in this context. We can anticipate that Caspian oil and gas could play a greater role in the global energy market as an alternative source of energy for Europe. Simultaneously, the transformation of the energy system towards renewable resources will be a great challenge for energy security policies in the region.

Third, the implementation of pipeline projects from the Caspian region is currently an enormous challenge, both in economic and geopolitical terms. Increasing competition for export routes for energy resources from the Caspian region under uncertainty about the sufficiency of supplies means that not all ambitious infrastructure projects can be implemented. The only chances for their implementation are the increase in the production of hydrocarbons in the region and favorable political circumstances.

Fourth, the importance of the Caspian region in the international energy market has evolved due to multiple geopolitical and economic conditions. The transformation of the international environment after the Cold War resulted in an increased interest of the international community in the post-Soviet Caspian states in the context of their energy potential. Both superpowers and transnational corporations saw an opportunity to pursue political and economic interests here.

The solution to the research problem undertaken in the monograph—that is to say, the determination of how and as a result of which conditions the energy security policies in the Caspian region evolve—was based on several assumptions. First, interdependencies in energy security policies determine the dynamics of international relations in the Caspian region. The possibilities of extraction and transport of fossil fuels affect not only the economic standing of states but also economic relations on a global scale because the actors of the energy market are not only states but also multiple non-sovereign actors which are increasingly involved in the production and distribution of hydrocarbons.

Second, energy security policies in the Caspian region result not only from objective economic premises but also from the balance of political forces. So the geopolitical dimension becomes a significant element in the development of the Caspian region. The Caspian region is a strategic area owing to the proximity of China, Russia and Iran, and the involvement of external actors, such as the EU or Turkey. Due to the multiple contradicting interests of these actors, the region is an area of geopolitical rivalry on a global scale.

Third, the indicator of international energy interdependence in the Caspian region is the policy of oil and gas transport. Serious threats to security in this dimension are technological and economic barriers as well as the slow but inevitable process of depletion of resources.

Fourth, the regional security environment in the Caspian region can be best understood through an analysis of phenomena in the intra-state and regional dimensions. Its dynamics is conditioned by a complex of interactions between state, sub-state, transnational, regional, and international levels of analysis.

Fifth, the Caspian region is both an opportunity and a challenge for the diversification of global energy supplies, as well as a crucial element of global energy security.

The solution to the research problem was based on the selection of appropriate theoretical and methodological assumptions.

Scholars who view geopolitics as a vehicle for integrating geography and international relations find it useful to "define geopolitics, not as a school of thought, but as mode of analysis, relating diversity in content and scale of geographical settings to exercise of political power, and identifying spatial frameworks though which power flows" (Cohen, 2003, p. 12). Geopolitical approach is understood here as the analysis of the interaction between, on the one hand, geographical settings and perspectives and, on the other, political processes. "The political processes include forces that operate at international level and those on the domestic scene that influence international behaviour" (Cohen, 2003, p. 12). Geopolitics was developed as an academic field in 1899 during the rapid changes in the global shift of power. According to David Criekemans, "At that time, the world was dominated by European powers that encompassed the whole world, in the wake of the colonial age and industrialisation. But this wave of Globalisation started to collapse; European powers were vying for geo-economic and geostrategic interests" (Criekemans, 2022, p. 61). Researchers have called geopolitics "applied Political Geography" (Criekemans, 2022, p. 62). "Geopolitics in combination with IR could offer us tools in the toolbox to better academically analyzes the various dimensions of these changes, and the implications and foreign policy options for countries but also regions around the world" (Criekemans, 2022, p. 62).

Based on research findings on the geopolitical dimension, an analysis of the Caspian region as a geo-energy space was made. Given the specific geopolitical location in the center of Eurasia and at the junction of the world's largest trade routes, this region is gaining both political and economic importance in contemporary international relations. The geopolitical (geo-energy) approach focuses on the power and structure of interests of power centers in the process of implementing the energy security policy. It can be a practical tool to describe, diagnose and forecast the current situation in the international energy market. Moreover, the concept assumes the significance of access to areas rich in energy resources, which may lead to conflicts between states.

The theory of complex interdependence, also known as the transnational approach developed by Robert Keohane and Joseph Nye, suggests that energy security policy is shaped by growing interdependence, transnational processes, and the emergence of new phenomena of a global character (Keohane, 2002). The transnational approach involves loosening traditional channels of communication between legal or sectoral systems at the intergovernmental or supranational level. The interdependence is evident in the activities of transnational actors who affect the development of energy policy or the energy sector. The interdependence in energy policy determines the dynamics of international relations in the Caspian region. The specificity of energy interdependence in the described region results from the complexity of relations between various actors involved in the implementation of energy infrastructure projects.

The concept of securitization is a very useful theoretical approach used to solve the research problem of this monograph. The Copenhagen Peace Research Institute (COPRI) emphasizes the necessity to expand the catalogue of security threats in international relations. It creates a vision of security that addresses both military and non-military threats. In this context, "security involves the survival" of a given actor (Buzan, 1997, p. 14). Threats may emerge on many levels of the actor's functioning, significantly limiting its development opportunities. The process of securitization is about defining activity as belonging to the sphere of security. The state has the authority to grant this activity specialty status. In other words, an issue becomes securitized when political or social leaders begin to talk about it as an existential threat to a given social group (Buzan, 1997). The threat, therefore, means a phenomenon or disproportion in resources that cause concern and fear. Both security threats and the objects to be secured (referent objects) are not given a priori but are created in a social process. What falls under the security domain is defined by the securitizing actor. The concept of national security evolved significantly already during the Cold War. The understanding of the concept of security expanded. Since the 1980s, as the likelihood of a global conflict decreased, the significance of the political and military dimension of security has also declined. At the same time two other dimensions of security were identified: economic and ecological.

Both of these security sectors correspond with the concept of energy security. Access to energy resources determines the development of a national economy, while their exploitation causes greenhouse gases emissions into the atmosphere, which has a fundamental impact on the condition of the natural environment. The increased importance of economic security (especially regarding energy) in international relations was related to the crisis in the United States due to the lack of oil supply liquidity and substantial dependence on oil imports in the 1970s. The dependence on oil supplies and the oil crisis linked to the embargo on this fuel imposed by the Arab states on the West can be considered a breakthrough moment in the process of conceptualizing the term "energy security." Since then, the term started to appear in national security strategies and literature. Therefore, one can conclude that the issues related to the energy market have been securitized. Currently, security is becoming multidimensional, having regard to, among other things, the political, cultural and economic conditions of the activities of both states and non-sovereign actors (Buzan et al., 1998, p. 24). "International security combines national security, but also the security of other actors in international relations [...] this means that national security interests are integrated into the broader structures of the international order" (Pietraś, 2006, p. 431). In the case of energy security, we are precisely dealing with sovereign and non-sovereign actors. The actors of the energy market are states, international organizations, transnational corporations and individual consumers. The analysis of the concept of energy security, therefore, challenges both the traditional understanding of security and the securitization theory.

In this analysis, it is worth considering realistic and idealistic approaches to energy security. Representatives of the realist strand who analyze national energy security perceive the world as a place enmeshed in a series of challenges that are becoming increasingly dangerous. They treat energy security as a component of the global power policy and a tool of foreign affairs. They believe that today's energy market is incapable of providing supplies in the long term. Thus, access to energy sources has always been and will continue to be a source of international armed conflicts. Michael T. Klare calls this system "a shrinking planet of rising powers" (Klare, 2009, p. 193, p. 44). The intensity of conflicts linked to access to energy is expected to increase. This forecast is pessimistic and is associated not only with international conflicts, but also with environmental degradation. Idealists are more optimistic. They believe that wars for territories rich in natural resources will be increasingly rare in the future. The fight for energy resources is pointless, because it is more profitable to buy oil, and the interests of buyers and sellers are not mutually exclusive. All actors in the energy market strive for stability, which is an indispensable element of profit for each of them. According to idealists, the basis of energy security is the belief in the power of the market and the concept of interdependence. They emphasize that because oil and gas are traded on a global scale, disruptions in this market will affect commodity prices all over the world. They believe in the rationality of energy market actors who strive to maximize profits. Idealists opt for the concept of the so-called "great transaction" between producers and consumers. They call for the development of multilateralism in energy security. Mechanisms ensuring collective energy security play a special role in liberal theory.

The network theory explains the specific nature of the energy system as a dynamic, multilevel, evolving phenomenon, which constitutes a structure of dispersed variable systems, combining order and randomness (Hoffmann & Magierek, 2015). A network-based approach to energy policy revolves around a broad spectrum of action models, in which preferences and specific relationships determine the scope of cooperation between the actors involved in initiating and implementing energy policies.

The study of regions and regionalisms became the object of broader interest to international relations studies after the Cold War for two reasons. First, a rise in the importance of the potential of integration in regionalization processes occurred in the face of globalization. Although the interests and policies of states are internationally diversified, regionally they face similar problems, risks, and challenges (Hurrell, 2005). Second, conceptually and analytically, in contrast to the state-centered model of international relations, the concept related to the functioning of regions constitutes an explanatory analysis model which elucidates the relationship between the state level and the broader international system. In this context, focusing on the regional level of analysis helps explain the behaviour of states. Thus, studies on the essence of regionalism are evolving. The concept of peripheral regions is a part of the studies on regionalization processes. The border zones of the regions differ from their core and even start to resemble the neighboring areas. Most often, the boundaries of regions are neither clearly defined nor clearly delineated, and do not even cover vast areas, encompassing a variety of states, nations, and cultures. Such areas illustrate the specificity of a given region or subregion in a broader context. Such regions are referred to as border regions. This concept challenges the traditional conceptualization of the region (Koter & Heffner, 1998). The concept of "peak regions" has been adapted to international relations studies by Philip Robins (2014). He created the concept of "a double gravity state." It referred to states that shaped the impact of various conflicting regional trends. Referring to this concept, one can analyze regionalism or the international policy of regionalism in border regions, such as the Caspian region.

Barry Buzan and Ole Wæver's work *Regions and Powers: The Structure of International Security* developed the concept of a regional security complex (Buzan & Wæver, 2003). This theory sought to place regions in an international structure. The scope of security autonomy of international systems stems from the level of centralization or consent to adapt a broader global security architecture.

The concept helps in the understanding of the importance of regions in the international system. It emphasizes the interdependence between the states of the region in terms of security and the key role of the neighboring states in defining the dynamics of regional security.

Benjamin Miller, in his eclectic approach, assumes that regional security dynamics stems from the specificity of states (especially the relations between the state and the nation) and the approach of forces from outside the region (Miller, 2007). The level of coherence between the aspirations of the state and society is directly proportional to a possible conflict. Also, the policy of external players towards the region may provoke tensions or motivate peace efforts. This situation is a reflection of the specificity of the security environment of the Caspian region.

The rentier state theory is part of the resource wealth theory or the "wealth paradox." A rentier state is an economic policy concept of social relations in states which derive most of their revenues from the energy sector. The theory assumes that such revenues have an impact on democratization processes, economic development, and issues related to security and social development. The revenue generated by the energy sector does not favor democracy, on the contrary, it limits it to a large extent, as it makes political elites richer, who effectively fight all forms of opposition. Many states in the world which produce important energy resources experience the "wealth paradox," the "resource curse," a situation whereby the resource wealth of a state does not translate into social and political development. Such states very often face economic and political problems related to system transformation. Richard

Auty was the first researcher to initiate the "wealth paradox" theory in *Sustaining Development in Mineral Economies: The Resource Curse Thesis*. He stated that: "new evidence suggests that not only are many developing and resource-rich countries not benefiting from their wealth, they are often worse off than countries that lack energy resources. This is the basis for thinking in terms of the wealth paradox" (Auty, 1993, p. 193). In addition, Jeffrey Sachs and Andrew Warner's studies on the economic achievements of resource-rich states in the 1970–1989 period made a significant contribution to the development of this theory. They proved the cause-and-effect relationship between energy resources and economic growth (Sachs & Warner, 1995).

There is no single theory that would comprehensively explain the specific nature of the Caspian region and its security environment. However, the theoretical dimension makes it easier to understand certain regularities that are characteristic not only of the region in question, but also of those that occur in other spaces.

Therefore, one should accept theoretical eclecticism in this respect (Sil & Katzenstein, 2010). At the same time, it is worth stressing that the realistic and geopolitical state-centered approach proved to be particularly useful in solving the research problem and in analyzing the specificity of the energy security policies and environment in the Caspian region as the energy security policies of state actors were analyzed. The theory of complex interdependence was helpful in the analysis of the complexity of relations between actors in the Caspian energy market, especially in terms of the implementation of energy infrastructure projects. The concept of securitization made it easier to define the specificity of energy security as an area of international security research. On the other hand, the concept of "peak regions" and the theory of the rentier state were particularly useful in defining the criteria for distinguishing the Caspian region and the economic specificity of the states in this region.

The methodological framework of the studies that were conducted for the book included those specific to international relations. The factor method was useful to identify, classify, and prioritize both the internal and external conditions for the construction of energy infrastructure from the Caspian region to the international market. It also became helpful to analyze the essence and specificity as well as the security environment of the Caspian region.

A comparative analysis made it possible to present the dynamics of relations between producers, consumers, and transit states in the Caspian region. The prognostic analysis proved to be helpful in the part of the work related to the prospects of energy security policy in the Caspian region. Research techniques useful in science include the analysis of literature, documents, and statistical data.

The complexity, dynamics, and specificity of the research area required familiarization with a wide range of sources and literature. The source documents used included mainly official documents published by individual states and international organizations, and official declarations made by their representatives. The documents on the strategies of energy security policies of the Caspian region states and external actors are especially noteworthy. Reference was also made to numerous statistics data published by the International Energy Agency (IEA), BP Statistical World Review of Energy, EU Energy Statistical Pocketbook, Index Mundi and CIA World Fact Book.

This monograph is a continuation of the author's long-term study of the energy security policy in the Caspian region. A search at the British Library of Political and Economic Science at the London School of Economics and Political Science in London, Jilin University in China, and the University of British Columbia in Vancouver, Canada, largely made it possible for the author to carry out the research project.

The structure of the book has been developed to solve the research problem posed and verify the hypotheses using the adopted methods. The work consists of an introduction, five chapters which contain the various stages of the research process, followed by the conclusion. The logic of the analysis is deductive: the first part of the work focuses on the theoretical dimension of the considerations and the next ones include a case study. A division into subjective and objective dimensions of the analysis was also applied.

The first chapter analyzes the subjects and the object of the energy security policy. The aim was to present the main subjects of energy security policy, namely state and non-state actors. It includes energy security as an area of international security research, along with its essence, specificity, and conditions. The chapter also presents an analysis of the development and a critical characterization of the main assumptions and trends in selected theories of energy security. This is followed by an examination of the essence and specificity of energy security, including its definition and dynamics in contemporary international relations. The threats to energy resources are discussed, including energy resource depletion and the structure of consumption and production, as well as economic, political, environmental, and infrastructural challenges.

The second chapter aims to analyze the essence and specificity of the Caspian region as a space for energy security policies. In this context, the criteria for distinguishing the Caspian region, the legal status of the Caspian Basin, the geopolitical and geoeconomic position of the Caspian region, and its energy potential have been analyzed. This region has been presented as an area of geopolitical competition on a global scale due to the proximity of China, Russia, and Iran, and the involvement of external actors, such as the US or the EU. Regionalism in this area has also been analyzed and the legal process of regulating the status of the Caspian Basin is reviewed. An important part of the monograph is the attempt to determine the energy potential of the Caspian states, which is not easy to do because of the diversity and divergence of available data. The chapter identifies the main threats to energy security in the Caspian region, which significantly reduce its position in the global energy market.

Chapter 3 analyzes the actors of energy security policies in the Caspian region, including the coastal states of the Caspian Basin and external actors such as the China, Turkey, and the European Union. The aim is to define the main priorities of energy security policies of both the Caspian region states and the external actors—with their specificity, interests, and activities.

Chapter 4 includes research findings on the matter of energy security policies in the Caspian region. The main routes of the transport of energy resources from the Caspian region to the world market have been included. The starting point for the analysis is the assumption that the main factor in international energy interdependence is energy transport policy. Pipeline routes are determined by economic considerations but are also the result of political action by states.

Chapter 5 of the monograph presents a prognostic analysis of energy security in the Caspian region. The perspectives of energy security policies in the region are analyzed, taking into consideration changes in the international energy market.

Considering the scope of the studies conducted for this book, the adopted theoretical framework, and the aim to understand and interpret energy security policies in the Caspian region, it can be concluded that the analysis presented here is pioneering, both on a national and international scale. This is because the subject matter is rarely analyzed in the academic literature. The analysis given in the book, and especially the method of solving the research problem posed for it, is not only an original approach, but also fills a gap in the discipline of international relations. In most of the literature on the subject, either the issues of the essence and specificity of energy security or the essence and specificity of the region of Central Asia or the Caucasus are taken into account. However, it is rarely deal with a comprehensive analysis and accumulation of these research areas. The originality of the study results from the fact that it combines the issues of geopolitics and energy in the context of international relations in the Caspian region. The research problem and the way it was solved undoubtedly contribute to the further development of energy security analysis. Taking into account a comprehensive analysis of the subject and object of energy security policies in the Caspian region, this innovative approach proves it to be a very interesting research field as a space for energy security policies and a field of geoenergy competition between various international relations actors. In addition, the powerful theoretical and methodological base used in the research process enabled an in-depth and comprehensive analysis of the research problem.

Critical remarks and kind advice on its entirety and individual parts had an invaluable influence on the shape and subject matter in this monograph and have been presented to the grateful author by Professor Marek Pietraś and Professor Katarzyna Marzęda-Młynarska of Maria Curie-Skłodowska University in Poland. However, most of all and from the bottom of my heart, I would like to thank my loved ones, Aleksandra and Marcin, for their patience and understanding.

Specificity of Energy Security Policy

The analysis in this part of the study focuses on the actors and the object of energy security policy. The analysis attempts to define the specific functioning of the international energy market actors. It also presents the possibilities of interpreting energy security in terms of selected theoretical approaches and definitions found in the literature.

The analysis presented is a kind of introduction to further considerations on security policies in the Caspian region. The author's goal is to capture, not only the specificity of energy security concept but also to present its various theoretical approaches and threats. It was not an easy task due to the complexity and multitude of literary sources on the subject. Thus, the following part of the work is intended to select theoretical approaches that facilitate solving the research problem of this study in the most representative way.

From an ontological perspective, the aim is to present the main sovereign and non-sovereign actors of the energy security policy. The role and position of states in the context of dynamics and dependence on the international energy market are defined. The specificity of selected international organizations and transnational corporations have also been analyzed. The epistemological approach was applied, then energy security as a field of international security research, and the essence and threats to energy security were all analyzed.

The approach presented towards the research problem shows that those specializing in international relations observe an evolution in the understanding of security, both in terms of the actors and the objects. The concept of security is no longer associated only with the activities of states in the military field. Currently, security is becoming multidimensional, having regard to, among other things, the political, cultural, and economic conditions of the activities of both states and non-sovereign actors (Buzan et al., 1998, p. 195). "No other concept of international relations packs the metaphysical punch, nor commands disciplinary power of security" (Collins, 2022, p. 1). In this sense, the broadening of the security studies "mirrors the wider blurring between international relations and political studies" (Collins, 2022, p. 1).

Interdependencies in energy security policy determine the dynamics of international relations. The possibilities of extraction and transport of energy resources affect, not only the economy of states but also economic relations on a global scale since the actors in the energy market are not only states but also numerous international enterprises, increasingly involved in the production and distribution of hydrocarbons.

Energy security results from objective economic premises but also from the balance of political forces. This is because states often use their resource potential as a foreign policy tool. The "oil shock" of the 1970s began a new era where the oil market became an instrument of political struggle between states. Since then we can also see a serious debate on national energy security. Henry Kissinger, the initiator of the Washington Energy Conference which adopted the International Energy Program (IEP) in 1974—the founding charter of the International Energy Agency (IEA)—stressed the need for importing states to work together to ensure their energy security (Kissinger, 1982, p. 906).

Serious threats to energy security include technological and economic barriers in the mining industry and the slow but inevitable process of resource depletion. As global demand for hydrocarbons rises, producers are forced to invest more in the exploration of new deposits, while consumers seek to diversify supplies.

This chapter is indispensable in the process of solving the research problem, as it explains the basic research categories, puts it in a specific theoretical framework, and takes into account the main challenges and threats that affect energy security policies in the Caspian region.

1   Energy Security Policy Actors

1.1   *States*

The main actor in energy security is the state, functioning with regard to other actors in the energy security system, such as international organizations and energy corporations, as well as individual and industrial consumers (Figure 1.1) (Młynarski, 2011).

The energy security policy is interpreted differently by states, depending on the geopolitical location, geological wealth, position in the international arena, political system, and economic development (Luft & Korin, 2009, p. 5; Yergin, 2006, p. 71).

There are variations in both the nature of state participation in international trade in energy resources and the motives behind the state actions to promote energy security. Philip Andrews-Speed divides the actors in this market into four groups:

a.   states exporting capital and technology, but importing energy (US, Japan, some EU countries);
b.   states exporting oil and gas, and technology and capital (Great Britain, Denmark, Norway, the Netherlands);

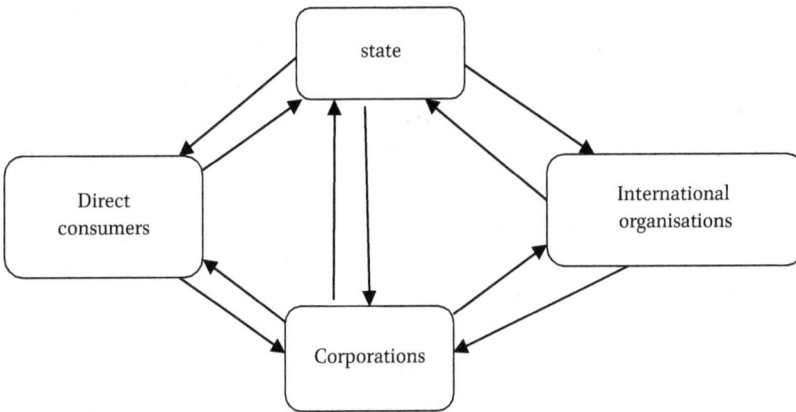

FIGURE 1.1   Relations between energy security actors
SOURCE: AUTHOR'S OWN WORK

c.   states exporting oil and gas, but importing capital and technology (Russia, OPEC states, Central Asia); and

d.   states dependent on the import of technology, capital, and energy (developing countries and new EU members).

The definition of energy security is individually interpreted by each state, depending on their position in the energy market (Luft & Korin, 2009, p. 10). For importers of energy resources, this means the security of supply and low energy resources prices. Diversification of supply sources is also essential for the energy security of consumers. Dependence on a single producer threatens to undermine import liquidity (Luft & Korin, 2009, p. 10). Therefore, states that depend on one or two energy sources attach particular importance to energy security. Their position in the energy market is very weak and they are susceptible to external pressures. Energy security is key to foreign policy for the states that are importers of energy resources. Hence, they try to maintain good relations with oil and gas producers and private companies in the energy sector.

Two categories of importers of energy resources can be mentioned: the poorest countries and highly developed countries. In the poorest countries, access to energy determines the satisfaction of essential needs. Poor countries lack a modern energy infrastructure, which leads to large energy losses and, consequently, increased demand. The highly developed countries, on the other hand, value continuous physical availability of energy resources in the right quantity, at any time, and at an acceptable price (Młynarski, 2011, p. 32). Their transmission system is more efficient, and increased investments mean that these states can use alternative energy sources. Consumers seek to reduce the risk of supply interruptions and mitigate their effects. This is made possible through the accumulation of strategic reserves and international mechanisms such as that of the IEA, which, in the event of an imbalance in supplies from abroad, distributes oil to consumer markets of the Organisation for Economic Co-operation and Development (OECD). However, despite the common goals and interests of consumer states, each of them pursues a specific energy security policy. The US is primarily an oil consumer, while Europeans are currently focusing on gas supplies. On the other hand, despite being key hydrocarbon producers, such states as Saudi Arabia, Russia, or Iran, energy security means the necessity to import processed petroleum products due to their limited refining capacity (Młynarski, 2011, p. 33). National energy security policy aims to define activities necessary to secure the current and predictable needs for energy resources, ensuring sustainable economic development (Jewell & Brutschin, 2021, p. 249). The main components of the national energy security strategy include: diversification of energy supply resources, establishing reserves of energy, limiting foreign access to the domestic energy market, or entering into international agreements (Figure 1.2) (Młynarski, 2011, p. 31; Klare, 2008, pp. 483–496). According to the guidelines of the US National Energy Policy, "concentration of world production of oil in any region is the major cause of the energy market instability, therefore production should be diversified, which will raise the profits of each actor" (Jewell & Brutschin, 2021, p. 249).

For producer states, energy security entails a constant need for energy carriers and the certainty that consumers will be able to pay the right price for energy in the long term. A serious challenge for producers of fossil fuels is the

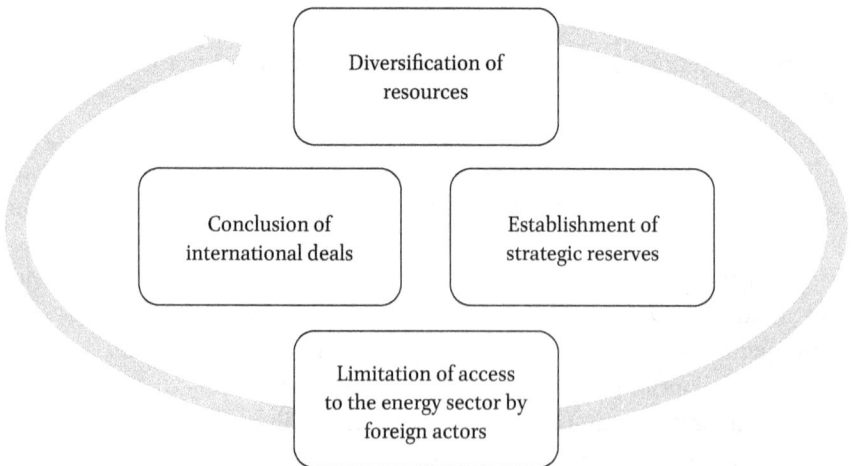

FIGURE 1.2   Objectives of the national energy policy
SOURCE: AUTHOR'S OWN WORK

need to increase the extraction and exploitation of new oil and gas fields. It often occurs that producer states simultaneously become importers of energy resources due to high domestic demand. So, meeting domestic consumption becomes a challenge of primary energy security policy for these states (Luft & Korin, 2009, p. 9). This requires modern, expensive technology, and huge investments. It is also crucial for producers to monitor export routes, especially pipelines (Sovacool, 2016). In this context, it is worth saying that the Caspian states can be included in this category.

Transit states have acquired a specific role in contemporary international relations. Their geopolitical position predisposes them to reap benefits, regardless of energy prices (Czarny, 2009, p. 47). The aim of the energy security policy of these states is to create on their territory an expanded system of pipeline infrastructures, connecting producers with consumers, the possibility of redistributing energy resources, and satisfying their own energy needs.

Quoting Jarosław Gryz:

> the current and future formula of the national energy security is tied to particular types of energy. They subordinate technologies of energy processing and distribution, and consequently both the civilian and military consumer market. In the context of national policies, energy and technological security serve as the foundation of all state efforts to project stable development and prosperity. (Gryz, 2018, p. 24)

The approach that states apply to energy security is determined both by dependent and independent variables. These variables form the basis of national energy policies (Gryz, 2018, p. 27). The dependent variables "form the instrumentation of the national and international policy" (Gryz, 2018, p. 27). The independent variables "generate objective conditions considered to project energy policy" (Gryz, 2018, p. 27). In this context, national interest is an important category as it provides a formula for social development related to the preferred form of energy (Gryz, 2018).

Energy culture in a given state is shaped by its society, its spiritual and material heritage, civilization, and historical tradition. National energy culture is related to the condition of science, the political dimension, technology, and every day-life routines. We could mention also the category of energy diplomacy, reflecting international relations in this dimension (Feldpausch-Parker, 2022, p. 222).

The determinants of energy culture include the level of greenhouse gas emissions, the structure of energy consumption, and the energy intensity of the economy (Kocon, 2013, p. 120). The types of energy culture are distinguished according to the dominant energy source in the structure of primary energy use (oil, coal, nuclear, mixed, hybrid, and so on) (Kocon, 2013, p. 121).

Gryz pointed to the added value resulting from the "holistic" approach of states to the issue of energy security, in both the intangible and tangible aspects (Gryz, 2018, p. 28). In the intangible dimension, it refers to the doctrine of energy security and the resulting policy objectives. In the tangible dimension, a "holistic" approach to energy security is manifested in the critical infrastructure (Gryz, 2018, p. 28).

Thus, the foundations of the energy policies of states change over time but relate to the category of national interest (Jewell & Brutschin, 2021, p. 249). It is also crucial for states to consider a variety of factors when managing energy. Following Gryz, attention should be paid to the: sets of patterns, values, and social attitudes; legitimization of the idea of energy security; and universally accepted intellectual and moral attitude which links political aims with scientific and technological development (Gryz, 2018, p. 29). It also includes "socio-political mechanisms which transpose the formula of obtaining and using energy and the idea of energy security to the will of a majority of citizens" (Gryz, 2018, p. 29). All of these conditions create a mandate to exercise power, its legitimacy, and the basis in the form of the national interest (Shneider & Peeples, 2022, p. 124; Pietraś et al., 2018).

Nowadays, various forms of energy management exist, depending on the national specificity. Gryz listed "fully open" states, with a stabilized economic, social, and political system. They represent a key element in the energy market, given the free competition, technological development, and transparency in the energy dimension (Gryz, 2018, p. 30). Open states belong to another category, with social security as an overriding imperative. In this case, the scope of economic freedoms and liberties is "regulated by the projection of the welfare of citizens, understood as a specific imperative of the actions of state institutions" (Gryz, 2018, p. 30). The third category consists of states of "competitive, authoritarian capitalism," which in the case of energy policy is expressed in the formula of "energy management oscillating between controlled openness and restrictive supervision" (Gryz, 2018, p. 30). The fourth category includes states with so-called "bureaucratic capitalism," and all processes occurring in the energy sector are subordinated to the politics of supervision and control (Gryz, 2018, p. 30). This is the most appropriate category for the Caspian countries.

The poor organizational structure of the state affects its ability to ensure energy security. Activities in this dimension require the skillful management of human resources, space, time, knowledge, and change (Gryz, 2018, p. 30).

1.2 *Non-state Actors*

1.2.1 International Organizations

Following Marek Pietraś, international organizations are becoming important actors in the energy market. As actors in energy security, they ensure that:

> it is identified not only with national security but also with international security. By their nature, they contribute an element of institutionalisation and multilateralisation [...] which in turn leads to the creation of structures of global or regional energy security management. (Pietraś, 2017, p. 24)

Their role is to encourage states to collaborate in energy security efforts. States remain responsible for their own energy security, but because of the progressive integration of energy markets and growing dependence on imports of fossil fuels, national strategies remain insufficient. The importance of individual organizations in the international energy market largely depends on their structure and ability to create an energy security policy. Taking this parameter into account, a distinction can be made between organizations that are supranational and those that are intergovernmental, as well as regulatory and coordinating.

The European Union is undoubtedly a significant international organization of a supranational, regulatory and coordinating nature, dealing with the energy security issues. As one of the most dynamic energy markets in the world, it is a key actor influencing international energy security. Energy issues were the basis of the European integration process as the European Coal and Steel Community or European Atomic Energy Community. To a large extent, the energy policy is still an individual choice of each EU country as regards the directions and conditions of energy imports. The actions of the European Commission in energy negotiations with third actors depend on the coherence of the interests of all member states, which to a large extent limits the decision-making capabilities of this institution (Kaveshnikov, 2010, p. 594). Under Article 194 of the Consolidated Version of the Treaty on the Functioning of the European Union, it is stated that:

> In the context of the establishment and functioning of the internal market and with regard for the need to preserve and improve the environment, Union policy on energy, in a spirit of solidarity between the Member States, shall aim to: ensure the functioning of the energy market; ensure the security of energy supply in the Union; promote energy

efficiency and energy saving and the development of new and renewable
forms of energy; promote the interconnection of energy networks.

The need to make the solidarity principle an actual instrument of action,
effective thanks to appropriate mechanisms for sharing costs, responsibility,
and risk among the various actors in the EU, is now a priority of their energy
policy. A key component of the current EU energy policy is the completion of
the internal energy market and an increase in energy connections between
member states.

The International Energy Agency is an example of an organization with
a primarily coordinating and informational character. It was created in 1974
in response to the so-called first oil shock after the embargo on Arab oil and
evolved towards a coordinated system of preventing the risk of disturbance in
energy supplies and oil distribution in the international energy market. Its seat
is located in Paris. It plays an active part in the OECD (International Energy
Agency, 2019). Initially, the organization's tasks were focused on the oil market, and were expanded in subsequent years. However, the system is imper-
fect because it does not include the most significant consumers of energy
resources, such as China and India, but also because it lacks effective decision-
making mechanisms among its actors. An important role of the IEA is to provide information on the situation in the international energy market and its
development prospects (Yergin, 2006, p. 76). As part of this organization, the
International Energy Forum collects information from energy producers and
consumers.

The Organization of the North Atlantic Alliance (NATO) is playing an
increasingly important role in energy security. However, in this dimension, it
mainly has a coordinating role. As a result of changes in contemporary international relations, the non-military dimension of security is becoming a new
challenge for the international community, and energy security, while playing
an increasingly important role, is becoming an issue that is increasingly discussed at the Alliance forum. This organization attaches greater importance
to energy security, especially the security of energy supplies. "Disruptions in
energy supplies may have an impact on the security of NATO states and thus
determine the effectiveness of the Alliance's military operations [...]. Therefore, these issues should be consulted within NATO. This organization is aware
of the impact of energy issues on the security of states" (NATO, 2019, p. 64).

NATO's strategic concept signals a growing vulnerability of the Alliance's
energy resources, but also commands NATO to "enhance capabilities that contribute to energy security by protecting critical energy infrastructure, transit
areas and routes, and by collaborating with partners and consulting NATO

members based on strategic assessments and contingency planning" (NATO, 2020, p. 67). Currently, NATO concentrates on the security of energy critical infrastructure and the relationship between a state's energy efficiency and its military effectiveness. The document *Energy Security: Operational Highlights* emphasized the need to ensure common energy security, diversification of energy resources supplies, compatibility of energy systems, and the necessity to increase the use of renewable sources (NATO, 2019).

The Organization of the Petroleum Exporting Countries (OPEC) brings together states that produce over 40% and have over three-quarters of the world's oil deposits (Organization of the Petroleum Exporting Countries, 2021). It is a cartel-type international intergovernmental organization, comprising most of the world's oil-producing states. Created in 1960 in Baghdad, its mission is to establish a unified policy for the production and sale of oil. The Organization of Petroleum Exporting Countries comprises fourteen states. The founding states include Iran, Iraq, Kuwait, Saudi Arabia, and Venezuela, followed by Qatar (1961), Libya (1962), the United Arab Emirates (1967), Algeria (1969), Nigeria (1971), Ecuador (1973–1992, again in OPEC since 2007), Gabon (1975–1995, again in OPEC since 2016), Angola (2007), and Equatorial Guinea (2017) (Organization of the Petroleum Exporting Countries, 2021). OPEC's supreme body is the OPEC Conference, which holds twice-yearly meetings of the member states delegations. The other OPEC structures are the Board of Governors and Secretariat, an executive body. The seat of OPEC has been located in Vienna since 1965.

The goal of OPEC is to unify the policy in the production and sale of oil by setting production and price limits, securing the interests of its producers, and carrying out research on energy use and the prospects of the petrochemical industry. OPEC coordinates the policy of the global oil market, ensuring its stability, and looking after the interests of its member states. The organization was a key influence on the world oil market in the 1970s and 1980s. It was then that OPEC contributed to the oil crisis by imposing sanctions on Western states in 1973 over the Israeli–Arab War that year. The organization had a significant impact on the shape of the oil market, mainly in terms of production and prices (Organization of the Petroleum Exporting Countries, 2021).

1.2.2   International Corporations

Transnational corporations, defined by the United Nations Conference on Trade and Development (UNCTAD) as "enterprises composed of a parent company and its foreign subsidiaries" (World Investment Report, 2005, p. 78), are actors playing a leading role and position in the globalization processes. As participants in international relations, they constitute a significant driving force for changes on economic, as well as political and social levels (Piórko, 2008, p. 462). This complex and specific impact of enterprises on various areas of the functioning and development of the international community results from their potential, which consists of financial and technological resources. This potential is accompanied by several organizational characteristics and capabilities which allow to "functionally integrate geographically dispersed activities" and the "global presence" of the corporations, manifested, among other things, in their numbers (Piórko, 2008, p. 462). At the same time, it should be noted that this is a very diverse and heterogeneous actor, one that eludes unambiguous evaluation and analysis.

As regards the participation of transnational corporations in global energy control, it should be emphasized that they are a source of changes that imply the need to transform the ruling powers of states. Corporations contribute significantly to changes in terms of the conditions under which states exercise their sovereignty. It is mainly about the relative decline in the importance of territory and precisely defined borders as a result of capital and information transfer. Thus, the activity of the corporation is of an "extra territorial" character (Piórko, 2008, p. 462). The control and jurisdiction of states in this dimension are also hindered by the evolution of corporate structures and their global expansion. In addition to locating foreign direct investments, the chief attribute of their activities today is maintaining control and coordination of the functioning of numerous economic actors on an international scale (Piórko, 2008, p. 463). Corporations create flexible, transnational networks with hundreds of subsidiaries, ventures, and partners (Piórko, 2008, p. 463). Strategic alliances and cross-border mergers and acquisitions are gaining importance in this context. So, problems emerge in determining the ownership as well as the nationality of corporations and their branches.

The potential of corporations and the specificity of their operations cause a change in the system, character, differentiation of components and forms of power, authority, and influence in the international environment (Pietraś, 2003, p. 162). The increasing effectiveness in achieving goals and the ability to control the processes of international relations (in a direction consistent with the interests of a given actor) guarantee "soft" manifestations of power in the form of economic resources, technological potential knowledge resources, innovation, mobility of activities, and flexibility of organizational solutions (Piórko, 2008, p. 465). Corporations hold these strategic resources, contributing to the transformation of the control system on a global scale. The intensification of the activity of transnational corporations and their growing power motivate states to cooperate with them in obtaining investments and resources to implement costly projects in the energy sector.

TABLE 1.1   Market position and financial resources of the largest energy corporations
(USD billions)

Company	2019 USD billions	2017 USD billions	Highest historical value USD billions	
BP	125.11	113.6	263.3	May 2006
Chevron	221.79	197.7	256.1	July 2014
CNOOC	63.85	48.9	120.9	April 2011
Conoco Phillips	57.67	54.4	112.6	June 2008
Eni	23.75	54.6	152.4	May 2008
Exxon Mobil	286.3	342.1	519.3	October 2007
Petro China	87.81	112.2	472.1	October 2007
Petrobras	85.31	52.1	329.9	May 2008
Royal Dutch Shell	223.57	218.7	458.6	January 2013
Sinopec	3.048	95.16	131.2	October 2007

Therefore, international corporations are increasingly important actors in
energy security in contemporary international relations (Table 1.1). They may
act as consumers of energy resources or as lobbying structures that exert pressure on states and even on international organizations which form structures
for global energy security management (Pietraś, 2017). Without their participation, states are often unable to make their own investments in energy infrastructure. They are thus forced to consider the interests of international energy
corporations in their energy security policy.

Today, oil companies dominate the international energy market. They control approximately 90% of reserves, 75% of production, and a significant por-
tion of the key transmission infrastructure (the *midstream* sector) (Tordo et
al., 2018 p. 23). Most of the 10 corporations with the largest reserves are owned
by states. Of these, ExxonMobil has the largest reserves. Saudi Arabia and the
Saudi Aramco concern occupy a unique position in the oil market, capable
of influencing the price of oil like no other actor by regulating supply. This is
made possible by having spare capacity (Ulatowski, 2017, p. 67).

In the 1950s and 1960s, seven international oil companies, the International
Oil Companies (IOC), which in the 1920s and 1930s obtained concessions for

the exploration and production of oil in the Middle East, transformed that region into the center of the world oil industry, and became the leaders of the energy sector (Ulatowski, 2017, p. 67). They were nicknamed the "Seven Sisters" by Eni Enrico Mattei, the president of the Italian concern (Hoyos, 2007, p.2).

In 2007, the *Financial Times* identified the "New Seven Sisters" by analogy with those seven private corporations that had dominated the energy industry in the 1950s and 1960s. They were: Saudi Aramco, Gazprom, China National Petroleum Corporation (CNPC), National Iranian Oil Company (NIOC), Petroleum of Venezuela (PDVSA), Petrobras and Petronas. According to the British newspaper, they were to dictate the "rules of the game" in the oil market in the future (Hoyos, 2007).

Energy corporations have a trade turnover and assets larger than those of medium-sized states. They pursue their own policies through which they influence energy security on a global scale. Some of them have cutting-edge technologies for extracting energy resources, being important actors in energy policy. The concerns have as much power and influence over energy policy as some countries. Consequently, having economic potential and capital in the form of accumulated energy reserves, they can dictate the terms of the game in the world market (Hoffmann & Magierek, 2015, p. 202).

To invest and operate in a given state, companies pay attention to a number of conditions that shape the so-called business environment, such as legal regulations or political stability (Svyatets, 2016, pp. 74–109). A significant example in further analyses is the involvement of transnational corporations in the post-Soviet energy market. The collapse of the Soviet Union caused many oil- and gas-rich states to seek investments from international corporations. In the 1990s, corporations signed large contracts in Azerbaijan and Kazakhstan (Ulatowski, 2017, p. 67). Multiple international companies are present in the Caspian region: Amoco, Chevron, Texaco, ExxonMobil, and others. They have invested around USD 50 billion in oil and gas production, especially in Azerbaijan and Kazakhstan (Molchanov & Yevdokimov, 2004, p. 423). ExxonMobil is also a major player in Turkmenistan. Since 1997, the Amoco Corporation has increased its involvement in the Caspian Basin. This corporation lobbied strongly for US interests (Molchanov & Yevdokimov, 2004).

The Caspian states attached a huge role to attracting foreign companies and their investments in the energy sector. Various instruments were used to encourage this type of actor. Azerbaijan passed a law to protect foreign investments. In addition, this state became a member of the Extractive Industries Transparency Initiative (EITI) in 2007 (Doing Business in Azerbaijan, 2008). The purpose of the EITI was to ensure that the society in a given country had access to the benefits of resource extraction. The initiative was supported by the largest corporations such as ConocoPhillips, BP, Chevron, and Royal Dutch Shell. The government of this state adopted the Law on the Protection of Foreign Investments as early as 1992, followed by the Law on Investment Activity in 1995, which states that if the government introduces any regulations unfavorable to foreign investors, they will be protected for 10 years against nationalization of property, and if this occurs, entrepreneurs will be able to apply for fair compensation. This guaranteed the same rights for foreign investors and domestic companies. Foreign investors were assured that their income would be transferred to their countries of origin (Sallis, 2003, pp. 50–52). This type of legislation has boosted the confidence of transnational corporations, which since the 1990s have increased their involvement in the energy sector in the Caspian states (Svyatets, 2016, pp. 74–109). In addition, foreign companies and the Azerbaijani Ministry of Energy and Industry have signed Production Sharing Agreements (PSAs) relating to the oil and gas sector. This further boosted the confidence of foreign investors. PSAs were signed as part of bilateral trade agreements that Azerbaijan negotiated with various states. In 2000, such an agreement was signed and ratified by the US Azerbaijan, which also simplified its business registration procedures, making them similar to the standards in Turkey and southern European states (Svyatets, 2016, pp. 74–109). For example, the time needed to set up a new business was reduced from 122 to 16 days, and the cost of setting up this type of business fell by 77% (Doing Business in Azerbaijan, 2008, pp. 40–41).

The simplification of procedures made it possible to finance large-scale energy projects involving businesses, states, and international institutions. The first contract between the Azerbaijani government and foreign corporations was the so-called "contract of the century" of September 20, 1994. It was not only the first agreement of this type in Azerbaijan but also in the entire Caspian region (Razavi, 2007, p. 278). The largest global energy corporations participated in the contract: Amoco, British Petroleum, Delta-Nimir, LUKoil, McDermott International, Pennzoil, Ramco, Statoil, Turkish State Oil Company, Unocal.

At the same time, other international contracts were signed between Azerbaijan and major oil corporations: BP, Chevron, Devon Energy, Amerada Hess, ExxonMobil, Statoil Hydro, Turkish Oil Corporation TPAO (Türkiye Petrolleri Anonim Ortaklığı), SOCAR (State Oil Company of the Azerbaijan Republic), Inpex, and Itochu (Yergin, 2011, p. 54; Svyatets, 2016, pp. 74–109; Molchanov & Yevdokimov, 2004, p. 418).

In 2008, the World Bank published the *Doing Business* report, in which it classified Azerbaijan as one of the major reformers in Eastern Europe and Central Asia (World Bank for Reconstruction and Development, 2008, p. 18). Then, in 2008, another report identified Azerbaijan as an attractive market for business (World Bank for Reconstruction and Development, 2008, p. 41). In 2014, the US State Department declared that: "a well-functioning administration supports US private investment in Azerbaijan's energy sector" (Nichol, 2014, pp. 193–279).

British Petroleum (BP) is a corporation involved in most energy projects in the Caspian region (Svyatets, 2016, pp. 74–109). In 2009, Greg Mattson, BP's vice president for environmental affairs in Azerbaijan, described Azerbaijan as a low political risk country and stated that oil production was a technological challenge here (Svyatets, 2016, pp. 74–109). According to Mattson, BP's "holy trinity" (energy, technology, and politics) contributed to technological development in the country, providing the country with a stable income for the government and promoting sustainable development there. He also positively assessed the business environment under the PSAs in Azerbaijan, which ensures the stability of contracts (Svyatets, 2016, pp. 74–109).

A significant tendency in the contemporary world, to quote Marek Pietraś, is "broadening the subjective scope of security, also known as vertical deepening" (Pietraś, 2017, p. 23). It consists in departing from the state-centered understanding of security and involving actors other than states. This tendency is essential for the "process of energy security autonomy," the analysis of which includes transnational corporations, international organizations, but also individuals who are consumers of energy carriers (Pietraś, 2017, p. 23).

2   The Object of the Energy Security Policy

2.1   *Energy Security as an Area of International Security Research*
The object of the energy security policy was both for state or non-state actors. Energy policy is a public policy (Cullingworth, 1990; Feldpausch-Parker, 2022, p. 222). It can be understood as a term denoting rationalized public activities and programs based on accumulated knowledge and the systematic process of designing and carrying out these activities (Hoffmann & Magierek, 2015, p. 181). The key questions, therefore, are how to study this area and which theoretical assumptions are most relevant in this context. Political science theorists have not developed appropriate research apparatus that can contribute to a deep exploration and explanation of the role and significance of energy policy in the area of international security. The interdisciplinary character of this concept and the changing research approaches justify the conclusion that energy policy can be studied using a variety of theories and research methods. Their multitude proves that energy policy as an explanatory space is very

broad. Each research approach seeks to demonstrate the differences in the perception of energy policy and identify its most important designations.

In the analysis of energy security, it is difficult to separate the theory of that concept from its practice. Paradoxically, the widespread discourse on this subject, on the one hand, links the concept of energy with security, and, on the other hand, hinders the process of conceptualizing and normalizing energy security (Ciuta, 2010, p. 124).

It is often questioned whether the energy issue should be analyzed in terms of security. Two determinants shaping the relationship between energy and security can be distinguished. First, energy is treated as a basic category that determines the existence and development of societies. It affects every aspect of the lives of individuals and social groups. The demand for energy rises as the population grows. The energy sector is essential for the development and productivity of agriculture and industry. The global energy demand is linked to demographic growth, technological advancement, and dependence on hydrocarbon fuels—the deposits of which may become insufficient to meet demand. The increase in energy consumption of a given state has a positive effect on its economic and social development (Demirbas, 2008, p. 41). Second, the concept of energy security is the result of theoretical debates on a broader understanding of security in contemporary international relations (Correlje & van der Linde, 2006, pp. 532–534). The expanding catalogue of participants in international relations and the constant development of internationalization processes result in the expansion of the set of values protected under the security policy as well as the expansion of the scope of applied measures. The means of national security policy are becoming more and more differentiated according to the nature, size, and strength of threats to values considered important to the survival and development of the state. According to Alan Collins: "the process of globalisation has led to the internal issues becoming externalized, and the external issues internalized" (Collins, 2022, p. 1).

Therefore, energy is a fundamental component of economic security, especially energy security. Energy security is a very complex concept. Many interpretations influence the understanding of this concept: competition for access to energy sources, changes in the natural environment, conflicts over the right to extract energy resources, and the increasing political instability of energy-producing countries (Neag et al., 2017, pp. 24–29). At the same time, energy security means achieving a stable, flexible, and sustainable energy market that ensures energy supplies for consumers, taking into account increased consumption of alternative sources.

Energy security also means securing the energy infrastructure against terrorist attacks (Neag et al., 2017, pp. 24–29; Cullingworth, 1990). The object of the study is the energy security of the state and its components, but also the internal and external conditions of the functioning of the state's energy system. The components of the state's energy security include fuels, energy, and economic resources, as well as infrastructural elements of the energy system in the state territory (Kyzym & Rudyka, 2018, pp. 18–23).

The components of the concept of energy security in research studies include:
- availability (supply diversification, geopolitical threats),
- infrastructure efficiency,
- energy price availability (competition in the energy market, price level),
- the social dimension: energy demand,
- the climate dimension, and
- energy efficiency (demand reduction, less energy-consuming technologies and energy consumption practices) (Kyzym & Rudyka, 2018, pp. 18–23).

The systematization of energy security components leads to the conclusion that the availability of energy is the main component of energy security. It is therefore important to identify the concept of energy security and security of energy supplies. This means taking into account energy interests as part of economic policy and the conditions of the energy market.

The concept of the so-called Copenhagen School (Copenhagen Peace Research Institute—COPRI) emphasizes the need to expand the catalogue of threats to security in international relations (Collins, 2022, p. 6; Misiągiewicz, 2015, pp. 393–448). Representatives of this school of thinking, "place primary importance on determining how an issue becomes a security issue, by how it is articulated" (Collins, 2022, p. 6). It is a subjective approach to determining what constitutes security, and seems to be particularly significant in studies on the energy dimension of security (Collins, 2022, p. 6). The securitization theory proposed by Barry Buzan is noteworthy. It creates a vision of security that addresses both military and non-military threats (Figure 1.3). In this context, "security involves the survival" of a given actor (Buzan, 1997, p. 13). Threats may emerge on many levels of the actor's functioning, significantly limiting its development opportunities. The process of securitization is about "defining activity as belonging to the security sphere. The state has the authority to grant this activity speciality status" (Czaputowicz, 2006, p. 24). An issue becomes securitized when political or social leaders start talking about it as an existential threat to a particular social group (Buzan, 1997, p. 13). "Security is the quality that an actor instils into an issue through securitization, which involves presenting a given issue in the political arena in a specific way and thus obtaining approval for the application of exceptional protective measures" (Czaputowicz, 2006, p. 26). For example, the securitization process may

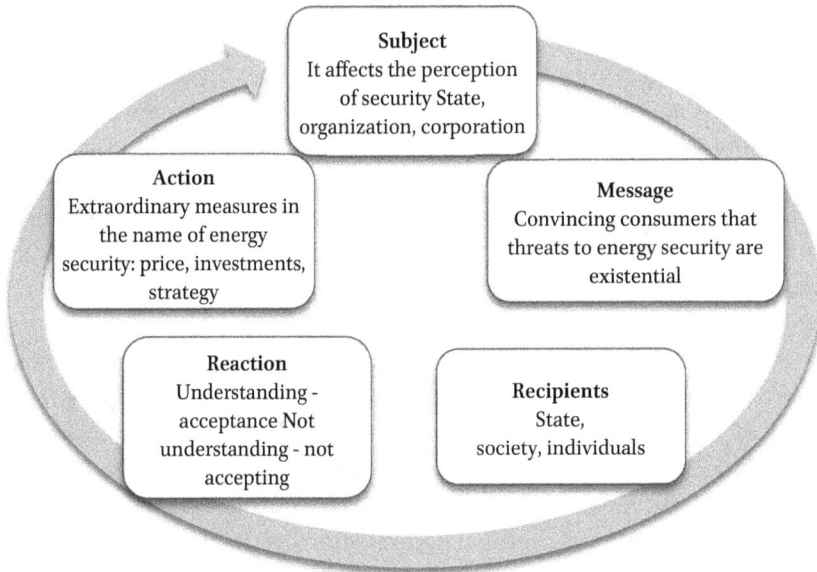

FIGURE 1.3 Securitization of energy security
SOURCE: AUTHOR'S OWN WORK

legitimize the use of force, more broadly, to quote Buzan, "it transfers a given issue from the realm of normal politics to the realm of panic politics" (Buzan, 1997, p. 13). In this context, "an existential threat requires special methods and justifies actions outside the bounds of normal political procedure" (Buzan, 1997, p. 14). Securitization can be seen as an extreme form of politicization (Buzan, 1997). According to the Alan Collins, "security is a matter of high politics; central to government debates and pivotal priorities they establish" (Collins, 2022, p. 1).

The sense of threat, sensitivity, and danger may be socially constructed and needs not be objective. So, the concept of a threat refers to the conscious sphere of a given actor. "Threat" means a certain mental state or consciousness caused by the perception of phenomena that are judged as unfavorable or dangerous (Pietraś, 2021, p. 441). The threat is not something that simply exists, it has to be articulated as such for it to become a matter of security (Collins, 2022, p. 6). Judgments formulated by a given actor are particularly important here, as they underlie the actions taken to minimize or eliminate threats. The perception of threats by a given actor may reflect the real state of affairs but may also be false (misperception). A threat refers to a phenomenon or disproportion in resources that causes anxiety and fear (Pietraś, 2021, p. 441). What counts as security is defined in this case by the securitization actor. At the same time, more and more often, two other dimensions of security are taken into account: economic and ecological. Both of these security sectors correspond with the concept of energy security. Access to energy resources determines the development of a national economy, while their exploitation causes greenhouse gas emission into the atmosphere, which has a fundamental impact on the condition of the natural environment. The increasing importance of economic security (especially in terms of energy) in international relations was related to the crisis in the United States as a result of the lack of oil supply liquidity and substantial dependence on oil imports in the 1970s (Buzan, 1997, p. 14). The dependence on oil supplies and the oil crisis related to the embargo on this fuel imposed by the Arab states on the West can be considered a turning point in the conceptualization of the term "energy security." Since then, the terms started appearing in national security strategies and literature. It can therefore be concluded that energy market issues have been securitized. Securitization, as regards energy, means "inclusion of energy carriers in the analysis of security problems, their threats and actions to ensure security" (Pietraś, 2017, p. 23).

To quote M. Pietraś:

> The complexity of security under conditions of growing international interdependence, the end of the Cold War, the dynamics of globalization and other processes has led to the securitization process, which resulted in individual sectors being distinguished – the dimensions of security and the process is not complete. Its effect is the progressive complexity of security, its threats and activities aimed at ensuring it. (Pietraś, 2017, p. 24)

The author further stated that:

> for the autonomy of securitization of energy problems and the emergence of the concept of 'energy security', the place of energy in contemporary social life, especially in economy but also in politics, is of key importance, followed by the securitization process and its stages. The result is an energy security category, understood in many ways, which reflects the complexity of the analysed phenomenon. (Pietraś, 2017, p. 24)

The analysis of the concept of energy security challenges both the traditional understanding of security and the securitization theory.

The securitization theory therefore becomes a very useful tool to analyze energy security of the Caspian countries. Income from oil and gas exports is the basis for the stability of the political systems of these countries and the survival of authoritarian regimes. Thus, the lack of access to the energy market or the reduction in the price of hydrocarbons is a highly politicized issue. Decision-makers often perceive threats to energy security as "a constraint on the political space" (Loschel & Rubbelke, 2010, p. 1665).

Securitization points to mechanisms and phenomena that are important for society, but become threatened at a given time (Bridge, 2015, pp. 328–339). They are referred to in the literature as "the breakdown of living conditions" (Loschel & Rubbelke, 2010, p. 1665). Considering the situation in the Caspian region, this would be sensitive, threatening social instability. Energy securitization takes various forms but this dimension is dominated by the prospect of "sovereignty" of the state (Lakoff, 2008, pp. 33–59; Cherp & Jewell, 2011, pp. 330–355). Other approaches emphasize the more comprehensive determinants of energy security. They focus on the state and its interests but also extend the meaning of energy security to infrastructure systems related to conversion, transmission, distribution, and production of energy on a global scale (Bridge, 2015, pp. 328–339). This is a particularly important issue in the context of the *upstream* and *downstream* infrastructure operating in the Caspian region.

The combination of various conditions of energy security and the development of their scenarios and visualizations was the basis for creating an interesting research model of short-term energy security, known as the Model of Short-Term Energy Security (MOSES). The creator of this concept is J. Jewell (2011). MOSES includes 30 energy security indicators, along with a methodology to combine and interpret them. The model is based on vulnerability assessment, and allows the determination of risk to energy supply disruptions and the system's resilience to such occurrences—that is to say, it defines the ability of the national energy system to cope with energy deficit. The model identifies risk and resilience as indicators resulting from domestic and international conditions. The specificity of energy security of a particular state is characterized in this manner.

The work of A. Cherp and J. Jewell (2011) on energy security indicators helped redefine its object. They argued that it should not be focused on states, but on energy systems such as nuclear and electricity, or on transport systems (Table 1.2). Today, the MOSES model reflects the official approach of the IEA regarding the specificity of energy security. The model positions the states of the world in terms of risk and stability of energy security (Kyzym & Rudyka, 2018, pp. 18–23).

Another methodological approach is presented by the Economic Research Institute for ASEAN and East Asia (ERIA) (World Economic Forum, 2013). A method was developed to determine energy safety with 16 indicators and nine components (Table 1.3).

TABLE 1.2   Methodology of energy security research study—the MOSES model

Component	Parameters		Indicators
Oil	External	Risk	Import dependence
			Political stability of suppliers
		Durability	Ports and pipelines
			Diversification of supply
	Internal	Risk	Production in the coastal area
			Diversity of domestic production
		Durability	Stock level
Petroleum products	External	Risk	Import dependence
		Durability	Diversification of supply
			Ports and pipelines
	Internal	Durability	Number of refineries
			Refinery infrastructure flexibility
			Stock level
Gas	External	Risk	Import dependence
			Political stability of suppliers
		Durability	Ports and pipelines
			Diversification of supply
	Internal	Risk	Production in the coastal area
		Durability	Daily production including LNG (liquefied natural gas) market
			Gas consumption intensity
Coal	External	Risk	Import dependence
		Durability	Ports and railroads
			Diversification of supply
	Internal	Risk	Share of extractive production
Atomic energy	Internal	Risk	Unplanned reactor shutdown
			Average age of nuclear power plants
		Durability	Variety of reactor models
			Number of power plants

SOURCE: AUTHOR'S OWN WORK BASED ON CHERP & JEWELL, 2011

TABLE 1.3   Methodology of energy security research study—the ERIA model

Energy security component	Evaluation component	Energy security index
Development of indigenous energy resources	Self-sufficiency	Energy distribution Energy production Energy consumption
Use of foreign resources	Diversification of imports from individual states	Diversification of energy import sources from individual states
	Diversification of energy sources	Diversification of the distribution of primary energy sources or sources of electricity production
	Dependence on the Middle East	Energy dependence on oil and gas resources from the Middle East
Providing a delivery system	Sufficiency of energy supply Development of institutional infrastructure	Reserve in terms of transmission capacity Access to energy
Demand management	Energy efficiency	Energy intensity per GDP
Preparedness for supply disruptions	Strategic reserves	Oil storage
Climate dimension	Coal consumption	Coal consumption in the energy mix CO_2 emission

SOURCE: AUTHOR'S OWN WORK BASED ON KYZYM & RUDYKA, 2018

Both of the above concepts can be useful when analyzing various determinants of energy security in the Caspian region. When analyzing the energy potential of individual Caspian countries in the region, the following determinants were taken into account: ports and pipelines, share of extractive production,

production in the coastal area, sources from individual states, energy dependence on oil and gas, and CO_2 emission.

An important dimension of the examination of the energy security policy is the geopolitical perspective, which enables the analysis of the Caspian region as a geo-energetic space. Geopolitics is the study of the state as a specific geopolitical organism, the study of the application of the principles of geography to world politics, or the study which deals with temporal-spatial relationships (Hoffmann & Magierek, 2015, p. 202). Criekemans described geopolitics as "the scientific field of study belonging to both Political Geography and International Relations, which investigates the interaction between politically acting (wo)man and their surrounding territoriality (in its three dimensions; physical-geographical, human-geographical and spatial)" (Criekemans, 2018, p. 37). "Geopolitics straddles two disciplines – geography and politics – its approaches vary according to frameworks of analysis common to each discipline" (Cohen, 2003, p. 12). Yves Lacoste defined geopolitics as "the scientific study of territorial power rivalries and their repercussions in/for the public opinion" (Criekemans, 2022, p. 128). His vision with regarded to the nature of geographical knowledge is "important to bear in mind because it asks attention for the complexity of the relation territoriality – politics" (Criekemans, 2022, p. 128). According to the Gyula Csurgai, the geopolitical method of analysis can be a useful tool "since it takes into account the strategic, historical, geographical, cultural and economic spheres" (Csurgai, 2022, p. 13). The logic of the geopolitical analysis method is multidimensional: "it seeks to identify the interactions between the different enduring factors and variables on the internal and external levels of states in a time and space dimension" (Csurgai, 2022, p. 14). In such an analysis, both objective and subjective factors have to be taken into consideration. Objective factors are connected with the size of a state, and the demographic dimension and subjective sphere are cognitive aspects of the geopolitical position (Csurgai, 2022, p. 14). So, geopolitics is defined as the "examination of interactions between political processes and geographical spaces in which these processes take place" (Csurgai, 2022, p. 14). Geopolitics is an interdisciplinary method of analysis. Furthermore, the external and internal dimensions related to the geopolitical position of the state need to be taken into account. Constant factors are connected with some physical geographic issues, and variable factors are connected with demography, sociopolitical structure, strategic motivation, alliance configuration, economic interest, or technological issues (Csurgai, 2022, p. 15). In such an analysis, the historical dimension is playing an important role. The roots of contemporary power rivalries are very often to be found in the past, which is important in the analysis of the international relations in the Caspian region. Csurgai pointed out some of the main components of geopolitical analysis:

1.   Geographical configuration;
2.   Natural resources;
3.   Boundaries;
4.   Geopolitical representations;
5.   Geography of populations;
6.   Historical factors; and
7.   Strategy of actors. (Csurgai, 2022, p. 16)

Most early theories and concepts of geopolitics were based on geographical thought. Later political scientists did not adapt such theories to the dynamic and complex nature of international relations. In 1990, Edward Luttwak coined the term "geoeconomics." According to him, "in some parts of the world where the role of military power was diminishing, states would continue to compete within 'a logic of conflict', but via 'methods of commerce' rather than military methods" (Criekemans, 2017, p. 115). Pascal Lorot can also be considered as one of the pioneers in the study of geoeconomics (Criekemans, 2022, p. 128). Mark P. Thirwell investigated the interconnection between geoeconomics and international security. He stated that: "if one wants to understand many of the most important strategic developments facing the world over the next couple of decades, then you are going to need to devote a reasonable amount of time to thinking about what's going on in the international economy" (Criekemans, 2017, p. 114). Energy policy, as a reference to fossil fuels resources, is significant in this context. Geopolitics is determined by economic interests and is associated with the term of geoeconomics, which is the use of economic policy instruments and energy resources to achieve political goals (Hoffmann & Magierek, 2015, p. 202). Geoeconomics can be used to describe, diagnose, and forecast the current situation on the international energy market. States and their energy concerns are competing for access to deposits of energy resources. Thus, the effectiveness of the energy policy depends to a large extent on the efficiency of economic policy. The geopolitical (geo-energetic) approach to energy policy allows states to gain an advantage through the development of modern technologies of energy resources extraction. Within geopolitics, the energy regime of the global system and the relations between producers, transit states, and consumers are important variables which can influence international relations (Criekemans, 2018, p. 37). Moreover, the theory assumes the importance of access to areas rich in energy resources, which may lead to conflicts between states. Energy policy as seen through the lens of geopolitics can facilitate political pressure, building political and economic influence.

Therefore, an effective energy policy can help shape international relations. According to David Criekemans:

> Geopolitical schools of thought may differ amongst each other with regard to how they conceptualise and operationalise the role which 'territoriality' plays in matters of foreign policy and international relations. Nevertheless, they all share in some fashion the analysis that spatiality remains at the core of problems with which humanity is being confronted. (Criekemans, 2022, p. 147)

The ontological and epistemological assumptions of different geopolitical schools of thought could be "weighed" against one another in light of their descriptive, exploratory, and predictive approaches (Criekemans, 2022, p. 146).

In this analysis, it is worth considering both realistic and idealistic approaches to energy security (Luft & Korin, 2009, p. 340). Analyzing the national energy security, representatives of the realistic trend perceive the world as entangled in a number of challenges that are becoming increasingly dangerous. They treat energy security as a component of the global power policy and a tool of foreign affairs, which is characteristic of the security environment in the Caspian region. They believe that today's energy market is incapable of providing supplies in the long term. Access to fossil fuels has always been and will continue to provoke armed conflicts between states. It is the system "a shrinking planet of increasing forces" (Luft & Korin, 2009, p. 340). It predicts an increase in the intensity of wars related to access to energy resources. His forecast is pessimistic and is associated, not only with international conflicts but also with the degradation of the natural environment. Realist energy policy is analyzed on a macroscale. Realism presents the rivalry between proponents of particular methods of obtaining energy. It means a conflict of interest in the form of a zero-sum game, because choosing one source means giving up another. However, some contradictions can be observed relating to various strands of realism.

According to the paradigm of defensive realism, the actor implementing energy security policy should avoid conflicts, while the paradigm of offensive realism speaks of the necessity to conduct an energy policy "at all costs," that is pursuing one's interests related to access to energy resources (Hoffmann & Magierek, 2015, p. 202). Proponents of neorealism, on the other hand, emphasize that states should develop an energy policy on their own because this is the only way they can obtain certain benefits. Proponents of this strand do not see the need for international organizations to develop an energy policy. They emphasize the interest of the state as the main actor on the international scene. Realists accept the concept of interdependence and cooperation to create common energy security, and at the same time they emphasize that the largest deposits of energy resources are found in Islamic countries, which causes additional civilizational conflicts between the East and the West. Realists also distinguish between state and non-state actors when it comes to the extraction and transport of energy resources. The resources at the disposal of states serve as tools of their foreign policy, while those managed by private businesses belong to a free market. The realistic approach seems to be particularly useful in the analysis of security policies in the Caspian region. The main actors of the energy market are states, and the interdependencies between them constitute the main element of the dynamics of implementing policies of energy security.

Idealists are more optimistic. They believe that wars for territories rich in natural resources will become increasingly rare in the future. The fight for energy resources is pointless, because it is more profitable to buy oil and the interests of buyers and sellers are not mutually exclusive. All actors in the energy market seek stability, which is an indispensable element of profit for each of them. According to idealists, the basis of energy security is the belief in the strength of the market and the concept of interdependence. They emphasize that since oil and gas are traded on a global scale, disruptions in this market will affect energy prices around the world (Luft & Korin, 2009, p. 340). They believe in the rationality of energy market actors, who seek to maximize profits. Idealists opt for the concept of the so-called great transaction between producers and consumers. They call for the development of multilateralism in energy security (Luft & Korin, 2009, p. 340). Liberalism promotes free trade as the basis for the functioning of the international system. In this context, a manifestation of thinking in these terms was the "contract of the century" concluded between Azerbaijan and international corporations.

Referring to the representatives of political realism, security is treated as access to resources, which is necessary for the development of the state regime and which represents the center of geopolitical confrontation. Contrary to realists, representatives of the liberal strand pay attention to the development of international relations. They highlight the importance of peace and cooperation in the energy sector. This can be done by creating certain rules, treating this system as based on universal principles and interests (Bihun, 2018, pp. 167–181). Referring to the classic paradigm, energy security can be achieved both through the use of force and through cooperation. The following analysis indicates the main debates regarding the interpretation of the essence and specificity of understanding the phenomenon of energy security, taking into account the challenges of the international energy market (Table 1.4). Thus, the conditions that were pointed out by both realists and idealists were taken into account.

TABLE 1.4   The main debates and theses present in the literature concerning energy security

Object of the analysis	Debate	Theses
Energy security	Oil and gas	Energy security means uninterrupted and reliable access to cheap oil and gas.
	Energy sector	Energy security refers to the oil, gas, coal, nuclear energy, renewables, extraction, distribution, infrastructure, and global energy markets.
Availability of natural resources	Depletion of resources	Oil and gas reserves are depleting. No new resource deposits are discovered. The peak of extraction took place in the 1960s.
	Resource sufficiency	We have enough energy. Technological achievements will optimize the extraction, and enable the discovery of new deposits and alternative sources of supply.
Historical trend	Continuation	Energy demand is a process. States deal with energy security threats in an unchanging manner over a long historical period.
	Radical change	Nowadays, the demand for energy is growing rapidly, which requires special remedies.
Context	State	Energy issues affect the ability of states to function. The state is thus the main actor in the energy market.
	International environment	Dependencies in terms of the extraction, production, transport, and consumption of energy resources affect the international environment and the global economic market.
Structure	Geopolitics	The energy sector can be an instrument for producers to influence import-dependent states.
	Economy	The politicization of energy has a negative impact on the economic situation of states and the functioning of the energy market.

TABLE 1.4   The main debates and theses present in the literature concerning energy (*cont.*)

Object of the analysis	Debate	Theses
Economic logic	Nationalization of the market	Energy scarcity causes nationalization of the energy market. Energy is a "strategic commodity" that should be controlled by the state.
	Market liberalization	The lack of stability in the energy market leads to a deficit of oil and gas. The functioning of the energy market eases deficit and sensitivity (susceptibility to influence) in this dimension.
Result	Confrontation	The scarcity of energy resources leads to international conflicts over access to deposits, transport routes, and transmission infrastructure.
	Cooperation	Energy problems require cooperation between energy market actors in order to exploit the available energy resources, discover new deposits, and use alternative fuels.
Optimal solution	Dependency	Potential disruptions in the supply of energy resources cause economic and political dependence and vulnerability. In such a situation, energy self-sufficiency is the only way to avoid dependence.
	Interdependence	Energy self-sufficiency is impossible. The interdependence between producers, consumers, and transit states is the main determinant of energy market activity.

SOURCE: AUTHOR'S OWN WORK BASED ON CIUTA, 2010

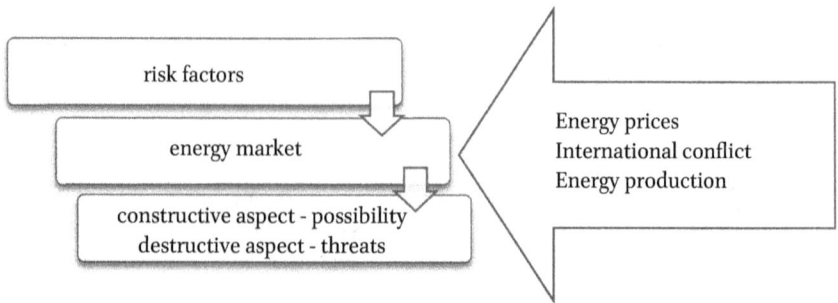

FIGURE 1.4   Risk factors in the Caspian energy market
SOURCE: AUTHOR'S OWN WORK

Undoubtedly, the risk category is the conceptual basis for analyzing energy security in the Caspian region (Figure 1.4). On the one hand, risk may cause a threat (the destructive aspect) and, on the other, it may affect economic security (the constructive aspect) through the emergence of alternative opportunities (Bihun, 2018, pp. 167–181).

Another theoretical approach, useful in the analysis of energy security policy in the Caspian region, is the theory of complex interdependence, also known as the "transnational approach." It was developed by Robert Keohane and Joseph Nye (Keohane, 2002, p. 379). In their opinion, political realism as a school did not propose a complex theory of international relations. Politics is shaped by growing interdependence, transnational processes, and the emergence of new global phenomena. A similar approach was represented by S. Huntington, J. Roseau, T. Rise-Kappen, and P. Willets. The transnational approach entails loosening of traditional channels of communication between legal or sectoral systems at the intergovernmental or supranational level. The interdependence is evident in the activities of transnational actors that affect the development of energy policy or the energy sector.

2.2   The Essence and Dimensions of Energy Security

The interdependencies in energy policy determine the dynamics of international relations. The possibilities of extracting and transmitting fossil fuels affect, not only the economic position of states but also economic relations on a global scale, because energy market participants are, not only states but also multiple international enterprises, which are increasingly involved in production and distribution of hydrocarbons. Energy security is not only based on objective economic premises related to free market principles but is also determined by political and geostrategic issues (Lixia, 2021).

Henry Kissinger pointed out "the necessity of cooperation of the importing states to ensure their energy security because they have a common problem that can only be solved through cooperation" (Kissinger, 1982, p. 906). Energy resources have a huge impact on the evolution of society, economic development, and the state of the economy in the national and global dimensions. Kissinger stated that: "Control oil and you control nations" (Neag et al., 2017, p. 24). M. Collon went even further, saying that, "if you want to control the world, you must control oil resources on a global scale" (Neag et al., 2017, p. 25). Access to energy resources is therefore central to the international community. Instability in this dimension may cause serious repercussions in the economy, environment, and society, and also in the military and political aspects of security.

The determinant of international energy interdependence is the policy of energy resource transport. Pipeline routes are determined by economic considerations but are also the result of political action by states. Serious threats to energy security include technological and economic barriers in the mining industry and the slow but inevitable process of resource depletion. As global demand for hydrocarbons increases on a global scale, producers of energy resources are forced to invest more in exploration, while consumers are seeking to pursue a policy of supply diversification. In contemporary international relations, energy security becomes a key issue as oil and gas resources shrink, increasing demand for them on a global scale and, as a consequence, the possibility of rising prices of energy carriers. Access to energy resources is the existential need of every state, conditioning its economic and social development.

Capturing the specificity of energy security is very difficult, given the complexity of the global energy market and the fact that it is a relatively new concept in international relations. It is therefore important to define the term "energy security," and identify its actors and the main factors determining the dynamics of the global energy market. In scientific studies, energy security often appears as an element of resource security, which is also one of the basic components of economic security (Raphael & Stokes, 2022, p. 362; Misiągiewicz, 2012a).

This approach is very relevant to the analysis of energy security policies in the Caspian region, given that access to energy resources is the basis for the economic development of the states in that area. Energy security is the ability of a national economic system to ensure the availability of energy resources of economic importance, that is to say energy carriers, both from domestic and foreign sources, in conformity to the needs of the economy and society (Lixia, 2021; Błoński, 2013, p. 15). Energy security relates directly to energy carriers in the context of ensuring their availability to specific recipients on acceptable terms. It is a state of no threat of energy supply interruption (Błoński, 2013, p. 16). Energy security is also defined as the constant availability of affordable energy, which comes from diverse sources and meets the appropriate quality and environmental parameters (Riedel, 2010, p. 19).

Oil security is understood as one of the components of energy security or one of its facets. What is meant by oil security is a constant, continuous, timely, and reliable system of supplies of oil and petroleum products. Oil must be available and it must be possible to transport this resource freely from the place of production to the place of consumption. In the context of the Caspian Sea region, this is reflected in the pipeline construction policy.

Energy security also means the ability of the national economy to supply energy on an ongoing and long-term basis to domestic recipients at socially acceptable prices while maintaining political independence (Pronińska, 2012, p. 306). This is a very general definition. Social acceptance of energy prices turns out to be a relative issue, and political independence is difficult to achieve with energy imports.

We can distinguish three areas as regards the essence of energy security:

1. energy security of the recipient—the energy user—that is, the level of guaranteed access to the necessary forms of energy at a given time and quantity, and at an affordable price;
2. security of energy supply—the readiness of a given energy system to cover the energy supply at socially acceptable prices; and
3. energy security of the state or region—which covers the energy security of recipients and the security of energy supply to these recipients in a given territory (Młynarski, 2011, p. 31).

Ensuring smooth energy supplies is a priority in the political agendas and economic strategies of states. The scope and intensity of the activities of actors in this dimension depend on the international context, including relations between importers and exporters, market trends, and the awareness of states regarding potential threats and challenges to energy security (Błoński, 2013, p. 15).

Energy security is very complex as it includes energy and economy issues, and also the political power of states. The variety of definitions of this concept creates a situation in which it is difficult to set clear boundaries of the meaning of energy security, in both theoretical and practical dimensions. Numerous terminological substitutes (for example, security of supply, geopolitics of pipelines) make it even more difficult to set specific boundaries for energy security. At the same time, it is hard to find a coherent definition of this term in documents and legal acts that link energy security to economic growth or the natural environment. Consequently, the literature contains much controversy regarding the scope of the term "energy security" and its specificity in the context of the international market dynamics.

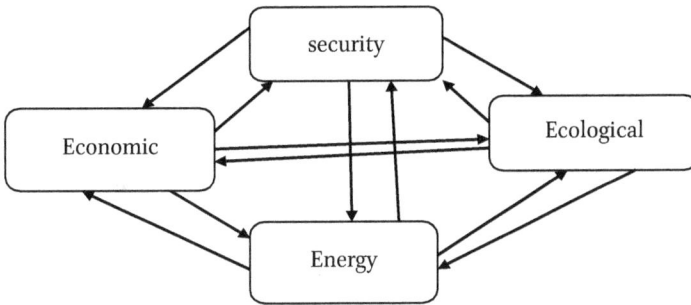

FIGURE 1.5   Relationships between different dimensions of energy security
            SOURCE: AUTHOR'S OWN WORK

Energy security is multifaceted and includes political, economic, and environmental considerations (Raphael & Stokes, 2022, p. 362) (Figure 1.5). In this context, economic security is of particular importance as a component of state
security. Such an approach is often present in the literature and it is hard to
question it. So, economic security can be understood as the state of development of the national economic system, which ensures its high efficiency
through the proper use of internal development factors and the ability to effectively resist external pressures which could lead to development disturbances
(Lixia, 2021). It determines the security of the national economy, which is the
situation where the economy of a given state receives the supply of production
factors necessary for its functioning and development, including energy sufficiency (Stachowiak, 2006, p. 386). The economic dimension of defining energy
security focuses on ensuring energy resource supply to national economic processes, which seems to be a proper approach, especially in states in the process
of economic transformation (Lixia, 2021). The energy sector directly influences
the efficiency and competitiveness of the state economy. This is characteristic
for the Caspian region states, whose economic development is based on revenues from the export of energy resources.

Part of the economic security of a state is energy resource security, food
security, financial security, and others. The economic dimension of energy
security mainly concerns the costs of obtaining energy and continuity of supplies (Pietraś, 2017). Energy is a specific product because it must be constantly
available, even during political or economic crises (Gradziuk et al., 2003, p. 76).

Lack of liquidity in energy supplies entails high costs for the entire national
economy. Therefore, the energy sector plays a fundamental role in shaping the
efficiency and competitiveness of the economy and has both a direct and indirect impact on the quality of citizen life (Gradziuk et al., 2003). Consequently,
energy resources are treated as a strategic product. Due to the intensified

competition in the international market of energy, the price of energy is increasingly significant as it determines the standard of living of consumers, industrial competitiveness, and economic growth (Gradziuk et al., 2003). In this context, the following economic conditions favoring the improvement of energy security can be distinguished:

1. liberalization of the energy market, which enhances the security of supply by raising the number of energy suppliers and by making the market system more flexible;
2. improving the quality of transport infrastructure;
3. reduction in energy consumption of the economy, which is connected with technological progress, which in turn mitigates both losses during energy transmission and the consumption of energy carriers; and
4. energy efficiency is defined as the percentage of energy generated from resources that is converted into a utility. It is usually measured as the relationship between energy gain and energy loss.

The above criteria expose the shortcomings of the energy market in the Caspian region, where the liberalization process is limited, the transport infrastructure needs to be expanded, and the national economies are largely energy-intensive.

Literature on the subject often touches upon climate issues when defining the matters of energy security (Emmons, 2021, p. 3; Konisky, 2020; Deitchman, 2016; Cannavo, 2011). "The reliability of energy supplies and its economically justified price are related to environmental protection, where the costs of natural environment restoration determine the choice of sources" (Gradziuk et al., 2003, p. 76). Environmental protection in a competitive energy market is a significant challenge for its participants. The application of the principles of sustainable development is key, that is to say, to combine economic growth with social progress and environmental protection, as well as to disseminate technologies which enable the reduction of greenhouse gas emissions into the atmosphere (Gradziuk et al., 2003).

Sustainable development, seen as an important part of civilizational development, is still only an addition to the economic and social policy of states. To ensure sustainable development one needs to use renewable energy sources and have governmental support for the industry (creation of appropriate legal regulations, supplementation of private research study investments, implementation of new clean coal combustion technologies, and subsidies for such investments). In the Caspian region, where states focus on oil and gas exploitation, environmental protection issues are not a priority for their energy security policies.

We have different geographic ranges of energy security. We can talk about security on a global or national scale, and about regions rich and poor in energy resources. Thus, the understanding of the essence of this concept will be shaped by various assumptions related to the logic of international relations, international trade, the world market, or the control of energy supplies (Gryz, 2018, p. 80).

No single, universal, and consistent definition of energy security exists. This term should be considered in relation to other dimensions of security. Energy security is a part of national and international security, as it covers internal and external aspects of interests of the state. However, it cannot be understood as the sum of the security of individual actors on the international scene. The division of state security into national and international security is a matter of convention because it is always international in nature. In contemporary international relations, security is a dynamic process, it is complex, multidimensional, multi-actor, and multilevel. Its multidimensionality means that it affects many areas of social life, including access to energy and its consumption (Pietraś, 2017, p. 23). Since energy security has become one of the dimensions or sectors of security (as defined in the previous subsection of this study), its distinctiveness and specificity are becoming an important research problem and are called "autonomy" by Marek Pietraś (2017).

The literature contains various definitions of the essence of the concept of energy security (Raphael & Stokes, 2022, p. 362; Dannreuther, 2017, p. 17). Lester R. Brown spoke in favor of broadening the definition of national security to include the issues of resources, economic and environmental threats, and demographic issues (Yergin, 2006, p. 69). Although it is a very general approach, it indicates the key trends in the analysis of energy security issues in contemporary literature. According to Daniel Yergin, energy security means the availability of affordable energy resources supply (Yergin, 2005, p. 52).

At the same time, it should be pointed out that most of the definitions of energy security are created while considering the viewpoint of energy resource consumers who are largely exposed to various turbulences in the energy market. However, such an approach seems insufficient and fails to take into account the threats to energy security faced by states exporting energy resources. Following Klare: energy security is a guaranteed supply of energy resources that ensures the basic needs of a state, even in crisis or international conflict (Klare, 2008, pp.483–496). Energy security includes activities aimed at reducing dependence on a single importer, that is to say diversification of energy sources. The second value, apart from diversification, is resilience. The "safety margin" relating to a supply system, which is designed to prevent the system from collapsing or to restore it after a crisis (for example, strategic reserves, additional production capacity, crisis response plans) (Yergin, 2006, p. 71).

The essence of supply security comes down to two basic issues: first, the readiness of a given energy system to meet the demand for energy under normal operating conditions (while maintaining continuity of supply, appropriate quality parameters, environmental protection requirements, and socially acceptable prices); and second, the ability to meet the energy demand satisfactorily, though incompletely, despite worse quality parameters, in various emergency and critical situations, natural disasters, and international conflicts (Klare, 2008, pp. 483–496). In such circumstances, the effectiveness of crisis management mechanisms (that is to say, strategic reserves and international cooperation) gain significance. Therefore, this category refers to both the security and stability of supplies of imported energy resources, and to the security and reliability of the domestic energy infrastructure (Yergin, 2006, p. 71). In this context, for the state to be able to ensure continuity of supply, its energy security strategy should take into account a variety of conditions, such as the level of risk associated with particular sources of supply. This is combined with the issue of the political and economic stability of exporting states.

Another issue is the flexibility of the energy system, that is to say, the ability to quickly convert from one resource to another and the scope of using internal resources. Defining the essence of energy security, University of Ottawa analysts Chantale LaCasse and André Plourde, stated that: "if security of supply means certainty of the physical availability of oil in times of disruption, then a state can be said to have achieved its objective if it is always able to ensure that the necessary quantity of oil will certainly reach the internal market" (LaCasse & Plourde, 1995, p. 24). Jan H. Kalicki and David L. Goldwyn defined energy security similarly—as a guarantee of a smooth, reliable, and affordable energy supply without any disruptions (Kalicki & Goldwyn, 2005, p. 10). Ensuring the energy security of the state is also interpreted as eliminating or limiting the possibility for external actors to use their status as an energy supplier in order to exert political pressure, which also applies to the situation of energy consumers who may be subjected to such pressure. Janusz Bielecki emphasizes the importance of energy resource prices, defining energy security as "reliable and sufficient energy supplies at affordable prices" (Bielecki, 2002, p. 237). Likewise, the Asia Pacific Energy Research Centre defines it as: "securing sufficient energy supplies at an affordable and stable price to achieve economic efficiency and growth" (Ciuta, 2010, p. 125). The most common definitions in the literature define energy security as "ensuring sufficient energy supplies that meet present and future basic needs, as well as the diversification of energy sources and investment in energy sector that are environmentally friendly and renewable, such as solar energy, biomass or wind farms" (Klare, 2008, pp. 483–496).

Energy security can be considered in the short term as the ability of the energy system to flexibly respond to sudden changes in supply and demand; and in the long term as the implementation of investments in the field of energy supply in accordance with the needs of the economic development of the state (Ciuta, 2010, p. 127). In 1993, the IEA recognized the diversification, energy efficiency, and flexibility in the energy sector as essential for long-term energy security. It added the mechanisms of the collective action of states, ongoing research, implementation of modern technologies, ensuring free trade, and a secure investment environment, as well as cooperation between all the actors in the energy market to exchange information and achieve mutual understanding (Skinner, 2005).

Daniel Yergin stated that: "energy security demands constant commitment and attention—both today and in the future" (Yergin, 2006, p. 52). He identifies many key features of the energy security of states. They include the diversification of energy supplies, strategic reserves, the diversity and multiplicity of key energy infrastructure, flexibility of energy markets, interdependencies between suppliers and consumers of resources, stimulating their mutual cooperation, and regular investments in technological modernization. For the purposes of the research problem of this study, the above definition seems to be the most useful and takes into account the most important elements of the energy security policy.

As the awareness of the importance of energy for the economy and security of states changed, so did the definition of energy security. According to Robert Skinner, defining and understanding the essence of energy security depends on "where and when we are" (Yergin, 2006, p. 52). Therefore, "context is everything" in analysis of the essence of this phenomenon (Yergin, 2006, p. 55). Thus, it is crucial to correctly understand this "context," that is, all and any proper functioning of the global energy market in a given period. Such an approach to energy security is very valuable and useful, as it defines it as a very complex issue that results from various conditions. So, we must analyze this problem, and consider the many factors which are constituents of the energy security category. At the same time, it is important to recognize the necessity to take, not only individual but also joint actions to ensure energy security on the regional and global scale (Skinner, 2005).

The political and military dimension of security was losing its importance in parallel with the decline of the Cold War system. Presently, security is becoming multidimensional, having regard to, among other things, the political, cultural, and economic conditions of the activities of both states and non-sovereign actors (Skinner, 2005). As Pietraś stated: "International security combines the security of the state but also other actors of international relations [...] this means that national security interests are integrated into broader structures of the international order" (Pietraś, 2006, p. 324). Since security is related to the survival of a given actor, we can undoubtedly treat energy as one of the most important dimensions of security. Threats in the functioning of society, a state, or international community limit their development, but most of all affect their further existence (Buzan et al., 1998, p. 195). Therefore, the energy infrastructure of states very often becomes the target of attacks by various types of actors, both sovereign and non-sovereign.

2.3   *Threats to Energy Security*

The challenges and threats of the international energy market present an important context of the energy security policy in the Caspian region. Energy security results, not only from objective economic premises but also from the balance of political power on the global scale. States often use their resource potential as a foreign policy tool (Mouraviev & Koulouri, 2019, p. 34).

In terms of energy security, a special place is given to oil, which is a very universal fuel, being a basis in the energy mixes of most countries in the world. It is estimated that oil will remain the primary energy carrier for at least two more decades. The main aspect of oil security was the continuous increase in demand for energy and oil products. On the other hand, this demand should be satisfied, which is associated with various types of threats (Table 1.5) (Dublaga, 2013, p. 61). Klare divided them into three groups:

1.   global oil depletion and doubts about the possibility to increase oil supply to meet the growing demand;
2.   shifting the center of gravity of global oil production and extraction towards politically unstable states, which may lead to more and more armed conflicts; and
3.   threats related to the functioning of the oil infrastructure and oil transport (attacks on oil facilities and tankers, accidents, and disasters) (Klare, 2008, pp. 483–496).

Serious challenges for energy security include technological and economic barriers in the mining industry and the slow but inevitable process of resource depletion. As global demand for hydrocarbons rises, energy producers are forced to invest more in the exploration of new deposits while consumers are trying to diversify supply. In this context, M. Pietraś's words deserve attention:

the variety of threats to the extraction and security of energy resources supply. These can be technical reasons related to the failure of

TABLE 1.5   Main threats of energy security

Short term	Long term
Related to the functioning of industrial transport infrastructure—supply shortages caused by accidents, weather conditions, or network failures. Increasing threats of terrorism and maritime piracy—a serious risk for the land and sea transport of energy. Cyberspace threats.	Geological—related to depletion of resources. Technical—problems with extraction and transmission systems due to underinvestment and poor technical conditions. Economic—the difference between supply and demand. Geopolitical—suspension of supplies for political reasons. This is also about competing for influence in resource-rich regions and the absence of rules for extraction in disputed territories. Environmental—related to environmental pollution caused by activities in the energy sector.

SOURCE: AUTHOR'S OWN WORK

transmission or transportation equipment. Political instability in the areas where the oil and gas are extracted or transported may be another threat, as can the activities of non-state actors such as terrorist organisations or sea pirates. One must not forget about natural disasters such as earthquakes or floods. (Pietraś, 2017, p. 23)

It is also hazardous for the volatility of energy resources prices and the failure of the global management of these resources to overlap (Pietraś, 2017). The variety of threats to energy security should be treated, according to Pietraś's view, "as another manifestation of the autonomy of this security, which is a dynamic process conditioned by various economic, technical, political, social factors, operating at different levels of social life, including global, regional and national levels" (Pietraś, 2017, p. 24). According to Daniel Yergin, international energy security is conditioned by threats posed by the activities of terrorist groups and political instability in mining regions, but also to weather anomalies, such as hurricanes Katrina and Rita in the US in 2005, which disrupted energy supplies in the international market (Yergin, 2006, p. 70). The aim of this part of the study, therefore, is to analyze major threats to international energy security and trends in the development of the global energy market

(Misiągiewicz, 2017a, p. 261). It takes into account the issues of energy demand
and its production, as well as political, economic, and ecological conditions,
significantly determining the state of energy security on a global scale.

2.3.1   Demand for Energy

Satisfying the needs of producers and consumers is an enormous challenge
for the global energy market due to the fact that the global demand for energy
has risen since the 1970s (Figure 1.6). It was estimated that this tendency would
continue in the coming years in connection with urbanization and industrialization processes, as well as the increase in consumption in the automotive industry (Klare, 2008, pp. 483–496). However, in the context of the global
Covid-19 pandemic, the situation changed drastically due to the lockdown
of the economy on a global scale. In this situation, energy demand declined
steadily, especially for coal and oil. Global energy demand in the first quarter
of 2020 fell by 150 million tonnes of oil equivalent (mtoe) compared to the first

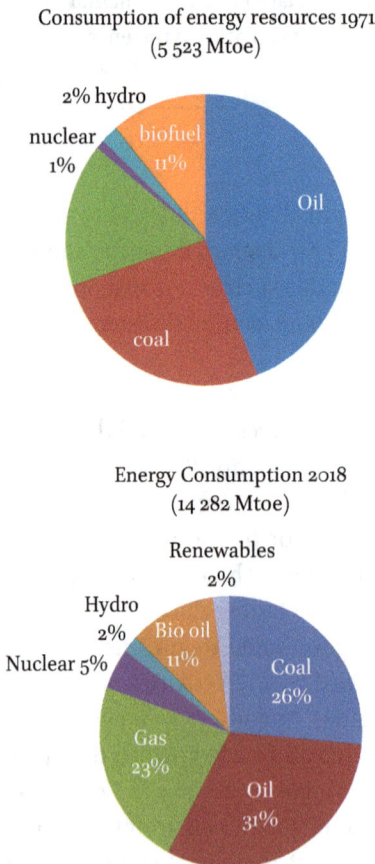

Consumption of energy resources 1971
(5 523 Mtoe)

Energy Consumption 2018
(14 282 Mtoe)

FIGURE 1.6
Consumption of energy resources, 1971 and 2018
SOURCE: AUTHOR'S OWN WORK BASED ON
INTERNATIONAL ENERGY AGENCY, WORLD
ENERGY BALANCES OVERVIEW 2018, 2020

quarter of 2019 (Global Energy Review, 2020, p. 14). However, the dynamics of the change in energy demand will largely depend on the pandemic control policies in individual countries and the pace of recovery of their economies. The IEA even estimated that the impact of the pandemic on energy demand in 2020 will be more than seven times greater than the impact of the 2008 financial crisis in that dimension (Global Energy Review, 2020, p. 16) (Figures 1.7 and 1.8).

Today, we see two primary energy sectors and the related challenges to energy security. The first is electricity generated from coal (41%), gas (20.5%), renewable resources such as water, biomass, sun, wind, and geothermal energy (18.5%), and nuclear energy (15%) (Figure 1.9).

The second energy sector is transport. In this sector, the contribution of oil is essential. According to the US Department of Energy (USDoE), oil accounted for 38% of the world's energy supply and it is estimated that this share would not change substantially by 2030. "Despite the increase in the

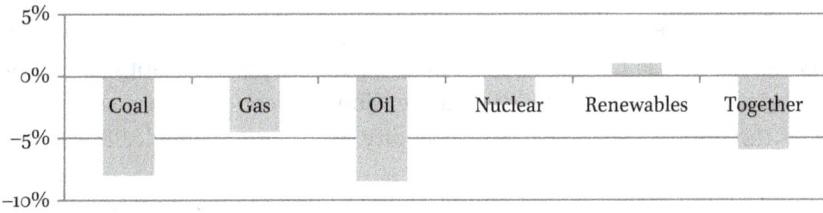

FIGURE 1.7   Change in energy demand, 2020
             SOURCE: AUTHOR'S OWN WORK BASED ON GLOBAL ENERGY REVIEW (2020)

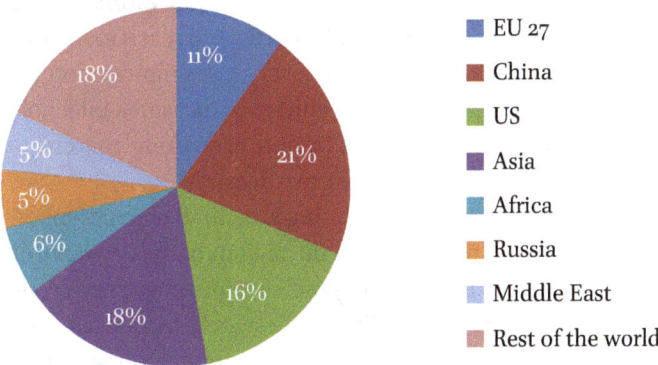

FIGURE 1.8   Energy demand by region, 2018
             SOURCE: AUTHOR'S OWN WORK BASED ON INTERNATIONAL ENERGY
             AGENCY, WORLD ENERGY BALANCES 2020

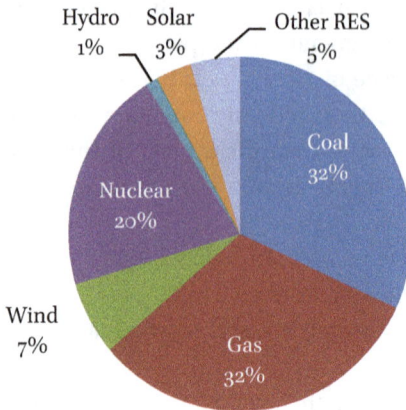

FIGURE 1.9
Electricity production in OECD countries
SOURCE: AUTHOR'S OWN WORK BASED ON
INTERNATIONAL ENERGY AGENCY, WORLD
ENERGY BALANCES OVERVIEW 2018

share of low-carbon energy sources, the global energy balance remains dominated by fossil fuels supported by subsidies" (Klare, 2008, pp. 483–496). While the world's largest consumers are able to exploit oil reserves to meet their basic needs, most states depend on imports. Their position in the energy market is very weak because they are susceptible to external pressure, not only in the economic but also in the political dimension. Dependence on a single producer threatens to undermine the liquidity of imports (Shneider & Peeples, 2022, p. 124; Klare, 2008, pp. 483–496).

The biggest problem for world energy markets is the concern over whether global production of resources will keep up with the growing demand. By 2030, the world's population will likely need 45% more energy than in the 1990s. However, it is unclear whether the production of energy resources will be large enough to meet the demand, especially for oil. The IEA estimated that global oil demand is projected to climb by 2.2 mb/d in 2023 to reach 102.1 mb/d. Growth will slow to 1.1 mb/d in 2024, as the "recovery loses momentum and as ever-greater vehicle fleet electrification and efficiency measures take hold" (International Energy Agency, July 2023, p. 23). Despite everything, this creates a necessity for increased production in the next two decades.

Global energy markets are currently undergoing structural changes following the increase in the number of producers (in the regions of the Persian Gulf, Central Asia, and Africa) and the emergence of new major consumers (countries of Southeast Asia). The Cambridge Energy Research Associates states that: "the global order is transforming: new alliances are emerging, reflecting interests that may fundamentally differ from those dominant in international politics over the past few decades" (Prońińska, 2006, p. 406). Thus, the transformation of the energy market has a direct impact on relations between producers and consumers of energy resources.

The imbalance in the world energy market may occur as a result of fewer discoveries of new sources of oil. The fact that the world's major oil fields are slowly depleting should be taken into account. Fewer and fewer new sources of oil are being discovered. Energy market analysts estimate that the current global production has already peaked and will steadily decline. More and more often they refer to the 1950s thesis of the geophysicist Marion King Hubbert, that after a period of growth, global production of fossil fuels will peak (peak-oil) and then decline until the reserves are completely exhausted (Proninska, 2011, p. 262). Colin Campbell wrote in 2001:

> Reality shows that there is no adjournment. Gradually, the market – not just for oil – will have to realise that the Organization of Petroleum Exporting Countries (OPEC) is not enough to deal with resource deple-tion. This will be a difficult experience as it means that there is no longer any barrier to price increases other than that resulting from a decline in supply. These events will result in a global recession and stock market crash. (Campbell, 2001, p. 21)

The peak of finding new oil fields occurred in the 1960s, when newly discovered reserves totaled 480 billion barrels (Klare, 2008, p. 483–496). Since then, fewer and fewer new reserves have been discovered, while the consumption of the exploited resources has risen in recent years. The international crisis related to the Covid-19 pandemic caused an imbalance in the energy market but once the situation normalizes, energy consumption will likely further increase. Based on an analysis of 800 key oil fields worldwide, the IEA estimated that the average annual decline in production would be 5.1%, reaching as much as 8.6% in 2030 (International Energy Agency, November 2008, p. 9). The largest decline in oil production occurred between 2000 and 2008 in Mexico, China, Norway, Australia, and the United Kingdom. North Sea oil production fell from 6.4 mb/d in 2000 to 2.1 mb/d in 2005. Production declines also occurred in Venezuela, Indonesia, and the Middle East.

Oil is the most important hydrocarbon for industrialized nations. It is an essential raw material for the production of fuels, lubricants, and other organic compounds (Dublaga, 2013, p. 63). Lack of access to oil is not the only threat to energy security. It is worth noting the issue of the so-called *peak oil* pro-duction, after which production begins to decline and never returns to its highest level. Oil market analysts disagree as to when this peak of production occurred. Geologist K. S. Deffeys determined it to be around 2009; J. Laharrere, also a geologist, set the range at 2010–2020; the American Energy Information Agency set it at 2016; and the Shell Corporation presented the most optimistic forecast at beyond 2025 (Gryz, 2018, p. 66). Analysts are not predicting a complete depletion of oil but rather, that a situation where oil that is cheap and easy to extract will run out. So, the main problem is not the lack of oil but the increasing difficulties with its extraction and refining (Gryz, 2018, p. 67). Most of the oil-producing countries and global oil fields have already passed their peak production or are at the so-called "flat peak," lasting several years (it is estimated to affect 54 of the 65 oil-producing states). As a result, a significant number of deposits have been depleted, and replacing the production capacity that is lost every year is becoming more and more expensive and difficult. Also, much less oil is being discovered than a few decades ago. The last significant discoveries were made in the 1960s. Also to be taken into account is that, since the 1980s, we have extracted more than we have discovered. Another problem is the difficulty of producing oil from newly discovered deposits. For example, oil sands in Canada or heavy oil in Venezuela are very abundant deposits but their exploitation is problematic (Gryz, 2018).

The most significant oil reserves are found in the OPEC cartel states (Figures 1.10 and 1.11). Many of them are politically unstable areas, with high rates of poverty among the population. Rebel movements, terrorist organizations, and corrupt, largely authoritarian governments are present there. Profits from the oil trade further exacerbate corruption and increase arms spending. Oil transport comes with numerous threats such as terrorism and maritime piracy.

More and more often energy market dealing with competition among consumers for supply sources and competition among producers for export routes (Fettweis, 2009, p. 67). A condition that fosters competition between the main consumption centers is the change in the structure of the global demand for energy and fossil fuels, and the loss of a leadership in this dimension by highly developed countries from the OECD. According to the EIA,

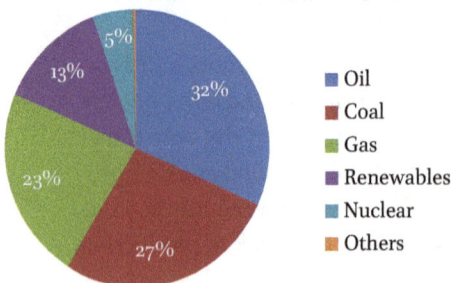

- Oil
- Coal
- Gas
- Renewables
- Nuclear
- Others

FIGURE 1.10
Production of energy resources
SOURCE: AUTHOR'S OWN WORK BASED ON EU
ENERGY IN FIGURES 2020

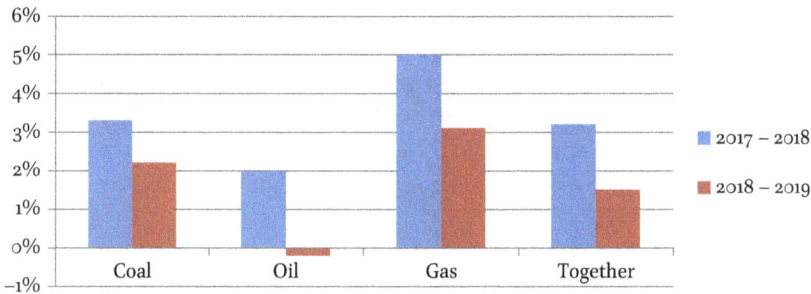

FIGURE 1.11   Change in global hydrocarbon production
SOURCE: AUTHOR'S OWN WORK BASED ON WORLD ENERGY
BALANCES 2020

global energy consumption will increase by 44% by 2030, while the share of OECD countries in global consumption will fall from 51% to 41%. Demand in the OECD, and Europe in particular, is languishing amid a grinding slowdown in industrial activity (International Energy Agency, July 2023, p. 203). The growth in demand for energy and hydrocarbon fuels is primarily driven by China and India, which are becoming major global importers (International Energy Agency, July 2023). The population of these countries accounts for one third of the world's population, and their dynamic economic development has created a new and very large middle class, which generates a rapid growth in energy demand. Thus, more than 80% of the rise in total oil consumption is attributed to the Asian countries. Strengthening the position of new global consumption regions increases competition in the market and improves the situation of exporters, who gain more freedom in their choice of markets (Pronińska, 2011, p. 264). This situation implies the energy market in the Caspian region is becoming more dominant. The countries of the region are becoming more and more important for the main importers of energy resources.

For the world's largest consumers of energy, the depletion of resources and the actions of exporters limiting access to resources are serious problems that may become a threat to their energy security. The consequences of the global energy deficit will have significant geopolitical implications. Importers will look for new sources of supply, which may increase the interest in energy resources in Africa, the Caspian region, South America, and the Arctic. The goal of the competition is to gain access to sources of energy and the transmission infrastructure. Simultaneously, the spatial and subjective scope of the competition has significantly expanded. It may take place in various regions of the world and between various actors, not only state actors. Klare considered the three facets of the rivalry for resources on a global scale: the US, China, and Russia. The three superpowers that constitute the so-called 'strategic triangle', determined the dynamics of the global energy market. However, due to economic sanctions imposed by Western countries on the energy sector related to the invasion of Ukraine [in 2022], Russian oil exports fell to 7.3 mb/d in June 2023, their lowest since March 2021" (International Energy Agency, July 2023, p. 231).

2.3.2   Geographical Conditions

The problem for the global energy market is that the deposits which are being currently exploited are located in regions that are difficult to operate due to geographic, environmental, or political conditions, which limits the global extraction of energy resources (Figure 1.12).

Until the 1950s, two-thirds of oil production was located in the US, Canada, and Europe. However, as demand grew, the search for new sources began. In 1990, the production of crude oil in the north accounted for 39% of global output (Klare, 2008, pp. 483–496). At the same time, there was an increase in the exploitation of resources in the south of the globe, that is to say, in Africa, the Persian Gulf, and the Caspian region. Such a shift in oil production raised the security risk of energy resources supply. It is greater given the political, social, and economic instability in those regions. The young inhabitants experience high unemployment, ethnic conflicts, instability of government, corruption, and the militarization of social life—the legacy of the colonial and totalitarian systems. Thus, the prospects for oil production are associated

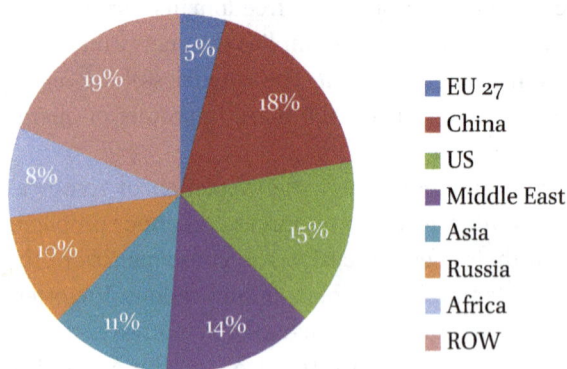

FIGURE 1.12   Global energy production (%)
SOURCE: AUTHOR'S OWN WORK BASED ON EU ENERGY IN FIGURES 2020, WORLD ENERGY BALANCES OVERVIEW 2018

with rising risk, which drives the price growth of this resource. Along with the price growth, the number of conflicts in regions rich in this commodity will probably increase (Ross, 2008, p. 123).

In addition, the profits from the sale of oil corrupt and strengthen authoritarian rule, and do not translate into the wealth of societies. Examples of such phenomena are visible in the countries of the Caspian region.

We are currently witnessing a transformation when it comes to oil exportation. Lower production from Saudi Arabia and core OPEC+ members since production cuts were first implemented in November 2022, has so far been offset by higher output from other producers: Iran and Kazakhstan (International Energy Agency, July 2023).

In this context, attention should also be paid to increasing oil and natural gas production in the US, caused by the use of extraction technologies that allow for the release of these resources from shale deposits (Figure 1.13). In the

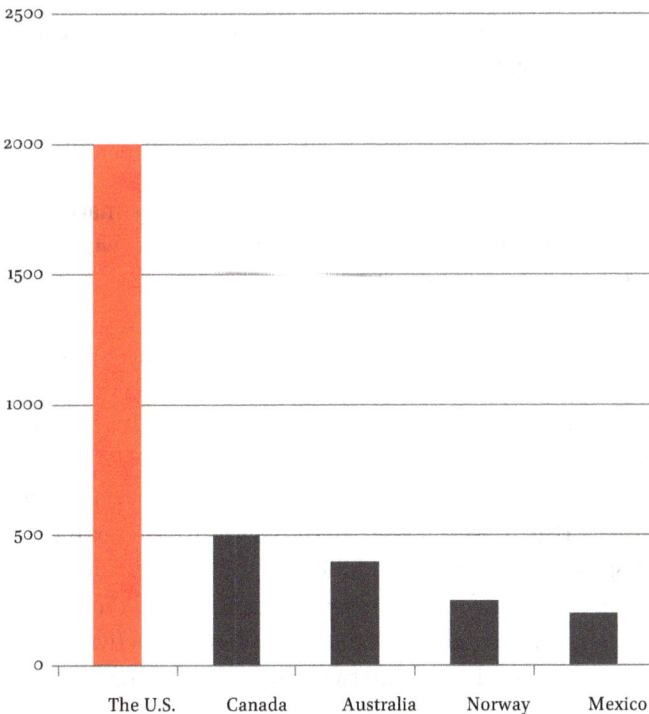

FIGURE 1.13   Major energy producers in OECD countries
SOURCE: OWN WORK BASED ON INTERNATIONAL ENERGY AGENCY, WORLD
ENERGY BALANCES OVERVIEW 2018

US, new shale gas extraction and up scaling technologies have been developed since 2001. With it, gas molecules trapped in rock formations can now also be extracted (Criekemans, 2022). This boosted business, gave the industry an additional competitive advantage in the form of cheaper electricity and natural gas, and gradually changed the role of the US in global energy trade. In 2020, the US became one of the world's largest producers of hydrocarbons (Geri, McNabb, 2019, p. 23; Emmons et al., 2021, p. 373). Currently, 30% of the country's energy comes from shale gas, the US is becoming nearly energy self-sufficient, which is unprecedented compared to most other energy-importing states. The geopolitical consequence is that the US wants to play a bigger role in the energy market in Europe after hydrocarbon supplies from Russia were limited. The declarative key concern of the US administrative was energy supply security in Europe. This explains why former US President Donald J. Trump and present Joe Biden pressured Germany over the Nord Stream II pipeline, which is being built in the Baltic Sea (Criekemans, 2022). The current geopolitical situation related to Russia's war in Ukraine has finally annihilated the plans to launch the gas pipeline, which was completed in 2021 and sabotaged a year later. Ultimately, the pipeline was destroyed and it will most likely not be possible to launch it in the future.

2.3.3   Supply System

The global supply system presents a challenge for the energy market. As J. Dyczka wrote, the functioning of the critical infrastructure within the following sectors is key to maintaining national energy security:
– gas, oil, liquid fuels;
– extraction equipment, processing and storage of gas, oil, and liquid fuels;
– power plants; and
– energy transmission and distribution networks that supply electricity, gas, oil, and liquid fuels (Dyczka, 2013, p. 73).

All these sectors can become the target of a wide variety of criminal groups. In the 21st century, terrorists most often attacked devices for the extraction, processing, and storage of gas, oil, and liquid fuels, in addition to water borne transport: maritime, ocean, and energy transmission and distribution networks that supply electricity, gas, oil, and liquid fuels. Terrorist activities that threaten energy security can be divided into two groups: sea-related and land-based (Dyczka, 2013, p. 74).

Transport infrastructure, that is to say pipelines or sea ways, is a vulnerable part of the energy market, being an easy target for terrorist attacks, making it increasingly problematic and costly to meet global energy needs. Transport routes very often pass through politically unstable territories, which increases the risk to the supply of resources. Energy security is thus linked to the military aspect of the activities of states (Klare, 2008, pp. 483–496). They are forced to protect energy resources and their transmission routes. Robert Ebel of the Center for Strategic and International Studies (csis) quoted by Klare, stated that: "pipelines are very vulnerable targets [...] you don't need sophisticated weapons or great effort to cause physical and psychological damage" (Klare, 2008, p. 483).

The intensification of the threats of terrorism and maritime piracy is a serious risk for land and sea transportation of resources, as two-thirds of the world oil trade is conducted by sea, and one-fourth of the world's oil and gas resources are located in the coastal zones (Map 1.1). The areas of the highest production and highest consumption are separated by enormous distances, which means that energy resources transporting units are exposed to attacks by terrorists to a very significant degree (Dyczka, 2013, p. 74). Energy security is closely connected with shipping security. The major threats include piracy, terrorism, and border conflicts between states. As for shipping, terrorist attacks can take diverse forms:
 – bombs in ports or at sea, using explosives delivered on a ship;
 – hijacking of a commercial vessel;
 – fire from the shore aimed at vessels maneuvering in coastal areas; and
 – actions using mines (Dyczka, 2013, p. 75).
Since September 11, 2001 and the destruction of the Twin Towers in New York, these threats became more common. The US Congress then passed the Maritime Transportation Security Act of 2002, and the International Maritime Organization issued the International Ship and Port Facility Security Code in the same year. Both documents deal with the problem of maritime terrorism, piracy, and other forms of maritime conflicts.

In this context, it is very important to secure transport routes for energy resources (Nincic, 2009, p. 31). The so-called "bottlenecks" through which oil is transported (Strait of Malacca, Hormuz, Bab el-Mandab, Suez Canal, Bosphorus, and Panama Canal) are being attacked by terrorist groups, which for them is the most effective means of hitting Western interests (Map 1.1).

Another category is waterways along the coasts of politically unstable states. The territorial waters of Indonesia, Nigeria, and Somalia experience the greatest number of acts of piracy, very often targeting tankers. Terrorists use various methods to disrupt the maritime oil and gas transportation system:
 – operations using high-speed units filled with explosives;
 – use of on-board armament: fast motorboats, ad hoc adopted commercial vessels, aircraft, submarines;

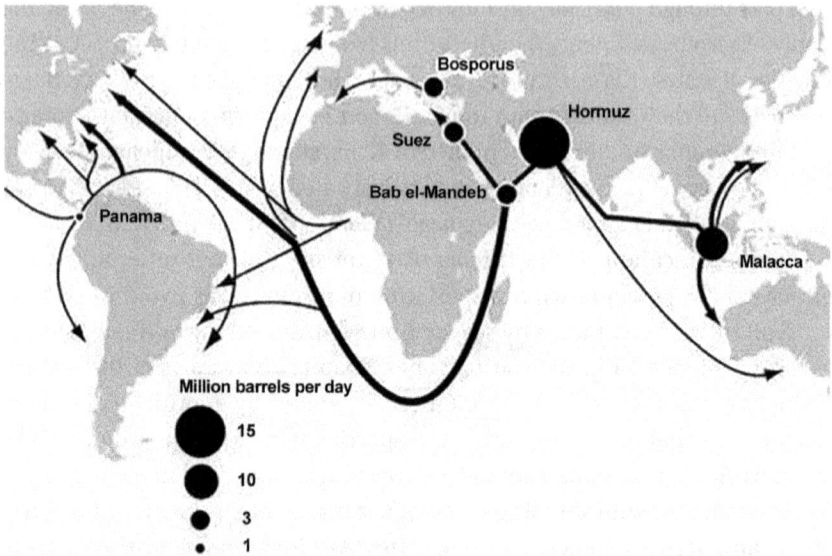

MAP 1.1   "Bottlenecks" in the transport of energy resources
          SOURCE: HTTPS://WWW.EIA.GOV/TODAYINENERGY/DETAIL.PHP?ID=330/

- seizure of a vessel: criminals can demand a ransom for the return of the cargo or make political demands;
- use of sea mines; and
- use of combat divers.

The consequences of such attacks include the following:

- increase in fossil fuel prices in the world market (economic costs—increase in transport costs);
- environmental disaster—social impact: oil contamination;
- costs of providing security to individuals; and
- fulfilment of terrorist objectives: political destabilization, meeting specific demands (Dyczka, 2013, p. 80).

Piracy is an illegal act of rape, detention, or looting committed for private ends by the crew or passengers of a private ship or aircraft (United Nations Convention on the Law of the Sea 1982) (Dyczka, 2013). Any act of piracy is also an act of terrorism, but terrorists can use methods characteristic of pirates to achieve political gain. What distinguishes pirates from terrorists is that the motive of pirates is the profit. Pirates often want to remain anonymous and avoid publicity.

Energy terrorism is not only closely related to armed attacks on energy infrastructure. This phenomenon also involves the theft of resources and the threat of an attack on infrastructures if the company or the state does not financially support a given criminal group. Regardless of the definition of energy terrorism that we adopt, it is undoubtedly an activity that causes enormous financial losses. The protection of energy infrastructure, that is to say, refineries, tankers, and pipelines, accounts for a large part of the financial expenditure of both states and corporations (Koknar, 2009, p. 18).

The technical condition of the infrastructure also poses a serious problem. For example, Russian installations leak as much oil every day as during the Exxon Valdez disaster in Alaska in 1989. Thousands of kilometers of rusty and damaged pipelines also lie in Canada and the US. The cause of the 2010 failure and disaster in the Gulf of Mexico was a faulty device used for emergency shutdown of the borehole. This is one of the effects of oil exploration in increasingly inaccessible locations (Dublaga, 2013, p. 69).

Digital technologies are now being used to control the entire global energy production and distribution sector. The ramification of this is enhanced susceptibility to cyber-attacks. The situation seems to be particularly dangerous in the context of the protection of this strategic sector, which is one of the key elements of critical infrastructure of the state (Saramak, 2014, p. 147). In the last few years, critical infrastructure has become the prime target of perpetrators of cyber-attacks: from government mercenaries, to political hacktivists and cybercriminals, and well-organized cyber-gangs. The attack on the Ukrainian energy network on December 23, 2015, is considered to be the first known successful cyber-attack on electricity networks. Hackers broke into the computer systems of three Ukrainian distribution companies and temporarily disrupted the electricity supply to consumers. Tens of thousands of people were left without electricity. This attack was a complex operation, elaborated in the smallest detail, with consequences in the physical world as well. It was undertaken by a group of exceptionally talented hackers, who had spent many months on planning their attack: they began by identifying electrical grids and the data of their operators, and finally launched a rehearsed, coordinated offensive. According to many analysts, the incident in Ukraine was only a rehearsal before the real attack. The cyber-attack consisted of the following stages: early breach of plant network security using email messages containing malicious software; taking control of the system and remote disconnection of power substations; blocking infrastructure elements; destruction of files stored on servers; an attack blocking the operation of the call center, thereby depriving energy consumers of up-to-date information on the situation. Electric grids are closely interconnected, and a breach of their security may have a cascading effect on other sectors of the economy. Single-operator problems can have cross-border implications. Cyber security involves the principle of the weakest link, according to which the resilience of interconnected systems is determined by their weakest element.

2.3.4   Politicizing
A serious threat to international energy security is the fact that the resource
potential may become an instrument of the foreign policy of producer states.
Such a situation arose in the 1970s, when the embargo imposed on oil by Arab
states on states supporting Israel caused fluctuations in the energy market and
a sharp increase in oil prices (Pronińska, 2006, p. 395). The so-called the "oil
shock" was a breakthrough in understanding energy security. Western states
reacted by establishing the International Energy Agency in 1974. The subsequent oil crises of the 1980s and 1990s were caused by the turmoil on the fuel
market due to the Iranian Revolution of 1979 and the suspension of oil exports
from Iran, the war in the Persian Gulf, as well as the constant fuel consumption growth and uncertainty as to the future supplies of resources. The consequence of these events was the limitation of oil supplies to global markets
(Bielecki, 2002, p. 242).

Russia also treats its energy policy as an instrument of foreign policy. It
perceives the energy-rich Central Asian and Caucasus region as its exclusive
sphere of influence, both economically and politically. Russia's activities in this
region clearly limited its integration with the global energy market (Cohen,
2009, p. 119). Russia maintains its troops there and influences the decisions
of the ruling elite in the newly created post-Soviet states. In 2008, it invaded
Georgia to defend the autonomous regions of Abkhazia and South Ossetia
(Stokes & Raphael, 2010, p. 112). The main reason for the operation in Georgia,
however, was Russia's desire to control the routes of the transport of hydrocarbons from the Caspian and Black Sea regions. The background to the conflict
in eastern Ukraine since 2014, was also related to energy. Russia's goal was to
undermine the credibility of Ukraine as a transit state for resources to Europe,
cut the country off from Russian gas resources, and even cut Ukraine off from
its own coal resources in the Donetsk region.

Following Pietraś, it is fully justified to "politicise" energy security, because
"energy carriers have become an instrument for achieving political goals, exerting influence in international relations, the object of political decisions at the
highest level, and not just economic transactions [...] They can change the geopolitical significance of regions in international relations" (Pietraś, 2017, p. 27).

2.3.5   Economic Conditions
The economic dimension of energy security is identified primarily with the
functioning of the market for energy resources. Until 1973, the law of supply
and demand governed this market. For many years after 1973, OPEC member
states dictated the price of kerosene oil (Pietraś, 2017). Regulatory action has
also been taken by Western countries. Deregulation of the energy commodity

market has contributed to a number of problems; and the fluctuation of energy commodity prices, market failure, and the involvement of states in regulatory activities have become a challenge for many countries (Harris, 2003, p. 158).

The energy sector directly influences the efficiency and competitiveness of the state economy. The economic dimension of security energy is mainly concerned with the cost of energy and continuity of supplies (Gradziuk et al., 2003, p. 76). Energy is a specific product, as it must be available on a continuous basis, even at times of political or economic crises. Lack of liquidity in energy supply entails high costs for the entire national economy. Therefore, the energy sector plays a fundamental role in shaping the efficiency and competitiveness of the economy and has both a direct and indirect impact on the quality of life of citizens (Gradziuk et al., 2003, p. 76). Consequently, energy resources are treated as a strategic product.

Contemporary analyses of the international energy market indicate numerous problems resulting from instability in the world economy caused by the crisis. According to a 2008 report by the IEA, the world's energy system is at a crossroads (International Energy Agency, November 2008). Today's global energy supply and consumption trends are completely unsustainable—in ecological, economic, and social terms. According to the report, these problems had their source in underinvestment in the energy sector with respect to production and transportation. In another 2010 report (International Energy Agency, November 2010), it was stated that the global energy industry was facing unprecedented uncertainty. The global economic crisis of 2008–2009 has thrown energy markets around the world into disarray, and the pace at which the global economy recovers will be critical to the development of the energy sector in the coming years (Pronińska, 2011, p. 261).

A consequence of the global crisis was a temporary decline in demand for energy resources. The economic crisis also affected the price of oil, destabilizing it significantly. As a result of falling demand, the energy sector first witnessed a severe drop in oil prices in 2008 (from USD 145 to USD 40 per barrel); prices then rose to USD 110 per barrel in late 2010 (Pronińska, 2011, p. 261). According to data provided by the IEA, in 2009, investment in the upstream oil and gas sector fell by 19% (Pronińska, 2011, p. 262). Underinvestment in the sector can pose a serious threat to the future security of supplies.

The macroeconomic crisis caused by the Covid-19 pandemic represents another watershed moment in terms of energy market stability. It brought a drop of about 6% in global GDP. Demand for energy decreased by 3.8% in the first quarter of 2020 (Global Energy Review, 2020). The reduction in demand for oil, caused mainly by the restrictions imposed on people's mobility on a global scale, was the most drastic measure. It caused a drop in oil prices on

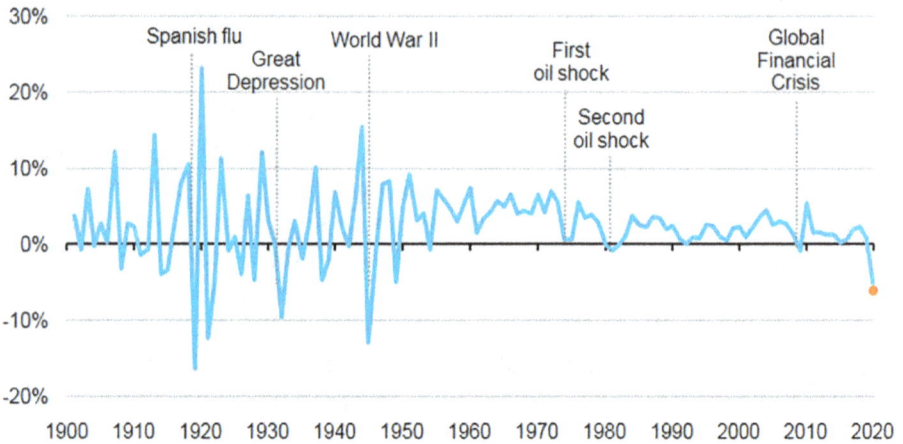

FIGURE 1.14   Changes in energy demand, 1900–2020
SOURCE: GLOBAL ENERGY REVIEW (2020)

the global market. The transport industry noted a 50% drop in activity compared to 2019, while activity in the airline industry decreased by 60% (Global
Energy Review, 2020, p. 23). The decline in demand for energy observed in
the face of the pandemic was the greatest in 70 years (Figure 1.14). The situation remains uncertain and unstable, as there is a prospect of prolongation
of Russia's war in Ukraine and energy transformation towards renewable
sources.

2.3.6   Ecological Conditions

Environmental protection under the conditions of a competitive energy market represents another significant challenge for participants in that market
(Dabelko, 2022, p. 248). In this context, the exploitation of renewable resources
is increasingly becoming an element of energy security strategies developed by
different countries (Kamenopoulos & Tsoutsos, 2019, p. 223). It was not until the
end of the 20th century that environmental problems emerged as a significant
issue in the discourse on energy security (Dabelko, 2022, p. 248; Pietraś, 2017).
Climate change will be counteracted by reducing greenhouse gas emissions,
which, in turn, will be achieved by reducing energy consumption, switching
to low-carbon sources and using energy from renewable sources (Pietraś, 2017,
p. 28). This means that there is a feedback loop between environmental security and energy security. The extraction and consumption of energy resources
cause environmental pollution. On the other hand, the requirements of environmental security, particularly with regard to combating climate change,

stimulate actions supporting energy efficiency, the development of new technologies, and the use of renewable energy (Kamenopoulos & Tsoutsos, 2019, p. 223; Pietraś, 2017; Froggatt & Levi, 2009, pp. 1129–1141; Sen et al., 2011, pp. 834–842). The main renewable technologies are hydropower, biomass energy, geothermal energy, wind energy, solar energy, wave energy, and ocean thermal energy (Demirbas, 2008, p. 42; Fridleifsson, 2001, pp. 99–312). Renewable resources were the principal sources of energy used by our ancestors (solar, wind, water energy). During the last 200 years, industrialized countries have relied mainly on hydrocarbon resources, as industrialization has changed the structure of energy resource consumption in favor of resources such as coal and oil, which generate more energy. The prospect of the abundant availability of these resources was very attractive, while rapid technological advances made their exploitation highly profitable (Bahr et al., 2021, p. 125). Meanwhile, renewable technologies could not provide such a rapid growth in productivity (Edinger & Kaul, 2000, pp. 295–313).

The greatest environmental threat posed by the exploitation of nonrenewable energy resources is the emission of carbon dioxide (CO_2). Nearly 29 billion tonnes of CO_2 enter the atmosphere each year, due to human activity, with 23 billion tonnes of CO_2 coming from hydrocarbon combustion and industrial activities (Demirbas, 2008, p. 45). CO_2 accounts for 50% of gases responsible for the greenhouse effect (Speight, 1996; Dincer, 2001, pp. 69–81).

The growth in greenhouse gas concentrations in the atmosphere leads to an increase in the earth's surface temperature. It is important to apply the principles of sustainable development, that is to say, linking economic growth to social progress, environmental protection, and the popularization of technology (Demirbas, 2008, p. 79). The use of renewable energy sources is one of the ways of ensuring sustainable development. Investing in such sources reduces the risk of supply shortages. However, it requires the construction of expensive infrastructure, with a high initial cost and a long payback period, and involves seasonal problems associated with the exploitation of wind and solar energy. The government's assistance to industry through the creation of appropriate legal regulations and supplementation of private investments in research is crucial in this context.

The economic crisis and the reduction in the use of fossil fuels it has caused have resulted in a drop in CO_2 emissions on a global scale. Greenhouse gas emissions in 2020 were 5% lower than in the previous year (Global Energy Review, 2020). This was due to the 8% decline in emissions from coal mining, 4.5% decline in emissions from oil mining, and a 2.3% drop in emissions from gas mining (Figure 1.15) (Global Energy Review, 2020, p. 17).

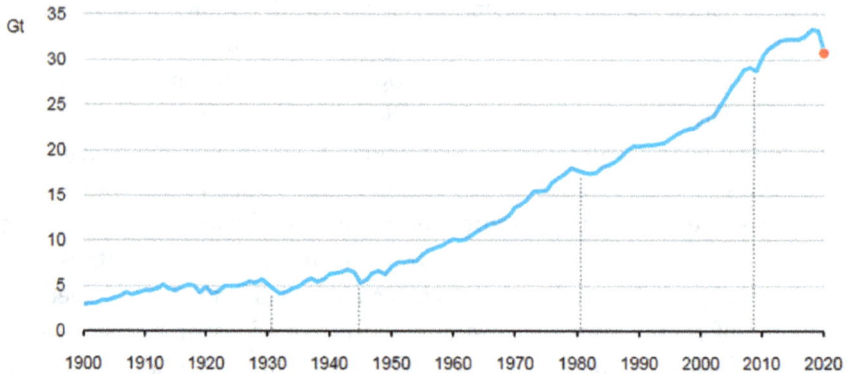

FIGURE 1.15 CO_2 emissions from energy sector activities, 1900–2020
SOURCE: THE IMPACTS OF THE COVID-19 CRISIS ON GLOBAL ENERGY DEMAND AND CO2
EMISSIONS, GLOBAL ENERGY REVIEW 2020

3   Conclusion

The analysis allows us to conclude that the emergence of the issue of energy security at the political level is tantamount to the emergence of the need for new state policy instruments to diagnose and manage the situation in the social sciences. The combination of security and energy creates a new quality for the social sciences. Thus, the science of energy security revolves around energy flow, access to energy, dependencies in the energy market, and the consequences of energy consumption for the climate.

We can identify various prerequisites for energy security: the availability of resources, their sufficiency, and the acceptability of particular fuels. The other prerequisites include: reserves, output, dependence on imports, political stability, the price of energy, and the sensitivity of particular sectors to changes in the price or supply of energy.

James R. Schlesinger (US Secretary of Defense in the Richard Nixon and Gerald Ford administrations, and US Secretary of Energy in the Jimmy Carter administration), stated that: "the world is facing a problem related to energy supply [...] we must get used to a certain level of danger in this dimension" (Klare, 2008, pp. 483–496). He further stated that:

> while we are dealing with modern technologies, we are exposed to multiple threats to energy security. Therefore, instead of addressing energy security, we should address threats to energy security, that is to say energy

insecurity. We are facing different levels of insecurity today. (Klare, 2009, p. 44)

Energy security is a dynamic phenomenon. Its definition depends on the specific character of the security policy actors and on relations in the international energy market. Access to energy resources is an existential need, not only for all states but also for non-sovereign actors, such as multinational corporations. Thus, under the conditions of the continuous growth in energy consumption on the one hand, and its politicization on the other, it has become an indispensable condition of social life and economic development, as well as an increasingly important factor in national and international security (Flaherty & Filho, 2013, p. 13).

The research presented above includes theories and concepts of energy security that relate to the environment of the Caspian region and helped in its analysis. The theory of securitization, the realist theory, and the geopolitical approach seem to be the most useful when analyzing the determinants of energy security policy in the discussed region. It seems that in this context, taking into account the threats and main challenges of the international energy market, it is of great importance for further analysis. Factor analysis implies this type of approach, which shows in which energy security/insecurity environment the countries of the Caspian region operate.

The Caspian Region as a Space for Energy Security Policies

The analysis in this part of the study focuses on the essence and specificity of the Caspian region as a space for energy security policies. The criteria for distinguishing the Caspian region, the legal status of the Caspian Basin, its geopolitical and geoeconomic position, and its energy potential were outlined in this context. The analysis covered regionalism-related processes in this area, as well as a review of the legal process of regulating the status of the Caspian Basin. An important element of this part of the study is an attempt to determine the energy potential of the Caspian states, which poses a major research challenge, due to the diversity and divergence of data on this topic. The subject of the analysis of this part of the study is the identification of the main security threats in the Caspian region that significantly reduce its position in the global energy market. The key issue affecting the regional (in) security environment is the Nagorno-Karabakh conflict.

The specificity of the Caspian region and its dynamics in the international system is conditioned by a complex set of interactions between state, sub-state, transnational, regional, and international levels of analysis. Thus, the systemic and structural specificity of the region is based on processes occurring at the local and regional scale. This logic of framing the research problem reflects its essence and facilitates the understanding of the importance of various processes in the political, economic, and geopolitical dimensions, as well as their impact on the development of energy security policies. The Caspian region is a strategic area owing to the proximity of China, Russia and Iran, and the involvement of external actors, such as the US, NATO, and the EU. Due to the multiple conflicting interests of these actors, the region is an area of geopolitical rivalry on a global scale. The interest in the hydrocarbon potential of the Caspian region was conditioned by the prospect of the depletion of these resources in the North Sea, Persian Gulf, and other regions in the world. The Caspian Sea is an area affected by numerous legal, economic, and environmental challenges related to the exploitation of energy resources. The area has been affected by conflicts between coastal states over access to resource deposits and the division of the seabed. Coastal states and corporations involved in the extraction and transport of energy resources must take greater responsibility for the natural environment in this sensitive region.

1   Criteria for Distinguishing the Caspian Region

A region is a limited geographical area with a shared history, culture, economic and social flows, common security concerns, common institutions, or common external threats (MacFarlane, 2018, pp. 143–160; Miller, 2007, pp. 143–160). Michael Schulz, Fredrik Soderbaum, and Joakim Ojendal define regionalism as "a process initiated by actors as a set of ideas, values, and goals aimed at creating, maintaining, or ensuring security, prosperity, and development within a region" (Schulzet al., 2001, p. 5). After the Cold War, regions and regionalism became a subject of broader interest to academics studying international relations (Hanckock et al., 2021, p. 173).

First, the integration potential of regionalization processes acquired greater significance in the face of globalization processes. Although the interests and policies of states vary internationally, regionally they face similar problems, risks, and challenges (Hurrell, 1995, pp. 331–358). Second, conceptually and analytically, in contrast to the state-centric model of international relations, the concept related to the functioning of regions constitutes an explanatory analysis model which elucidates the relationships between the state level and the broader international system (Altunisik & Tanrisever, 2018, pp. 30–45). In this context, focusing on the regional level of analysis helps explain why states behave the way they do (Hurrell, 2005, pp. 38–53).

Thus, studies on the essence of regionalism are evolving. It seems, however, that although there are many theoretical approaches, there exists a common foundation for these considerations based on the assumption that regionalism is grounded in a common identity and policies of the actors located in a specific geographical and cultural space, which is separated from the external environment by identifiable borders (Altunisik & Tanrisever, 2018, pp. 30–45). The functioning of regional cooperation in economic, political, and cultural dimensions existing between actors is the key issue here (Hajizada & Marciacq, 2013, pp. 305–327). However, this dominant approach to defining regions and regionalisms is useful for analyzing the center of regions that are characterized by shared values, institutions, and integrative processes (Okolo, 1985, pp. 121–153). The integration potential of regionalization processes becomes weaker in the region's peripheral area in proportion to the distance from the center, where the regionalization process has been initiated, promoted, and monitored.

Thus, peripheral areas are part of regionalization processes, but their integrity with regions becomes weaker, as they are removed from the core of the region towards its borders (Altunisik & Tanrisever, 2018, pp. 30–45). The border zones of the regions differ from their core and even tend to resemble the neighboring areas. In most cases, the boundaries of regions are neither clearly defined and nor clearly delineated, and may even include vast areas of different countries inhabited by diverse nations and cultures, illustrating the specificity of a given region or sub-region in a broader context. Such regions are referred to as "border regions." This challenges the traditional conceptualization of a region (Koter & Heffner, 1998, p. 34). The existence of border regions requires a new approach, and their specificity is difficult to grasp. In contrast to the center of the region, the "intermediaries" or border regions can be referred to as "peak" or "on the edge" regions (Altunisik & Tanrisever, 2018, pp. 30–45). This means that they are located on the dividing line between two systems. Conceptualizing border regions as "peak regions" enables the study of simultaneity, complementarity, and conflicting regionalization processes in a given region (Altunisik & Tanrisever, 2018).

The concept of "peak regions" has been adapted to international relations studies by Philip Robins (2014). He developed the concept of the "double gravity state," which referred to states shaped by the interaction of various conflicting regional trends (Altunisik & Tanrisever, 2018, pp. 30–45). Then, in 2014, Mark Herzog and Robins (2014) published *The Role, Position and Agency of Cusp States in International Relations*, which considers the concept of "peakiness" in relation to countries such as Turkey, Ukraine, Taiwan, and Mexico.

One can analyze regionalism or the international politics of regionalism in border regions, such as the Caspian region, with reference to this concept (Altunisik & Tanrisever, 2018, pp. 30–45) (Map 2.1). In this sense, a border region can be treated as a peak region when it is located at the edge of two or more regions and is subject to the diverse dynamics of regionalization processes. Border areas have local, national, and regional characteristics that link them to regional processes initiated by regional centers. The cores of regions can also be analyzed using the conceptualization of peak regions, especially when the full integration of regions is regarded as an idealization (Altunisik & Tanrisever, 2018, pp. 30–45). In this sense, peakiness is not treated as an anomaly, but rather as a specific feature of regions that have diverse histories, sociopolitical, and international dynamics, regardless of whether we consider them as central, peripheral, or border regions. It all depends on the context in which we view a given region (Tanrisever, 2014, pp. 60–79).

In contrast to the centers of regions, where consolidated processes of regionalization occur, peak border regions cause the processes of regionalization to be contested and replaced by a discussion of regionalism and its multidimensionality (Altunisik & Tanrisever, 2018, pp. 30–45). In the case of border peak areas, concepts of regionalism are evolving, undergoing transformation and

MAP 2.1   The Caspian region: Between Central Asia and the Caucasus
SOURCE: HTTPS://COMMONS.WIKIMEDIA.ORG/W/INDEX
.PHP?SEARCH=CENTRAL+ASIA&TITLE=SPECIAL:MEDIASEARCH&GO=GO&TYPE=IMAGE

manipulation by various sociopolitical actors both from outside of the region and inside it. Such processes of regionalization reflect different economic and geopolitical interests. Thus, the policy of regionalization in border regions is shaped, taking into account the internal specificities of these areas, which creates opportunities and constraints for regional actors. Regional actors can also make an instrumental use of a region's peak and frontier role to enhance their own power and counterbalance the power of other players (Altunisik & Tanrisever, 2018, pp. 30–45). To achieve this end, regional actors impact not only on the regions in which they operate, but also on neighboring regions, as they create cross-border links based on regional problems concerning border areas, central areas, and neighboring regions (Koter & Heffner, 1998).

Iver Neumann's concept describes the region-building process (Neumann, 1994, pp. 53–74). He argues that basing this phenomenon on cultural integration (*inside-out*) and geopolitics (*outside-in*) is insufficient. Instead, he proposes a debate on "how and why the functioning of a region is postulated, who promotes its existence, what their intentions are, and how the definitions of processes of inclusion and exclusion define a given region and its transformation" (Neumann, 1994, p. 53).

According to the liberal approach, which refers to shared democratic values and the presence of international organizations in the region, the Caspian states are neither democratic nor do they have established significant regional organizations that would be of major importance for regional security (MacFarlane, 2018, pp. 143–160). Although there is a progressing economic co-dependence in the region, its countries have not developed common principles of cooperation in solving problems, which is largely due to the Soviet legacy. Consequently, the Caspian region is unstable and exposed to various risks (MacFarlane, 2018, pp. 143–160).

The realist trend, represented by Kenneth Waltz (1979) or John Mearsheimer (2001), does not directly address regions composed of small states. The thinking in this case is based on the relations between powers on the international scale, which regard strength and power as fundamental values. In an anarchic environment, states seek to achieve strategic equilibrium. The stronger ones try to obtain control over the weaker ones by treating them as peripheral areas. However, the realistic insistence on the uniformity of behavior among the strongest players is often questioned: "What also matters are differences between states and their goals, which lead them to choose different policies: the search for security may lead them to choose international cooperation or rivalry" (Glaser, 1997, pp. 171 - 201). This approach makes it possible to analyze the region, and not only in terms of the "Great Game" between superpowers (MacFarlane, 2018, pp. 143–160).

One can apply the alignment theory to analyze the specificity of the Caspian region. Structural realism points out that states will seek to achieve balance (alignment) against force (Walt, 1987; Schweller, 1994, pp. 72–107). According to this trend, "balance is preferable to joining a stronger entity" (Walt, 1987, p. 147). Stephen Walt suggests that states seek balance not against force, but against threats that have a variety of backgrounds: geopolitical, military, and others. Balancing against threats generates different behaviours than balance of power does. Paul Schroeder contests the existence of a dichotomy between balance and submission to the influence of powers, arguing that many states face a different dilemma, namely, whether they should protect themselves or hide (Schroeder, 1994, pp. 108–148).

In a sense, the specificity of the Caspian region confirms all the behavioural possibilities outlined above. Assuming that Russia is the dominant power in the region, the balance of power theory proves that the post-Soviet states will try to act in such a manner as to balance the influence of this power

(MacFarlane, 2018, pp. 143–160). However, there is a variety of perceptions of threats in the region, so the balance of power is not dominant here. Balance against threats is a more adequate concept. This concept makes it easier to understand how the states of the Caspian region define threats and how to oppose them (MacFarlane, 2018, pp. 143–160).

The last issues considered by Walt are perception and intention (Walt, 1987). This approach makes it easier to understand the specificity of the security environment in the Caspian region. There are two variants in this context. Samuel P. Huntington points out that the structure of international relations evolves from the contradiction between the major centers of influence towards a conflict of civilizations. Within this meaning, the security challenges in the Caspian region can be interpreted in terms of civilizational rivalry (Huntington, 1997). However, various international relations cut across the civilization lines: Azerbaijan—the West, Iran–Russia, Turkmenistan–China. Such a situation calls into question civilizational determinism (MacFarlane, 2018, pp. 143–160). Walt points out that "ideology is less important than balance as a motive for cooperation" (Walt, 1987, p. 181). Another question arises: how do global players use identity and identity-related policies? It can be concluded that they promote regional cooperation where an identity community comes together. If such links are absent, international players are less involved in cooperation. The Caspian region is not therefore a priority for US global policy, however, it is a key region for Russia due to the need to pursue geopolitical and economic goals.

Another theory that helps to capture the specificity of the regional security environment in the Caspian region is the concept of Buzan, who, like Walt, focuses on the perception of intentions (Buzan, 1991). He argues that regional security stems from the way in which states interpret a threat. The relationships between members and regional neighbors define the specifics of security. They function together, and none of them is able to define its security policy without considering the position of other states within and around the region.

The work of Buzan and O. Wæver titled, *Regions and Competences: The Structure of International Security* (2003), developed the concept of a regional security complex (RSC). This theory aimed to place regions in the international structure. The extent of autonomy of international systems with respect to security follows from the level of centralization or acquiescence to the adaptation of the broader global security architecture. This concept helps us understand the importance of regions in the international system. It emphasizes the interdependence between states in the region in terms of security and the key role of the neighboring states in defining the dynamics of regional security (MacFarlane, 2018, pp. 143–160).

In his eclectic approach, B. Miller believes that the dynamics of regional security arise from the specificity of states (and especially the relationship between the state and the nation) and the approach of forces outside the region (Miller, 2007). The level of coherence between the aspirations of the state and society is directly proportional to the possibility of a conflict breaking out. Also, the policy of players external to the region may provoke tensions or motivate peace efforts. This situation reflects the specificity of the Caspian region.

The historical approach shows the specificity of the regional security environment, taking into account determinants operating at the deeper level. In this context, questions arise about the role of regional powers: namely, Russia, Iran, and Turkey, in the process of creating security structures and about their relations in the historical context. Another important issue is the shared historical identity of countries in the region, which originated in the Soviet area and gained independence around the same time (MacFarlane, 2018, pp. 143–160).

There is no single theory that would comprehensively explain the specific nature of the Caspian region and its security environment. However, the theoretical dimension makes it easier to understand certain regularities that are characteristic not only of the region in question, but of other spaces, too.

Regional actors became the focus for A. Acharya, who argued that regions form from the bottom up, rather than being created by structures of the broader system (Acharya, 2007, pp. 123–130). Weak states give rise to instabilities that affect external actors. Their partners are also weak as they do not have sufficient capacity to commit to mutually beneficial cooperation. Thus, divided and poorly institutionalized regions consist of weak states that are susceptible to influence from external actors. Newly formed Caspian states have experienced various difficulties when it came to creating durable, transparent, and representative state structures.

The economy is another important dimension of regional security. The development of countries in the region is based on revenues from the exports of energy resources. In this context, we observe developmental disparities and diversification of activity in the global market (MacFarlane & Weiss, 1992, pp. 12–13).

In terms of social and ethnic issues, there is diversity in the Caspian region, too, despite a long-standing policy of homogenization. As the countries regained independence, the ruling elites were deprived of support from the Soviet state and nationalism became a real threat, which was reflected in the armed conflicts in the region (in Nagorno-Karabakh, South Ossetia, and Abkhazia). Authoritarian regimes frequently use ongoing armed conflicts to consolidate their power (MacFarlane, 2018, pp. 143–160).

With regard to the prospects for the distribution of power in the region, conflicts can result in new divisions and subject it to the geopolitical influence of external actors. For example, the conflict in Nagorno-Karabakh provoked Turkey to impose a trade embargo on Armenia and led to the freezing of Azerbaijan's relations with Armenia. Actors who seek to achieve their aspirations and goals in the region play an important part in its development, too. Turkey has strong cultural and ethnic ties with Azerbaijan and has supported the country in the Nagorno-Karabakh conflict. Iran's relations with Azerbaijan are complicated, due to the presence of a significant Azeri minority in that country. In the early days of Azerbaijan's statehood, the People's Front governments contested the border with Iran, treating the northwestern part of that country as the southern part of Azerbaijan. Iran sees this as a threat to the territorial integrity of the state (MacFarlane, 2018, pp. 143–160).

The implementation of energy infrastructure projects opened the Caspian Sea to foreign markets. In this context, cooperation between Azerbaijan, Georgia, and Turkey was very significant. These states cooperate not only in the construction of pipelines but also in the transport, as part of the railway line projects from Baku via Tbilisi to Kars (MacFarlane, 2018, pp. 143–160).

2   Legal Status of the Caspian Basin Region

The Caspian Sea is a strategic body of water, which plays an important role in terms of diversifying the supply of energy resources to the global market. The Trans-Caspian Pipeline project, connecting Türkmenbaşy in Turkmenistan with Baku in Azerbaijan, is currently a challenge to energy security in the Caspian region and Europe, but its implementation depends on the willingness of the two countries to cooperate and on the legal possibilities of regulating the status of the Caspian Sea (Contessi, 2017, pp. 25–40).

The first legal regulations on the status of the Caspian Basin region were formulated in 1921 and 1940 between Soviet Russia/USSR and Persia/Iran. Based on these agreements, the basin was defined as "Soviet–Iranian Sea" (Cutler, 2019, pp. 1–19). None of the treaties included boundaries for shipping or rules for exploiting energy resources. The only geographic criterion defining the ability to exploit resources was the right to fish in the coastal zone of up to 10 nautical miles. However, the area was not strictly defined either as a fishing zone or as a territorial sea.

In 1950, the Soviet Union delimited individual sectors of the Caspian Basin remaining under the jurisdiction of specific republics, with the proviso that the Soviet administration was to exercise control over the exploitation of oil and gas. The division was therefore irrelevant to post-Soviet solutions. This is because, at that time, the formal coastal states of the Caspian Basin were the USSR and Iran. The "Astara–Hosseingholi Line" was established on the basis of mutual agreements. According to the division, Iran obtained 13–14% of the Caspian Basin (Cutler, 2019, pp. 1–19). In the 1970s, the Soviet Ministry of Oil and Gas divided its part of the basin into four zones belonging to the coastal republics of Azerbaijan, Kazakhstan, Russia, and Turkmenistan (Grison, 2013, pp. 83–94). Further modifications to the legal status of the Caspian Basin followed after the disintegration of the USSR. Although the Alma Ata Declaration in 1991 established that treaties signed during the Soviet era would be maintained, the newly formed coastal states did not approve of this solution and sought to impose a new division of the basin and to obtain access to its resources.

The possibilities of extracting energy resources were restricted by the unclear legal situation. Given these circumstances, the Caspian states signed bilateral and multilateral agreements on the division of the reservoir and the exploitation of resources. For example, in 1997, Kazakhstan signed an agreement with Turkmenistan. In 2001 and 2003, Azerbaijan entered into agreements with Russia and Kazakhstan. Iran refused to recognize any bilateral agreements reached by other states on this matter. Thus, the southern part of the Caspian Basin, which has the largest reserves of energy, became the most unstable and problematic area (Grison, 2013, pp. 83–94).

This led to the creation of a dual system of division in the region. The northern part of the basin was divided on the basis of an agreement reached by Russia, Azerbaijan, and Kazakhstan in 2003. At the same time, the status of the southern part of the Caspian Basin remained unregulated. It turned out that the largest energy reserves remained outside of the territory of Russia, which initially sought to establish a consortium that would exploit resources in the Caspian Basin on equal terms. However, the post-Soviet states opted for dividing this reservoir into national zones. Iran, on the other hand, opted for dividing it equally among all coastal states (Islamova, 2015, pp. 484–489). Rejecting all agreements, it sought to establish a system of joint use of the Caspian Sea. The situation was further complicated by territorial disputes between Azerbaijan and Turkmenistan, and between Azerbaijan and Iran (Contessi, 2017, pp. 25–40).

Following the collapse of the Soviet Union, the new Caspian states of Azerbaijan, Kazakhstan, and Turkmenistan began to pursue their economic interests in the Caspian Sea. Summits of Caspian coastal states were held, however, they did not bring the final settlement of the basin's legal status (Grison,

2013, pp. 83–94). A dispute over its division arose. The controversial question was "whether it was a sea, where exploitation zones were determined according to the United Nations Convention on the Law of the Sea, or a lake, where each coastal state is entitled to an equal share" (Legucka, 2018, pp. 1–3).

Since 1996, negotiations on the status of the Caspian Sea were conducted by Azerbaijan, Iran, Kazakhstan, Russia, and Turkmenistan. At the same time, these states were "pursuing the policy of accomplished facts and performed drills on territories which they regarded as their own, treating the basin either as a lake (Iran) or as a sea (the other countries)" (Legucka, 2018, p. 2).

The three legal models for regulating the status of the Caspian Sea included: joint use, international sea, and internal lake.

2.1   *Joint Use*

Under the agreement signed during the CIS summit in 1992, member states were obliged to respect the 1940 treaty. The problem was that the Soviet legal regime divided the basin without taking the existence of new coastal states into account. The Caspian Basin was then defined as a "common Soviet-Iranian sea" (Cutler, 2019, pp. 1–19). This idea was proposed by Russia in the early 1990s and was backed by Iran. It defined the basin and its resources as a "common facility" for the coastal states (Cutler, 2019, pp. 1–19).

2.2   *International Sea*

An alternative solution to the problem of the legal status of the Caspian Basin was to recognize it as an international sea, located between independent states. This situation allowed for the application of the Law of the Sea of 1958 and 1982. This way, each state would have jurisdiction within 12 nautical miles of its coastline and an Exclusive Economic Zone (EEZ) of additional 24 nautical miles. Under this arrangement, some oil reserves held by Azerbaijan would be outside of the country's EEZ. The system of division consistent with the rules applying to an "international sea" does not regulate the division of natural resources among countries and does not facilitate the operations of individual coastal states outside of the EEZ. Moreover, according to the Law of the Sea, the Caspian Sea would have to be connected with other basins of this type by navigation canals. Supposing we treat the Volga and Don rivers as canals connecting the Caspian Basin to the Sea of Azov, which, in turn, connects it to the Black Sea, these canals would not be salt water canals, and would thereby create the need for additional legal regulation. If the Volga–Don Canal is awarded international status, Russia will have to ensure that all coastal states have free passage along this route (Cutler, 2019, pp. 1–19).

2.3   *Internal Lake*

This solution would mean that no state could take unilateral action regarding the exploitation of energy resources in the Caspian Basin without the consent of all of the other coastal states (Cutler, 2019, pp. 1–19). In practice, the difference between the concept of an "inner lake," with Russia playing a central role, and of "joint use," with the body of water being accessible to all coastal states, was small (Cutler, 2019, pp. 1–19; Boban & Loncar, 2016, pp. 77–100). Russia's importance both in economic and geostrategic terms, was growing in this situation, too.

In the early 1990s, Russia proposed to apply the Law of the Sea Treaty to the Caspian Basin. Such a stance, however, contradicted the policy of Russia's Ministry of Fuel and Energy, which had given Lukoil permission to participate in a consortium intended to exploit oil fields in Azerbaijan and support the exploitation of resources in the Kazakh part of the Caspian Basin. Lukoil's activities in Azerbaijan restricted Russia's political position in the Caspian Basin with respect to the negotiations over its legal status (Cutler, 2019, pp. 1–19). However, Lukoil was unable to influence the policies of the Foreign Ministry, which was critical of Azerbaijan's actions in the Caspian region. Eventually, in 1994, Russia proposed that each coastal state be given 20 nautical miles as its "sphere of influence" and that a condominium (joint control) system be created (Cutler, 2019, pp. 1–19). Iran was the only state that supported this idea. Azerbaijan and Kazakhstan did not approve of this solution.

Russia changed its position on the matter in December 1996. It proposed a 45-nautical-mile exclusive economic zone for each coastal state and joint access to the central part of the basin, which would be under the control of an interstate commission, responsible for issuing licenses for the exploitation of energy resources (Cutler, 2019, pp. 1–19). Russia also appealed to countries in the region to a joint corporation that would exploit energy reserves, and to adopt a common navigation law, and the joint management of fisheries and environmental protection. Iran again supported Russia's proposal. Azerbaijan opposed it, while Kazakhstan supported Azerbaijan in opposing the designation of national sectors, but agreed to cooperate in the areas of environmental protection, fisheries policy, and navigation.

In 1998, the presidents of Russia and Kazakhstan signed an agreement on the delimitation of national sectors. However, these provisions did not result in the signing of a common international treaty. Russia proposed to draw the boundary between sectors belonging to the two countries along the so-called "center line," running along the deepest canal between them (Cutler, 2019, pp. 1–19). However, the area is seismically active, which causes shifts in the bottom of the reservoir. Due to this, Kazakhstan refused to accept the solution. Consequently, Russia amended its proposal, suggesting a "revised centre line." This method involved drawing a boundary between sectors controlled by coastal states by defining a line that would reflect an equal distance between the outermost coastal areas of each state (Map 2.2) (Cutler, 2019, pp. 1–19).

Between 1998 and 2000, Russia concluded bilateral agreements with Kazakhstan and Azerbaijan on the division of the Caspian Basin along the modified center line. This concept was opposed by Iran and Turkmenistan. Ultimately, however, Turkmenistan accepted the Russian proposal. Iran did not accept it and insisted on the concept of a condominium, or "joint use" of the basin.

In 2003, Russia, Kazakhstan, and Azerbaijan divided the northern part of the seabed and shelf of the Caspian Sea into national sectors. The division method

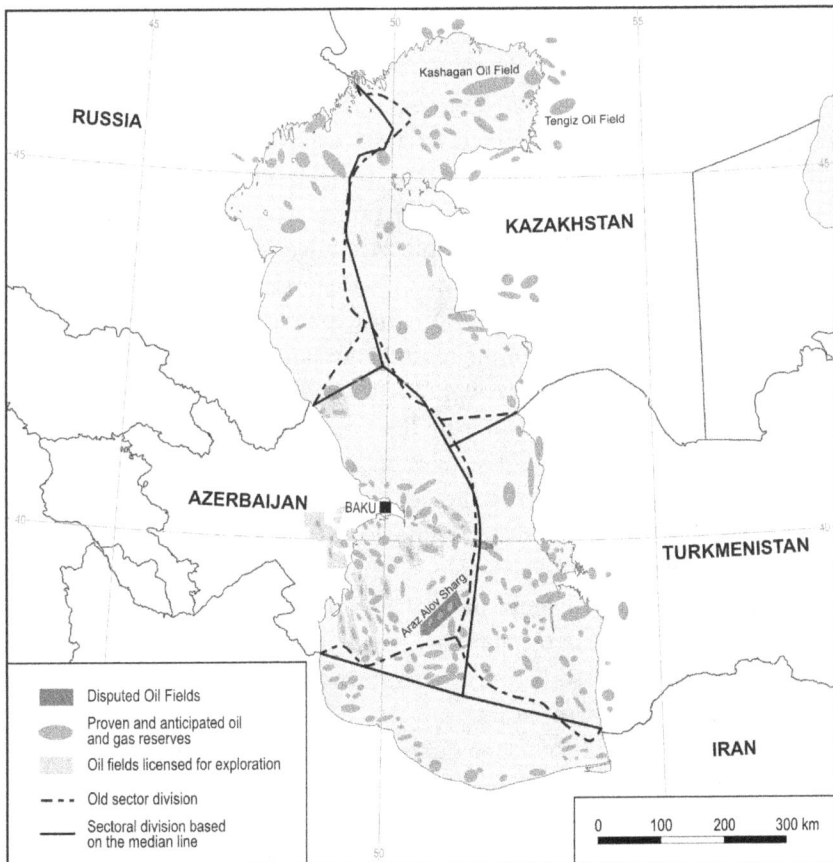

MAP 2.2   The division of the Caspian Basin by the center line
SOURCE: MADE BY W. JASIŃSKI IN MISIĄGIEWICZ, 2014

proposed by Russia was the modified center line (Map 2.2). Iran rejected such a model because it only had 13–14% of the shelf. Tehran proposed a division used for border lakes, which would give each state a 20% share of the shelf (Legucka, 2018, pp. 1–3). At the same time, Teheran drilled boreholes in the Sardar Jangal field, to which Azerbaijan claimed rights. Azerbaijan, in turn, disputed with Turkmenistan over the exploitation of the Kapaz, Azeri, and Chirag fields (or Serdar, Osman, and Omra in Turkmen terminology), located in the southern part of the Caspian Sea. Kazakhstan concluded an agreement on the division of the shelf with Turkmenistan in 2014 (entered into force in 2015) (Legucka, 2018, pp. 1–3). The main controversy over the division of the Caspian Sea remained between Azerbaijan, Iran, and Turkmenistan.

The key issues to be decided were the principles for laying underwater pipelines and cables. So far, such actions required the consent of all the coastal states, which often led to the blocking of projects unfavorable to Russia and Iran (Legucka, 2018, pp. 1–3).

In terms of the delimitation of state borders in the Caspian Sea, the 2010 Baku Summit was a breakthrough. It proposed a division into zones of 25 miles long from the coastlines of individual states. Next, the summit in 2014 specified that each state had the right to jurisdiction over a zone of 15 nautical miles from the coast and the right to fish within 25 nautical miles. The waters outside this area were to be exploited jointly. This agreement regulated the access to the reservoir's waters, separating it from the exploitation of the bottom of the reservoir, and allocated most of the reservoir for joint use. Such a solution was in line with Russia's vision. Following President Vladimir Putin, the agreement would eliminate "future misunderstandings and tensions over differing positions on Caspian waters" (Contessi, 2017, pp. 25–40).

Pursuant to the provisions of the Tehran Declaration of 2007, all vessels operating in the Caspian Sea must be under the flag of coastal states. The 2010 Baku Summit clarified this principle, adding that only coastal states could participate in solving problems, in particular those related to security in the Caspian Sea. The Astrakhan Summit in 2014 stressed that only commercial and military ships of coastal states might operate in the Caspian Sea, which would trust and respect mutual interests.

An important part of the agreements between the coastal states was the peaceful use of the Caspian Sea. It was raised for the first time in 1995, during a conference in Almaty. Under the Tehran Declaration of 2007, coastal states undertook not to use military force against one another and to prohibit the actions of third states from their territories against any coastal state (Art. 14–15). Then, at the Baku Summit of 2010, the Caspian Basin was proclaimed the "Sea of Peace" (Contessi, 2017, pp. 25–40). Its signatories pledged to resolve all disputes by peaceful means and to renounce the use of force against any Caspian state. In addition, they reaffirmed their commitment not to make available their territories by third states to carry out hostile actions against any of the signatories of the agreement.

During the 2014 Summit, the Caspian states specified that their aim was to ensure "a stable military balance in the Caspian Sea" (Contessi, 2017, pp. 25–40). As part of mutual arrangements, the coastal states decided to regulate their presence and military activities based on the principles of mutual security, limited to "establishing military installations taking into account the interests of all parties and not threatening the security of any of them" (Contessi, 2017, pp. 25–40). Besides, Russia demonstrated the initiative to create a collective security system in the Caspian region. Defense Minister Sergei Shoigu mentioned this concept during a visit to Baku after the Astrakhan summit in October 2014. He proposed to establish a security system based on the council of naval fleet commanders and a five-party agreement on the prevention of incidents in the Caspian Sea and in the air space above it (Kucera, 2014, p. 34). In connection this concept, in July 2015, the commander of the Russian Navy, Admiral Viktor Cherkov, received in St. Petersburg delegations from Azerbaijan, Iran, and Kazakhstan. The purpose of the meeting was to discuss the creation of a consultative body for all Caspian navies and a collective security system (Kucera, 2014, p. 13).

The issue of security of the Caspian Sea involved many contradictions. First, there was the problem of Iran's approach, as the country did not approve of any division of the basin that would grant the country less than a 20% share in it. Thus, Tehran rejected all bilateral agreements on the status of the Caspian Sea, in the absence of any comprehensive treaty. Second, the rivalry over the question of where to draw the center line, especially given the competition for access to strategic reserves of Kyapaz/Serdar, Azeri/Khazar, and Chirag/Osman, was problematic, too. Azerbaijan claimed rights to these deposits under resolutions of the Soviet Ministry of Oil and Gas of 1970. Meanwhile, Turkmenistan disapproved of taking the outermost area of Azerbaijan, the Absheron Peninsula, into account when drawing the central line. In addition, Azerbaijan and Iran were in conflict over the Alborz/Alov field. This led to a display of force in the region. In 2001, Iran sent combat ships to the area (Caspian Sea Region, 2016, p. 22). Third, there is the prospect of the Trans-Caspian Gas Pipeline project, which would transport gas from Turkmenistan to Azerbaijan and which faces opposition from Russia and Iran (Misiągiewicz, 2022, p. 598; Contessi, 2017, pp. 25–40).

Eventually, in November 2014, Turkmenistan and Kazakhstan reached an agreement on the demarcation of borders on the bottom of the Caspian Sea.

Their parliaments ratified the new maritime border in May 2015. The agreement in Article 3 ensures a full right of exploitation of the seabed, allowing for the possibility of laying cables and pipelines along specific national sectors. In October 2015, Russia and Kazakhstan revised their treaty of 1998 and expanded its wording to include the question of cooperation in the area of energy production (Levit, 2016, pp. 34–44). This solution could serve as a model for Azerbaijan, Turkmenistan, and Iran (Babayeva, 2016).

After 22 years of negotiations, on August 12, 2018, during the Fifth Caspian Summit in Aktau, Kazakhstan, Azerbaijan, Iran, Kazakhstan, Russia, and Turkmenistan signed the Convention regulating the legal status of the Caspian Sea. It was agreed that "the Caspian Sea is a closed body of water with special legal status" (Legucka, 2018, pp. 1–3). The nature of the document is very general, as it contains no direct references to the UN Convention on the Law of the Sea, and its status has not been clearly specified, which may give rise to problems with its interpretation in the future. The Convention sets out general rules for the division of the Caspian Basin but does not specify how to divide the seabed into national sectors. It merely states that "their delimitation will be based on an agreement between the Caspian states, taking into account generally recognised principles and norms of international law" (Legucka, 2018, p. 3).

The waters of the Caspian Sea were the subject to regulations similar to the 1982 Convention on the Law of the Sea, which divide them into internal waters, territorial waters (up to 15 nautical miles), and fishing zones (up to 10 miles). The remaining waters and the biological resources of the basin are to be used jointly by the coastal states (Legucka, 2018, pp. 1–3).

One of the main obstacles in the negotiations on the adoption of the convention were the differences of opinion on the division and exploitation of the bottom and waters of the Caspian Sea. The stake in the game are the energy reserves in the basin, estimated at 8.3 trillion m3 of natural gas and 48 billion barrels of oil. The Caspian Sea Convention provides the basis for the division of the Caspian Basin floor, taking its resources into account (Map 2.3) (Cutler, 2019). The Caspian Sea is also of considerable importance to the fishing industry, for example 80–90% of the sturgeon caviar consumed in the world is obtained there (Legucka, 2018, pp. 1–3).

The Convention is a comprehensive solution, taking into account various areas of international cooperation, such as: security, environmental protection, navigation, the fishing industry, and the construction of offshore pipelines and telecommunications infrastructure. The Third Agreement was signed by the states after more than 50 Working Group meetings (Bayramov, 2019, pp. 15–20, 2022, p. 13). The other two are the Tehran Agreement and the Security Cooperation Agreement. The Caspian Sea Convention acknowledged these

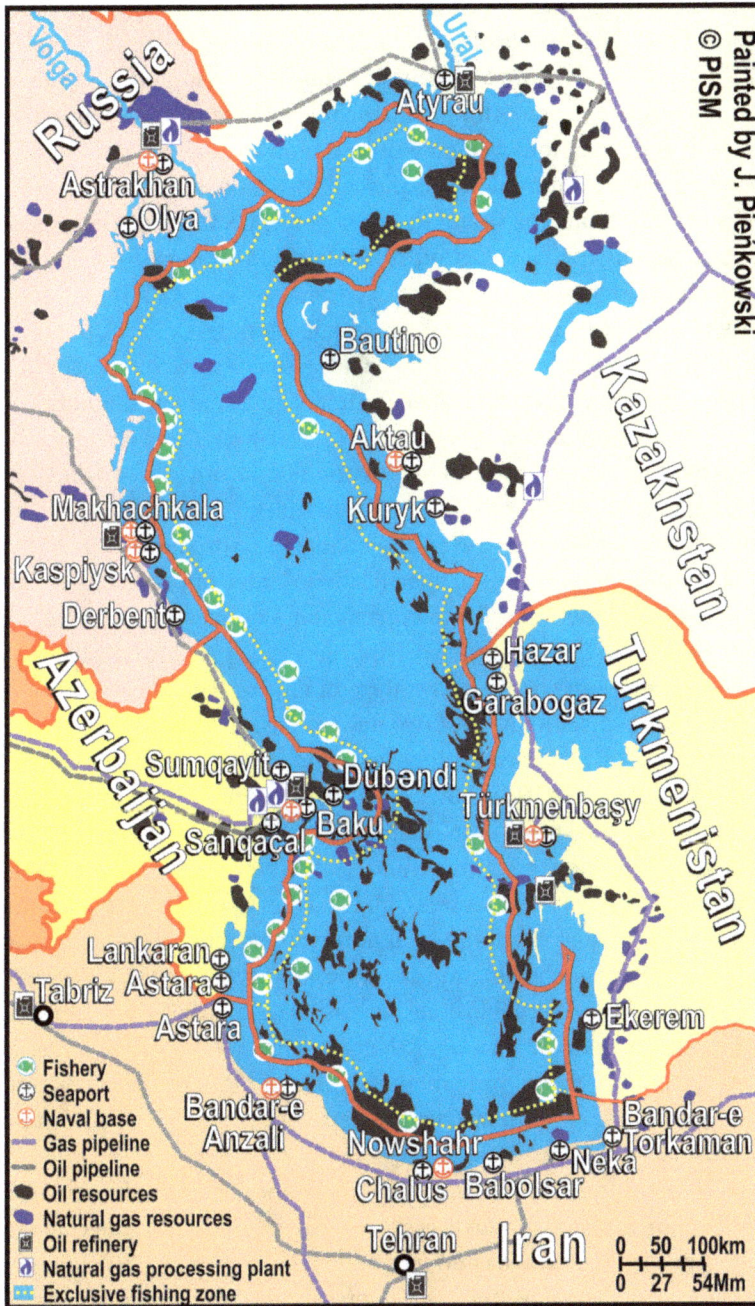

MAP 2.3   The division of the Caspian Sea according to the 2018 Caspian Sea Convention
SOURCE:. LEGUCKA, 2018

two documents. Should coastal states wish to construct an underwater pipeline, they must meet the criteria of the Tehran Convention (Art. 14) (Bayramov, 2019, pp. 15–20). Moreover, the Convention regulated the important issue of security in the Caspian region. All warships shall fly the flags of Caspian states (Legucka, 2018, pp. 1–3). Moreover, only these countries shall be permitted to build military ports. This provision was pushed by Russia and Iran. Their primary aim was to eliminate the risk of the presence of US forces in the region. This provision led to the cancellation of the agreements on supplying US troops stationed in Afghanistan through the Caspian ports of Aktau and Kuryk, which were negotiated by the US and Kazakhstan (Marszewski, 2018, p. 2).

The agreement does not specify whether it is a sea or a lake. State borders have not been determined, which will necessitate additional negotiations and agreements (Art. 8) (Bayramov, 2019, pp. 15–20). However, there is a risk that Iran and Russia may take advantage of the environmental provisions of the Convention (Art. 1, 11, 14, 15) to block the exploitation of oil and gas fields (Anceschi, 2019, pp. 6–8). Some analysts have even argued that the two countries included these provisions in the Convention specifically in order to prevent the construction of a pipeline between Turkmenistan and Azerbaijan (Garibov, 2018, pp. 179–195; Gurbanov, 2018, pp. 159–179; Ismayilov, 2019, pp. 5–10). To quote A. Garibov: "Russia and Iran will take advantage of environmental issues to halt the progress of the project for at least two decades, while the implementation of the Convention will create conditions for a wider debate on requirements and standards for pipelines" (Garibov, 2018, p. 193). L. Anceschi also made the argument that the Convention would allow Russia and Iran to use the new instrument to monitor any infrastructure projects which do not include them as participants (Anceschi, 2019, pp. 6–8). M. Ismayilov spoke in a similar vein: "Russia and Iran are using environmental norms to prevent the construction of the Trans-Caspian Gas Pipeline in the future" (Ismayilov, 2019, p. 9). Some researchers reached similar conclusions long before the Caspian Sea Convention was signed. For example, in 2015, E. Nuriyev argued that Iran and Russia were taking advantage of environmental concerns to block or delay the construction of the oil transport infrastructure between Azerbaijan, Kazakhstan, and Turkmenistan (Nuriyev, 2015).

All these opinions indicate that there is no difference between the situation that existed before the Convention was signed when the status of the Caspian Sea was unclear, and after. Russia and Iran benefited in both cases (Bayramov, 2019, pp. 15–20). At the same time, the quoted scholars do not address the question of how Azerbaijan, Kazakhstan, and Turkmenistan have adapted the environmental protocols of the Convention. They have also provided no justification why post-Soviet countries have signed the Convention, despite its being a tool in the hands of Russia and Iran. It is unclear whether it was possible to regulate environmental issues differently so that they would not be treated instrumentally by Russia and Iran (Bayramov, 2019, pp. 15–20).

The provision enabling the laying of pipelines and telecommunications cables on the seabed is crucial to the region's energy security policy. Such a solution could result in the resumption of the work on infrastructure projects (like the Trans-Caspian Pipeline). A principle was adopted, assuming that consent would be obtained only from that country through whose sector the infrastructure would pass (Legucka, 2018, pp. 1–3). The remaining coastal states would be informed about such activities. This formally eliminated the possibility of blocking the construction of pipelines. At the same time, the Convention stipulates that projects of this type must obtain the environmental consent of all states. This provided Russia and Iran with an instrument which would enable them to delay the construction of infrastructure that would be unfavorable from their point of view (Legucka, 2018, pp. 1–3).

Climate protection is an important aspect of cooperation under the Convention. According to studies on the environment of the Caspian Sea, the problems observed there include water-level fluctuations, coastal degradation, lack of biodiversity, and environmental pollution (Firoozfar et al., 2012, pp. 667–672). Back in 1998, the *Caspian Environmental Program* (CEP) was developed as a region-wide system of intergovernmental cooperation. It was created in cooperation with international institutions (*United Nations Environmental Program* – TACIS, EU program, *Global Environment Facility, the United Nations Development Program,* and the World Bank). The CEP has developed regional and national solutions to environmental problems. The Tehran Convention (*Framework Convention on the Protection of the Marine Environment of the Caspian Sea*) was signed in November 2003 (United Nations Environment Programme, n.d.). It came into force in August 2007. This document laid out the basic principles for protecting the biological resources of the basin while the Tehran Convention provided an institutional mechanism for the protection of the marine environment in the Caspian region (Bayramov, 2019, pp. 15–20, 2022). It included four protocols:

1. the Protocol for the Conservation of Biological Diversity (*Biological Diversity*) of May 2014;
2. the Protocol for the *Protection of the Caspian Sea against Pollution from Land-based Sources and as a Result of Land Activities* of December 2012;
3. the Protocol for *Regional Preparedness, Response and Cooperation in Combating Oil Pollution Incidents* of August 2011; and
4. the Convention on Environmental Impact Assessment in a Transboundary Context (Espoo) (Bayramov, 2019, pp. 15–20).

By 2006, the Caspian states had ratified the Tehran Convention, which represented significant progress in mutual cooperation. The rapid ratification demonstrated the willingness of states to work together to protect the environment (Bayramov, 2019, pp. 15–20). All protocols were signed by coastal states. Thus, it should be emphasized that environmental cooperation provided the basis for regulating the status of the Caspian Sea (Tables 2.1 and 2.2).

The two summaries in Tables 2.1 and 2.2 illustrate the relationship between negotiations on the legal status of the Caspian Sea and the protocols on environmental protection in the area, which serve as the basis for the current Caspian Sea Convention. The Protocol on the Environmental Dimension of Cooperation—*Environmental Impact Assessment* (EIA)—governs the construction of

TABLE 2.1   The stages of introducing regulations on the status of the Caspian Sea

Date	Regulation
September/ October 1992	First stage of negotiations
May 1995	Establishment of a Working Group at the Almaty Conference
July 1998	Russia and Kazakhstan signed the first bilateral agreement on the division of the Caspian Sea
November 2001	Azerbaijan and Kazakhstan signed an agreement on the division of the Caspian Sea
April 2002	First Caspian Summit in Ashgabat
September 2002	The division of the North Caspian Sea under the treaty between Azerbaijan and Russia
May 2003	Trilateral agreement between Azerbaijan, Kazakhstan, and Russia on the Caspian Sea division
October 2007	Second Caspian Summit in Tehran
November 2014	Third Caspian Summit in Baku. Signing of the Agreement on Security Cooperation
September 2014	Fourth Caspian Summit in Astrakhan
December 2014	Agreement between Kazakhstan and Turkmenistan on the delimitation of the Caspian Sea
August 2018	Fifth Caspian Summit in Aktau. Signing of the Caspian Convention

SOURCE: BAYRAMOV, 2019

TABLE 2.2   Steps in the implementation of the CEP and the Tehran Convention

Date	Regulation
May 1994	Almaty Declaration on Environmental Cooperation
June 1995	The CEP project, initiated by the World Bank, UNDP, and UNEP
May 1998	Official launch of the Caspian Environmental Programme
November 2003	Signing of the Tehran Convention by the Caspian states
August 2006	Entry into force of the Convention
May 2007	First Conference of the Parties to the Convention in Baku
November 2008	Second Conference of the Parties to the Convention in Tehran
August 2011	Third Conference of the Parties to the Convention in Aktau. Signing the Protocol on International Convention on Oil pollution Preparedness, Response and Cooperation
December 2012	Fourth Conference of the Parties to the Convention in Moscow. Signing the Protocol for the Protection of the Caspian Sea against Pollution from Land-Based Sources and Activities
May 2014	Fifth Conference of the Parties to the Convention in Ashgabat. Signing the Protocol on the Conservation of Biological Diversity
August 2018	Extraordinary Meeting of the Conference of the Parties to the Convention in Moscow. A Protocol on the Environmental Dimension of Cooperation was signed—*Environmental Impact Assessment* (EIA)

SOURCE: BAYRAMOV, 2019

underwater pipelines and their impact on the state of the natural environment in the Caspian Sea (Bayramov, 2019, pp. 15–20).

The Convention is the result of a broad compromise. Russia yielded on the principle of laying underwater pipelines. This state is likely to strengthen its military presence in the basin and make it difficult for other Caspian partners to conduct military cooperation from the US or the PRC (Legucka, 2018, pp. 1–3). The beneficiaries of the Convention are Azerbaijan and Turkmenistan, which could build the Trans-Caspian Gas Pipeline after resolving disputes over the division of the seabed and obtaining EU financial support (Legucka, 2018, pp. 1–3). The signed protocols are to promote further discussions on the implementation of the provisions of the Convention. All parties must honor the

Caspian Convention, even if they have not yet ratified it (currently, all Caspian countries have ratified the Convention except Iran). The division of the basin bottom was the most problematic issue.

Iran has consistently rejected proposals to obtain less than 20%, but following the application of the delimitation methods, it obtained only 13–14% of this area. According to the Convention, delimitation will be carried out "in accordance with the principles of international law," which rules out Iran's aspirations (Cutler, 2019, pp. 1–19).

For many years, coastal states in the Caspian region have relied on a "modified center line" to identify their sectors in the Caspian Basin. It allowed for the joint exploitation of oil and gas resources located near the borders between them. Details of the delimitation of individual sectors in the basin were not included in the provisions of the Convention. These issues will be governed by supplementary protocols (Cutler, 2019, pp. 1–19). The modified center line enables the adjustment of boundaries. However, in terms of relations between Azerbaijan and Iran, the two countries have finalized a bilateral agreement, which allows Iran to participate in the exploitation of resources in Azerbaijan's sector. It did not specify the deposits concerned, however, they certainly included the Alov field, where Iran attacked a BP research vessel in 2001. At the same time, a similar agreement was made between Iran and Turkmenistan. Iran thus gained greater opportunities to engage in the exploitation of the Caspian Sea.

According to international law, Azerbaijan and Turkmenistan will not need the Convention to build a pipeline at the bottom of the Caspian Basin. However, the Convention currently guarantees such a right. It includes a provision that each coastal state has the right to lay pipes and cables at the bottom of the Caspian Sea within its sector. Article 14 (3) specifies that states have the right to install such infrastructure across sectoral boundaries, without the need for third-party consent. The sectors of Turkmenistan and Azerbaijan intersect roughly in the middle of the basin, however, the countries do not need consent to cooperate bilaterally on the construction of a common pipeline. Pursuant to Article 8 (1) of the Convention, states may delimit boundaries between their sectors of the Caspian Sea, without requiring the approval of the other coastal states, in accordance with "generally recognised principles of international law" (Cutler, 2019, pp. 1–19). Azerbaijan and Turkmenistan could thus build a pipeline without officially delineating boundaries between their sectors. To do so, the states would only have to agree to implement a specific project.

Pursuant to Article 14 (2) of the Caspian Sea Convention any pipeline project would have to comply with international environmental agreements and refer to the 2018 Moscow Protocol of the Tehran Convention. Moscow Protocol

(Art. 10, 1 (a)) provides that any decision to implement any infrastructure project must be made in accordance with its provisions. This means that no third country can use a unilateral veto on the implementation of such a project. Article 15 of the Moscow Protocol emphasizes that "any conflict between parties to the agreement should be resolved in accordance with Art. 30 of the Tehran Convention" (Cutler, 2019, p. 19). The parties to the agreement "shall resolve conflicts by consultation, negotiation, or by any other peaceful means consistent with their preferences" (Cutler, 2019, p. 12). It is up to the parties involved to choose how to resolve the dispute. Thus, the other coastal states have no right to interfere in this matter. The Convention gives preference to regular consultations or diplomatic negotiations between the parties. It is worth mentioning here that, according to studies of the World Bank and the EU, the Trans-Caspian Gas Pipeline project will not have an adverse impact on the natural environment in the region. Therefore, the project is not inconsistent with the Tehran Convention. Thus, its implementation cannot be blocked on environmental grounds. The final decision on the implementation of such infrastructure will be made, not by the five coastal states, but by the initiating states, which the Moscow Protocol refers to as "core parties" (Cutler, 2019, p. 13).

According to A. Legucka, "the success of the negotiations is a result of the tightening of cooperation between Russia and Iran and the compromise between the remaining Caspian states" (Legucka, 2018, p. 3). Although the division of the Caspian Sea has been regulated, there is no guarantee that disputes over its exploitation will end. Problems with interpreting the Convention may arise in the future, as it does not unambiguously resolve the maritime status of the basin (Legucka, 2018, pp. 1–3).

3   The Geopolitical and Geoeconomic Position of the Caspian Region

On the specifics of the "geopolitical" approach, it is important to mention the classical researchers of the term. Rudolph Kjellén, who coined the term in 1899, described geopolitics as "the theory of the state as a geographical organism or phenomenon in space" (Weigert, 1942, p. 106). Geopolitics was developed by Kjellén from the perspective to "develop a scientifically based instrument that could also advise key decision makers in foreign policy and defense to avoid war" (Criekemans, 2022, p. x). Influenced by Friedrich Ratzel, one of the first political geographers, Kjellén believed that "the state is foremost a territorially embedded entity, and more than the sum of legal or constitutional articles" (Criekemans, 2022, p. x). Kjellén proposed an "organic Political Science," in which geopolitics played a key role.

Karl Haushofer, described geopolitics as the "new national science of the state, [...] a doctrine on the spatial determinism of all political processes, based on the broad foundations of geography, especially of political geography" (Gyorgy, 1944, p. 183). Derwent Whittlesey dismissed geopolitics as "the faith that the state is inherently entitled to its place in the sun" (Whittlesey, 1939, p. 8). Richard Hartshorne defined geopolitics as "geography utilized for particular purposes that lie beyond the pursuit of knowledge" (Hartshorne, 1939, p. 404). Thus, for Geoffrey Parker, geopolitics is "the study of international relations from a spatial or geographical perspective" (Parker, 1998, p. 5). While, John Agnew defined the researched area as "examination of the geographical assumptions, designations and understandings that enter into the making of world politics" (Agnew, 1986 p. 2). Similarly, Gearold O. Tuathail argues that "geopolitics is culturally and politically varied way of describing, representing and writing about geography and international politics" (Tuathail & Dalby, 1998, p. 3). In the 1990s, a school of thought-critical geopolitics was developed. It presented a different point of view, whose thinking comes from the criticism on geographic determinism. It critically put into question the "naturalization" of geography in foreign policy and issues of world affairs (Criekemans, 2022).

In the context of the above-mentioned definitions, we can safely assume, that the Caspian region is an interesting area in international relations, with an important position in world politics. The Caspian region, which serves as a bridge between the Middle East, the former Soviet republics, and the Euro-Atlantic zone, is at the center of the geopolitical and geoeconomic game. In addition to its strategic location, it is estimated to hold between 6% and 10% of the world's gas reserves and between 2% and 6% of the world's oil reserves (BP, 2020; Grison, 2013, pp. 83–94).

In geographic terms, the Caspian Basin is a body of water measuring about 390,000 km², bordering on the Elbrus Mountains of Iran to the south and the Caucasus Mountains to the northeast. It is more than four times the size of Lake Superior, the largest of the Great Lakes in North America. Its size approximates the combined size of Germany and the Netherlands (the Caspian Sea is 1,200 km long, while its minimum width is 196 km and its maximum width is 435 km) (Zhiltsov et al., 2016, pp. 7–37).

The Caspian Sea (Azeri: *Xəzər dənizi*, Persian: خزردریا or مازندرندریای, Russian: Каспийское море, Kazakh: Каспий теңізі, Turkmen: Hazar deňzi) is the world's largest enclosed saline marine reservoir (Bajrektarevic & Posega, 2016, pp. 237–264). The total length of the coastline is nearly 7.000 km. It is not directly connected to the ocean, but is connected to the Black Sea via the Volga River and other minor rivers (Mehdiyoun, 2000, p. 183). The Volga flows into the northern part of the Caspian Sea, forming a huge delta near Astrakhan

(Newman, 2008, p. 93). The southern part of the basin is its deepest part and holds the most productive oil and gas fields.

The controversy over whether the Caspian Sea is a sea or a lake can be resolved by considering the hydrological specificity of the reservoir. The northern part of the basin is a shallow lake, fed by water from Europe's largest river, the Volga River, in addition to the Ural River and other minor Russian rivers. Its southern part, on the other hand, consists of deep water without river tributaries and with a high level of salinity, which meets the criteria of a sea.

The collapse of the USSR and the end of the Cold War in 1991 led to significant changes in the geopolitical configuration in Eurasia. The new reality gave rise to a "security vacuum" in the Caspian region as an area of influence for neighboring states and global players. Some analysts describe this geopolitical rivalry as the "New Cold War" or the "Great Game" between the key actors, namely: the US, China, and Russia. The "Great Game" is a British term referring to the strategic rivalry and conflict between Great Britain and Russia in Central Asia (Kurecić, 2010, pp. 21–46). The end of the Cold War changed the geopolitical situation in the Caspian region. The collapse of the USSR contributed to the emergence of new states in the Caucasus and Central Asia. However, independence resulted in economic and political instability in the emerging region. The security vacuum that appeared there was related to the collapse of the former system.

New states experienced a severe economic and social crisis (Kurecić, 2010, pp. 21–46). Their leaders, who emerged from the Soviet system, introduced authoritarian rule. The borders of post-Soviet states were artificially drawn. Ethnic groups, scattered across various post-Soviet states, sought to annex the territories they inhabited to the states they recognized as their homelands. This caused instability in the Caspian region.

The situation gave rise to a new strategic game in the Caspian region, the rules of which were not yet known. New states emerged on the ruins of the USSR, while external actors began to get involved in the region and to show interest in its potential. "The Caspian region has become internalized to a level not seen before and there has been a reconfiguration of power and influence" (Chufrin, 2001, p. 11).

There are currently five Caspian coastal states. They can be divided into traditional and historically established, such as Russia and Iran, and newly formed ones, which include Azerbaijan, Kazakhstan, and Turkmenistan. Only Iran and Russia have access to the open sea, while the remaining states are surrounded by land (Bajrektarevic & Posega, 2016, pp. 237–264). Their common goal is the exploration and exploitation of hydrocarbon resources (Bahgat, 2005, p. 3; Zamnitskaya & von Geldern, 2011, p. 10).

Azerbaijan is a state whose economy depends on the energy sector. The state established close cooperation with foreign corporations, taking advantage of the boom on the global energy market. The objective of its foreign policy was balancing between Russia and the West (Dekmejian & Simonian, 2003, pp. 92–95). Kazakhstan has the largest oil reserves in its sector of the Caspian Sea. Kazakhstan's decision on the direction of export routes will thus be crucial for the balance of power and geopolitics in the Caspian region. The state has three options when it comes to transporting energy. The first involves developing functioning roads to the Black Sea through Russia's territory. The second assumes that Kazakhstan may join the Baku–Tbilisi–Ceyhan pipeline, building the Aktau–Baku offshore pipeline (Marketos, 2009, p. 4). The third assumes that it is possible to increase the capacity of pipeline infrastructure from Kazakhstan to China. Turkmenistan is a country of great geostrategic and geoeconomic importance. Thus, it attracts the interest of powers outside the region (Kurecić, 2010, pp. 21–46). Although it is an authoritarian state that does not attach importance to human rights in the Western sense, its strategic location and abundance of energy resources mean that both the US and the EU are interested in closer cooperation with this country. Russia and China pay even less attention to internal problems in Turkmenistan, as long as Turkmenistan does not change its foreign policy orientation (Kurecić, 2010, pp. 21–45). As a result of tightening its cooperation with China, Iran, and Western countries, Turkmenistan has entered the energy game in the Caspian region.

Russia plays a key role in the Caspian region. It is the largest trading partner for the newly formed post-Soviet states. Moreover, it has a significant position on the energy market in the region in both the *upstream* and *downstream* sectors (Iseri, 2009, p. 39). Russia possesses scarce energy resources in the Caspian Sea area, and is therefore trying to interfere in the energy projects of the coastal states, which are rich in oil and gas resources (Bajrektarevic & Posega, 2016, pp. 237–264). Following the collapse of the USSR, Russia has sought to maintain its strategic position in the post-Soviet area. In the early 21st century, the country focused on economic development. In that context, bilateral and multilateral agreements were signed with post-Soviet states to secure interests in the region. This gave rise to rivalry between Russia and the EU and US in the Caspian region (Dekmejian & Simonian, 2003, pp. 92–95). Russia's strategy is mainly defensive and based on a "policy of obstruction," that is, preventing the expansion of external players who could limit its influence both in political and economic terms (Labban, 2009, p. 7). Forced to adapt to the post-imperial reality, the country also tried to limit the influence of Turkey and Iran in the Caspian region, preventing "the pull of the new states towards their main rivals" (Brzeziński, 1999, p. 143). Russia is also trying to hinder the

emergence of independent cooperation between post-Soviet states and foreign markets. The tools for achieving these aspirations are the system of the
Commonwealth of Independent States (CIS), military power, and effective
diplomacy. The strategy pursued by Russia in the Caspian region can thus be
interpreted with reference to the following four determinants:
– rivalry with the West, which conditioned international relations in the region;
– an ambivalent attitude to China's strategy (however, cooperation with this
  superpower would be possible in the event of confrontation with the West);
– relations with the newly formed post-Soviet states based on the "near
  abroad" doctrine; and
– pipeline geopolitics—maintaining transit of oil and gas exports through
  Russia (Misiągiewicz, 2012a, pp. 61–79; Işeri, 2009, p. 39).
Russia's primary geopolitical objective in the Caspian region is the political
subjugation of Azerbaijan and Kazakhstan, which would cut off other players'
access to this strategic area. This is a difficult task, especially since Azerbaijan,
supported by Turkey and the US, has rejected Russia's demands to deploy military bases on its territory. It refused to accept Russia's monopoly for the exports
of hydrocarbons to foreign markets. Kazakhstan has also been increasingly
assertive in political and economic terms, tightening cooperation with China,
as has Turkmenistan, which is increasingly diverting fossil fuel shipments to
the eastern and southern markets.

Iran is one of the world's leading producers of hydrocarbons, but, like Russia,
it does not have significant resources in the Caspian region. Its ability to export
oil and gas is largely limited due to sanctions imposed by the US in response
to the development of the nuclear program by Iran (Dekmejian & Simonian,
2003, pp. 120–123). However, from the geopolitical point of view, Iran is a very
convenient transit territory for the export of resources from the Caspian Sea
(Bajrektarevic & Posega, 2016, pp. 237–264).

The prospect of access to new sources of energy has also become attractive to external actors (Chufrin, 2001, p. 11). The newly formed Caspian states,
supported by extra-regional players, sought to limit Russia's role in the region,
especially its dominance in oil and gas exports (Mcarthy, 2000, p. 21). The interests of world powers in this region are determined by geostrategy and geoeconomics. The West and China are the main active forces in the region. Their
involvement is due to the oil and gas potential of the Caspian Basin. A strategic presence in the region is necessary to control the oil and gas production
and transportation sectors. This situation leads to competition between the
superpowers.

External players entered the "Caspian game" and succeeded in it for three
main reasons. First, the post-Soviet states needed technology and capital to

exploit energy resources. The inflow of foreign investment was therefore nec-essary for the development of new sources of oil and gas and the construction of export infrastructure, as well as to pursue an independent energy policy and assert independence from Russia. Second, the Caspian Sea is surrounded by land, which means that importing oil and gas from that area is only possible through pipelines and requires international cooperation (Bajrektarevic & Posega, 2016, pp. 237–264). In this situation, a new, technologically advanced energy infrastructure is required. Third, post-Soviet Caspian states were not strong enough to play a significant role on the international stage. They were weak in military, political, and economic terms and susceptible to numerous internal and international conflicts, which made them an "easy target" for external players who tried to take advantage of these circumstances in pursuit of their own interests (Kubicek, 2013, pp. 171–180).

It was probably Napoleon who stated: "if you know the geography of a coun-try, you can understand its foreign policy" (Brzeziński, 1999, p. 37). It is safe to say that, due to its geopolitical position in the center of Eurasia, the Caspian region is becoming increasingly significant in global international relations, both politically and economically.

The significance of Eurasia as a "World Island" was emphasized by Sir Halford J. Mackinder in his 1919 book *Democratic Ideas and Reality* (Mackinder, 1919). The book also introduced the term "Heartland." Mackinder referred to the area situated in the center of Eurasia as the "Geographical Pivot of His-tory" as early as 1904. He defined the area as the most important place in the world, from the geostrategic point of view (Sloan, 1999, pp. 15–36). According to Mackinder, the Caspian region is part of the Eurasian Heartland (Dalby, 2001, pp. 171–188). Thus, control over this territory provides the basis for domination over the whole of Eurasia and, consequently, the entire world. The Eurasian continent is the location of the majority of those states that are the most expansive and active in political, economic, and military terms (Brzeziński, 1999, p. 31). Mackinder's theory was developed at a time when the "Great Game" was being played out in Central Asia. He was aware of the importance of controlling this strategic territory, which was sparsely popu-lated and undeveloped, and had difficult access to the sea (Kurecić, 2010, pp. 21–46). Mackinder altered the boundaries of the Heartland according to the strategic context of 1904, 1919, and 1943. However, Central Asia has always been its key element. The region has also been called "the greatest natural fortress in the world" (Seiple, 2004, p. 22). Contemporary strategic and eco-nomic relations in the Caspian region cannot be separated from the situation in Eurasia as a whole, which is viewed as the World Island (Kurecić, 2010, pp. 21–46).

Mackinder's ideas relating to the foundations of geostrategy should be analyzed to understand the significance of the region as a field of competition among world powers for energy resources. If, according to Mackinder's theory, Eurasia is the World Island, then the strategic and economic relations in that region should be interpreted as significant in geostrategic and geoeconomic terms (Kurecić, 2010, pp. 21–46). The significance and specificity of international relations in Central Asia, the influence of the superpowers, and the rivalry among them make this region crucial on a global scale. It thus becomes a stake in the game and a testing area for the strategic game between the powers (Kurecić, 2010, pp. 21–46). A map depicting Mackinder's vision was first published in the article "The Geographical Pivot of History" in 1904. Central Asia and the Caspian region formed the southern part of Mackinder's "pivot area." They also constituted elements of the "Heartland" concept (Kurecić, 2010, pp. 21–46). Halford Mackinder describes the Caspian region and adjacent areas as the "Eurasian Heartland," or "the heart of the continent" (Kurecić, 2010, pp. 21–46). He stated: "Who rules East Europe commands the Heartland; who rules the Heartland commands the World Island (Europe, the Arabian Peninsula, Africa, South and East Asia); who rules the World Island commands the world" (Brzeziński, 1999, p. 31). Also, Nicholas Spykman is widely known for his geopolitical vision of international relations. He was inspired by Mackinder's Heartland thesis and suggest an alternative adage, the "Rimland" thesis: "Who controls the rimland controls Eurasia; who rules Eurasia controls the destinies of the world" (Criekemans, 2022, p. 119). The Heartland theory provides the intellectual basis of the US Cold War strategy. Its renaissance occurred after the collapse of the USSR, in the 1990s, and especially after September 11, 2001 (Labban, 2009, p. 2). Thus, Central Asia and the Caucasus acquire importance in geostrategic terms as the "pivot of the pivot" (Labban, 2009, p. 2).

The geographical position of the Caspian region is characterized by its detachment from Western influence and lack of access to the sea. Being a transit territory, rich in energy resources, it acquired more importance in the 1990s. It became a region of opportunity, but also of instability, conflict, and rivalry between great powers. The following considerations can be distinguished in this context:

– energy resources are located in an area which is very unstable and difficult to exploit for countries located in neighboring regions, due to physical barriers and the lack of appropriate infrastructure;
– there are many competing, or even hostile, players in the area, whose aim is to prevent other participants from getting involved in the energy market;
– the US, which is a distant superpower, and China, which is a superpower bordering on the region, seek to diminish Russia's role as a major player in

terms of resource extraction and transportation in the region of Central Asia; and

- at the same time, Russia and China aim to limit US influence in the region (Kurecić, 2010, pp. 21–46).

Three main geopolitical strategies can be observed currently in the Caspian region:

- the strategy of the US is an element of the superpower's global policy intended to penetrate the region and expand its influence there. It is linked to the Broader Middle East strategy. The strategy refers to the US interests, which are supported by its European allies (NATO members);
- the strategy of Russia, which is a regional superpower that seeks to eliminate US influence in Central Asia. Russia's goal is also to weaken China's role in the region, at the same time using the country's power to oppose the influence of the West, and especially of the US; and
- the strategy of China, which is another regional superpower that aspires to expand its influence in this significant region. However, the country's involvement in Central Asia is driven chiefly by economic motivations (Kurecić, 2010, pp. 21–46).

The geopolitical confrontation between the US and Russia in the Central Asian region demonstrates that the new "Great Game" is constantly evolving. The US aims to increase its influence in the region, while Russia lost its dominating role there in the 1990s. Following the collapse of the USSR, a "security vacuum" emerged in Central Asia and in the Caucasus, which the US intended to fill. That plan was partially fulfilled as a result of the war in Afghanistan and the establishment of US military bases in the region. Meanwhile, Russia focused on regaining its influence in this strategic region. China emerged as a new player. Turkey and Iran also sought to increase their influence in the region. However, their role seems negligible when compared to that of the global superpowers.

According to Zbigniew Brzeziński, "Eurasia is thus a grand chessboard on which the struggle for global primacy continues to be played" (Brzeziński, 1999, p. 31). That "megacontinent" is "too large, too populous, culturally too varied, and composed of too many historically ambitious and politically energetic states to be compliant toward even the most economically successful and politically preeminent global power" (Brzeziński, 1999, p. 31).

After the collapse of the Soviet Union, the Caspian region became an area of competition between external powers, interested primarily in the exploitation of energy resources in the newly established post-Soviet states. The strategic goal of states and transnational corporations has been to build a variety of export routes (pipeline geopolitics). In many cases, decisions regarding the selection of a particular energy infrastructure project reflected the geopolitical and geoeconomic rivalries among actors. At the same time, the capacity to build infrastructure and its economic efficiency will depend on the political, economic, and environmental stability in the region. Most energy infrastructure is built and managed by multinational corporations, which play a significant role in the region (Misiągiewicz, 2015, pp. 393–448).

The collapse of the USSR created new geoeconomic and geopolitical opportunities in the Caspian region. It was then that the Russian–Iranian lake became a sea, which provided development opportunities for the newly formed coastal states, but also attracted the interest of global players. The interests of external participants had a symbolic, geostrategic, or theoretical character, conditioned by the balance of power in the region and by economic pragmatism. We can distinguish three main categories of interests in the Caspian region:
– economic and political interests related to energy and referring to oil and gas reserves and their exploitation;
– economic interests not related to energy, such as fishing, and especially the harvesting of expensive caviar;
– the strategic position of the Caspian region is related not only to its treatment as a political link between Europe and Asia, but also as an attractive area in the geoeconomic sense, where pipelines can be laid, reflecting both political thinking and economic calculation (Zeinolabedin et al., 2009, p. 116).

The world's major consumers of energy, such as China and the EU, operate here, seeking to satisfy their basic needs, and looking to the Caspian region to supplement their oil and gas supplies. Thus, the dimension of energy security conditions geopolitical thinking in the Caspian region. Consequently, the region became the object of a "New Great Game," involving competition for influence and domination in the area of exploitation and transportation of energy (Bajrektarevic & Posega, 2016, pp. 237–264).

Due to the geographical specificity of the Caspian Basin, which has no connection to the seas and oceans, pipelines serve as the only means of exporting fuel to foreign markets. However, many of the planned pipelines were not built, due to the existing political and economic conditions. The actions of external players in the Caspian region also stem from international tensions and relations. The conflict in Ukraine, which antagonized Western states and Russia, and motivated the EU to seek alternative sources of energy supplies to become independent of Russia, can be quoted as an example of this tendency. In this context, some authors replace the term "New Great Game" with that of the "New Cold War," playing out between the West and Russia (Bajrektarevic & Posega, 2016, pp. 237–264).

Tensions in the region, resulting from an increased international involvement, were a consequence of the new geopolitical reality and strategic rivalry

between different powers (Chufrin, 2001, p. 11). The new geostrategic situation in the Caspian region was characterized by the following features:
- increased involvement of external actors (both sovereign and non-sovereign);
- energy security being the fundamental condition of the strategic role played by the Caspian region; and
- growing competition between Russia and extra-regional players, especially the West (Chufrin, 2001, p. 11).

Energy is crucial to the economic development in the Caspian region. The geopolitical balance of power is important, too. Thus, there is a competition for the implementation of various energy infrastructure projects, and the selection criteria are based not only on economic calculation, but primarily on geopolitical conditions and the influence and position of various actors (Chufrin, 2001, p. 11). The future exploitation of energy resources and the routes for exporting them to foreign markets are conditioned by the development of the Caspian region in both economic and political terms (Chufrin, 2001, p. 11).

The region's vulnerability in terms of security is also an issue. The USSR drew the borders of the republics in Central Asia and the Caucasus in an arbitrary and artificial manner. The states that emerged after the collapse of Soviet structures are ethnically heterogeneous. The policies that guaranteed the cohesion of the Soviet state caused instability in the Caspian region in the post-Cold War period (Gungormus, 2006, p. 188). It was the result of a number of conditions, including the collapse of the Soviet system and the growth of national consciousness in the newly established states. Moreover, there were no clearly defined mechanisms for preventing international conflicts in the region and instability within states. This created the risk of international armed conflicts or the spread of internal conflicts in the region and across Eurasia (Flint, 2017, p. 270).

Therefore, Zbigniew Brzeziński called this area the "Eurasian Balkans" (Brzeziński, 1999, p. 124). The term "Balkans" implies a certain level of instability in the national or religious dimension. There is tremendous diversity in Eurasia, which is the center of geopolitical rivalry.

Transport networks connecting the western and eastern ends of Eurasia run through the Eurasian Balkans. They are of great significance for the security of Russia, Turkey, Iran, and China. The region's rich energy reserves enhance its role as a stake in the geopolitical game between the superpowers. Issues related to access to resources "fuel national ambitions, attract the interest of great concerns, reawaken historic territorial claims, revive imperial ambitions, and inflame international rivalry" (Brzeziński, 1999, p. 126). The question of security in the Caspian region is as important as the question of development in the area of energy (Misiągiewicz, 2012a, pp. 61–79). At the same time, energy and security are closely connected due to the fact that the effective exploitation of energy resources requires a stable security environment resulting not only from the ability and capacity of the states in the region to cooperate, but also from the position and influence of external players (Chufrin, 2001, p. 12).

Active geopolitical players in the region are states that are willing and able to use their own power and influence beyond their borders to change the existing geopolitical state of affairs (Brzeziński, 1999, p. 40). These include Russia, China, the US, and the strongest EU member states. They have aspirations and sufficient potential, conditioned by a variety of factors: national, ideological, and economic, to gain dominance in various regions, and even on a global scale.

Geopolitical pivot points, on the other hand, are states whose importance is not based on their power or ambition, "but rather on their important geographical location and the effects of their potential instability on the behaviour of geopolitical players" (Brzeziński, 1999, p. 41). In the Caspian region, such a role is played by Azerbaijan, Turkey, or Iran. Azerbaijan is of great geopolitical importance, despite its small size and small population. Brzeziński described it as the "cork in the bottle containing the riches of the Caspian Sea basin and Central Asia" (Brzeziński, 1999, p. 43). Subordinating this state to Russia would not only enable Russia to take over Azerbaijan's rich energy resources, but could also have political consequences for the newly formed post-Soviet states in the region. Azerbaijan, connected to the Western market by an energy infrastructure that bypasses the Russian territory, has become a bridge between developed countries and former Soviet republics in the Caspian region. The state has thus been highly vulnerable to external pressures.

Turkey and Iran are also trying to maximize their influence in this strategic area, taking advantage of Russia's weakness and Azerbaijan's precarious position (Gungormus, 2006, p. 188). They can also be categorized as geostrategic players or even geopolitical powers (Flint, 2017, p. 44; Brzeziński, 1999, p. 47). Yet, they both experience numerous internal problems, which largely limits their ability to influence policy in the Caspian region. Iran fears Azeri separatism, as there are twice as many Azeris living in the northwestern part of the country than in Azerbaijan itself. As a result, Azerbaijan has been pressurized by both Russia and Iran, which sought to have it limit its relations with Western countries. Kazakhstan is also of great importance in this geostrategic analysis, as it represents the "shield" that protects other countries in the region against pressure from Russia, due to its geographical location (Brzeziński, 1999, p. 131). The strong position of the Russian population that inhabits the northern part of its territory is a problem to the country, too, making it necessary for Kazakhstan to take Russia's interests into account in its foreign and security policies, due to the fear of possible emergence of separatism. Turkmenistan, on the other hand, is not as ethnically diverse, while its geographical location makes it less susceptible to Russian influence. The stability of the Eurasian Balkans is largely conditioned by the situation in Iran and Turkey, which are "unstable in their geopolitical orientation" and susceptible to serious internal conflicts (Brzeziński, 1999, p. 134). These are post-imperial states with great strategic ambitions. They can be categorized as both regional players and geopolitical pivots.

In the post-Cold War period, Turkey became a pragmatic and assertive player (Lesser, 1992, pp. 86–103). It was a significant intermediary between Asia and Europe, both in political and economic terms. Its involvement in the Caspian region was based on ethno-cultural ties with post-Soviet states and a convenient geopolitical position (Bal, 2000, p. 43). In the early 1990s, when prospects of the energy sector's development in the Caspian region were promising, Turkey's ambition was to play the role of a leader in the area, relying on the cultural and ethnic community of Azeris, Turkmen, and Kazakhs. Turkey, a country which shares the same language, history, and culture with the Central Asian nations, is also one of the most active players in the Caspian region (Ataman, 2018, p. 4).

Despite commonly held perceptions that Turkey was more interested in Europe and the Middle East, President Recep Tayyip Erdoğan has never neglected the Turkic states and has visited them regularly over the past two decades (Balci & Liles, 2018, p. 16). The multidimensional foreign policy of Erdoğan's government "aimed to make new friends rather than create enemies and rested on the principle that more contact would mean a deeper relationship with others" (Akdoğan, 2019, p. 194). Due to the precarious international and regional geopolitical (geoenergetical) context, Turkey will probably devote more attention to its Caspian policy in the years to come. It's complicated relations with the Western states could catalyze this process (Balci & Liles, 2018, p. 18). However, the country's aspirations proved too ambitious and could only be fulfilled with regard to the transit of hydrocarbons. Although Turkish companies were active in the Caspian region's energy market, the newly formed states preferred Russian, American, and European investments. Due to its geopolitical position, Turkey can play a much more significant role as a natural intermediary between the Caspian region and the European market.

Iran's situation is even more precarious due to its hostile relationship with the US and concerns over possible Azeri separatism. The country is also leaning towards cooperation with Russia as part of the balance of power policy in the region.

The geostrategic importance of the Caspian region for US policy is not limited to energy security issues, but has implications in the so-called US grand
strategy for the 21st century. The US is not interested in direct acquisition of
energy resources from the Caspian region, and its interests extend beyond the
issue of energy security. The superpower not only seeks to control the energy
infrastructure, but, more importantly, competes with China and Russia in
geopolitical terms (Flint, 2017, p. 40; Iseri, 2009, p. 26). The Americans want
to prevent Russia from gaining exclusive geopolitical dominance and control
over the energy sector in the newly formed post-Soviet states. According to the
National Security Strategy Document of 1998:

> stability and prosperity in the Caucasus and Central Asia will contribute
> to security in the area extending from the Mediterranean to China and
> facilitate the dynamic development of the transportation of the vast oil
> and gas resources from the Caspian region to international markets with
> the involvement of the US. (Iseri, 2009, p. 35)

The priorities of the superpower's policy in the Caspian region are an element
of its broader strategy, which assumes the strengthening of its hegemony in
the region as a guarantor of security and stability (Iseri, 2009, p. 35). The US
seeks to maintain geopolitical pluralism in post-Soviet Eurasia:

> The new organisation of the European space created by the West is in fact
> based on the idea of supporting young, relatively small and weak nation-
> states in this part of the world by drawing them, more or less forcefully,
> into the orbit of NATO, the European Community and so on. (Brzeziński,
> 1999, p. 51)

In this context, oil and gas are viewed as strategic commodities on international markets, while the priority objective is to control the territory and its
resources as "strategic assets" (Brzeziński, 1999, p. 51). This approach applies
to the Caspian region, which is located at the center of the Eurasian Heartland, and which has an energy potential that makes it a playing field for strategic rivals (Rioran, 2019, p. 8; Amineh & Houweling, 2005 p. 82). The US is not
linked to the countries of the region by geographic or cultural ties, yet, it has
been seeking to mark its presence in the region. It consisted predominantly in
investments made by US companies, which contributed to the development of
the energy sector in Azerbaijan and Kazakhstan. Encouraged by its successes
in this area, the US has been expanding its influence in the region. In line with

the idea of creating a unilateral system on a global scale, it initiated a strategic objective in the Caspian region: to determine energy export routes that would bypass the territory of Russia, diminishing the country's role in the region. "However, the implementation of this scenario did not go exactly according to Washington's plan, nor did it cause any concern in Moscow" (Kurecić, 2010, p. 30). Russia's strategic influence did not disappear, while the US did not gain any significant allies in the region (apart from Azerbaijan). "While the US and NATO states are trying to spare Russia humiliation as much as they can, they are also decisively and consistently destroying the geopolitical foundations that allow Russia, at least in theory, to maintain the hope of becoming the world's number two superpower that the USSR once was" (Kubicek, 2013, pp. 171–180). This is manifested in the rivalry between the US and Russia in the Caspian region. According to Z. Brzeziński: whatever happens in terms of the distribution of power in the territory of Eurasia must also be significant for the role and historical mission of the US on a global scale (Brzeziński, 1999, p. 51; Labban, 2009, p. 9).

"The New Great Game" in the region began after September 11, 2001, when the US established its military bases in Central Asia as part of its occupation of Afghanistan, and of its fight against international terrorism, drug trafficking, human trafficking, and arms trafficking. Since that time, Caspian states have been benefiting from US support, especially in the area of security.

To sum up, America is too far away to dominate the Caspian region, but is also too powerful to abstain from getting involved there. Thus, the US is mainly interested in ensuring that no superpower gains exclusive control over the Caspian geopolitical space and that the international community has unfettered access to it. Pursuing the policy of geopolitical pluralism depends on the construction of diverse export pipelines in the region. Like Russia, the US has been focusing its attention on cooperation with Azerbaijan.

China is another active geopolitical player in the region (Xuetang, 2006, p. 123). Being the world's largest consumer of energy resources, it has taken interest in the Caspian hydrocarbon reserves. The aim of this superpower is to divert energy infrastructure away from the region of Central Asia towards the East, which would be contrary to the interests of the Western states (Labban, 2009, p. 42). China's involvement in Eurasia is underpinned by the "Belt and Road" initiative and the need to diversify energy sources and supplies. Shortly after the collapse of the USSR, the country's activity in the Caspian region was modest. China's interest in Central Asia intensified in the 2000s and was related to the huge demand for energy resources. At the same time, China could count on success because it posed no real threat to Russian or US interests, as was the case with Africa or the Middle East.

The EU, which is a major global importer of energy resources, is also a key player in the Caspian region. It has sought to establish closer cooperation with the post-Soviet states and promoted energy infrastructure projects extending in a western direction. The EU is a specific player in the Caspian region, consisting of both states and corporations. The policy of EU governments in the region was similar to that pursued by the US and based on diversifying energy supplies while bypassing Russia and Iran (Misiągiewicz, 2022, p. 483). The good example of EU engagement in the region is the eighteenth Cooperation Council meeting it had with the Republic of Azerbaijan in Brussels on July 19, 2022. Thus, Azerbaijan is both an important partner of the EU and a strategic partner one, providing natural oil and gas, and hence contributing to EU's efforts to diversify its energy resources (European Commission–Council of the European Union, 2022).

The strategic game in the Caspian region, which is the center of the Eurasian Balkans, thus involves a variety of actors, sovereign and non-sovereign, geopolitical players and pivots. Their relations are, in many cases, distinguished by natural enmity that results from historical reasons, as is the case with relations between Russia and Turkey or between Turkey and Iran. However, the game is a dynamic phenomenon and requires the formation of various coalitions to cooperate on eliminating the strongest player that could upset the balance in the region. Moreover, ambitious plans for the creation of spheres of influence in the Caspian region are often verified by confrontation with other players. Turkey, for example, wanted to play the role of the natural leader for the Turkish-speaking countries in the region. However, it was unable to implement this vision. Similarly, Russia, which sought to renew its power in the post-Soviet area, had to reckon not only with competition from geostrategic players, but also with the increasing assertiveness of newly emerging states in the region. Iran's ambitions are even vaguer. They are built on the legacy of the Persian Empire and on the idea of integrating Islamic states.

Competitors in the Caspian region are driven by different motives. Some want to gain geopolitical power, others would like to obtain access to natural resources, while still others seek to fulfil their national or religious mission or to ensure their own security.

Until the collapse of the USSR, Russia had a complete monopoly in the area of transport, both rail and pipeline, in Central Asia and in the Caucasus. Russian geopolitical scholars realized that "whoever controls access to the region stands a better chance of benefiting in geopolitical and economic terms" (Brzeziński, 1999, p. 141). Thus, the issue of pipeline geopolitics became crucial to the future of the newly formed Caspian states.

The shape of the new geopolitical game in the Caspian region will depend on a variety of political and economic conditions, yet, it is unlikely that any player may seek to build an empire or achieve a monopoly of power. States in the region will have two options to choose from in terms of their future geoeconomic role. The first is the "delicate balance of power in the region," which would allow them to gradually join in the global economic system and strengthen particular states. The second is a situation of conflict, political breakdown, or even an armed conflict, which would destabilize the Caspian region and the whole of Eurasia (Brzeziński, 1999, p. 142). The likelihood that the Caspian region may remain outside of any sphere of influence is also very low. This is because it is exposed to the instability associated with influence from different centers of power. On the other hand, there is no superpower in the region that would be strong and acceptable enough to act as an effective guarantor of security. The Caspian region is ethnically, politically, and economically fragmented. It has seen tensions and conflicts, as none of it has been strong enough to emerge as a leader that would organize international relations (Kurecić, 2010, pp. 21–46). The region is thus prone to fragmentation and instability. Following the collapse of the USSR in the 1990s, Russia was too weak to play the role of a guarantor of security in the region. At the same time, the other superpowers also failed to gain a dominant influence over the countries of Central Asia and the Caucasus because they feared the reaction of Russia, which, despite its weakness, treated this area as its exclusive sphere of influence. The region opened up to external influences, which became increasingly intense due to its strategic importance, especially as the power elites in individual post-Soviet states sought the involvement of the superpowers, hoping to increase foreign investment and to strengthen their position on the international energy market.

4   Energy Potential of the Caspian Region

Due to its wealth of energy resources, the Caspian Basin became a geoeconomic target for many participants in international relations. The area's oil and gas resources play a vital role in the energy strategies of the superpowers, which aim to control these resources, exploit them, and export them to international markets. However, exporting hydrocarbons to global markets faces many geographic constraints and geostrategic challenges.

In geological terms, the Caspian region can be divided into two basins: the North Caspian (Pre-Caspian) and the South Caspian, along with smaller basins, the North Ustyurt, Mangyshlak, and Amu-Darya, located between these two major basins to the east (Lerche et al., 1997; Belopolsky et al., 1998, p. 34). The area between the northern and southern parts of the Caspian Sea is the Central Caspian Basin (Hall & Sturrock, 2001, pp. 13–17). The northern part of the Caspian Sea consists of the shallow waters of the continental shelf (about 20 m) in the part that extends furthest to the north towards the Russian Platform. Most of this part of the Caspian Sea is located in Kazakhstan, while its western part is located in Russia. This area of the basin contains the highly significant Tengiz and Karachaganak, and Kashagan deposits.

The basin is divided into the western and northern parts, where the boundary is formed by elements connected to the south-eastern part of the Russian Platform, while the eastern and south-eastern borders are formed by the Ural Mountains, Southern Emba, and the Karpinsky Belt (Rabinowitz et al., 2004, pp. 19–40; Zonenshain & LePichon, 1986, pp. 181–211; Zonenshain et al., 1990, pp. 211–224; Nevolin & Fedorov, 1995, pp. 453–470; Lerche et al., 1997; Nadirov et al., 1997, pp. 389–400). The evolution of the Caspian Sea basin occurred during three major tectonic events, taking place during the Cambrian and Cenozoic eras.

The Caspian Sea and the surrounding region, especially Azerbaijan, have a long history of oil exploitation (Narimanov & Palaz, 1995, pp. 32–39; Abrams & Narimanov, 1997, pp. 451–468; Cullen, 1999, pp. 2–35; Daniloff, 1998, pp. 24–35; Sagers & Matzko, 1993, pp. 1093–1103). The presence of oil in the region was first mentioned in the 4th century in reports from Alexander the Great's soldiers (Rabinowitz et al., 2004, pp. 19–40). Then, Marco Polo reported on the region's abundance of oil during his journey along the Silk Road in the 13th century. Deposits in Baku were first exploited in 1848. However, this involved problems, such as the issue of oil storage, processing, and transportation. Oil wells were located at very close distances from one another, blowouts were common, cavities in the ground were used to store oil, and special canals were dug to transport it. The building of oil-refining facilities started in the 19th century. In that period, 23 refineries were established in Baku and two in Surakhan. Many private installations were in operation, too. Due to frequent fires, and spills of soot, smoke, and dust, the installations were moved to the outskirts of Baku, to the so-called "Black City" (Huseynzade & Aliyev, 2016, pp. 169–196). Sand was collected and water reservoirs were created to prevent fires. Oil was transported by horse-drawn carriages. This is how it was delivered to merchants and refineries, however, the costs of such transports were very high and exceeded the value of the resource.

In 1870, the Russian government allowed private businesses to operate in the region and exploit oil resources for the first time (Rabinowitz et al., 2004, pp. 19–40). The year 1920 marked the beginning of the next stage of the development of the oil sector in the Caspian region.

The first offshore well was drilled in 1924. According to 1940 estimates, Azerbaijan was responsible for the production of 70% of oil within the USSR.

Fearing Hitler's expansion in the region, the Soviets took full control over the deposits. However, oil production in the Caspian region declined significantly in the post-war era, as the USSR focused on the newly discovered deposits in Siberia (new oil fields, such as Gala and Buzovna-Mashtaga were launched at the time) (Rabinowitz et al., 2004).

In 1941, the output of oil in Azerbaijan reached 23.6 million tonnes (which accounted for 76% of the total output in USSR). This high output of fuel has probably contributed to the USSR's victory in World War II, and Baku was named the "Hero City" (Huseynzade & Aliyev, 2016, pp. 169–196). In 1949, the Neft Dashlari (Oil Rocks) deposits were discovered beneath the Caspian Sea, 40 km off the coast. This added to the significance of the Caspian Sea as a potential reserve of energy resources.

In 1950, mining operations in the offshore area began for the first time on a global scale. Special platforms were built, which resembled artificial cities (Huseynzade & Aliyev, 2016). Production was then developed in the Azeri sector of the Caspian Sea, in Gyurgan Deniz, Pirallahi, Chilov Island, Palchyg Pilpilasi, Sangachal, Duvanny, Khara Zira, Bulla Deniz, Bahar, Alyat Deniz, and Gunashli. New oil and gas condensate deposits were also discovered in the coastal area, in Kyurovdag, Mishovdag, Kyursanga, Garabagly, Galmaz, and Garadag. During this period, intensive geologic exploration was conducted and a lot of drilling was performed in the maritime area. New mining and transportation technologies were developed. The first pipeline from the Caspian Sea was laid in 1964 and ran from the Pirallahi Island towards the coastline (Huseynzade & Aliyev, 2016). In 1975, the total oil and gas output in the area reached 27.1 million tonnes of oil equivalent. In the 1980s, there were 11 offshore drilling units exploring underwater structures at depths ranging of 80 to 350 m, in areas with huge hydrocarbon reserves (Gunashli, Chirag, Azeri) (Huseynzade & Aliyev, 2016). By 1990, there were about 3.000 oil sources, which, at that time, were estimated to account for nearly 50% of global oil production.

The collapse of the USSR brought a dramatic change in the geopolitical situation in the Caspian region. Newly formed states opened up to foreign investment in the energy sector. At that time, it was estimated that the region would hold between 17 and 39 billion barrels of oil; according to some scenarios, the reserves could reach 230 billion barrels (Rabinowitz et al., 2004, pp. 19–40). The US Department of Energy maintained that the Caspian region held about 33 billion barrels in terms of proven oil reserves and nearly 220 billion barrels of potential oil reserves. Gas reserves were estimated at 243–248 trillion m^3 (Hill & Spector, 2001).

The oil produced in this region is of good quality and is located near the world's major trade and communication routes. Most of the oil produced in the region is destined for export, especially since domestic demand for this resource in oil-producing countries is not high. Moreover, countries in the region do not have the capital and technology required to develop their mining and transport potential independently. Thus, the importance of Western investment is growing (Kurecić, 2010, pp. 21–46).

The higher figures for oil reserves in the Caspian region noted in the early 21st century were due to the discovery of the Kashagan Oil Field in Kazakhstan (Mcutcheon & Osborn, 2001, pp. 18–25). It was estimated at the time that energy reserves in the entire Caspian region could be as high as 233 billion barrels (Kurecić, 2010, pp. 21–46). These optimistic figures were primarily based on the estimates of the US Energy Information Administration (EIA) of July 2001. At that time, the Caspian region and its resources were compared to the potential of the North Sea, North America, Africa, Latin America, the Far East, and Oceania. Taking into account the unproven but probable oil reserves, it could be concluded that they represented as much as 17% of the world's oil reserves, while gas reserves were estimated at about 12% of the world's reserves. However, these extremely optimistic scenarios were subject to revision, which set the region's reserves at 2% of the global reserves for oil and 5% of the global reserves for gas (Rabinowitz et al., 2004, pp. 19–40). At the turn of the 1990s and 2000, the output of oil in the area amounted to 1.1 million barrels per day (mb/d); the value was expected to grow steadily and even to triple in 2010, when it would reach 3.7 mb/d, with 85% of the output being destined for export. According to the British Petroleum Statistical Review of World Energy, oil reserves in the Caspian region (excluding Russia and Iran), account for about 3% of the global reserves; the same applies to gas reserves (Table 2.3) (BP, 2017, 2020). Meanwhile, according to the International Energy Agency (IEA), the region is the world's largest potential reservoir of hydrocarbon resources (Caspian Oil and Gas, 2022). Studies by the US Energy Information Administration estimated the reserves at 6.5 billion tonnes for oil and 8.3 trillion m^3 for gas (US Energy Information Administration, 2015). The World Energy Outlook estimated that oil production in the Caspian region would increase from 2.9 mb/d in 2009 to 5.4 mb/d between 2025 and 2030 (IEA World Energy Outlook, 2010). It was also estimated that gas output in this region would go up from 159 billion m^3 in 2009 to 260 billion m^3 in 2020, and possibly even to more than 310 billion m^3 in 2035 (IEA World Energy Outlook, 2010). According to Richard Jones, Deputy Executive Director of the IEA: "oil and gas exports from the Caspian region could double in the next 25 years" (Caspian Oil and Gas Exports, 2011).

Various internal and international sources estimate that oil reserves in the area range from 2 to 40 billion tonnes, while gas reserves range from

TABLE 2.3   Energy potential of the Caspian region countries

State	Proven oil reserves (billions barrels)	Proven oil reserves (share in global reserves, %)	Oil production (barrels per day)	Oil production (global share, %)	Proven gas reserves (trillions m^3)	Proven gas reserves (share in global reserves, %)	Gas production (billions m^3)	Gas production (global share, %)
Azerbaijan	7.0	0.4	779	0.8	2.8	1.4	24.3	0.6
Kazakhstan	30.0	1.7	1931	2.0	2.7	1.3	23.4	0.6
Turkmenistan	0.6	?	264	0.3	19.5	9.8	63.2	1.6

SOURCE: BP (2020) STATISTICAL REVIEW OF WORLD ENERGY 2020

2 to 12 trillion m³ (Zhiltsov et al., 2016). Offshore fields account for 41% of total oil reserves and 36% of gas reserves in the Caspian region (Zhiltsov et al., pp. 7–37). Most oil reserves are located in the North Caspian Sea, while most gas reserves are located in the South Caspian Sea (US Energy Information Administration, 2015). The energy reserves in the Caspian Sea are located far from export markets in Europe, Africa, and Asia. This necessitates the development of expensive transportation infrastructure, such as offshore and onshore pipelines, terminals, and tankers. The Caspian region was therefore treated as a significant energy reservoir on a global scale. States in the region, as well as the US, Great Britain, Turkey, and many transnational corporations, competed for the rights to exploit oil and gas in the Caspian Basin (Table 2.4). Furthermore, the involvement of international institutions, such

TABLE 2.4   Actors involved in the Caspian energy market

Participant	Interests	Activities
Private businesses	Maximum long-term profits Management risks	Infrastructure development Promoting government subsidies
Countries rich in resources but with poor infrastructure (Azerbaijan, Kazakhstan, Turkmenistan)	Maximum profits Energy and political independence Strong market position	Attracting foreign direct investment Access to profitable markets
Countries rich in energy and having well-developed infrastructure (Russia and Iran)	Maintaining the status quo when it comes to position on the energy market, especially in transporting energy	Maintaining competitive infrastructure Restructuring existing infrastructure
Poor transit states (Georgia)	Stable income, smooth deliveries	High transit fees Maximum utilization of transport position
Neighboring countries in need of energy (Turkey, EU, China)	Low-cost, smooth deliveries from various directions	Support for various infrastructure projects Revaluation of demand Guaranteeing the position of a redistributor state that has a strong impact on the price of the resource

TABLE 2.4   Actors involved in the Caspian energy market (*cont.*)

Participant	Interests	Activities
The US	Promoting independence of post-Soviet country Supporting non-OPEC supply Support for US companies	Support for the development of various infrastructure projects involving countries friendly to the US

as the International Finance Corporation (IFC), which is a component of the World Bank, was evident. It invested USD 3.6 billion in the construction of the BTC oil pipeline. Meanwhile, environmental NGOs are protesting against the exploitation of energy resources in this region, due to the risk of leakage of substances that could pose a threat to the ecosystem (Molchanov & Yevdokimov, 2004). The transportation of hydrocarbons from the Caspian Sea has become a problem.

Operating post-Soviet pipelines were inadequate, and most of them were directed to Black Sea ports, which involved increased risks to the environment and security of supplies. After the collapse of the Soviet Union, foreign companies started investing in the region and first conflicts emerged between coastal states over access to energy and the division of the Caspian Basin. Other problems were related to the cost of extraction and transportation of resources, and to environmental issues. The intense exploitation of deposits could cause natural disasters, such as earthquakes or eruptions of mud volcanoes. To quote US Assistant Secretary of State Marc Grossman, "access to Caspian energy is the most significant development of this decade" (Ivanovich, 1998, p. 8).

Most countries in the region are open to foreign investment. They are in the process of economic transformation and their goal is to integrate with the global free market economy. Regional producers are unable to consume the energy they produce, as individual post-Soviet states are abandoning the industrial economy model (Mahnovski, 2003). Moreover, post-Soviet states are unable to exploit their own energy resources, due to infrastructural deficiencies. All this makes the Caspian region more and more attractive to foreign actors, especially as the market has not been fully penetrated by investors (Karagiannis, 2003, p. 12; Molchanov & Yevdokimov, 2004, p. 434).

Numerous international companies are present in the Caspian region. Amoco, Chevron, Texaco, ExxonMobil, and others have invested about USD 50 billion in oil and gas extraction, especially in Azerbaijan and Kazakhstan (Misiągiewicz, 2022, p. 214). ExxonMobil is also a major player in Turkmenistan. Since 1997, the Amoco Corporation has increased its involvement in the Caspian Basin. The corporation lobbied heavily for US interests (Molchanov & Yevdokimov, 2004). Amoco is the principal shareholder in the Azeri consortium International Operating Company (AIOC) (President of the Republic of Azerbaijan, n.d.). Amoco's goal was to bring the strategic value of Azerbaijan to the attention of US authorities. The oil industry attracted nearly 70% of all investments. Thus, competition among foreign corporations with respect to the exploitation of energy resources in the Caspian Basin was on the rise. Western states interested in oil and gas production in the Caspian region include the United States, Great Britain, Germany, Italy, Norway, and Finland. After September 11, 2001, the US and British presence in the Caspian region increased notably. Currently, American corporations are trying to limit the development of independent local energy producers in Central Asia and the Caspian region. Moreover, they compete against Russian and European enterprises. At the same time, disputes between countries over the access to resources are not conducive to the involvement of foreign corporations, as the unstable situation makes investments riskier (Misiągiewicz, 2022, p. 203).

In addition to this, capital markets in the region's countries need modernizing, the productivity of the labor force is low, and people's standard of living in post-Soviet states leaves much to be desired. Common standards of international cooperation in the area of exploitation of energy resources are the only thing that can contribute to the development of the energy sector in the region (Molchanov & Yevdokimov, 2004).

Apart from political issues, there are other problems related to the exploitation and discovery of energy deposits in the Caspian region. These are due to the geographical and geological specificity of the Caspian Sea, which is a closed basin that faces many natural hazards. The Caspian states' export capabilities depend on how quickly they can develop the necessary infrastructure. Another important question is whether new export infrastructure projects will attract foreign investments.

The pipelines stretching from the Caspian Sea through the Black Sea, the Caucasus, the mountains in Turkey and Iran, the Karakum Desert, and various rivers are exposed to a variety of environmental hazards, such as storms, glaciation (especially in the northern part of the Caspian Sea), water-level changes, tides, high waves, coastal-water rise, and geological and geomorphological hazards (Zonn & Kostianoy, 2016). In addition, mountainous areas in Azerbaijan, Georgia, Turkey, Iran, Turkmenistan, and Russia form natural barriers to pipeline construction and operation (Zhiltsov et al., 2016, pp. 7–37). Thus, it seems reasonable to analyze a variety of geographical and geological phenomena, which seriously threaten the processes of exploitation and distribution of energy resources in the Caspian region.

The geographical area of the Caspian Sea is relatively small if we compare it to other producing regions such as the Gulf of Mexico, North Sea, and West Africa. The Caspian Sea has a closed character, which makes access to it difficult for larger vessels (Zonn & Kostianoy, 2016, p. 23). The only transport route by which ships can reach the Caspian Sea is through Volga River canals running from the Black Sea. However, the canal system permits only seasonal navigation and there are problems with shallow water and narrow areas, which do not allow large vessels to pass freely. For this reason, transport on specific vessels often requires their modification, which increases transportation costs. The same applies to the transportation of large mining equipment. The procedure in these situations is very complicated because such systems must be transported in parts. Therefore, huge mining systems cannot operate in the area. High transportation costs mean that equipment, once installed in the region, operates for a very long time, which is a challenging commitment for mining companies (DeLuca, 1998, p. 12, pp. 68–70; Kosarev & Yablonskaya, 1994, p. 259; Rodionov, 1994, p. 243; Kosarev, 2005, pp. 5–31).

5   International Conflicts in the Caspian Region

The subject of the analysis of this part of the study is the identification of the main security threats in the Caspian region that significantly reduce its position on the global energy market. The key issue affecting the regional security environment was the Nagorno-Karabakh conflict. This creates a risk of social stress, but also of an international conflict (Charlick-Paley et al., 2003, pp. 7–39; Alieva, 2012, pp. 443–453).

There are many conditions for the outbreak of conflicts in the Caspian region. One is the state-led "ethnic reconstruction" policy. In the process of transformation towards democratization or authoritarianism, conflict becomes more likely. In addition, the emergence of new political groups, citing ethnic, religious, or other sources, may constitute a conflict element, as in other groups they begin to perceive opponents (Oliker & Shayna, 2003, p. 307).

There are also conditions that indicate how the states of the region and their neighbors cooperate with each other and whether their relations may lead to conflict. However, complicated international relations do not always lead to conflict. For example, the military presence or economic domination of Russia may stabilize the situation in the region—although it can also make a conflict more likely. It depends, however, on the specific situation in the region and the possibilities of support from external actors. The likelihood of a conflict increases when, for example, Russia's actions are viewed as hostile by one or more countries in the region (Oliker & Shayna, 2003, p. 358).

The Caspian region became a source of tensions and conflicts after the collapse of the USSR, which was largely related to the energy security policies of the newly established states. They have started a competition for energy resources of this reservoir. This situation also led to the militarization of the region. There have been many incidents in this dimension that disturbed an already unstable area (Grison, 2013, pp. 83–94).

The presence of the armed forces causes a lack of confidence in the intentions of individual states, in line with the principle of the security dilemma (Oliker & Shayna, 2003, pp. 307–358). The lack of formal regulation of the status of the Caspian Basin region caused conflicts between coastal states. At the same time, the deposits of this reservoir were exploited, which led to military incidents between Azerbaijan, Iran, and Turkmenistan (Grison, 2013, pp. 83–94). In 1999, Azerbaijan accused Iran of exploration activities involving Royal Dutch Shell in the Azerbaijan sector. In July 2001, the Ministry of Petroleum of Iran issued a warning for foreign corporations not to operate in the coastal zones of the Caspian Sea, where territorial disputes are taking place (Rabinowitz et al., 2004, pp. 19–40). The day after this warning, Iranian ships intercepted the British Petroleum (BP) research vessel Geofizik-3, which was exploring the Araz–Alov–Sarq fields in the southern part of the basin, located approximately 90 miles southeast of Baku. The government of Azerbaijan handed over the license to exploit them to the BP consortium. At the same time, Iran is claiming rights to these deposits. Iran's actions are the first military incident in the Caspian Basin after the collapse of the USSR (Rabinowitz et al., 2004). Quoting Elmar Mamedjarov, chargé d'affaires of the Azerbaijani Embassy in Iran: "The conflict between Azerbaijan and Iran over the legal status of the Caspian Sea is an element of tension that has arisen in the region" (Calabrese, 2009, p. 3). This tension had its implications in the Karabakh conflict, where Iran supported Armenia. Another problem was that the US excluded Iranian companies from its energy projects in the Caspian region. In 2000, an Azerbaijani ship was blocked by the Iranian Navy on its way to oil fields in the southern part of the Caspian Basin (Grison, 2013, pp. 83–94).

A similar incident happened in 2009. In the face of such situations, Azerbaijan strengthened its military cooperation with the US.

Territorial conflicts also occurred between Azerbaijan and Turkmenistan. The reason for the tension was the marking of the central line from the shores of Azerbaijan, the farthest to the east, namely the Apsheron Peninsula. In this way, Azerbaijan controlled most of the central Caspian Basin. There are abundant oil deposits here. Turkmenistan declared that Azerbaijan illegally exploits oil deposits in the Caspian Basin. It claimed the rights to the Azeri and Chirag fields, where the Azerbaijan International Rating Company operated. The conflict also focused on the Kyapaz/Serdar fields, with reserves estimated at 500 million barrels (Mahnovski, 2003, p. 120). According to the information provided by the Turkmen border service, the Azerbaijani patrolling unit undertook "illegal actions" against the civilian Turkmen unit which conducts scientific research in the Kapaz/Serdar oil fields, to which both Turkmenistan and Azerbaijan have claims (Grison, 2013, pp. 83–94). In 2008, after a similar incident, the two countries reached an agreement aimed at limiting all exploration in the area until the status of these deposits was determined. Through unofficial sources, Russia threatened to take military steps if Azerbaijan and Turkmenistan reached an agreement on the construction of a joint pipeline (Grison, 2013, pp. 83–94).

The level of competition and distrust increased, resulting in increasingly intense militarization in the region. Numerous incidents and the expansion of military potentials threatened to escalate the conflict in the region towards an open military confrontation (Grison, 2013, pp. 83–94). Currently, each Caspian state has a certain military potential, located in or around the Caspian Basin. However, Russia and Iran clearly dominate in this dimension. If this trend continues, the military potential of Azerbaijan, Turkmenistan, and Kazakhstan in the Caspian Basin will increase significantly in the coming years. Relations between Azerbaijan and Turkmenistan, and between Azerbaijan and Iran, have become very tense since Azerbaijan signed contracts with Western corporations to exploit the disputed oil fields. As long as the Caspian states compete with one other in terms of access to deposits, as long as there is increased militarization of this region (Grison, 2013, pp. 83–94). Russia is the undisputed military power among the states of the region. From the beginning of the 2000s, the elite of this power defined the Caspian Basin as a zone of national strategic interest. In May 2011, the commander-in-chief of the country's navy declared that the Caspian fleet would increase its number by 16 new ships by 2020. With 148 ships with various tasks and functions, Russia has the greatest military potential in the Caspian region. Additionally, the country continues to strengthen its presence in this dimension in order to force Western players out of the region (Grison, 2013, pp. 83–94). In addition, Russia is able to prevent other Caspian states from expanding their navies. It controls the Volga River, which is the only waterway to the Caspian Basin. So far, Russia allows vessels of the Caspian states to use this channel, but this situation may change at any moment.

To develop its independence, Azerbaijan built its own shipyard. Kazakhstan and Turkmenistan have undertaken similar projects. Iran has the second-largest navy in the Caspian region. Since the beginning of the 1990s, the state has been systematically modernizing this industry. In 2001, Iran pledged to strengthen its armed forces with 75 warships. Iran announced that it would place submarines and a destroyer in the Caspian Basin. Such a policy worries Russia and increases the militarization of the region (Grison, 2013, pp. 83–94).

Rivalry and distrust lead to situations of tension and uncertainty. The post-Soviet states of the region, that is to say Azerbaijan, Turkmenistan, and Kazakhstan, feel threatened in the face of the increasing potential of Russia and Iran. Azerbaijan focuses largely on shipping safety. Until the collapse of the USSR, the Soviet Caspian fleet was stationed in Baku. Azerbaijan took over this infrastructure after independence. In addition, the country received 30 patrol boats and three motorboats from the USA and Turkey (Laruelle & Peyrouse, 2009, pp. 17–35). The US helped install a radar system along Azerbaijan's Caspian coast. The US Department of Defense conducted a series of exercises for the country's fleet to protect critical energy infrastructure (Grison, 2013, pp. 83–94). Azerbaijan also purchased torpedoes from Israel. The main threat to this country in the region was Iran and Russia. Both powers could have prevented negotiations between Azerbaijan and Turkmenistan on the construction of the Trans-Caspian Pipeline.

At the same time, Kazakhstan began to strengthen its military position in the region. The state has five ports in the Caspian Basin, but none of them were used for military purposes during the Soviet era. In 1994, Kazakhstan withdrew from the agreement promoted by Russia regarding the safety of shipping. In 2003, N. Nazarbayev announced that Kazakhstan was going to become a military force in the region. In 2012, he presented his first manufactured warship. In addition, in 2011, an air base was opened in Aqtau, a port city in the western part of Kazakhstan (Grison, 2013, pp. 83–94).

Turkmenistan has been present in the Caspian Basin to a minimal extent for many years. It was only in the 2000s, when its relations with Azerbaijan worsened, that the country decided to focus on securing its interests in the Caspian Basin by expanding the fleet. The state has only seven patrol units, three warships, two Sobol patrol units, and two Molniya ships. Despite the fact that Turkmenistan is a neutral state, its maritime doctrine says: "The purpose

of the maritime forces is to protect the state's interests in the Caspian region"
(Fitzpatrick, 2011, n.p.). In 2011, with the participation of Turkey and Ukraine,
the first Naval Academy was established in Turkmenistan. In the same year,
the country purchased two modern warships (Grison, 2013, pp. 83–94). In 2012,
Turkmenistan conducted naval maneuvers with the official goal of combating terrorism, but in reality the state intended to increase its influence in the
region. These maneuvers provoked Azerbaijan, as well as the Caspian component of the Collective Security Treaty Organization, engaging the forces of
Russia and Kazakhstan to undertake similar actions (Grison, 2013, pp. 83–94).
In October 2005, Russia's Minister of Foreign Affairs, S. Lavrov, proposed the
creation of a joint armed force in the Caspian region—CASFOR. Kazakhstan,
Turkmenistan, and Azerbaijan, however, rejected this proposal for fear of
Russia's domination in the dimension of regional security (Grison, 2013, pp.
83–94). In such a situation, there is a high probability of a conflict between
the countries of the region. Another problem may be the deepening of cooperation in the military dimension of the countries in the region with external
actors, in particular with the US. In addition, countries such as Azerbaijan and
Georgia are tightening relations with Turkey, which may also cause Russia to
react (Oliker & Shayna, 2003, pp. 307–358).

The countries of the region have their own internal problems that may
contribute to regional instability:
– wide variation in the standard of living, awareness of economic handicap,
  and deprivation among people living in poverty;
– deepening of problems in the macroeconomic dimension; and
– high mortality rate, health problems, and drug abuse (Oliker & Shayna,
  2003, pp. 307–358).
The above-mentioned problems have existed for many years and may even
worsen in some countries of the region. In such a situation, the risk of a conflict outbreak largely depends on the ability of states to respond to economic
and social challenges and various types of crises. A weak state is the lack of
institutional possibilities necessary in the case of anti-crisis measures. In addition, one of the main determinants of conflicts in the Caspian region may be
the crisis related to the succession of power in some countries. This can cause
social tensions, especially in the case of authoritarian systems in the process
of transformation. The very process of transformation may be a cause of conflict, due to the possibility of the activity of extremist political parties (Oliker
& Shayna, 2003, pp. 307–358).

The conflict between Armenia and Azerbaijan is the most dramatic
humanitarian tragedy in the post-Soviet Caucasus (Map 2.4). The number of
refugees and displaced persons from the occupied territories in Karabakh and

MAP 2.4   The Nagorno-Karabakh conflict area
SOURCE: HTTPS://COMMONS.WIKIMEDIA.ORG/W/INDEX.PHP?SEARCH
=NAGORNO-KARABAKH+&TITLE=SPECIAL:MEDIASEARCH&GO=GO&TYPE
=IMAGE

the seven districts outside this area numbered approximately 1.010.000. In addition, approximately 20.000 people died, 50.000 were injured, and 4.866 missing (Ipek, 2009, pp. 228–239). The Khojaly massacre was portrayed by Azerbaijani leaders as an ethnic cleansing of the occupied territories, which provoked anger among the Azerbaijani society and hatred towards Armenia. During the bloodiest clashes in the Karabakh region, the people of Khojaly were brutally attacked by the armed forces of Armenia on the night of January 25–26, 1992. As a result, 613 people were killed, 1.275 were taken hostage, and the fate of the remaining 150 was unknown (Haydar Aliyev Foundation, 2005, pp. 7–8). The conflict caused significant migrations and demographic changes. The population of Azerbaijan had to leave both Armenia and the former NKAO (Mountain-Karabash Autonomous Oblast), together with the adjacent areas, which came under the control of Armenian forces (Górecki, 2020a, pp. 1–88). The total number of displaced people in Azerbaijan was nearly 750.000, which in 1994 accounted for around 10% of the country's population (Górecki, 2020a, pp. 1–88). The forced migrations also affected the Armenian population. Almost all Armenians had to leave Azerbaijan. Their number is estimated at over 330.000 (Górecki, 2020a, pp. 1–88).

The subject of the conflict that has been going on for over 30 years was the nationality of Nagorno-Karabakh, an area inside Azerbaijan, inhabited by Armenians, functioning as a quasi-state under the political and military patronage of Armenia. The actual power was exercised there by the so-called Nagorno-Karabakh Republic (NKR), a para-state not recognized internationally even by Armenia. Formally, in line with international law, all disputed territories remain part of Azerbaijan. The international community recognized it as the territory of Azerbaijan under Armenian occupation. The main city of the area and the de facto capital of the RGK is Stepanakert (Chankendi). There was also a dispute over the future ethnic composition of these territories (Górecki, 2020a, pp. 1–88). The separatist Republic of Nagorno-Karabakh was in practice "a branch of the Armenian state and was dependent on it in the political, military, economic and social dimensions" (Górecki, 2020a, p. 70). Thus, he was not the subject of the peace process. At the same time, the RGK felt a certain separateness, which manifested itself in a separate political system, separate presidential, parliamentary and local elections, or its own state symbolism.

The settlement of the conflict since 1992 was handled by the so-called OSCE Minsk Group, consisting of Armenia, Azerbaijan, Russia, France, and the US (Legieć, 2019, p. 13). Although there was a ceasefire between Azerbaijan and Armenia since 1994, the displacement of Azerbaijanis from the territory of Nagorno-Karabakh was not conducive to a peaceful process in the region.

The ceasefire agreement stopped the main fighting in Nagorno-Karabakh and opened the door to peaceful negotiations and the final settlement of the conflict. Negotiations have been going on for over two decades. The situation of "stable equilibrium" resulted from the fact that none of the parties to the conflict showed the initiative to change it (Gasparyan, 2019, pp. 235–250). Thus, despite many years of negotiations, Azerbaijan and Armenia did not want to finally resolve the conflict until November 10, 2020. The reason for such a situation was the fact that both sides sought to achieve their maximum aspirations (Gasparyan, 2019, pp. 235–250).

The conflict has its roots back in the early 1920s. Then, after the Soviets took over the Caucasus, the Bolsheviks granted the area of Nagorno-Karabakh to Soviet Azerbaijan as an autonomous region, 94% inhabited by the Armenian population. This decision was often contested by Armenia, but to no avail (Górecki, 2020a, pp. 1–88). Within the USSR, Nagorno-Karabakh was an autonomous region—(NKAO, Nagorno-Karabakh Autonomous Oblast) and belonged to the Azerbaijan Soviet Socialist Republic (Górecki, 2020a, pp. 1–88).

In the early 1990s, Armenia's armed forces took control of the entire area (with the exception of parts in the north and east of the former NKAO) as a result of hostilities (Górecki, 2020a, pp. 1–88). In the initial phase of the war, Armenian armed forces succeeded in conquering all areas controlled by Azerbaijan, including strategically important regions: the city of Shusha and the Lachin region outside Karabakh. A land corridor between Armenia and Nagorno-Karabakh was also created (Gasparyan, 2019, pp. 235–250). In 1993, Armenian forces took control of six Azerbaijani districts bordering Nagorno-Karabakh:

Kelbajar, Agdam, Qubatli, Jebrayil, Fizuli, and Zangelan (Gasparyan, 2019, pp. 235–250). In the same year, the UN Security Council adopted four resolutions: 822, 853, 874, and 884, calling for a ceasefire, withdrawal of the occupying forces from the Azerbaijan province, resumption of negotiations, lifting of all economic blockades in the region, and called for the Republic of Armenia to persuade the Nagorno-Karabakh authorities to comply with the above resolutions and the Minsk Group's initiatives Minsk OSCE (Gasparyan, 2019, pp. 235–250).

At the same time, Russia's defense and foreign ministers worked on a ceasefire agreement between the parties to the conflict. Such an agreement was finally signed by the defense ministers of Azerbaijan and Armenia and the commander of the Nagorno-Karabakh armed forces on May 12, 1994. From August 1994, representatives of Armenia, Azerbaijan, and Nagorno-Karabakh began regular meetings in Moscow (Gasparyan, 2019, pp. 235–250). Thus, the Russian Federation became a mediator in the preparation of a political agreement between the parties to the conflict. At the same time, the OSCE declared its readiness to deploy an international peacekeeping force in Nagorno-Karabakh. However, it was decided to suspend these actions until the ceasefire becomes a fact and a political agreement is signed between the participants in the conflict. In line with the decisions of the Budapest summit in March 1995,

> The Chairman of the Minsk Group will create a structure for resolving the conflict as a result of the negotiation process; reaching a solution by the parties following an agreement to cease armed conflict; and promoting the peace process by deploying OSCE multinational peace forces. (OSCE, 1995, p. 10)

In 1997, the leaders of the Group (France, Russia, and the US) presented the "package" and "phases" of the peace process to all parties to the conflict. The "package" plan was rejected by Nagorno-Karabakh and Azerbaijan. Armenia, on the other hand, decided to implement the "phased" plan and President L. Ter-Petrossian initiated a public debate in order to approve it and guarantee a lasting peace. In the article, "War or Peace: Time for Thoughtfulness," he declared that "the opposition should not convince the public that there is an alternative to compromise: an alternative to compromise is war. The rejection of the compromise will lead to the destruction of Karabakh and the deterioration of Armenia's situation" (Ter-Petrossian, 2018, p. 22). At that time, the dominant view was that a possible resumption of fighting carried a threat of supra-regional destabilization and problems in the field of "soft security," including mass migrations of refugees (Ter-Petrossian, 2018).

However, other key problems appeared in the Caucasus, obscuring the Kara-bakh conflict, such as the launch of new energy transport routes (2005–2006), the Russo-Georgian War (2008), or the annexation of Crimea by Russia and the outbreak of the war in Donbas (2014). Thus, the conflict between Azerbaijan and Armenia ceased to be a priority for external players, who treated it as non-developmental or even "frozen."

In April 2016, Azerbaijan, which had so far declared that it would not use force to regain the territories lost in the 1990s, launched a military attack, destroying the status quo and thus attracting the attention of international opinion. The situation in the line of fire between the forces of Azerbaijan and Nagorno-Karabakh became unpredictable, both sides used force, and more and more victims were killed (Gasparyan, 2019, pp. 235–250).

On May 16, 2016, the Russian minister of foreign affairs, the US secretary of state, and the minister for European Affairs of France, representing the OSCE Minsk Group chairmen, met with the presidents of Armenia and Azerbaijan in Vienna in order to work out a peaceful solution to the conflict. It was declared impossible to solve it by military means, and it was important to respect the 1994 ceasefire agreement (Organization for Security and Co-operation in Europe, n.d.). The presidents agreed to the next round of talks, which held in St. Petersburg on June 20, with the participation of President Putin. The presidents of Russia, Armenia, and Azerbaijan adopted a joint position, in which they undertook to normalize the situation and agreed to increase the number of OSCE observers in the conflict zone. In addition, they committed to creating the necessary conditions for the negotiation process to resolve the conflict politically (Organization for Security and Co-operation in Europe, n.d.). The intensification of fighting in 2016 showed that the threat of a new war was real, although the main actors were interested in maintaining the status quo (Górecki, 2020a, pp. 1–88).

The Karabakh conflict, which is an international dispute over territory, is primarily a political one, but its important catalyst was also the reluctance between two nations: the Azerbaijan and the Armenians (Górecki, 2020a, pp. 1–88). Thus, the conflict was also of an ethnic and national character. In the initial phase, it was a provincial rebellion against the metropolis, although Karabakh separatism was supported by the society and the Armenian authorities, and even inspired by Armenia. The social dimension of the conflict was related primarily to the issue of refugees, especially internal refugees. As a result of the conflict, the areas controlled by Armenian forces became ethnically homogeneous (Górecki, 2020a, pp. 1–88).

At the regional level, Russia was and still is the most involved actor in the conflict. It was an arbiter (contributing to the conclusion of the ceasefire agreement) and an intermediary (as one of the three—apart from France and the US—co-chairmen of the OSCE Minsk Group to settle the conflict). Over time, it became the most important and indispensable mediator (Górecki, 2020a, pp. 1–88).

For Russia, the conflict was an important instrument for maintaining its influence in the region. In the initial phase, it supported Azerbaijan

> by defending the Soviet *status quo* and wishing to prevent the collapse of the USSR. Then it supported Armenia in order to prevent Azerbaijan from getting closer to Western states and institutions, and to prevent Turkey's expansion in the region. (Górecki, 2020a, pp. 1–88)

Since the suspension of arms in 1994, Russia acted as a mediator between the parties to the conflict. Thanks to good relations with Azerbaijan and Armenia, it pursued the "Divide and rule" policy, pushing for solutions that were beneficial to it. Russia, although linked to Armenia by a defense alliance, was the main supplier of weapons to both sides of the conflict. The concepts proposed by Russia are based on the so-called Kazan document of the Minsk Group of 2011 (Legieć, 2019, p. 13). According to it, the territory outside the former NKAO, controlled by Nagorno-Karabakh (seven Azerbaijani provinces), should be returned to Azerbaijan, with the exception of the territorial corridor connecting Armenia with the GK (Legieć, 2019, p. 13). According to Russia, the final status of Karabakh itself should be determined in a referendum.

The West accepted Russia's dominant role in the region, as it usually acted as the co-chairman of the OSCE Minsk Group responsible for the Karabakh peace process. Despite the fact that after the collapse of the USSR, the South Caucasus was an area of rivalry between Russia (wishing to control it) and the West (supporting the independence of the former republics and forcing the construction of a new pipeline network) (Górecki, 2020a, pp. 1–88). Western states reduced their ambitions and are primarily interested in stability Caucasus and preventing the resumption of fighting.

In the international dimension, the conflict was initially considered to be the main obstacle to access to Caspian oil and gas deposits (Górecki, 2020a, pp. 1–88). Despite the lack of progress in settling the Karabakh conflict, regional energy projects have been successfully implemented. The West also supported the emerging post-Soviet states in promoting regional stability and democracy. For Turkey and Iran, involvement in the conflict as intermediaries and mediators was, in turn, an attempt to "return to the Caucasus" and rebuild their influence there (Górecki, 2020a, pp. 1–88). Turkey aspired to create a bloc of Turkish-speaking countries (which would include

Azerbaijan), while Iran tried to limit the American presence in its immediate neighborhood.

The conflict over Nagorno-Karabakh's nationality determined the post-Soviet history of Armenia and Azerbaijan, constituting "the most important security challenge for both countries and significantly influencing the overall foreign and domestic policy" (Górecki, 2020a, pp. 1–88). The conflict resulted in displacements and forced migrations, as well as intensive propaganda of both countries building around Karabakh "narratives of the state and consciously creating images of the enemy" (Górecki, 2020a, pp. 1–88).

The Karabakh conflict largely shaped the contemporary map of the South Caucasus, creating a system of alliances (Armenia with Russia and Azerbaijan with Turkey) and the course of transport and communication routes, including oil and gas pipelines. The conflict also increased the role of Georgia, which became the main transit country for the export of energy resources from Azerbaijan to the Western market. According to W. Górecki, it remains an important element of politics in the Caspian region, as it takes place in a crucial area: between Russia and the Middle East (Górecki, 2020a, pp. 1–88). Important transport corridors run in this region, and a possible resumption of the conflict in Karabakh may lead to a supra-regional crisis (Krüger, 2010).

On November 24, 2019, the ministry of defense of Azerbaijan reported about 23 shellings of its positions, on November 25 at 23, November 26 at 22, November 27 at 21, November 28 at 20, November 29 at 23, and on November 30 at 20 (in total—about 152 cases) (Górecki, 2020a, pp. 1–88). In February 2020, both sides reported about 20–30 daily cases of violations of the ceasefire by the opponent (Górecki, 2020a, pp. 1–88). At the same time, they did not care about the escalation of the conflict, as it would entail too high a risk of failure, which for the ruling elite would mean the risk of losing power (Górecki, 2020a, pp. 1–88). The intensification of hostilities was also very risky due to the possible involvement of external forces on both sides of the conflict.

Over the past 20 years, both the OSCE Minsk Group and Russia have unilaterally attempted to resolve the conflict. However, there has always been a conflict of interest on both sides. The key question, then, is why the parties to the conflict have not been able to bring about a permanent political solution. There are two perspectives that suggest an answer to this question.

First, even if maintaining the status quo entailed significant costs, it is preferable to bear the cost of any solution that does not require territorial concessions. Second, territorial concessions will fundamentally change the balance of power between Azerbaijan and Armenia, making them more vulnerable to influence (Gasparyan, 2019, pp. 235–250). In such a situation, Azerbaijan may become more aggressive. The negotiating positions of both sides can be

analyzed in the context of the theory of possibility developed by Daniel Kahneman and Amos Tverski (Kahneman & Tversky, 1979, pp. 263–292). It presents
a model of the decision-making process in a risk situation. The value in this
context is the gains and losses and, to a lesser extent, the final solution. The
probabilities of creating a solution are not as important as the decision bur-
den. When this theory is applied in international relations, Jack S. Levy argues
that the tendency to maintain the status quo is stronger than the prospect of
strengthening one's position in a comparable amount due to the risk of loss
(Levy, 2003, pp. 215–241). Thus, in the theory of possibility, loss is a greater
threat and risk than the prospect of gaining benefits. Therefore, the negotiations over the status of Nagorno-Karabakh for many years did not lead to a
solution to the conflict, as neither side wanted to make concessions, even if it
could get some benefits in return. Randall Schweller stated that "rational states
countless on benefits than they try to avoid losses" (Schweller, 1996, pp. 22–30).

   In the context of Nagorno-Karabakh, although the communities of all parties to the conflict were bearing its economic and social costs over a period of
more than two decades, political leaders did not want to bear the costs of a possible agreement. As J. Snyder noted, democratization can cause nationalism
when the ruling elite uses the state's potential for conflict and economic development, while avoiding the weakening of political authority for the benefit of
citizens (2000). Such argumentation is appropriate in the case of the situation
in Armenia, where political leaders preferred and sought the status quo, rather
than a peaceful agreement that could fundamentally change the state's position in the region. Although maintaining the status quo in Nagorno-Karabakh
posed the risk of resuming the armed struggle, the Armenian authorities did
not opt for a permanent agreement that could result in political and economic
stabilization.

   Similar regularities occur in Azerbaijan. Åslund commented that the state
maintained an equilibrium that was favorable for the leaders, but not for the
citizens. Authoritarian stability allowed the ruling elite to develop a system of
corruption at the expense of society (Åslund, 2017, pp. 89–101). The current
regime in Azerbaijan is associated with economic and social problems, which
also resulted from the conflict in Nagorno-Karabakh. It has also become an
instrument of manipulation in the hands of the ruling elite in order to justify
the repressive policy. The ruling regimes in both countries used the conflict
before the next elections and during various crises. In this way, they wanted
to maintain the mobilization of societies in order to divert their attention
from various problems (economic difficulties, human rights violations, social
unrest, and so on) (Åslund, 2017, pp. 89–101). Thus, both in Armenia and Azerbaijan, the Karabakh conflict was an important state and nation-building

factor, playing an important role in building identity and national consolidation (Górecki, 2020a, pp. 1–88).

There have been various reasons for the failures of the Nagorno-Karabakh peace process to date. First, the parties to the conflict preferred to maintain the status quo. Second, any change in the status of the disputed region could have fundamentally disrupted the balance of power between Azerbaijan and Armenia to the detriment of the latter. In such a situation, Azerbaijan could use its strategic advantage and take over provinces outside Nagorno-Karabakh. Authoritarian regimes benefited from the conflicts, despite the social and economic costs, as often authoritarian propaganda justified any problems in the state with the need to conduct a conflict. There were also tensions between the mediators involved in the peace process, which manifested itself in relations between the West and Russia.

As a result of the change of power in Armenia in 2018, Armenian–Azerbaijani talks on the conflict over Nagorno-Karabakh were intensified. However, they did not bring any results due to strong internal social pressure, limiting the possibility of reaching a compromise (Legieć, 2019, p. 2). However, an unexpected breakthrough took place on November 9–10, 2020. The prime minister of Armenia, Nikol Pashinyan, and the presidents of Azerbaijan and Russia, Ilham Aliyev and Vladimir Putin, signed a declaration to stop fighting in the area of the Nagorno-Karabakh conflict.

The deal came after six weeks of intense fighting in the region. The truce assumes that "the warring parties will stop in their positions" (Górecki, 2020b, p. 12). Azerbaijan will maintain the southern part of the Nagorno-Karabakh and the safety belt in the form of seven Azerbaijani oblasts occupied by Armenia during the war in 1992–1994, and will gain a corridor connecting its territory with Nakhichevan (Legieć, 2020). The 5 km belt, the Laczyński corridor, will enable the maintenance of land communication between Armenia and Stranakert (Górecki, 2020b, p. 12). The prime minister of Armenia declared that: "it is not a victory, but it is not a defeat either" (Łukaszewski, 2020, n.p.). Arayik Harutyunyan, the leader of the Nagorno-Karabakh region, declared: "Taking into account the present situation and wanting to avoid further human losses, I agreed to end the war and sign a tripartite truce" (Łukaszewski, 2020, n.p.).

The Russian peacekeeping force has been deployed along the border line (15 Mechanized Brigade, 1.960 soldiers). The peacekeepers are to be stationed there for five years, with the possibility of extending their stay for further five-year periods. All roads and communication routes in the region are to be unblocked, and refugees and forced displaced persons may return to their places of residence. The parties will also exchange prisoners and fallen. The agreement does not regulate the status of the part of Nagorno-Karabakh remaining under Armenia's control (formally, it will remain as part of Azerbaijan, and the enclave of Armenia will be given an autonomy smaller than that of the Nagorno-Karabakh Republic so far). The "new Nagorno-Karabakh" will probably be a demilitarized zone. It will most likely be the subject of additional arrangements between the parties to the conflict (Map 2.5).

According to W. Gorecki's commentary, "the ceasefire at the current stage of fighting and in the form outlined above marks the triumph of Azerbaijan and the *de facto* capitulation of Armenia, which loses most of the territories occupied in the early 1990s" (Górecki, 2020b, p. 12). The deployment of a contingent of Russian peacekeepers to the conflict area is a guarantee that the truce will be maintained (Górecki, 2020b, p. 12). In this way, Russia strengthened its presence in the South Caucasus region. The declaration of the parties to the conflict did not, however, provide for a fundamental role for Turkey, which had hoped to participate in the peace process (Górecki, 2020b, p. 12). However, the significance of this state in "the security architecture in the conflict area will only become symbolic and will be based on the presence of military observers in the future Russian-Turkish ceasefire control centre" (Górecki, 2020b, p. 12). The agreement takes into account the elements of conflict settlement developed by the Minsk OSCE Group: returning the territories around Nagorno-Karabakh to Azerbaijani control; maintaining the corridor linking Armenia to Nagorno-Karabakh; ensuring that all refugees and internally displaced persons have the right to return to their previous places of residence; international security guarantees; granting Nagorno-Karabakh itself a temporary legal status that guarantees its security and self-governance; and establishing a final legal status for Nagorno-Karabakh through a referendum (Górecki, 2020b, p. 12). The truce will have an impact on the internal situation in Azerbaijan and Armenia. The agreement is a success for Azerbaijan, as it legally sanctions the incorporation of most of the territory of the Nagorno-Karabakh and offers a chance for the takeover of full control over it in the future (Legieć, 2020, p. 12). It will also empower the position of Ilham Aliyev, who managed to end the occupation of Azerbaijan lands. Thanks to the territorial corridor to Nakhichevan, the country will have a land connection with Turkey (Legieć, 2020, p. 12). The return of the territories around Nagorno-Karabakh to Azerbaijan in accordance with the provisions of the peace agreement may make the area vulnerable to possible attack by that state in order to take over the entire disputed area (Łukaszewski, 2020).

In turn, in Armenia, the terms of the truce were perceived as a humiliating defeat (Łukaszewski, 2020). The society of that state rejected the terms of the agreement. There were violent demonstrations in the capital of the state, Yerevan (Górecki, 2020b, p. 12). They may lead to the loss of power by Prime

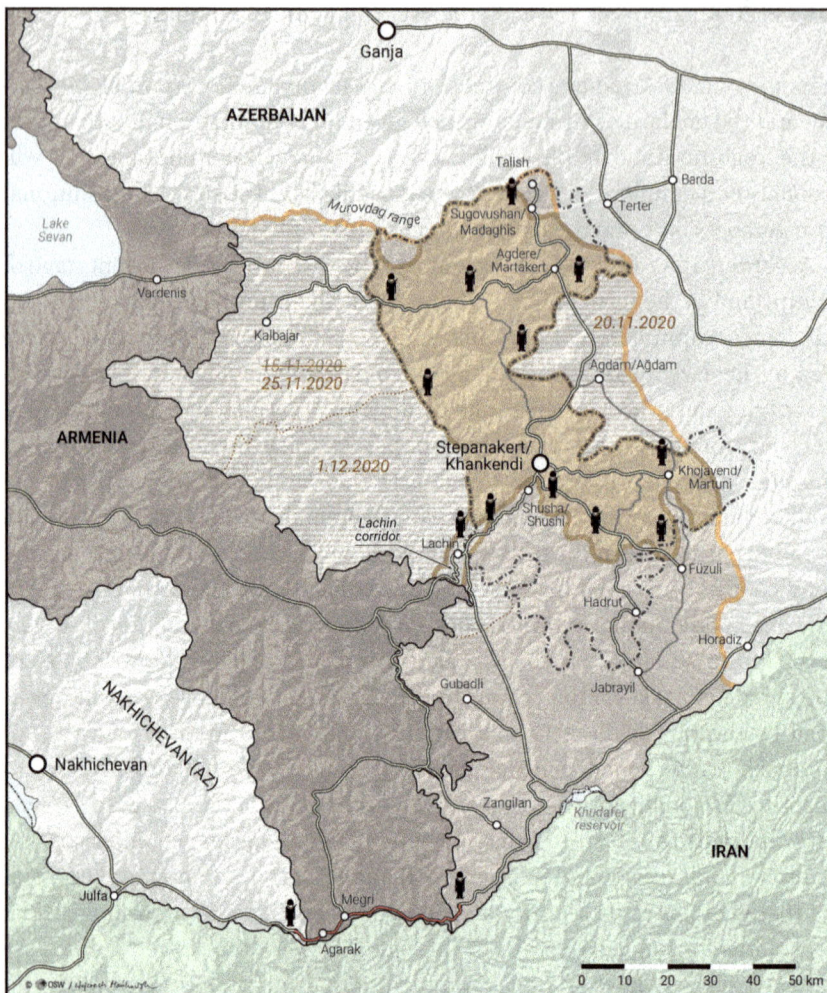

Likely extent of the areas that will come under Azerbaijan's control in accordance with the truce of 10 November 2020 (with dates when each area is to be handed over):

- Agdam district: 20 November 2020
- Kalbajar district (raion): 25 November 2020 (new date)
- Lachin district: 1 December 2020

Areas in block colours were captured by Azerbaijani troops during the fighting (27 September – 9 November 2020)

Probable shape of the 'new Nagorno-Karabakh'
(Russian peacekeepers will be stationed along the contact line, including in the Lachin corridor)

Russian presence in the conflict zone (peace forces and border troops)

Border of the former Nagorno-Karabakh Autonomous Oblast (as part of the USSR)

Future land connection to Nakhchivan (under the control of Russian border troops)

Main roads

MAP 2.5   The Nagorno-Karabakh conflict area after the entry into force of the truce of November 10, 2020

SOURCE: © OSW, WOJCIECH MAŃKOWSKI, HTTPS://WWW.OSW.WAW.PL /EN/PUBLIKACJE/ANALYSES/2020-11-10/NAGORNO-KARABAKH-ARMENIAS -SURRENDER-RUSSIAS-SUCCESS

Minister N. Pashinyan and destabilize the political situation (Legieć, 2020, p. 12). According to Arkadiusz Legieć, the undermining of the agreement may become a priority of Armenia's policy, "because it does not end the Armenian-Azer conflict, the basis of which is both the dispute over the membership of the Nagorno-Karabakh and ethnic determinants" (Legieć, 2020, p. 12).

On March 24, 2022, Azerbaijani forces entered the village of Farrukh located on the border of Nagorno-Karabakh, northwest of the town of Agdam. According to the Armenians, this was an act of aggression, although the Azerbaijani side referred to the action as "establishing positions and deployment locations" (Górecki, 2022, p. 13). Baku also denied using force: the separatist authorities in Stepanakert stated that over the next few days, the Armenian positions came under fire, from weapons including drones. Three Armenian soldiers were killed in the attacks. The entry into the village of Farruch is part of a broader strategy adopted by the Azerbaijani government since the end of the second Karabakh war (fall 2020). This consists of maintaining the tension around the conflict area and along the border with Armenia, and creating facts on the ground. From the perspective of Baku, its deadline to bring a complete end to the conflict is 2025, which is when the Russian peacekeepers in the Nagorno-Karabakh region should leave (Górecki, 2022).

The resolution of the Karabakh conflict will not improve the economic situation in the participating states, but the political stabilization in the region will undoubtedly increase foreign investments and trust on the part of international corporations. It has a fundamental influence in attracting capital (Polachek et al., 2012, pp. 736–755). According to E. Gartzke et al.: "If a state is dependent on capital markets, it is also dependent on political stability" (Gartzke et al., 2001, pp. 391–438). The normalization of relations between the Caucasian states will not only optimize the security environment, but may also increase the possibilities of transporting energy in the region (Gartzke et al., 2001).

The conflict in Nagorno-Karabakh was the oldest conflict in the post-Soviet area. It influenced domestic and foreign policy, as well as the identities of Armenia and Azerbaijan. Quoting W. Górecki: "It also left his mark on the entire region, violating the internal cohesion of the South Caucasus and creating new networks of political, economic and social ties" (Górecki, 2020a, pp. 1–88). "The conflict between Armenia and Azerbaijan (as well as Armenians and Azeris) over Nagorno-Karabakh was multi-level and multi-dimensional. At individual levels – bilateral, regional and international – the following dimensions can be distinguished: political (including military), economic (especially transport and energy), and social" (Górecki, 2020a, pp. 1–88).

It is also worth noting that the conflict had a major impact on the geopolitics of building pipelines from the Caspian region to the European market.

The elimination of Armenia as the main transit country for energy resources exported from Azerbaijan has strengthened Georgia's role in this dimension.

6   Conclusion

To sum up, energy security in the Caspian region can be best understood through an analysis of intra-state and regional developments. This conclusion agrees with studies conducted by Benjamin Miller, who focused on the state and nation on the one hand, and on the involvement of the so-called great powers on the other (Miller, 2007). He suggested that states and nation groups do not act cohesively, while external actors do not tend to cooperate. This situation gives rise to tensions and conflicts in the region. Commenting on this multilevel concept, T. V. Paul concluded that this approach is interesting, and many regions experience this type of imbalance that makes peace impossible (Paul, 2012, pp. 17).

The Caspian region is no exception in this respect. Questions related to border demarcation, navigation, and contradictions concerning strategic issues, such as energy transport routes, affect energy security in the Caspian region, Europe, and even the whole of Eurasia. Many transnational corporations have invested billions of dollars in oil and gas exploitation projects in the Caspian region. At the same time, there are numerous problems that cause investment risk. At the level of declarations, states view the Caspian region as a "sea of peace," however, in practice, the area is a region of strategic play between states and a place where the armed forces of coastal states are stationed. This geostrategic game determined the political and economic dynamics. The players here include: regional states; major regional powers: Iran, Turkey, Russia, and China; and global players: the US, the EU, and transnational corporations. Each of these participants vies for access to the region's energy resources. Russia and the US are the main players that are trying to eliminate each other. If Russia renews its control over the Caspian region on the basis of a system of international agreements, it will become the main actor and beneficiary of the energy market formed by the region's countries.

In view of the growing consumption of energy resources on the global scale, the "Great Game" in the Caspian region may gain momentum. At the same time, there is the prospect of a shift in the structure of energy consumption towards the exploitation of renewable resources, which will diminish the geopolitical significance of the region. In addition to that, the drop in the price of oil diminishes competition for this fuel on a global scale, and thus limits the Caspian region's potential for economic and political development.

Based on the presented analysis, it can be concluded that the Caspian region is exposed to many potential threats to energy security. An important issue is the rivalry between the great powers in the Caspian region. After September 11, 2001, this area gained importance in the geostrategic dimension. The main players are China, Russia, and the West. In this situation, there is no coordinated response from the newly established states of the region. On the contrary, each of them develops independent relationships with different external players. Powers compete for spheres of influence in the region. Foreign governments influence Caspian states to promote their interests and block the influence of opposition groups. This may lead to manipulation and internal tensions, and as a result—to deeper divisions in the region. Consequently, the situation in the Caspian region seems more unstable than during the collapse of the USSR. Internal and external pressures make the former republics vulnerable. National and state-building processes are exposed to various challenges that states have not always coped with.

In the context of geopolitical instability due to the armed conflict between Russia and Ukraine, the Caspian region will most likely gain in importance in the global energy market. By imposing sanctions against Russia, the European Union is looking for alternative sources of hydrocarbon materials, and is increasingly tightening cooperation with Azerbaijan. In addition, as a result of the weakening of Russia's geopolitical position on a global scale, the balance of power in the Caspian region will also change. Russia will cease to be the "point of reference" for EU and Chinese policies in the region. The new security architecture has not yet taken shape, but one thing is certain, the Caspian states should adopt proactive approach to increase their resilience to the turbulence of the international system. Thus, we can confidently say that a new "Great Game" is beginning regarding the energy policy and geopolitical position of the Caspian region.

Energy Security Policy Actors in the Caspian Region

The subject of the analysis of this part of the study is to define the main priorities of energy security policies of both the Caspian region states and external
participants (taking into account their specificity, interests, and activities).

The energy security policies of the countries of the Caspian region are an
outcome of many factors, such as: the specificity of the regime created after
the collapse of the USSR, the issue of national identity, the influence of social
groups, the geopolitical position of the state, interests and influence of external actors, and investments by foreign corporations.

A specific element of the dynamics of international relations in the region
is Azerbaijan's energy security policy. The country is becoming an increasingly
valuable and assertive participant in the international energy market, effectively developing its mining potential. Pipeline geopolitics and security threats
influence the strategic policy goals of Azerbaijan, a pioneer in the development of the energy sector in the Caspian region. It is a country at a geopolitical
and identity crossroads. In the geopolitical dimension, it is a post-Soviet and
European state; in the religious dimension, it belongs to the world of Islam;
and in terms of culture and civilization, it represents Turkophone values. On
the one hand, Azerbaijan participates in many structures and forms of international cooperation, and on the other, it is exposed to various types of conflicts
and instability in the regional and sub-regional dimension.

It is impossible to analyze the issue of energy security in the Caspian region
without taking Azerbaijan into account. Kazakhstan's economy is mainly
based on oil exports. At the same time, the transport of this raw material is
a major challenge for the country's energy security policy. Turkmenistan, in
turn, is developing its energy position and is becoming an assertive partner in
this dimension for Russia, China, and Western countries. The country plans to
develop a policy of diversifying hydrocarbon exports, but its activities in this
respect so far have encountered many problems, which have blocked the possibility of implementing various pipeline infrastructure projects. After the collapse of the USSR, when most analysts pointed to the risk of a political vacuum
in the Caspian region, Iran pursued a pragmatic policy towards post-Soviet
states, devoid of ideological influences. The country realized that it did not
have enough resources to play the role of a leading player in the Caspian region
(Hunter, 2003, pp. 133–134). Being aware of the limited possibilities, Iran tried
to implement its economic and cultural goals in the region, taking into account

© JUSTYNA MISIĄGIEWICZ, 2024 | DOI:10.1163/9789004697614_005

the specificity of the environment and the resulting threats and opportunities. Russia, in turn, treats its energy policy as an instrument of political influence. It still perceives the Caspian region as its exclusive sphere of influence, both in the economic and political dimensions. Russia's actions in this region are limiting its integration with the global economy. Russia maintains its troops here and influences the decisions of the ruling elite in the newly created post-Soviet states. It also aims to play the role of a monopoly as a supplier of energy resources to Western markets.

The Caspian region has furthermore become an area of interest for external participants. They see here the possibility of obtaining energy resources, and are also influential geostrategic players. At the end of the 20th century, China's energy security policy focused on efforts to seek cooperation with oil and gas suppliers. In return, the state offered a range of support, including for the construction of energy infrastructure. Undoubtedly, Chinese oil companies are a significant player in the energy market. Their relations with Kazakhstan, Turkmenistan, and Russia are specific due to the political regimes operating in these countries. After the end of the Cold War, Turkey lost its strategic importance as an ally of Western countries against the expansion of the Soviet Union. However, new opportunities arose, resulting from the change in the international system. In the Caspian region, countries with a majority Muslim population and ethnically related to the Turks were established. Therefore, the situation in this region forces a re-evaluation of the foreign policy objectives of the Republic of Turkey. Its location at the junction of the European and Asian continents influences its specific role as a transit country for energy resources. The European Union is a special subject of energy security in the Caucasian region. This structure is now one of the major energy consumers worldwide. The priority of the EU energy security policy is to guarantee the smooth supply of oil and gas in the face of increasing dependence on imports. In such a situation, an effective policy of diversifying sources is indispensable, as, too, is increased EU activity in order to strengthen economic relations with alternative suppliers.

1   Energy Security Policies of the Caspian Region States

1.1   *Republic of Azerbaijan*
When analyzing Azerbaijan's energy security policy, one should take into account geopolitical and geoenergetic conditions, as well as those related to political and social changes in the country. Azerbaijan's strategic interests are mainly related to the process of the exploitation of energy resources and

cooperation with sovereign and non-sovereign actors. The actions of this state are reflected in numerous agreements and contracts concluded by Azerbaijan, relating to the *upstream* and *downstream* sectors. Azerbaijan's energy security strategy in the Caspian region is conditioned by its geopolitical identity, which is a complex phenomenon that determines its double-track policy (Mammadov, 2017, pp. 12–20).

In this context, the Commonwealth of Independent States is an important point of reference. The historically conditioned relations between Azerbaijan and the CIS states are somewhat natural in the context of belonging to the USSR during the Cold War.

At the same time, the country has strong cultural ties with Turkey. A manifestation of this is the participation of Azerbaijan in the Co-operation Council of Turkish-speaking countries. In this way, the country implements its foreign policy and geopolitical aspirations (Mammadov, 2017, pp. 12–20).

Moreover, the geopolitical dimension of Azerbaijan's position results from the fact that it is a European state and that cooperation with European structures is a priority of its foreign policy (van Gils, 2020, p. 20). Azerbaijan is a member of the Parliamentary Assembly of the Council of Europe and maintains good relations with EU states and institutions (Mammadov, 2017, pp. 12–20). As a result, the Cooperation Council meeting between the European Union and the Republic of Azerbaijan was held in Brussels on July 19, 2022. Its aim was to review the overall state of EU–Azerbaijan relations and to discuss mutual interests for future cooperation (European Commission–Council of the European Union, 2022). The NATO operation in Afghanistan after the 9/11 terrorist attacks on the United States, was also a platform for deepening cooperation with Azerbaijan as part of the Partnership for Peace structure (NATO, 2014). The cooperation of Azerbaijan and NATO countries concerns in particular the protection of energy critical infrastructure (NATO, 2014).

At the same time, it is a Muslim state and identifies itself with the community of Islamic states. It is a member of the Organization for the Cooperation of Islamic States (Goble, 2009, p. 3). Azerbaijan thus plays a significant geopolitical role in the international environment. It is a member of the Black Sea Economic Cooperation Organization (BSEC), the Economic Cooperation Organization (ECO), and the Organization for Democracy and Economic Development (GUAM) (Mammadov, 2017, p. 12). Thus, the policy of this state has multi-sectoral features and is based on the principle of balance in international relations (Strakes, 2015, pp. 5–8).

In the security dimension, Azerbaijan saw the following issues as conditioning its foreign policy:

1. geopolitical rivalry regarding the routes of energy exports;
2. strategic positioning in the context of the fight against international terrorism;
3. neutrality, despite the alliance with the US regarding the proliferation of nuclear weapons in Iran; and
4. the specificity of the state-building process based on energy resources (Ipek, 2009, pp. 228–239).

Since independence, Azerbaijan has built a coherent and predictable foreign policy that reflects national interests. The combination of activities, economic and social development, and the political influence of this country in international relations guarantee that Azerbaijan is able to independently carry out the decision-making process, regardless of external processes and actors.

Due to its geopolitical and geoeconomic position, this state has various foreign policy interests. It is increasing its role not only in the region, but also on a global scale. The challenge for Azerbaijan in this context was the instability of the Caspian region and the increasing rivalry between various actors. The Russo-Georgian War or the conflict in Nagorno-Karabakh made the region both politically unstable, and exposed it to various threats in the context of building critical energy infrastructures (Ipek, 2009, pp. 228–239). Mention must be made here to Russia's ongoing war in Ukraine, which has increased the role of Azerbaijan as an alternative supplier of gas to European markets.

Azerbaijan's resource potential essentially determines its energy security strategy. The country was a pioneer in the development of the energy sector in the Caspian region and on a global scale. Since ancient times, Azerbaijan has been known for having energy resources. Inhabitants of this area were afraid of flammable gas escaping from the face of the earth, and Azerbaijan was called "the land of fire" (Huseynzade & Aliyev, 2016, pp. 169–196). Oil has always been treated as a national good. The country was the first in the world to have a kerosene factory, an oil field, and an oil platform.

The main oil resources in this country are located on the Apsheronian Peninsula, near Baku. Their discovery started a long history of the oil sector in the Caspian region. In 1846, the world's first official oil production took place here (Huseynzade & Aliyev, 2016, pp. 169–196). However, citing historical sources, oil in this area was mined much earlier, and even in ancient times. Industrial-scale oil production began in 1847 in the Ramana, Balakhana, Sabunch, and Bibi-Heybat fields. Behind the former SOCAR's head, Rovnag Abdullajew is: Azerbaijan was the first country to exploit coastal and marine oil deposits and the first to use tankers to transport oil (Svyatets, 2016, pp. 74–109).

Baku is a unique example of a city with a significant energy potential, rich history, and traditions, combined. Oil deposits have been used since the time of their discovery as a basic fuel, insulation material, and even medicine (Huseynzade & Aliyev, 2016, pp. 169–196).

Already in medieval times, the Arab geographer Abdul Hasan Ma'sudi, Italian traveler Marco Polo, German explorer Engelbert Kaempfer, and others reported on the presence of oil in Azerbaijan. National entrepreneurs, such as Haji Zeynalabdin Taghiyev, Aga Musa Naghiyev, Murtuza Mukhtarov, Aga Shamsi Asadullayev, Isabey Gadjinski, and Ashurbeyovs, played a special role in the development of the oil industry in this country (Huseynzade & Aliyev, 2016, pp. 169–196). Since the 19th century, the Baku region has been one of the world's richest in energy resources. About half of the world's oil resources were mined here at that time (Bahgat, 2005, p. 6). This impressive level of production was due to the investments of the brothers Robert, Ludwig, and Alfred Nobel and Royal Dutch Shell, which enabled Russia to exploit the Caspian deposits. In the 1960s, Azerbaijan started competing with the USA in the development of engineering knowledge and new technologies in the oil industry, and foreign investments in the oil sector played an increasingly important role. The first tanker in the world was built in Baku by Ludwig Nobel at the end of the 19th century (Yergin, 2011, p. 50). During this period, oil production in Azerbaijan attracted the first foreign investors and was controlled by powerful entrepreneurs: the Nobel and Rothschild brothers as well as Taghiyev, Naghiyev, Mukhtarov, and Hajinsky (Svyatets, 2016, pp. 74–109). The oil company of the Nobel brothers was the largest of its kind in the world.

Caspian oil was a strategic value during both World Wars. The Germans were unsuccessful in their several attempts to conquer Baku. The inability to obtain Caspian resources was one of the reasons for their failure both in 1918 and 1945 (Bahgat, 2006, p. 3). Azerbaijan's oil fields were the Soviet Union's main source of oil during World War II (Terterov, 2018, pp. 213–230). In the 1950s, after the discovery of oil resources in the Urals and Siberia, Russia shifted its energy investments from the Caspian region. This reduced production in the area. After the collapse of the USSR, Azerbaijan began to pursue an energy policy independent of Russia (Kolundzić, 2009, pp. 203–212). The country's energy industry developed in the 1990s and early 2000s. Azerbaijan's economic strength is largely based on revenues from the oil trade (Terterov, 2018, pp. 213–230) (Table 3.1).

The production of this raw material increased from 22.2 million tonnes in 2005 to 50.8 million tonnes in 2010. Following SOCAR data, after reaching the peak of production in 2009–2010 in 2011 and 2012, the level of production

TABLE 3.1   Azerbaijan oil production (barrels per day)

2001	2004	2005	2008	2009	2010	2011	2012	2016	2018	2020
307.200	312.800	477.00	1,099.000	1.011.000	1.041.000	987.000	931.9000	842.000	789.300	798.000

SOURCE: HTTPS://WWW.INDEXMUNDI.COM/G/G.ASPX?C=AJ&V=88

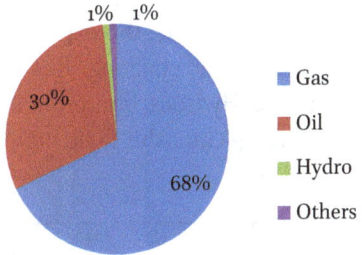

FIGURE 3.1
Energy consumption in Azerbaijan
SOURCE: MADE BY THE AUTHOR, HTTPS://WWW
.EIA.GOV/INTERNATIONAL/ANALYSIS/COUNTRY
/AZE

TABLE 3.2   Natural gas production in Azerbaijan (billions m^3)

2001	2003	2004	2007	2009	2010	2011	2013	2016	2018	2020
5.7	5.1	5	9.7	16.5	16.6	17.8	18.2	29.3	16.9	16.9

SOURCE: HTTPS://WWW.INDEXMUNDI.COM/G/G.ASPX?V=136&C=AJ&L=EN

dropped significantly to 43.5 million tonnes per year (Kosowska et al., 2018, pp. 267–274). Currently, Azerbaijan produces 779.000 barrels per day, which accounts for 0.8% of the global share (BP, 2020). Geology has ceased to favor this country's policy, since its oil reserves are estimated at around 7–10 billion barrels (Terterov, 2018, pp. 213–230).

Oil and gas are the main component of the country's energy mix in its consumption of energy resources (Figure 3.1).

Azerbaijan continues to be a significant player in the global energy market. It is a key producer of hydrocarbons in the post-Soviet area (Tables 3.1 and 3.2). After Russia and Kazakhstan, Azerbaijan has the largest oil and gas reserves in the region. According to BP data from 2020, Azerbaijan's documented oil reserves amount to 7 billion barrels (1 billion tonnes), which is 0.4% of world reserves, and 2.8 trillion m^3 of gas, which accounts for 1.4% of world reserves (BP, 2020). The International Energy Agency reported that Azerbaijan is a major producer of crude oil (32.7 million tonnes, including natural gas liquids in 2022) and of natural gas (35 m^3 in 2022) (International Energy Agency, 2023a). The country's estimated oil reserves are around 10 billion barrels. On the other hand, the estimated gas reserves are about 3 trillion m^3.

The country is located on the Caspian Sea, with significant potential reserves of oil and gas (International Energy Agency, 2023a). Its energy resources are located in the Caspian Basin, both confirmed and potential ones, may contribute to the diversification of satisfaction and stabilization of supplies on an international scale (Ipek, 2009, pp. 228–239). At the same time, the exploitation of energy potential for a closed water reservoir, is a huge challenge due to the need to build an extensive pipeline infrastructure. Hydrocarbon production in Azerbaijan is concentrated in the Azeri–Chirag–Gunashli (ACG) and Shah Deniz fields (Map 3.1) (Hall & Grant, 2009, p. 66).

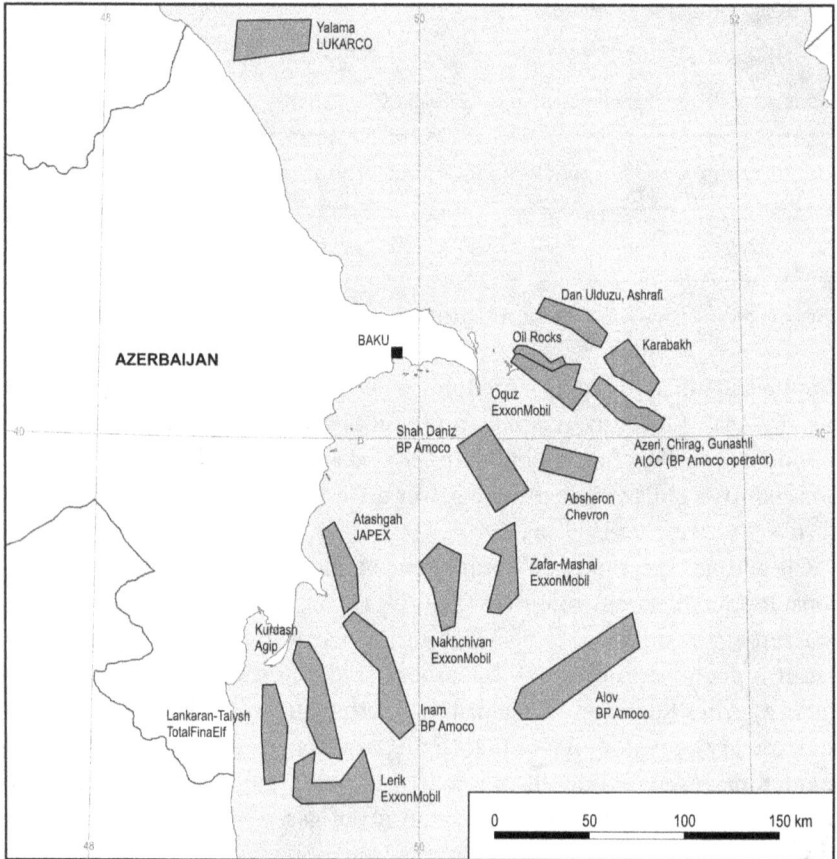

MAP 3.1   Oil and gas fields in Azerbaijan
SOURCE: MADE BY W. JASIŃSKI IN MISIĄGIEWICZ, 2014

The main oil reserves in the region are in the Baku region (Apsheron) and in the Apsheron-Pribalkhash zone, where the Azeri-Chirag-Gunashli (ACG) field is located. Currently, 75% of oil from the Caspian region of Azerbaijan is produced from these fields. The remaining 25% comes from the old resources of the Baku region. Among the oil fields in the Azerbaijan zone of the Caucasian Sea, ACG deserves special attention, as its resources are estimated at 1.2 billion tonnes of oil and 360 billion m^3 of gas (Opening speech by Ilham Aliev, 2021).

Most of Azerbaijan's gas reserves are located in the Shah Deniz fields, the reserves of which are estimated at 1.2 trillion m3 of gas. These fields were developed in two stages. In the first phase, production started at the end of 2016, and in the second from 2018. TBP is the main operator and shareholder of this gas field. Under the Caspian Sea, the Shah Deniz field conceals at least twice as much gas as the EU's annual gas consumption (Kublik, 2018). These fields are located in the Caspian coastal zone, and the extraction from these fields accounts for 80% of energy production in Azerbaijan (Stokes & Raphael, 2010, p. 116).

According to forecasts, the second phase of the field expansion will increase gas production to 24 billion m^3 annually (Senderov, 2019, pp. 5–11). The Shah Deniz gas field was discovered in 1999 and Azerbaijan became self-sufficient in gas resources in 2007.

Another 600 billion m^3 of gas is obtained from the Apsheron, Umid, Ashrafi, and Karabakh fields (Senderov, 2019, pp. 5–11). In addition to the main oil and gas fields, there are five prospective gas extraction structures: Babek (400 billion m^3), Nakhchivan (300 billion m^3), Zafer-Mashal (300 billion m^3), Araz–Alov–Sharg (700 billion m^3), and Shafag–Asiman (500 billion m^3). The overproduction of gas, estimated at 10 billion m^3, increased the interest of Western markets in cooperation with Azerbaijan in gas exploitation and export (Senderov, 2019, pp. 5–11). The importance of this country as a gas producer and exporter has been steadily increasing. Azerbaijan has evolved from the main exporter and producer of energy resources towards a transit country, connecting the Central Asian region with Europe.

An important condition for Azerbaijan's security strategy is its geopolitical position. Azerbaijan, situated at the intersection of the east and west, north and south of Eurasia, is a key country in transportation. It initiated and actively participated in strategic trans-regional transport projects, such as the Baku–Tbilisi–Kars railway connection, the International Sea Trade Port in Baku, or the Trans-Eurasian Information Super Highway. The International Port of Baku is the main trade and logistic hub in the region, it is an element of the Transport Corridor Europe–Caucasus–Central Asia (TRACECA) project, which connects Asia and Europe in the commercial dimension (Jafarova, 2017, pp. 41–44). In addition, Azerbaijan, Kazakhstan, and Georgia are interested in expanding the possibilities of freight transport through the Trans-Caspian International Transport Route and agreed to establish the Trans-Caspian International Transport Consortium in April 2016 (Jafarova, 2017, pp. 41–44). Due to its favorable geostrategic position, Azerbaijan plays a transit role as the shortest route connecting Europe with Asia. In August 2016, the Azerbaijan, Russia, and Iran summit in Baku took place in order to implement the North–South Transport Corridor project (Jafarova, 2017, pp. 41–44).

Security threats in the early years of Azerbaijan's independence became a key element of the country's foreign policy strategy, which was largely based on economic development through cooperation with transnational energy corporations. Due to the economic crisis resulting from the collapse of the economic system centrally controlled by the USSR, direct foreign investments in Azerbaijan's oil and gas sectors of have become an opportunity for its economic reconstruction. Azerbaijan focused on the extraction and production of energy resources. However, its experience differed from that of other former Soviet republics due to its geographic position and cultural heritage.

The conflicts that took place after Azerbaijan regained its independence largely influenced its economic reconstruction and national security. Thus, Azerbaijan aims to strengthen its independence and economic development in the context of the geopolitical rivalry resulting from the diversity of interests of state and non-state actors involved in the construction of export roads for oil and gas (Ipek, 2009, pp. 228–239). There were two main conflicts within the Caspian region influencing the shape of the country's foreign policy. First, the Karabakh conflict between Armenia and Azerbaijan, and second, the unresolved status of the Caspian Sea.

Azerbaijan perceived the Karabakh conflict as a threat to its territorial integrity and independence. According to the Concept of National Security of 2007, "aggression against the state is the main determinant of the security environment and a key factor in the process of creating the National Security Policy" (National Security Concept of the Republic of Azerbaijan, 2007, p. 4). The Azerbaijani Military Doctrine of 2010 notes that Armenia's occupation of Nagorno-Karabakh, apart from the control of Azerbaijan, destroys not only national security, but also affects the security of the entire region (Republic of Azerbaycan, 2010). Azerbaijan President Ilham Aliev stated that the failure to resolve the Karabakh conflict not only affected Azerbaijan's security environment, but also the region as a whole, and set a dangerous precedent for other conflicts in various parts of the world (Aliyev, 2013).

The dispute over the status of the Caspian Sea was another challenge for Azerbaijan's foreign policy. The conflict over the division of this body of water was of fundamental importance for the exploitation of hydrocarbons off its coast, especially after the significant oil contract of 1994 was signed (Goldberg, 1998, p. 67). Azerbaijan argued that the basin should be divided into national sectors, within which each coastal state would exercise exclusive jurisdiction.

Energy resources have become a tool for implementing Azerbaijan's fundamental strategic interests and the basis of its activities in international relations. During this period, the long-term strategy of Azerbaijan's president was to attract foreign investment in the energy sector, which was to strengthen national security. Quoting Vafa Guizade, foreign policy advisor to President Aliyev: "Oil is our strategy, it is our defence and our independence" (Ipek, 2009, pp. 228–239). Such a policy meant that most of the transnational oil corporations were present in Azerbaijan (Ipek, 2009, pp. 228–239). This was also confirmed by Sabit Bagirov, the then president of the State Oil Company of the Azerbaijan Republic (SOCAR), declaring that: "the only way to establish economic and political relations between Azerbaijan and the West is to use oil and open Azerbaijan territory to the West as a new strategic way to Central Asia" (Bagirov, 2001, pp. 179–180). Thus, the Azerbaijani administration made it a priority to establish cooperation with Western oil corporations, ensuring that the country was open to signing lucrative contracts. The situation developed dynamically, as already in 1992 two contracts were signed with BP–Statoil and Pennzoil–Ramco for the exploitation of the Chirag and Gunashli fields.

The political consequence of this move was the pro-Western course of Azerbaijan's foreign policy and the deterioration of relations with Russia, which was excluded from these oil contracts. The US also turned out to be interested in entering Azerbaijan's energy market through the Amoco and Unocal corporations. In 1994, a consortium of Western companies signed the aforementioned "deal of the century" with the Azerbaijani government (Ipek, 2009, pp. 228–239). This agreement included oil exports to the West, reducing the dependence of the West and Azerbaijan on Russia.

The aim of this project was to increase the energy security of Western European countries, as well as the economic independence of the Caspian region. This cooperation resulted in the construction of the Baku–Tbilisi–Ceyhan pipeline and the project to build the Nabucco gas pipeline. Azerbaijan was thereby able to become a strategic partner for Western countries. It can also play the role of a transit state for energy resources from Central Asia in the event of the construction of the Trans-Caspian Pipeline (Socor, 2007, p. 25). The "contract of the century" had a major impact on the development of the oil and gas industry in Azerbaijan through significant investments, the introduction of modern technologies in the process of exploring fields in the maritime area, modernizing the oil and gas infrastructure, increasing oil production, and strengthening the market leader position. In addition, the export of oil and gas to neighboring countries and Europe was initiated, projects for the construction of export roads were implemented, research and development in the oil and gas sector was developed, and the National Oil Fund was created to collect income from trade in oil (Kosowska et al., 2018, pp. 267–274). The agreement thus reflected Azerbaijan's energy security strategy. In the years 1994–2008, 26 agreements were signed on the management and exploitation of Azerbaijani oil fields, in which 41 corporations from 19 countries participated. As a consequence, Azerbaijan became one of the most significant producers in the region, and the BP corporation became the main operator of energy reserves and transmission infrastructure in the country. There was a kind of symbiosis between BP and Azerbaijan, which in the event of economic problems of one of the parties may lead to a serious crisis (Kosowska et al., 2018, pp. 267–274). In 2017, a new agreement was signed in Baku, which is an extension of the "contract of the century." It concerned the development of the ACG fields until 2049. BP (30.37% share), SOCAR (25%), Chevron (9.57%), INPEX (31%), Equinor (7.27%), and ExxonMobil (6.7%) participated in it (Senderov, 2019, pp. 5–11).

Successive international agreements concerning the exploitation of energy deposits reflected the strategic interests of Azerbaijan and their implementation. On September 19, 2013, an international consortium exploiting the Azerbaijani Shah Deniz field signed contracts for the supply of 10 billion m^3 of gas annually from the second phase of the exploitation of this field (Jarosiewicz, 2013, pp. 12–14). Contracts were concluded for 25 years with nine European companies: Axpo, Bulgaraz, DEPA, Enel, EON, Gas Natural Aprovisionamientos, GDF Suez, Hera, and Shell (Jarosiewicz, 2013, pp. 12–14). Not all companies have disclosed the amount of contracted gas. According to a statement by the Azerbaijani state-owned company SOCAR (which plays the most important role in the consortium), 8 billion m^3 of gas is to go to Italy (and hence to Western Europe), 1 billion m^3 to Greece, and 1 billion m^3 to Bulgaria. Deliveries started in 2019. Regional supplies of Azerbaijani gas to Italy will increase their role on the EU gas market and give them a growing importance as a southern gas hub. The choice of Italy indicates that Azerbaijan hopes that, through the already integrated gas market in Europe, its raw material will also go to Western European countries (Jarosiewicz, 2013, pp. 12–14). The significant number of contracts also means that Azerbaijan is trying to diversify its gas recipients.

Over the last 10 years, Azerbaijan's position has strengthened notably, both in relation to individual consortia and to the EU itself. The failure of EU efforts to secure additional gas for the Southern Gas Corridor (Iraqi and Turkmenistan) made Azerbaijan the only reliable supplier to the Corridor. Baku's oil export revenues also increased, accompanied by an increase in assertiveness. In addition, Azerbaijan began to implement its own initiatives, such as transporting gas in the form of LNG to Romania (the AGRI project) and diversifying gas exports to put pressure on Turkey.

The changing geopolitical circumstances have created new challenges for Azerbaijan's policy. For this country, the Southern Gas Corridor is a pillar of economic development and an element of strengthening energy security. It seems that in the face of limited supplies of energy resources from Russia, Azerbaijan should fill this gap.

After gaining independence in 1991, Azerbaijan, as a result of active measures on the energy market, began to systematically increase its income from the export of hydrocarbons. For example, its GDP grew from USD 1.3 billion in 1994 to USD 25 billion in 2008. At the same time, revenues from oil and gas exports accounted for 52% of the country's GDP (Azerbaijan to Turn into Non-oil, 2013).

Most of the oil produced in Azerbaijan is exported. According to SOCAR data, in 2014 only 6.5 of the 41.9 million tonnes were used by the state. It means that year, Azerbaijan exported over 35 million tonnes of oil (Kosowska et al., 2018, pp. 267–274). There is also a noticeable decline in gas production in Azerbaijan. This trend is also reflected in the value of exports. For example, in 2011, the total value of Azerbaijan's exports was USD 26.6 billion, of which oil and gas exports amounted to USD 25.1 billion, which accounted for 94.5% of the total. In 2016, the total value of this country's exports amounted to USD 9.1 billion, of which oil and gas exports amounted to approximately USD 8 billion, which accounted for 87.4% (State Statistical Committee, 2016). Thus, the decline in Azerbaijan's exports amounted to 21.8%. The total value of Azerbaijan's exports in 2011–2016 decreased almost three times, of which oil and gas exports decreased 3.14 times. This situation was largely due to fluctuations in commodity prices on a global scale (Senderov, 2019, pp. 5–11).

A manifestation of the implementation of the energy security policy was the reaction of the Azerbaijani government to the fall in oil prices and the establishment of the SOFAZ Oil Fund by a decree of President H. Aliyev in 1999. Its main goal is both the short- and long-term protection of the state's macroeconomic stability. The priority of this system is to collect financial resources from oil exports so that they can be used in times of economic downturn related to the international energy markets. The fund is also used to finance strategic infrastructure projects, such as BTC, BTE, and the Southern Gas Corridor (Kosowska et al., 2018, pp. 267–274). The system appears to be effective, has a legislative basis, and is managed transparently. It functions as a separate state financial institute. Over USD 34 billion accumulated on the Fund's account is

TABLE 3.3   Export directions for gas from Azerbaijan (billion m³)

Trail	Transmission in 2014	Transmission in 2020	Transmission in 2030	Capacity in billion m3 of gas per year
To Russia	0.2	1	1	5 (operational) 13 (technical)
To Iran	0.4	0.5	0.5	10
To Georgia	1.4	1.4	1.4	8
To Turkey	6.6	6.6	6.6	8
TANAP	–	16	26	16 (2021)
		Share in total exports, 41%	Share in total exports, 73%	32 (2026)
Total	8.6	25.5	35.5	39 (2021) 49 (2026)

SOURCE: JAROSIEWICZ, 2015

not only a safety valve for public finances and the entire economy, but also a platform for modernization in the economic dimension (Kosowska et al., 2018, pp. 267–274).

Since independence in 1991, Azerbaijan has not transformed into a free market economy, despite huge profits from the sale of crude oil. The process of democratization progressed slowly due to the government's oppressive rule, nepotism and corruption in the echelons of power (Ipek, 2009, pp. 228–239). Azerbaijan's energy security policy is conditioned by many problems in the energy sector, such as:
– the geological structure of newly discovered and exploited fields;
– gaps in know-how;
– the need to attract foreign capital and investments necessary for the exploitation of energy; and
– the issue of effective methods of supplying the world market with Azeri oil (Kosowska et al., 2018, pp. 267–274).

Azerbaijan's success in terms of hydrocarbons has turned out to be a threat since the country became dependent on oil and gas exports (Asian Development Bank, 2014). Currently, the share of the energy sector in Azerbaijan's GDP is over 60% (Asian Development Bank, 2014). This one-dimensionality is a threat to the country's economic stability. The development model carries a high risk of the so-called "Dutch disease," that is, susceptibility to negative external phenomena. As a result, the dominant energy sector determines the development of the state, which reduces the competitiveness and importance of other industries in the economy. The reduction in the price of energy commodities then causes a drastic decline in the state's income, and can even lead to a serious crisis. Thus, the energy sector is the basis of the state's development and its main source of income.

There are also negative consequences to Azerbaijan's dependence on the export of energy resources which are related to the sensitivity to hydrocarbon prices on the world market (Asian Development Bank, 2014). At the same time, the decline in domestic oil production may reduce Azerbaijan to the role of a transit state. The reduction in the production of hydrocarbons was an alarm signal, indicating the need to generate profits from other sectors of the economy, not only energy (Terterov, 2018, pp. 213–230).

Azerbaijan shows the features of a rentier state, in line with the theory of H. Beblawi (1990, p. 23; Auty, 1993). First, it is a country rich in energy resources. Second, revenues from commodity exports account for a significant proportion of GDP and total exports. Third, the state maintains a strong position in the process of generating and distributing revenues from the oil and gas trade through the state oil company, SOCAR (Almaz, 2015, pp. 60–72; Schwab, 2014 p. 23; Auty, 2004, p. 109; Ross, 2012, p. 335).

Azerbaijan is playing an increasingly important role in international relations. The country's importance increased as a result of its activity in the energy market. The perception of Azerbaijan in the region as a significant investor and supplier of energy has also changed. Azerbaijan is an expansive country in the economic dimension, it is also exerting an increasing influence on the situation in the whole of Eurasia. Failure to take this fact into account by Western states would be a mistake that can cause not only measurable economic costs, but also political ones, as well as those related to regional security (Blank, 2014). Thus, more and more actors are interested in the situation in Azerbaijan.

For Azerbaijan nowadays, the issue of security is a priority goal. In this context, the case of Ukraine assumes special significance. The problem is that Western countries have so far treated Azerbaijan as a country belonging to Russia's sphere of influence. However, in the context of Russia's full-scale war in Ukraine, the geopolitical situation in Eurasia is likely to evolve.

1.2 Republic of Kazakhstan

The energy security policy of Kazakhstan is conditional on its energy potential and its geoeconomical position. Kazakhstan pursues its interests in this respect through cooperation with states and international corporations to exploit and transport hydrocarbons (International Energy Agency, 2023b). Kazakhstan's activities have been involved in the geostrategic development of pipelines, and are also a result of the geostrategic play between powers in the Caspian region.

Kazakhstan is one of the largest producers and energy redistribution centers in Central Asia, which determines the country's energy security policy. It has significant reserves of oil and gas and raw materials such as uranium, chromium, zinc, and magnesium. It is a global leader in coal, iron, and gold. Oil and gas, on the other hand, constitute the national economy of that state (Assanbayev, 2016, pp. 127–137). According to the International Energy Agency, the country is the largest oil producer in Central Asia, with the 12th-highest proven crude oil reserves in the world (International Energy Agency, 2023).

In the light of various studies and reports by the World Bank, the IMF and the Asian Development Bank, Kazakhstan is an economic leader in the Caspian region and throughout Central Asia, generating 60% of regional GDP, mainly due to its energy potential in terms of oil, gas, carbon, and uranium (Khan, 2020, pp. 22–36). According the World Bank in Kazakhstan (2023), Kazakhstan recorded a 3.2% GDP growth in 2022. Growth was driven by non-oil exports to neighboring countries and investment growth of 7.9%, primarily in resource sectors, while consumer demand weakened as real incomes shrank under the weight of high inflation. In 2014, according to the IEA, Kazakhstan exported about 1.69 mb/d of oil. Revenues from the oil trade constitute the largest share in the country's budget, amounting to approximately 60% and to 33% of the GDP (Assanbayev, 2016, pp. 127–137). It is estimated that oil production in Kazakhstan will increase, which will result in significant budget revenues.

Kazakhstan has a comprehensive energy security strategy that reflects market dynamics, is forward-looking, and takes into account regional interdependencies (Mantel, 2016, pp. 139–143). In its policy, the country emphasizes the diversification of supply and demand for energy and attaches importance to security issues, climate policy, and efficiency in this dimension. Figures 3.2 and 3.3 illustrate the main pillars and objectives of Kazakhstan's energy policy strategy.

Energy potential is the basis for defining Kazakhstan's main interests, goals, and activities not only regionally, but also globally. Kazakhstan clearly attaches great importance to the issue of foreign investments, the functioning of energy corporations, and the stability and security of energy prices. The State Commission on Energy Resources indicates that Kazakhstan is among the top 10 countries in terms of hydrocarbon resources and among the top 15 in terms of potential resources (Tables 3.4–3.7) (Khan, 2020, pp. 22–36).

Oil was first exploited in Kazakhstan in 1911, in an area near Guriev (Atyrau), in the Emba fields, in Dossor and Matat. US Shell was the first to obtain licenses

Dialogue between energy consuming and producing countries	Cooperation with corporations from different countries of the world	Reduction of oil market volatility	Diversification of energy transport routes	Improving the investment climate

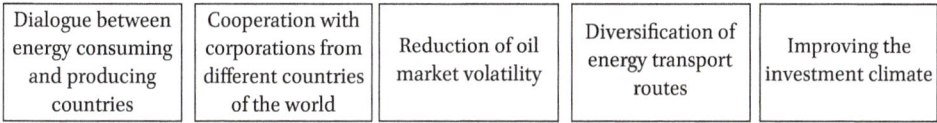

FIGURE 3.2   Pillars of the energy policy strategy of Kazakhstan
SOURCE: AUTHOR'S OWN WORK BASED ON KHAN, 2020

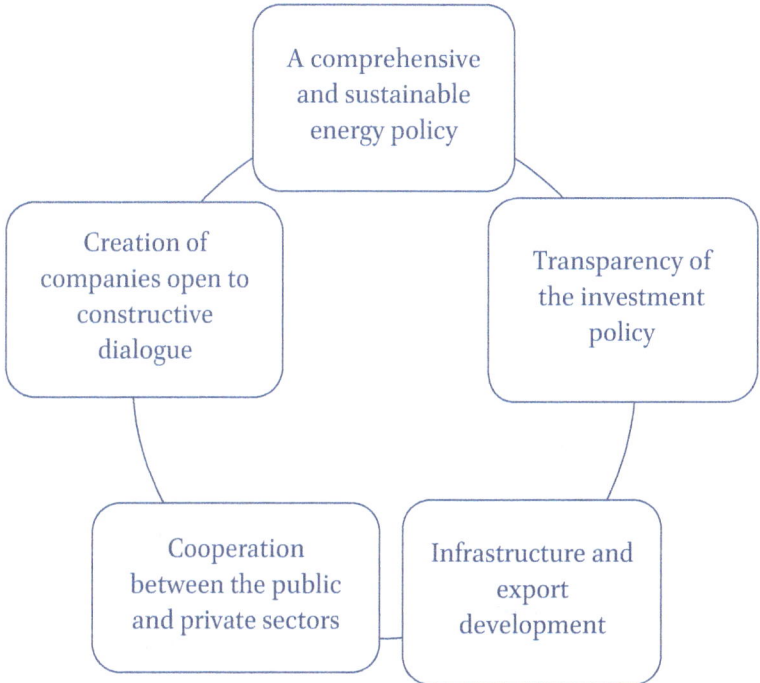

FIGURE 3.3   Energy policy objectives of Kazakhstan
SOURCE: AUTHOR'S OWN WORK BASED ON KHAN, 2020

TABLE 3.4   Kazakhstan oil reserves (billion barrels)

2002	2003	2004	2008	2010	2011	2012	2013	2016	2020
2.7	2.7	26	30	30	30	30	30	30	30

SOURCE: HTTPS://WWW.INDEXMUNDI.COM/G/G.ASPX?V=97&C=KZ&L=EN (12.06.2022)

TABLE 3.5   Kazakhstan gas reserves (billion m³)

2002	2003	2004	2008	2010	2011	2012	2013	2016	2020
920	920	3	2.8	2.4	2.4	2.4	2.4	2.4	2.4

SOURCE: HTTPS://WWW.INDEXMUNDI.COM/G/G.ASPX?V=98&C=KZ&L=EN

TABLE 3.6   Oil production in Kazakhstan (bbl/day)

2001	2004	2005	2007	2009	2011	2012	2016	2018	2020
798.2	1.2	1.3	1.4	1.5	1.6	1.6	1.6	1.7	1.8

SOURCE: HTTPS://WWW.INDEXMUNDI.COM/G/G.ASPX?V=88&C=KZ&L=EN

TABLE 3.7   Natural gas production in Kazakhstan (billion m³)

2001	2004	2007	2009	2011	2013	2016	2018	2020
10	20.4	27.8	35.6	20.2	20.4	21.3	22.4	22.4

SOURCE: HTTPS://WWW.INDEXMUNDI.COM/G/G.ASPX?V=136&C=KZ&L=EN

for oil exploitation in this region (Bun, 1999, pp. 86–87). The company became the operator of the Ural Caspian Oil Corporation. After 1943, the amount of oil produced reached 979.000 tonnes (Zhiltsov et al., 2016, pp. 23–25).

During that period, construction of the Guriev refinery began. After World War II, oil fields were opened on the Mangyshlak Peninsula and south of the Emba area, where oil production reached 1.6 million tonnes. In 1954, the Uzen field was discovered, with reserves of 140 million tonnes and estimated reserves of 680 million tonnes (Kolchin, 1998, pp. 97–103).

Kazakhstan faces many obstacles in the security and production of oil and gas (Table 3.8). Development is limited due to high exploitation costs, the lengthy source discovery process, and technological difficulties (Zhiltsov et al., 2016).

The Caspian shelf is an important area of hydrocarbon exploitation by Kazakhstan. The Caspian shelf is an important area of hydrocarbon exploitation by Kazakhstan, and measures 100.000 km². In the mid-1990s, only 7% of its land was exploited. Kazakhstan's reserves are estimated at 8 billion tonnes,

TABLE 3.8   Challenges of energy security policy in Kazakhstan

Difficulties	Statement of reasons
Exploitation of the Caspian Basin	Restrictions resulting from disagreements over access to resource deposits by individual coastal states
High costs	Costs associated with long-distance transport of resources
Foreign intervention and control	Most of the pipelines pass through Russian territory and is controlled by Transneft. It discriminates against non-Russian oil by intervening in the price market
Geographical conditions	Kazakhstan's resources are located in the northern part of the Caspian Basin, remote from other parts of the state. The transport of resources is therefore limited due to the poor of development infrastructure and tough weather conditions

SOURCE: AUTHOR'S OWN WORK BASED ON KHAN, 2020

or even 15 billion tonnes for all hydrocarbons (Mantel, 2016, pp. 139–143). About 70% of the oil is found in the western part of the country, especially in the Caspian Basin.

In total, 90% of the oil reserves are concentrated in 15 large deposits in the west of the country and in the Caspian Basin: Tengiz, Kashagan, Karachaganak, Uzen, Zhetybai, Zhanazhol, Kalamkas, Kenkiyak, Karazhanbas, Kumkol, North Buzachi, Alibekmola, Prorva, Kenbai, and Roya. About 80% gas reserves are located in four fields: Kashagan, Tengiz, Karachagak, and Imashevskoe (Khan, 2020, pp. 22–36).

As part of the implementation of the energy security policy, Kazakhstan is trying to encourage potential partners to cooperate in joint energy projects (Table 3.9). A key element of the country's energy policy is the expansion of the Tengiz and Karachaganak oil fields and the Kashagan field in the Caspian Basin. While Tengiz and Karachaganak are currently tapped, Kashagan is a difficult and expensive to exploit. The total cost of exploitation of this field is estimated at USD 136–187 billion (Butyrina, 2013, pp. 20–24). Investments will increase in proportion to the technological difficulties in extraction of the resources.

In this context, a growing body of analysis on the development of the Kashagan project appear. The field was discovered in 2000 in the Kazakhstan

TABLE 3.9   Major foreign business involved in the Kazakhstan energy sector

Enterprise	Explored field
British Gas	Karachaganak
CNPC	Aktobe
CNPC, KMG,	Mangistau, North Buzachi
Eni Agip, Chevron, Lukoil	Kashagan, Karachaganak
Maersk Oil	Dunga
Petrom	Tasbulat, Aktas
Repsol YPF	South Zhambai
Royal Dutch Shell	Kashagan
Tengiz Chevroil, Exxon Mobil, KMG, LukArco	Tengiz
Total E & P Kazachstan	Kashagan
Turgai, Lukoil, Petro Kazachstan	Kumkol

SOURCE: AUTHOR'S OWN WORK BASED ON KHAN, 2020; MANTEL, 2016

zone of the Caspian Basin. Its geological resources are estimated at 4.8 billion tonnes. Oil reserves are 38 billion barrels, of which 10 billion barrels are produced. Also, gas reserves are found there, estimated at 1 trillion m³. The Kashagan Field is located 4.200 meters below the water surface, in the northern part of the Caspian Basin. The oil extracted there contains the so-called acid gas (Assanbayev, 2016, pp. 127–137). The low salinity level associated with the inflow of waters from the Volga River, low water levels and winter temperatures down to -30°C cause the northern part of the Caspian Basin to freeze for more than five months of the year. All these factors make the exploitation of energy resources difficult (Assanbayev, 2016, pp. 127–137).

The Field Development Project Kashagan was initiated by the Offshore Kazakhstan International Operating Company (OK-IOC) consortium. This consortium was later named Agip KCO (Kazakhstan Operating Company), and then North Caspian Operating Company (NCOC). It consists of Western companies, such as Eni, Exxon-Mobil, Dutch Royal, Dutch Shell PLC, Total, and Inpex (Kretov, 2013, pp. 18–23).

Since 2013, the Chinese company CNPC has been involved in the project, replacing Conoco Phillips. The consortium's plans show that oil production in this region was to reach 180.000 barrels per day, reaching 370.000 barrels per day in further stages of development. According to the plan made in 2000 by Nurlan Balgimbayev, the then director of the state-owned company

Kazakh Oil (the predecessor of KazMunaiGaz), commercial production of oil from the Kashagan field was to begin in 2005. That same year, Italian Eni became the international operator in the North Caspian Operating Company (Assanbayev, 2016, pp. 127–137). It was then estimated that in the first stage of expansion (2013–2017), production would reach 50 million tonnes per year, and 75 million tonnes in the second stage (2018–2019). The implementation of these plans would place Kazakhstan among the world's top five oil exporters. However, technical problems delayed the start of exploitation of that field until September 2013. Two weeks after the deposit was put into service, mining operations had to be stopped. This was caused by, among other things, the toxic hydrogen sulphide, which caused the pipes to rust. Production was also suspended due to a gas leak from the pipeline running from the borehole towards Bolashak and the Eskene complex (Assanbayev, 2016, pp. 127–137).

Kazakhstan must therefore take into account various problems related to the exploitation of resources and the operation of pipelines in the Caspian area (Parkhomchik, 2016, pp. 139–152). Despite the optimistic prospects for the development of the oil field, the limitations resulting from the difficulties of operating in this region due to climatic and technological constraints should be factored in. The average water depth in the Kashagan area is only 3–4 meters. The sea is covered with ice for three to four months, from November to March (Assanbayev, 2016, pp. 127–137). Tokamys Mendebayev, an analyst and expert on mining technologies in Kazakhstan, stated that oil production in such harsh conditions could even lead to an earthquake.

Kazakhstan does not have direct access to the sea (the Caspian reservoir is closed), and there is also a large transit distance between this country and other oil producers and exporters. Due to the geographic location, energy exports are therefore dependent on pipelines. This requires large investments and long-term planning because after Kazakhstan gained independence, all export pipelines ran through the Russian territory.

Diversification of export routes is the main goal of Kazakhstan's energy security policy. In the 2000s, in pursuit of this goal, the pipeline to China was built, energy cooperation with Iran was established, and exports via tankers through Azerbaijan began. However, the majority of Kazakh oil is still exported via Russia. Due to geographic and infrastructural barriers, the regions producing energy in the western part of the country are not connected with consumers and industry in its eastern part. Kazakhstan is also a significant transit territory for gas from Turkmenistan and Uzbekistan to Russia and China.

Due to their growing energy demands, both Europe and China are particularly interested in cooperation with Kazakhstan. Kazakhstan is therefore seeking to build a pipeline infrastructure directly to Europe, eastern markets, and China, bypassing Russian territory (Assanbayev, 2016, pp. 127–137). Kazakhstan's energy independence is guaranteed only if it is able to maintain the oil supply system for consumers through Russia or without its participation. In terms of the geopolitics of the transport of energy, Kazakhstan focuses on securing supplies for Europe, Turkey, and China, and on cooperation with transit states (Table 3.10). Kazakhstan experienced significant economic growth in the 2000s, becoming the strongest economy in Central Asia. The main driving force behind this growth was foreign investment in the oil and gas sectors (Tables 3.10 and 3.11). Energy is a major factor in the economic development of Kazakhstan. The country can therefore be defined as a rentier state, based on Beblawi's theory, discussed in the previous part of the study (Beblawi, 1990, p. 34). In 2014, due to its dependence on oil exports, Kazakhstan experienced a financial crisis following the fall in oil prices (Table 3.10). This led to a reduction in export volumes and a currency devaluation of 82% in 2015.

Given that energy is a key issue for Kazakhstan's interests and activities in the Caspian region towards external actors and for its economic position, it is necessary to identify the types of energy consumed in this state (Figure 3.4). The publication *Fuel Energy Balance of Kazakhstan*, issued annually by the Committee of Statistics of the Republic of Kazakhstan (CSRK), is one of the main sources of information on the production, consumption, and transformation of

TABLE 3.10   Kazakhstan oil exports (billion barrels per day)

2003	2005	2009	2010	2011	2016	2018	2020
890.000	1.236.000	1.078.000	1.406.000	1.390.000	1.292.000	1.409.000	1.409.000

SOURCE: HTTPS://WWW.INDEXMUNDI.COM/G/G.ASPX?V=95&C=KZ&L=EN

TABLE 3.11   Kazakhstan gas reserves (billion m³)

2001	2003	2004	2007	2008	2011	2013	2016	2020
4.1	11	7	8.1	17.6	9.7	11.2	13.7	12.8

SOURCE: HTTPS://WWW.INDEXMUNDI.COM/G/G.ASPX?V=95&C=KZ&L=EN

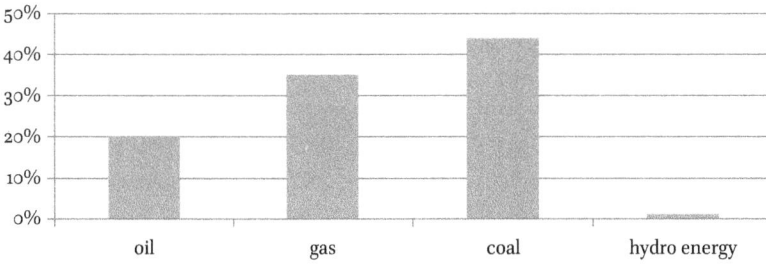

FIGURE 3.4   Energy mix in Kazakhstan
SOURCE: AUTHOR'S OWN STUDY BASED ONKHAN, 2020

this state in various economic sectors (Committee of Statistics of the Republic of Kazakhstan, 2016; Kerimray et al., 2018, pp. 315–335). The dominant resource in Total Primary Energy Supply (TPES; the sum of production and imports after deducting exports and in-storage changes) is coal, although its share fell from 63% in 2000 to 49% in 2014. This resource is mainly used in power plants and heating.

Crude oil is used in the transport sector, while gas is mainly used in the household sector. The share of gas increased from 17% in 2000 to 25% in 2014. This was, among other things, a consequence of the expansion of gas transport systems located along the main gas pipeline in the western and southern parts of Kazakhstan. The share of crude oil also dropped from 29% in 2000 to 32% in 2014, driven by demand in the transport industry (Kerimray et al., 2018, pp. 315–335).

In this context, the importance of renewable sources is growing. Kazakhstan has plans to develop this industry within its energy policy. In its strategy, it assumes that in 2050, 50% of its consumption will be met by the exploitation of renewable resources. The hydropower potential of Kazakhstan is approximately 62 billion kW (Kuchukova et al., 2016, pp. 244–255). Production comes from 15 large power plants, with a total capacity of 2.248 GW (Kerimray et al., 2018, pp. 315–335).

Trends in energy consumption in Kazakhstan are determined by the economic development of the state (Kerimray et al., 2018, pp. 315–335). Economic growth in Kazakhstan increased the demand for energy.

1.3   *Turkmenistan*
Similarly to other states in the Caspian region, Turkmenistan bases its energy security policy on its resource wealth and geopolitical position (Jarosiewicz & Lang, 2015). Its interests are pursued through cooperation with importers of

gas. At the same time, the main challenge and threat to Turkmenistan's energy security policy is the economic crisis, largely caused by the sharp fall in gas prices and an ineffective strategy for diversification of gas exports (Karatayev et al., 2016, pp. 120–136). Turkmenistan's energy security policy depends on its energy resources, which include around 19.5 trillion m³ of gas (Kerimray et al., 2018, pp. 315–335; Jakubik, 2017). According to the World Bank, Turkmenistan's gas reserves are estimated to be the world's fourth largest, representing about 10% of global reserves (World Bank in Turkmenistan, 2023) (Table 3.12).

In addition to cotton and natural gas, the country is rich in petroleum, sulfur, iodine, salt, bentonite clays, limestone, gypsum, and cement—all potential inputs to chemical and construction industries (World Bank in Turkmenistan, 2023). However, according to the declarations of Myrat Archajew, president of the state-owned company Turkmengas, Turkmenistan's total gas reserves are estimated at 50 trillion m³ (Kerimray et al., 2018, pp. 315–335). "Turkmenistan, by ensuring a stable and uninterrupted supply of environmentally friendly hydrocarbons, seeks to contribute to the sustainable development of humanity, while promoting energy efficiency and reducing the negative effects on the environment," declared Archajew (Kerimray et al., 2018, p. 315). Thanks to the favorable geopolitical position and rich hydrocarbon resources, Turkmenistan has great potential to increase gas exports. However, the fact that this country is located on the "wrong side" of the Caspian Basin limits its export possibilities to European markets, especially in the absence of pipeline infrastructure (Gotev, 2018). Despite having significant oil and gas reserves, the country had no access to global markets. Turkmenistan became a key gas producer in the region, while its oil reserves were poorly exploited.

Turkmenistan began producing oil in the southeast part of the Caspian Sea at the beginning of the 20th century, where the Nobel brothers had been drilling since 1887. In 1908, the first oil flowed from a depth of 140 meters at a rate of 24.5 tonnes per day (Zonn & Zhiltsov, 2008, p. 348). This region was called "Black California" because oil deposits appeared close to the surface of the earth.

Between 1911 and 1912, on the Cheleken Peninsula, south of Turkmenbashi (Krasnovodsk), 208.000 tonnes of oil was produced. In the Soviet period from

TABLE 3.12   Turkmenistan gas reserves (billion m³)

2002	2003	2005	2008	2010	2011	2013	2014	2016	2018	2020
2	1.4	2	2.8	7.5	7.5	17.5	17.5	7.5	7.5	7.5

SOURCE: HTTPS://WWW.INDEXMUNDI.COM/G/G.ASPX?V=138&C=TX&L=EN

1949, oil production began in two onshore oil fields: Nebit-Dag and Gum-Dag. In the first one, the maximum oil production (1.25 million tonnes) was achieved in 1949. Once the pressure was reduced, however, production began to decline. The same situation occurred for the Gum-Dag field, where the maximum production was achieved in 1955 (1.8 million tonnes), and then fell systematically (Leizerovich, 1968, p. 157).

Turkmenistan's oil belt stretches from west to east over an area of 200 km. It runs through the land area and partly through the Caspian Sea along the Apsheronian Peninsula. Turkmenistan's sector of the Caspian Sea consists of two geological blocks: the Depression shelf of the South Caspian Sea and the Central Caspian Sea with a total area of 70.000 km^2. The South Caspian Depression area covers an area of 40.000 km^2 and extends to the southern edge of the South Caspian Sea (Kerimray et al., 2018, pp. 315–335). According to data from Turkmen geologists, oil reserves in this region may amount to 2 billion tonnes. Research found that oil and gas deposits are at the middle Pliocene level. The boreholes therefore need to reach depths of 5 to 6 km. The mining area covers 25.500 km^2. The Central Caspian Sea block extends over an area of 30.000^2. Sources in Turkmenistan declare that a billion tonnes of oil are located there but the region has not been thoroughly researched. Total oil reserves were estimated at 3 billion tonnes, and were even projected at 6.6 billion tonnes (Batyrov, 1994, pp. 102–106) (Tables 3.13 and 3.14).

The largest area of oil production is the Caspian coast (the regions of Balkanabat and Cheleken, and the cities of Okarem and Goturdepe). However, oil and gas structures are found virtually throughout Turkmenistan. The US

TABLE 3.13   Turkmenistan oil reserves (million barrels)

2002	2003	2005	2008	2010	2011	2016	2018	2020
273	273	546	600	600	600	600	600	600

SOURCE: HTTPS://WWW.INDEXMUNDI.COM/G/G.ASPX?V=138&C=TX&L=EN

TABLE 3.14   Oil production in Turkmenistan (bbl/day)

2001	2003	2004	2007	2009	2010	2011	2012	2015	2018	2020
162.5	203.4	213.7	180.4	197.7	216.0	222.2	244.1	243.1	244.	244.

SOURCE: HTTPS://WWW.INDEXMUNDI.COM/G/G.ASPX?V=138&C=TX&L=EN

Western Geophysical Company estimated that the oil reserves in the Caspian shelf of Turkmenistan amount to 11.5–16.5 billion tonnes (Zhiltsov et al., 2016). In 2008, the government of Turkmenistan released new data on oil reserves, indicating a potential of 21 billion tonnes. The government declared that thousands of prospective oil structures were identified, both onshore and offshore, and about 150 fields were discovered, 50 of which are in operation. Then, in 2013, Turkmenistan reported the availability of 12 billion barrels of oil in the Caspian shelf (Zhiltsov et al., 2016).

Gas resources were discovered in the coastal zone of Turkmenistan and cover an area of 2–4.5 km². No deep boreholes have been drilled here, but seismological research has identified 23 gas-bearing structures (Kerimray et al., 2018). The largest gas fields are located in the southern and eastern parts of the state: Dovletabad–Donmez and Yashler, and near the cities of Gazodzhak, Darvaz, Zhatlyk, and Bayramali (Zhiltsov et al., 2016).

In 2007, the company, Turkmengeologia, announced the opening of 150 gas fields, representing reserves of 6.1 trillion (tln) m³. The onshore areas were estimated at 5.7 tln m³, and offshore resources at 400 billion m³ (Zhiltsov et al., 2016). In 2009, new data was released showing that the Galkynysh field with gas condensate had over 26.2 tonnes m³, which ranked it second only to the South Pars fields in the Persian Gulf. The Galkynysh field was put into service in 2013. Three refineries were built here and gas extraction works were carried out by Korea's concern Hyundai Engineering Co. Ltd. and China's CNPC Drilling Engineering Co. Ltd. Extraction capacity was at 30 billion m3 per year (Zhiltsov et al., 2016). In 2013, Turkmenistan declared that 25 tonnes m3 of gas could be extracted and 6 tonnes m³ in the offshore area. According to the Turkmenistan oil industry development program, gas production in this country is to reach 230 billion m³ annually by 2030, and 110 million tonnes of oil (Zhiltsov et al., 2016).

The key determinant of Turkmenistan's energy security policy is its geoenergy position. After the collapse of the USSR, Turkmenistan was able to transport its resources only through Russian territory. It was due to the geographic location of the state and the pipeline infrastructure that was a legacy of the Soviet system (Zhiltsov et al., 2016). This way, Turkmenistan became completely dependent on Russia's transport infrastructure. The need to change the situation proved to be a strategic priority. Therefore, the state became active in efforts to create new pipeline infrastructure projects to enable an independent export policy. Additional motivation for such activities was the discovery of new deposits of oil and gas, both onshore and offshore (Zhiltsov et al., 2016). Turkmenistan needed foreign investment to exploit these fields, and new pipeline systems would enable them to be exported, generating significant fiscal gains. The choice of export routes depended on investment opportunities, security, the level of competition between hydrocarbon producers, geostrategic interests of states in the region, and external actors. As a rule, it is the result of a compromise between various interests, not only in the economic but also in the geopolitical, military, and strategic dimensions.

Production and export of hydrocarbons, especially gas (Tables 3.15 and 3.16), is of particular importance in the implementation of Turkmenistan's energy security policy. Its activities in the energy market depend on gas reserves. The country has relied on gas exports since the 1990s. In 2005, based on EU data, energy resources accounted for 60–80% of its total exports. In 2014, the energy sector generated 35% of Turkmenistan's GDP, 90% of total exports, and 80% of fiscal profits (World Bank, 2015).

According to the estimates of the American geophysical company Western Geo, the reserves in the Turkmen sector of the Caspian Sea are about 11 billion tonnes of oil and 5.5 trillion tonnes of gas. Turkmenistan therefore focused mainly on the exploitation of the Caspian shelf resources. However, no conclusive data on the actual hydrocarbons reserves in Turkmenistan is available. Most estimates are based on data provided by the Turkmen government. They are usually inflated to boost Turkmenistan's importance in the region (Zhiltsov et al., 2016). The country has focused on the exploitation of its oil and gas fields. Consequently, the government prepared a long-term program for the development of the energy sector, assuming that gas production would amount to 230 billion m³ annually by 2020 (Zhiltsov et al., 2016). The strategy of the development of the country's mining complex contributed to its increased hydrocarbon mining.

TABLE 3.15   Gas production in Turkmenistan (billions m³)

2001	2004	2007	2009	2010	2011	2012	2013	2014	2018	2020
48.2	58.57	68.88	34.0	42.4	59.5	64.4	84.8	76.0	77.45	77.45

SOURCE: HTTPS://WWW.INDEXMUNDI.COM/G/G.ASPX?V=138&C=TX&L=EN

TABLE 3.16   Turkmenistan gas exports (billions m³)

2001	2004	2007	2009	2011	2012	2013	2014	2018	2020
38.6	42.0	49.4	18.0	34.5	41.1	60.8	45.79	38.14	38.14

SOURCE: HTTPS://WWW.INDEXMUNDI.COM/G/G.ASPX?V=138&C=TX&L=EN

Simultaneously, Turkmenistan maintained its willingness to open up to the European market, bypassing Russian territory (Zhiltsov et al., 2016).

Turkmenistan's energy policy is a function of the country's gas contracts with foreign partners. Until 2008, Russia was the main recipient of gas from Turkmenistan (over 80% of that state's exports) (Anceschi, 2017, pp. 409–429). Since 2015, Russia has significantly reduced its imports of Turkmen gas, resulting in excessive dependence on China. In 2015, Iran became the second importer of gas from Turkmenistan, and China bought no less than 73% of Turkmen gas.

In January 2016, Gazprom officially declared it would stop buying gas from Türkmengaz. The decision deprived Turkmenistan of one of the main routes for gas exports in the post-Soviet era (Anceschi, 2017, pp. 409–429). The sudden and unexpected closure of gas exports to Russia put considerable economic pressure on the Berdymuhamedov regime. Since Turkmenistan had problems with gas exports via Russia, it became isolated from foreign market. It therefore began efforts to attract foreign investors in the energy sector.

Over the last decade, the directions of Turkmenistan's gas exports have reversed, and starting in 2011, China replaced Russia as the main recipient of Turkeminstan's gas (Fredholm, 2011, p. 8). This has been facilitated by China's investments in transmission infrastructure (construction of a gas pipeline to China), loans (approximately USD 10 billion), and access to Turkmen fields by CNPC (China National Petroleum Corporation) (Jarosiewicz & Lang, 2015). Turkmenistan exported about 30 billion m³ of gas do China, 11 billion m³ to Russia, and about 7 billion m³ of gas to Iran (Jarosiewicz & Lang, 2015). Fears of Russia and reluctance to increase dependence on China are currently the main drivers of changes in Turkmenistan's foreign policy (Jarosiewicz & Lang, 2015).

With increased demand for energy resources, China has long tried to strengthen cooperation with the Caspian states to build a pipeline infrastructure (Xuetang, 2006). Turkmenistan was a very attractive partner in this context. On April 3, 2006, China and Turkmenistan signed an agreement to build a gas pipeline and long-term gas supply. Within a short period of time, the dependence of Turkmenistan's economy on China grew very dynamically. In 2013, as much as 60% of Turkmenistan's gas was sold to the PRC (Anceschi, 2017, pp. 409–429). However, this did not translate into a marked rise in the income from the exports of this resource.

Turkmenistan's energy security is thus threatened by a fluctuation in gas prices and dependence on China as the main recipient of Turkmen gas. The export of energy resources accounts for about 70% of the country's revenue. In such a situation, Turkmenistan had to focus on the strategy of diversifying gas import routes. It required cooperation with alternative gas importers. Despite the fact that Iran has significant gas resources, imports from Turkmenistan complement the gas supply in the northeastern part of the country, which is poorly connected to the internal gas infrastructure. In January 2018, Turkmenistan stopped gas supplies to Iran due to a price conflict (Turkmenistan, 2018).

In this context, the gas pipeline to India seems promising, not only in terms of economy but also geographic issues. It could provide a solution to the revenue crisis (Anceschi, 2017, pp. 409–429). However, the approach of the Turkmen elites to this project is unclear (Anceschi, 2017, pp. 409–429; Menga, 2015, pp. 479–494).

The European Union is another important actor interested in close cooperation with Turkmenistan for gas supplies. The EU sees Turkmenistan's resources as an opportunity to diversify its gas supply sources. After Azerbaijan, Turkmenistan may be the second supplier of gas to the EU-promoted Southern Gas Corridor (Anceschi, 2017, pp. 409–429). The EU's efforts were welcomed by Turkmenistan President Berdimuhamedov after Gazprom unilaterally announced a threefold reduction in gas imports from Turkmenistan in 2015 (Anceschi, 2017, pp. 409–429). Turkmenistan saw this as a breach of the existing agreements and declared its intention to supply between 10 to 30 billion m^3 of gas annually to the EU (Anceschi, 2017, pp. 409–429). Turkmenistan's turn towards the European gas market is caused by disappointment with the profits from gas contracts with China and the uncertainty about cooperation with Russia in this sector. The construction of the Trans-Caspian Gas Pipeline would strengthen Turkmenistan's position on the European market (Misiągiewicz, 2014b).

Turkmenistan's economic situation is largely dependent on China, which is virtually the exclusive recipient of Turkmen gas and, at the same time, its main creditor. The contractual terms between these states (for example, linking gas prices to oil prices, according to J. Jakóbowski and M. Marszewski, "leads to the drain of Turkmen resources with a markedly reduced inflow of foreign currency" (Jakóbowski & Marszewski, 2018, pp. 13). As Turkmenistan's main creditor, China has an interest in the economic stabilization of Turkmenistan, so as to engage in "rescue operations" (Jakóbowski & Marszewski, 2018, p. 13). At the same time, Russia may use the crisis to rebuild its influence in Turkmenistan, offering military assistance in the possible stabilization of the regime, as well as in the resumption of gas cooperation. In the current difficult economic conditions, global increase in resource prices would be the most favorable scenario for Turkmenistan's government.

1.4   *Russian Federation*

Russia's energy security policy is part of its broader strategy towards Europe and the post-Soviet area (Balmaceda & Heinrich, 2021, p. 465; Misiągiewicz, 2016). Russia was increasingly tightening its economic cooperation with European countries (Fredholm, 2011, p. 3). It developed on a large scale and was based primarily on the export of Russian natural gas using the pipeline infrastructure (Gawlikowska-Fyk & Terlikowski, 2018, p. 12). At the same time, following the Polish Institute of International Affairs (PISM) analysts and the authors of the report "Energy and defense in the Nordic-Baltic region," some states mistakenly believed that, "This cooperation will lead to the reduction of threats from Russia by gradually building good economic relations and trust" (Gawlikowska-Fyk & Terlikowski, 2018, p. 12).

In 1990, Russian gas exports to Europe already reached 110 billion m^3, twice as much as just a decade earlier (Gawlikowska-Fyk & Terlikowski, 2018, p. 14). After the end of the Cold War, energy cooperation continued, accompanied by the expectation in the West that Russia would gradually liberalize its economic and political system (Gawlikowska-Fyk & Terlikowski, 2018, p. 14). Thus, after the collapse of the USSR, economic relations between Russia and Western and Eastern European states were formed and developed. The first challenge for Russia resulting from the fall of the USSR was the prospect of losing control over strategic transmission or storage infrastructure to the newly created post-Soviet states. At the same time, Russia had to rely on transit states (Gawlikowska-Fyk & Terlikowski, 2018, p. 12).

More than 20 years after the collapse of the USSR, Russia is the major actor in the Caspian region (Nanay & Stegen, 2012, pp. 343–357). According to B. Buzan's and O. Wæver's theory quoted in T. German, this region can be interpreted as a "sub-complex" of the regional security complex covering the territory of the former USSR and was within the reach of Russian hegemony (German, 2018, p. 181). After the USSR collapsed, researchers argued whether Russia would withdraw from the post-Soviet area and gradually limit its influence there, or whether it would strengthen its presence there and pursue its interests. P. Baev argued that, "Russia's gradual retreat from the Caucasus region seemed irreversible" (Baev, 1997, p. 59). Similarly, J. Nixey, in his article "The Long Goodbye," sees the declining influence of Russia in the post-Soviet area as being due to limited ambitions and possibilities (Nixey, 2012, p. 2). S. Blank, in turn, argued that Russia's military presence in the Caspian region would steadily increase after the war in Georgia (Blank, 2013). Also, R. Suny did not believe that Russia would withdraw from this area, as it "seeks to be a regional hegemon" (Suny, 2007, p. 68).

Russia's interests in the region are shaped by security, economic, and ideological considerations (Balmaceda & Heinrich, 2019). Security issues are related to competition with the West, especially with NATO, and the stability of this area (Duncan, 2018, pp. 235–252). The region is exposed to separatism and terrorism, which triggers concern for Russian decision-makers. As a relic of the Cold War, NATO is a structure that Russia could cooperate with but only if NATO is not involved in the post-Soviet region (Duncan, 2018, pp. 235–252).

The Ottoman Empire and Persia are Russia's eternal competitors in the Caspian region. After the collapse of the USSR, Russia feared that Turkey and Iran would offer an alternative development model in the Caspian region, based on the Muslim identity of the newly established states. However, Russia's influence has not been eliminated in this context. Concerns about the ideology of pan-Turkism were only valid in the case of Azerbaijan. Nevertheless, after the Azerbaijan Popular Front fell and Heidar Aliyev took power in 1993, the concerns were dispelled. In addition, relations between Russia and Turkey steadily improved thanks to growing trade and the implementation of the Blue Stream gas pipeline (Duncan, 2018, pp. 235–252).

Despite the contradictions regarding the division of the Caspian Basin and the exploitation of the natural resources located there, Russia and Iran established economic cooperation. Russia helps Iran develop their nuclear energy industry and sells it weapons. At the same time, Iran is not considered to be competing with Russia in the Caspian region.

Russia's economic interests in the Caspian region are mainly related to transporting energy resources to foreign markets (Balmaceda & Heinrich, 2019). Russia seeks to eliminate export routes that bypass its territory. In this context, the main problem is Azerbaijan, which cooperates directly with European states in supplying oil and gas (Duncan, 2018, pp. 235–252).

Since 2005, when the "contract of the century" was implemented and the BTC pipeline was launched, mainly promoted by the USA, Azerbaijan became independent of Russian routes for exporting energy. In 1997, Azerbaijan, Georgia, Ukraine, and Moldova founded the Organization for Democracy and Economic Development (GUAM), which received the support of the West and was merged with the EU structure—TRACECA (Duncan, 2018, pp. 235–252). Russia was unable to prevent the establishment of this organization or the implementation of the BTC and BTE energy infrastructure. Only when the EU initiated plans in 2002 to build an ambitious and wide-ranging Nabucco project, transporting gas from the Caspian region to the European market, did Russia propose a competitive project—South Stream. When it turned out that both projects were not viable due to insufficient gas supplies, Russia became a competitor of the EU (Duncan, 2018, pp. 235–252).

The ideological aspect of Russia's involvement in the Caspian region, as the main actor in the post-Soviet area, is also significant (Duncan, 2018, pp. 235–252). In this context, Vladimir Putin emphasized the character of the Russian Federation as a superpower. One of its attributes is the defense of the Russian diaspora and citizens of other states who share common ethnic roots with Russia. The key issue related to the concept of Russia as a superpower is the geopolitical dimension, that is to say the sphere of influence. In 1993, former Soviet President Boris Yeltsin declared that international organizations should provide Russia with special rights to establish peace and stability in the post-Soviet region (Lynch, 2000, p. 52). In August 2008, after the war with Georgia, former President Dmitry Medvedev, announced that the Russian Federation viewed that area as a "region of privileged interests" (Duncan, 2018, p. 235). He did not specify its geographic boundaries, but declared that it was not only about Russia's immediate neighbors.

Russia's aim is therefore to integrate the former Soviet republics into the Commonwealth of Independent States and to promote political and economic projects in the post-Soviet region. After this structure failed to prove effective, President Putin initiated a new integration project in 2001: the Eurasian Economic Community, followed in 2010 by the Customs Union, which in 2012 became the Common Economic Zone (Duncan, 2018, pp. 235–252). The concept of the Eurasian Union also has an ideological dimension related to Russia's role as the keystone of the post-Soviet system. Furthermore, it stems from Putin's anti-Western vision (Duncan, 2018, pp. 235–252). The Eurasian Union is a structure consisting of authoritarian and undemocratic states. At the same time, there is no willingness to create supranational bodies.

An important element of Russia's policy towards the Caspian region is its relations with Azerbaijan. Putin strengthened relations with Azerbaijan after H. Aliyev took power (probably the shared experiences of the presidents of both countries within the KGB structures facilitated reciprocal relations), and later on his son Ilham. The tensions between the two states were broken when Azerbaijan banned Chechen separatists from its territory (Duncan, 2018, pp. 235–252). The resumption of diplomatic relations between Armenia and Turkey in 2009 motivated Azerbaijan to tighten relations with Russia. In this context, he began negotiations with Gazprom about the sale of gas. Azerbaijan supported the UN resolution opposing the Russian annexation of Crimea in 2014. Russia is opposed to the activity of Azerbaijan's activities in seeking to be the main supplier of gas to European markets. Russia views Azerbaijan's gas exports as competition in the European market and tries to sabotage its efforts to expand the gas pipeline infrastructure. Following A. Dugin, a Russian conservative columnist: "If Baku pursues an anti-Russian policy, Moscow will not guarantee its territorial integrity" (Shlapentokh, 2014, p. 10). Currently, Azerbaijan focuses on exporting gas to Europe via Turkey. In addition, the country is tightening cooperation with NATO, that further worries Russia, which fears an enhanced the role of the Alliance in the Caspian region. The prospect of closer cooperation between Azerbaijan and Turkmenistan in the construction of the Trans-Caspian Pipeline has also met with criticism from the Russian superpower. The Russian Federation threatened to use force against Azerbaijan. In April 2014, the Southern Military District of Russia announced the "unscheduled combat readiness test of the Caspian flotilla," involving approximately 10 ships and 400 soldiers (Shlapentokh, 2014, p. 10). These actions were aimed to dissuade Azerbaijan and Turkmenistan from cooperating in the joint pipeline.

The main determinant of Russia's energy security policy is the resource potential (Balmaceda & Heinrich, 2021, p. 465) (Tables 3.17–3.22). The Russian Federation is one of the world's major exporters of fossil fuels (this role is losing importance now with the sanctions related to the war in Ukraine). In December 2005, at a session of the Security Council of the Russian Federation, Putin, called Russia an "energy superpower" (Wyciszkiewicz, 2008, p. 7). He added that "energy is the most important driving force of world economic development" (Balmaceda & Heinrich, 2021, p. 465). Russia's ruling elites are convinced that the abundance of energy resources will ensure Russia long-term prosperity and a powerful position in the international arena (World Bank, 2021; Bahgat, 2010, p. 163).

TABLE 3.17 Oil reserves in Russia (billion barrels)

2002	2003	2005	2008	2009	2011	2012	2013	2016	2020
51.2	69	74	79	74.2	60	60	80	80	80

SOURCE: HTTPS://WWW.INDEXMUNDI.COM/G/G.ASPX?V=97&C=RS&L=EN

TABLE 3.18 Natural gas reserves in Russia (billion m^3)

2002	2003	2008	2010	2011	2012	2013	2015	2016	2020
47.860	47.570	44.650	47.570	44.8	47.57	47.8	32.6	47.8	47.8

SOURCES: HTTPS://WWW.INDEXMUNDI.COM/G/G.ASPX?V=98&C=RS&L=EN

TABLE 3.19   Oil production in Russia (barrels per day)

2001	2003	2005	2007	2009	2010	2012	2013	2016	2018	2020
7,286,000	8,420,000	9,400,000	9,980,000	9,932,000	10,270,000	10,370,000	10,440,000	10,830,000	10,580,000	10,759,000

SOURCE: HTTPS://WWW.INDEXMUNDI.COM/G/G.ASPX?V=88&C=RS&L=EN

TABLE 3.20   Gas production in Russia (billion m³)

2001	2003	2005	2007	2009	2010	2012	2013	2014	2015	2018	2020
580.8	578.6	641	654	583.6	588.9	653	669.7	578.7	635.5	665.6	665.6

SOURCE: HTTPS://WWW.INDEXMUNDI.COM/G/G.ASPX?V=136&C=RS&L=EN

The size of documented natural oil and gas deposits shows that Russia is the world's third largest oil producer behind the United States and Saudi Arabia. In January 2022, Russia's total oil production was 11.3 mb/d (International Energy Agency, n.d.b). It also has the world's largest natural gas reserves (Ronek, 2017; Bodio, 2009, p. 79; Molo, 2008, p. 76).

In recent years, the largest oil production in Russia has been concentrated in West Siberia, between the Ural Mountains and the Central Siberian Plateau. The largest confirmed gas resources in Russia are in West Siberia (Uregoj, Medwiez, Jamburg, Zapolarnoye), in the European part of the Federation, as well as in East Siberia and the Russian Far East (Wyciszkiewicz, 2008, p. 16).

Before the dissolution of the USSR, the industry in the Caspian Sea sector belonging to Russia was not being developed. The reason for this was, first, Russia's use of energy produced by the republics, and second, the northern part of the Caspian Sea was the spawning ground of sturgeon and the production of black caviar (Zhiltsov et al., 2016). In 1975, it was established as a protected zone. Meanwhile, Russia's coastal marine area has been very poorly studied geologically and geographically, which limited the potential for energy exploitation. Despite this, oil reserves in this sector of the Russian-owned Caspian Sea are estimated at 2–2.5 billion tonnes (Zhiltsov et al., 2016). Many areas in the region are highly prospective for oil and gas reserves. Russia possessed three areas on the Caspian Sea, rich in the main resources: the Republic of Kalmykia, the Republic of Dagestan, and the Astrakhan Region. Six oil and gas fields within the Mesozoic strata and two natural gas condensate fields within the Paleozoic strata were discovered in Astrakhan. Three fields (Astrakhansky, Promyslovskoye, Beshkulsky) were exploited, and the Verblyuzhie oil field and the Alekseevsky gas condensate field are under study. However, the Bugrinsky and North Shadzhinsky fields have been closed. The small Promyslovskoye and Bugrinsky gas fields were discovered in the 1950s. In the 1980s and 1970s, the Beshkulsky oil field was in operation from 1960, the Astrakhansky gas condensate (AGCF) field was opened in 1976, unique in terms of its reserves, not only in Russia but also globally (Vostokov, 1997, p. 76; Shorokhov, 1997, p. 65). It is located 70 km northeast of Astrakhan. This gas field extends over 2.500 m². Its

TABLE 3.21   Russia's oil exports (billion barrels)

2003	2004	2005	2007	2009	2010	2012	2013	2016	2018	2020
6.110.000	5.150.000	7.000.000	5.170.000	5.430.000	5.010.000	4.690.000	4.720.000	5.116.000	4.921.000	4.921.000

SOURCE: HTTPS://WWW.INDEXMUNDI.COM/G/G.ASPX?V=95&C=RS&L=EN

TABLE 3.22   Gas exports by Russia (billion m³)

2001	2003	2004	2007	2009	2010	2012	2013	2014	2016	2018	2020
205.4	171	216.8	173	179	199.9	200	196	201.9	222.9	210.2	210.2

SOURCE: HTTPS://WWW.INDEXMUNDI.COM/G/G.ASPX?V=138&C=RS&L=EN

importance stems from the fact that it probably has reserves of gas condensate that amount to 3.6–5.0 trillion m³.

Reserves in the continental part of the region are estimated at 1 billion tonnes of oil, 6 tonnes m³ of gas and 1.2 billion tonnes of gas condensate. The hydrocarbon reserves found at a depth of 5.000–7.000 m are the most promising. It is primarily a right-bank block of North Astrakhan resources. According to geological forecasts, sulfur-free oil reserves could amount to 5–8 billion tonnes (Zhiltsov et al., 2016). Hydrocarbon reserves were discovered during drilling in the North Caspian Sea in the Khvalynsky, Rakusherny, and Korchagin fields (estimated at 450 million tonnes) and the Filanovsky field with possible reserves of 600 million barrels of oil (Zhiltsov et al., 2016).

Russia pursues its interests in energy security policy through expansion into international markets (Balmaceda & Heinrich, 2021, p. 465). The reconstruction of the energy sector in Russia after the collapse of the USSR, made possible thanks to the involvement of many private companies, quickly led to the establishment of strong state control over it and an attempt to utilize energy supplies to boost political influence abroad. Russia aims to control the entire energy infrastructure in the post-Soviet states. State monopolists such as Gazprom, Transneft, and Lukoil play the main role in Russia's energy security policy (Cohen, 2003 p. 119). Russia promotes the participation of Russian companies in the world energy market, which is not only of economic but also of political significance (Poussenkova, 2010, p. 103; O'Sullivan, 1996, p. 7; Cohen, 2003, p. 119).

In 2003, Russia presented its energy security policy strategy, which assumed protection of the state, its citizens, and the economy against internal and external threats to energy supplies, as well as geopolitical and factors related to the energy market (Ministry of Energy of the Russian Federation, 2010). Putin stated that "Russia's place in global energy relations directly determines its present and future prosperity" (Cohen, 2003, p. 119). Thus, Russia's energy strategy aimed at maximizing the benefits from the energy sector and the fact that it is the main energy producer and owner of huge fossil fuel reserves.

The basic aims and assumptions of Russia's current energy policy are set out in the government's document, "Russia's Energy Strategy until 2030," published in late 2009, and in the new energy security doctrine of that state, established in May 2019 (Energy Strategy of Russia, 2009). The strategy assumes a stronger influence of Russia on the international markets of energy carriers in order to minimize internal threats resulting from the strong dependence of the Russian economy on the global demand for energy resources (ibid). The introduction to the document emphasizes that "the task of Russia's energy policy is to optimize the use of natural energy resources and the potential of the energy sector in order to stabilize the economy, improve the quality of life of citizens and strengthen the country's position in the world economy" (ibid, p. 10).

One of the main priorities of Russia's energy security policy is the development of the energy infrastructure and exerting a greater influence on the price of energy resources through dialogue with producer and consumer states (ibid). Russia further aims to use its energy potential and logistic advantage in the European market and ensure stable and high revenues from hydrocarbon supplies to the European market. Other strategic challenges include increasing Russian investments in the global energy market, as well as the purchase of shares in foreign energy companies. The government's strategy also emphasized the priority of transmission infrastructure projects directly connecting Russia's resources with Western markets.

In line with Russia's energy strategy, the following actions are required to achieve the set goals:
– boosting the efficiency of production, extraction, and processing of fuel and energy resources to meet internal and external demand;
– modernization of the existing infrastructure and construction of new energy infrastructure by modernizing the energy sector;
– shaping the institutional environment conducive to the development of the energy sector; and
– integration of the Russian energy sector into the world energy system (ibid).
It can therefore be concluded that Russia's role in the post-Soviet region is offensive relative to the activity of other actors, in particular the West (Penerliev, 2012, p. 4). Russia sabotages any energy projects that are not in line with its interests and do not run through its territory.

The future of Russian energy supplies is uncertain. The scenarios in 2023 assume a persistent reduction in Russian exports of fossil fuels (BP, 2023). In the near term, this reflects the impact of sanctions on Russian energy exports. Further out, it stems from the assumption that sanctions affecting Russia's access to foreign investment and technologies ease only gradually (ibid). From an energy perspective, the impact of the Russia war in Ukraine is operating through three main channels: energy security, economic growth, and composition of global energy supplies (ibid). The war is continuing with no end in sight. Hence, this analysis should be treated as preliminary and subject to change, depending on future developments.

1.5   *Islamic Republic of Iran*

Iran's energy security policy is mainly determined by its geopolitical position. Iran is an Asian country with access to the Caspian Sea and the Persian Gulf. In the post-Soviet period, it became a significant actor in the energy market of the Caspian region, a convenient transit area for the export of energy resources to foreign markets (Zhiltsov et al., 2016). Iran's economy is characterized by its hydrocarbon, agricultural, and service sectors, as well as a noticeable state presence in the manufacturing and financial services (World Bank, 2022b).

Given its energy abundance, strategic position between the East and West, the Persian Gulf and the Caspian region, Iran undoubtedly plays a significant role not only in the region, but also on a global scale. It can be an attractive partner for the newly established states in Central Asia and the Caucasus, as a link state within the Eurasian corridor. Iran provides the shortest route from the Caspian region to the Persian Gulf. It has major oil terminals and essential export infrastructure. Iran is an active player within the ECO, and promotes the construction of pipelines from Central Asia to the south. However, Iran is not strong enough to become the major actor in the region. It is noteworthy that it is not making use of its geoenergy position. Adequate infrastructure is needed to transport resources to the EU market from the Persian Gulf region and the Caspian Basin (Misiągiewicz, 2022, p. 408). In this context, the risk of US sanctions does not encourage potential investors in Iran's energy sector. US policy towards Iran results from Iran's nuclear program and its destabilizing role in Iraq. The US obstructed any plans for the transit of Iranian energy resources via Turkey to Europe (Abolhosseini et al., 2017, pp. 224–238). Iran is moving towards China and is an attractive economic partner for Russia.

The evolution of Iran's policy in the Caspian region (including its main determinants and interests) is noteworthy. Iran and the Caspian region have historical ties dating back to the 6th century (Misiągiewicz, 2022, p. 410; Rakel, 2005, pp. 235–256). Since the founding of the Safavid Empire in 1501, with the Shiite branch of Islam as the state religion, Iran has had no actual chance to establish a sphere of influence in this region.

In the 19th century, it was included in the "Great Game" between Russia and the British Empire. At that time, Iran's policy was to seek a balance between the two empires and maintain independence. This strategy failed, as evidenced by the occupation of the country by Great Britain and the USSR during World War II.

After the 1979 revolution, Iran became a radical and independent actor on the international stage. Following the Iran–Iraq War (1980–1988), its foreign policy was perceived as pragmatic, and the hallmarks of its foreign policy were independence, anti-Americanism, and, to a lesser extent, anti-Russianism. Such a policy was described as "neither eastern nor western, but an Islamic Republic," stemming from reliance on Shiite principles (Sadri, 1999, pp. 29–46).

After the revolution, Iran's foreign policy was without a doubt conditioned by its image problems on the international stage (Pahlavi & Hojati, 2010, pp. 215–238). These experiences taught Iran an important lesson, valid to this day: never allow international isolation and strategic vulnerability (Hilterman, 2005). Iran therefore needs a prudent and pragmatic foreign policy focused on regional issues. As early as 1985, Tehran tried to diversify its trade and technology partners in order to avoid dependence on any foreign power. During the presidency of Hashemi Rafsanyani, the "dearabisation" of Iran's foreign policy was inaugurated, starting from 1989 (Rakel, 2005, pp. 159–187). The focus on regional interests and multilateralism, including trade and military relations with Russia and China, gained importance in Iranian politics. The state thus attempted to compensate for the lack of relations with the US.

Iran's previous conservative approach to international relations, which relied on independence, turned into a realistic policy "both northern and southern" (Pahlavi & Hojati, 2010, p. 215). It was only after the fall of the USSR that Iran was determined to renew its position in the Caspian region, especially economically. Since then, Iran has joined the "New Big Game" in the region (Rakel, 2005, pp. 235–256). With the emergence of the new Caspian states, Iran began pursuing a balanced policy, both bilaterally and regionally. However, despite this, Iran has not become a leader in this region but an economic partner and a state supporting regional integration processes. In the early 1990s, despite high expectations, Iran neither had the material capacity nor the interest to play a superpower role in the Caspian region, using the mechanisms of power politics (Misiągiewicz, 2022, p. 410; Pahlavi & Hojati, 2010, pp. 215–238). Rivalry between different political factions in the country, from the conservative right (Rast-e Sonati), the conservative left (Chap-e Sonati), the revolutionary New Left, or Hezbollah, to the Conservative Modern Right, made Iran's foreign policy inconsistent and the state was not treated as a reliable partner in the region (Malek-Ahmadi, 2015).

Being aware of many limitations and its isolation in international relations, Iran focused on the development of regional ties by using its geopolitical, cultural, and economic position. Engagement in the Caspian region increased its international role and was one dimension of the country's broader strategy. It thrives on limiting the influence of the West and building an image as a credible state, a partner for the newly established post-Soviet states.

In 1991, Iran recognized the independence of the Caspian states, hoping for economic benefits. The former president of Iran, H. Rafsanjani, often declared that independent states in this region would create an economic and trade center to link the Caspian Sea and the open waters. Accordingly, Iran intended to achieve the following objectives:
– develop its infrastructure;
– gain political and economic influence in the Caspian region through the Economic Cooperation Organization; and
– obtain shares in projects related to the exploitation of oil and gas in the Caspian region (Misiągiewicz, 2022, p. 409; Buchta, 2000, p. 50).

Iran's rational realism results from its unique geostrategic position, which is a significant condition for the development of regional relations (Muñoz, 2008, pp. 22–23; Pahlavi & Hojati, 2010, pp. 215–238). Obviously, Iran's regional relations cannot be interpreted solely through the lens of geopolitics. Iran's internal policy, driven by its needs or interests on the one hand, and tense relations with the West on the other, forces this state to seek areas of economic, trade, or investment cooperation with other actors. Thus, the Caspian region is an important part of Iran's strategy (Pahlavi & Hojati, 2010, pp. 215–238).

An important factor in Iran's energy security policy in the Caspian region were its tense relations with the US. In the 1990s, the US toughened its policy towards Iran. In 1992, the Iran Non-Proliferation Act was introduced, which extended export sanctions to Iran and Iraq, and the Iran Libya Sanctions Act 1996 (ILSA), which prohibited any investment in Iran's oil sector (Iran and Libya Sanctions Act, 1996). President George W. Bush extended these regulations in 2001. Tension in Iran's relations with the US limited cooperation between Iran and the newly established Caspian states and the investment activity of transnational corporations in Iran. In March 2002, US Deputy Secretary of State Richard Armitage and other White House officials warned Iran not to put pressure on its neighbors in the Caspian region to limit US political and economic influence. Iran's activities in the Caspian region became more radical on July 23, 2001, when two Iranian Air Force planes attacked the BP/Amoco research vessel, which was exploring the Azerbaijani Araz–Alov–Shargh fields. On the same day, an Iranian warship crossed the waters of Azerbaijan and threatened to use force against the research vessel. Iran thereby sought to enforce its claims in this part of the Caspian Basin. Following this incident, BP/Amoco then suspended work in the Araz–Alov–Shargh fields (Rakel, 2005, pp. 235–256).

Iran's aim was to limit Western influence in the Central Asian region. During his visit to the countries of the region, Iran's president, Muhammad Khatami, declared, "our nations have the right to solve their problems on their own and decide what is right and what is wrong" (Recknagel, 2002, p.23). He linked his realistic approach with the emphasis on the regional nature of Iran's foreign policy. During a speech at the UN General Assembly in 1997, Iran's minister of foreign affairs declared, "our greatest foreign policy priority is to strengthen trust, confidence and peace in our immediate neighbourhood" (Pahlavi & Hojati, 2010, pp. 215–238). President Mahoud Ahmadinejad and his minister of foreign affairs, Manucher Mottaki, continued this direction of foreign policy. During his visit to Kabul, Iran's vice president, Ali Saeedlou, confirmed that the promotion of security and cooperation with the states of the region was a priority in Iran's foreign policy (Misiągiewicz, 2022, p. 412).

Iran's cautious policy in the post-Soviet region follows a rational model that effectively describes the dynamics of political and security relations. Relations between Iran and the Caspian states developed immediately after the collapse of the USSR. They stemmed from a community of interests, ethnic and cultural conditions, and geostrategic matters. For the newly established states, Iran was an important partner for their integration with the global economy (World Bank, 2022b; Dannreuther, 2003, pp. 32–46). At the same time, Iran needed to liaise with them to strengthen its security and pursue economic and political interests (Frappi & Garibov, 2014, p. 40).

In terms of regionalization processes and in the bilateral and multilateral dimensions in the Caspian region, the basis of Iran's interests was to support the independence of the newly established states and eliminate non-regional powers (Herzig, 2004, pp. 503–517). Taking advantage of its historical regional ties and the vacuum following the collapse of the USSR, Iran sought to form a broad coalition of Islamic states which would provide a strategic barrier against US influence.

However, Iran was unable to implement the strategy of exporting the radical Shiite model due to the fact that most of the Caspian states are under the influence of Sunni Islam and Turkish culture (Misiągiewicz, 2022, p. 410). Iran was therefore aware that it would not become the dominant regional actor.

Iran's policy towards the Caspian region has been largely driven by the security situation that evolved and was favorable to the state, and resulted from a number of conditions:

– departure from the policy of "containment" towards balancing geopolitical influences and increasing influence in the region, with particular emphasis on specific objectives: political, economic, and especially energy-related;
– Iran's policy is conditioned by the broad Eurasian and Middle Eastern context, and especially by the strategy of limiting the influence of the West in Iran's immediate environment; and
– a vision of Iran's foreign policy, based on the conviction that it occupies a prominent position in the neighboring regions; such a position enables

Iran to set limits on the influence of foreign actors (Malek-Ahmadi, 2015; Kupchan, 2005, pp. 106–110).

Thus, Iran's policy towards the Caspian states is a part of a broader approach to international relations, known as the "grand strategy" of Iran's power. However, despite high ambitions, this strategy is largely one of cautious pragmatism. The rationalization of Iran's ambitions may enhance the importance of this state in the region as an economic and cultural partner. The priorities of Iran's strategy are to enhance its ethnic and cultural ties with the Caspian region, strengthen its geostrategic position, and develop its energy policy. Therefore, Iran's policy is focused on development, trade, and to a lesser extent, political or military domination. Iran's pragmatic approach to the Caspian region results from a multidimensional strategy. To understand Iran's role in this region, three main features of its foreign policy activities must be considered:

1. a strategy based on the development of bilateral political and economic relations with individual countries;
2. a strategy related to the development of regional infrastructure, in particular the "pipeline policy" (energy infrastructure projects); and
3. a strategy for regional integration through the establishment of international organizations such as the ECO or the Shanghai Cooperation Organization (Misiągiewicz, 2022, p. 410; Mackenzie, 1993, pp. 13–34).

The relations between Iran and Turkmenistan are an example of good relations resulting from the common interests of both states, based on a policy of alignment and neutrality in security (Peyrouse, 2015). In his first foreign visit, President Khatami went to Turkmenistan, which was a symbolic confirmation of mutual relations.

Both countries strengthened their cooperation in the field of energy, strategic transport links, and pipelines. About 10 bilateral agreements and 57 international agreements have been signed to this extent (Pahlavi & Hojati, 2010, pp. 215–238). Iran has become Turkmenistan's second largest trade partner. Relations between Iran and Kazakhstan have also grown stronger in recent years. Kazakhstan was especially interested in energy-related exchanges. Such cooperation was mutually beneficial, leading to broader economic cooperation (Misiągiewicz, 2022, p. 410; Mesbahi, 1997, pp. 109–139).

Iran's involvement in bilateral relations in the Caspian region can be considered a success. However, deeper economic cooperation was largely limited due to structural problems in the Iranian economy and its overdependence on oil and gas (Misiągiewicz, 2022, p. 410; Pomfret, 2006, pp. 657–668). After the collapse of the USSR, the Caspian states, especially Turkmenistan and Kazakhstan, focused on the transport of hydrocarbons to Iran. A number of pipeline projects have been developed that run through the territory of Iran.

Nevertheless, due to turbulences in Iran's relations with Western states, they could not be implemented.

For objective reasons, Iran did not play the "ethnic card" in the region (Kalehsar, 2016, pp. 136–142). For example, it never showed solidarity with Azerbaijan, fearing nationalist sentiment among the Azerbaijani population in Iran. Although Azerbaijan identified linguistically with the Turks, it also had strong cultural ties with Iran.

The second dimension of Iran's strategy in the region is the development of large-scale infrastructure projects, mainly pipelines and road and rail systems. Tehran expected that this type of infrastructure would not only connect the Caspian region with the world via Iran but would also transform the country towards a hub in the exploitation and transport of energy resources (Kucera, 2006). Iran's involvement in the "pipeline policy" was related to efforts to support political and economic stability in the Caspian region. The aim was to create a pipeline network involving Iran as a link between the Central Asian and the Caspian and Persian Gulf regions. This geopolitical zone was called "Pipelineistan" in connection with the development of the oil and gas pipeline networks in this area (Blanche, 2008, pp. 22–25).

A key dimension of Iran's energy security policy is its resource potential. Iran is the second country in the world in terms of gas reserves. Its resources amount to 32 tonnes m^3, which constitutes 16.1% of the world's reserves (BP, 2020). Iran has 32 gas fields, 26 of which are onshore and 6 that are offshore. The country produces 244.2 billion m^3 of gas annually. However, this is not enough to meet domestic demand. Iran's resources are located in the south, the Gulf Coast, and the center of the state. However, they are far from the northern part of the country, where trade and industry are concentrated.

Iran is the third country in the world and the second within OPEC for oil reserves. It has 21.4 billion tonnes of this oil, which accounts for 9% of the world's resources (BP, 2020). It produces 3.535.000 of barrels per day (3.7% globally), and exports around 3 mb/d of oil, or 1.3% of global exports. Oil accounts for 80% of the country's exports (BP, 2020).

The reserves of the Iranian part of the Caspian Sea are estimated at 199 million tonnes of oil. Based on US data, they amount to 12 billion barrels (Zhiltsov et al., 2016). In 2000, the reserves from operating fields, according to the estimates of the National Iranian Oil Company (NIOC), amounted to 10 billion barrels of oil and 560 billion m^3 of gas (Zhiltsov et al., 2016). Geological work in this region was carried out by the British Lasmo corporation and the British-Dutch Company Royal Dutch in the area of 100 km^2. Iran has discovered oil and gas fields in its part of the Caspian region. One of them is Sardar Jangal, located in the province of Gilan. There are reserves of 275.000 tonnes of oil and 1.42 billion m^3 of gas (Zhiltsov et al., 2016).

Iran has played an important role in resource exploitation and exportation. It had an appropriate and extensive pipeline infrastructure to which pipelines from the Caspian region could be connected. Thus, Iran can be a significant source and transit state for hydrocarbons to the EU (Abolhosseini et al., 2017, pp. 224–238). However, this scenario has not manifested so far. Due to US sanctions, Iran's potential in terms of investment attractiveness has significantly declined. The Iranian gas industry is mainly concentrated on the domestic market. In addition, this state attaches great importance to the development of the oil sector.

In order to implement its energy security strategy, Iran has engaged in the construction of various infrastructure projects. One of them was the Korpeje–Kurtkui project, a gas pipeline running from Central Asia without Russia's participation, exporting gas from Turkmenistan to Iran. The Iran–Pakistan–India pipeline was also an important project. Due to possible challenges related to oil and gas supplies from Russia to the European market, Iran could be an alternative source. In 2016, Iran gained access to the EU energy market. The economic sanctions were then lifted and oil exports from Iran to the EU market amounted to 497.323 billion barrels per day (Abolhosseini et al., 2017, pp. 224–238).

The geographical position and geostrategic importance for the world energy market are therefore the key dimensions of Iran's policy towards the Caspian region. This policy focuses largely on building and promoting significant pipeline systems that aim to connect the region to the global market, given that the area is not connected to the seas and oceans. At the same time, it is important to note that Iran's role in this sensitive sector results from conditions beyond its direct control (Pahlavi & Hojati, 2010, pp. 215–238). Commentators point out that "new rivalry between national interests is causing tensions over fuel prices, transit fees and, more generally, energy resources and transport corridors in the post-Soviet area, which has economic and often irrational consequence" (Kandiyoti, 2008, pp. 75–93).

It is difficult to unequivocally assess Iran's strategy towards the Caspian region. It can be concluded that it was a failure, as Iran was unable to have the role of the dominant player. Iran was aware of its strengths and weaknesses. Consequently, it chose a cautious pragmatic approach, aimed at increasing confidence among the newly emerged states of the region. Iran is aware of its weakness compared to other international actors and applies a balancing strategy in the international environment (Walt, 2005, p. 120).

Most likely, Tehran will maintain a multidimensional approach in the Caspian region through the use of a combination of hard and soft (smart power) foreign policy instruments. The country aims to increase investment to gain economic, political, and security benefits. Iran's international relations with neighboring regions show that it is a very patient partner. It seems that Iran will gain more benefits by pursuing a consistent and pragmatic policy in the Caspian region (Misiągiewicz, 2022, p. 427).

2   The Caspian Region in the Energy Security Policies of External Actors

2.1   *People's Republic of China*

Following the English geographer, James Fairgrieve, China was in an excellent position to dominate Eurasia, according to the "Heartland" theory (Fairgrieve, 1915, p. 329). The policy of the People's Republic of China (PRC) in the Caspian region is conditioned by the superpower's increased demand for energy resources and its geographical proximity to oil and gas fields located in Turkmenistan and Kazakhstan. In pursuit of its main interests, China has focused on expanding its pipeline infrastructure and strengthening bilateral relations with hydrocarbon suppliers.

The PRC became interested in the hydrocarbon resources of the Caspian region immediately after the collapse of the USSR. At that time, the superpower's energy security policy was implemented in several stages: from gaining access to the region's oil and gas reserves to building export pipelines to supply the absorptive Chinese market (Nahm, 2021, p. 533). Cooperation between the Caspian states and China in the field of energy developed rapidly. China invested in developing energy reserves and pursued export pipeline projects (Zhiltsov & Grishicheva, 2016, pp. 105–116).

According to S. Howell, there are three dimensions of vulnerability in China's energy security policy:
a.   insufficient geological potential;
b.   huge demand for hydrocarbons; and
c.   pressure on the Communist Party of China to raise the standard of living of the population in order to perpetuate the regime (Howell, 2009, p. 192).

In the first half of the 1990s, the economic and political weakness of the newly formed countries enhanced the PRC's expansion opportunities in this market. China's policy in the Caspian region was conditioned largely by strategic competition for access to energy resources and to routes for their export to foreign markets. Interest in the Caspian region coincided with economic development in China, which was experiencing an increasing demand for energy resources (Lixia, 2021). The geopolitical aspect, related to the competition for influence in the region, was also important. In this context, China was concerned about the US military presence in the Caspian area. The country focused on energy cooperation with Kazakhstan and Turkmenistan (Zhiltsov, 2009, pp. 174–178).

The key element of China's energy security policy was the "Going Out" strategy, initiated in the 1990s. During this period, Chinese energy corporations took advantage of the international crisis to implement their own strategic plans in relation to foreign partners. The main instruments of the "Going Out" strategy included:

1. buying foreign companies because of their technological capacity, efficiency, and market position;
2. investing in oil and gas abroad and diversifying transportation routes; and
3. guaranteeing access to energy markets and development investments in the commodities market (Cutter, 2014, pp. 673–698).

The main feature of China's energy security policy is the simultaneous development of the renewable energy sector and continued investment in fossil fuels (Nahm, 2019, pp. 1–29; Mori, 2019, p. 23; Li, 2018). The policy is therefore full of contradictions. Each successive Five-Year Plan issued by the government outpaces the previous one in terms of the transition to clean energy sources. In 2016, the country accounted for 81% of the global solar panel production and 42% of the global wind turbine production (Ball et al., 2017). Although China aimed to obtain 315 gigawatts (GW) of clean energy from wind and solar, its rapid economic growth has increased the demand for nonrenewable energy sources, and their overexploitation has led to severe environmental pollution (Ball et al., 2017; Li, 2018). Since the beginning of the 1978 reforms, China's economy has been growing very rapidly. Its GDP grew from USD 395 billion in 1980 to USD 9.2 trillions in 2015. Between 2000 and 2015 alone, the superpower's economic growth tripled. This led to a growing demand for energy in China. The country's economy, focused on exports, development of energy-intensive sectors (such as steel, aluminum, and cement industries), and raising the living standards of its citizens, generated an intensive growth in energy consumption (International Energy Agency, 2017). China's economy was much more energy intensive than the economies of OECD countries. As a result, lower GDP per capita (in 2017, it accounted for no more than 23% of the OECD average) coexisted with high energy consumption per capita. China is also the largest energy consumer in the world, with a population exceeding 1.4 billion people. China's economy slowed down in 2022. After a strong start in early 2022, the largest Covid-19 wave in two years disrupted China's growth normalization (World Bank, 2022a). China's GDP growth was 5.6% in 2023, led by a rebound in consumer demand (World Bank Report, 2023).

In 2015, industry generated half of China's energy demand (Tables 3.23 and 3.24). Households and transportation accounted for 16.4% and 15.7% of consumption, respectively. Renewable sources account for a small percentage of energy demand. An increase in the number of cars is likely to contribute to a significant rise in the demand for oil (Table 3.23, Figure 3.5).

At the same time, the country's population is largely dependent on coal consumption (Where India's, 2016). Coal accounts for two-thirds of the energy supply (Figure 3.5). China's electricity sector is about 70% based on coal, but this dependence has declined since 2005, when coal accounted for 80% of the

TABLE 3.23   Production and consumption of oil in China

		2002	2010	2012	2016	2019	Global share 2019
Production	Thousand barrels/day	3.351	4.077	4.155	3.999	3.836	4.0%
	Million tonnes	166.9	203.0	207.5	199.7	191.0	4.3%
Consumption	Thousand barrels/day	5.262	9.272	10.221	12.381	14.056	14.3%

SOURCE: BP STATISTICAL REVIEW OF WORLD ENERGY, 2017

TABLE 3.24   Production and consumption of gas in China

		2002	2010	2012	2016	2019	Global share 2019
Production	bln m3	32.7	94.8	107.2	138.4	177.6	4.5%
Consumption	bln m3	29.2	106.9	143.8	210.3	307.3	7.8%

SOURCE: BP STATISTICAL REVIEW OF WORLD ENERGY JUNE 2013, 2017

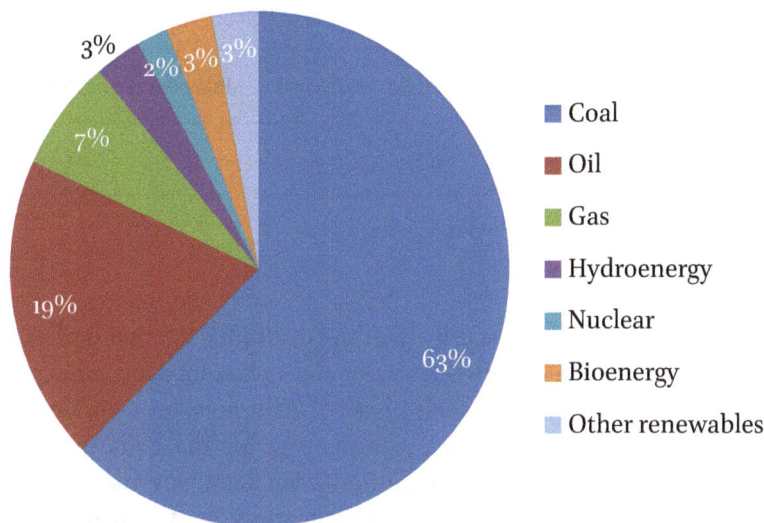

FIGURE 3.5   Energy consumption in China
SOURCE: MADE BY THE AUTHOR, HTTPS://WWW.ENERDATA.NET
/PUBLICATIONS/EXECUTIVE-BRIEFING/CHINA-STRATEGY-IN
-AFRICA.HTML

TABLE 3.25   Oil import sources in China (%)

Kazakhstan	Saudi Arabia	Angola	Russia	Oman	Iraq	Iran	Venezuela	UAE	Kuwait	Colombia
2	16.8	9.5	15.3	6.9	9.9	3	1.9	3.1	4.5	2.3

SOURCE: HTTP://WWW.WORLDSTOPEXPORTS.COM/TOP-15-CRUDE-OIL-SUPPLIERS-TO-CHINA/

production of electricity (Nahm, 2019, pp. 1–29). Coal-fired power plants generated 4,109 terawatt-hours (TWh) in 2015 (meanwhile, in the US, they generated 1,471 TWh) (International Energy Agency, 2017). This results in increased CO_2 emissions into the atmosphere. Since 1993, China has also been dealing with the problem of dependence of imported energy (Tables 3.25 and 3.26). The country is the world's largest importer of oil. In 2015, 62% of the oil consumed in China was imported (Andrews-Speed, 2012; Hornby, 2017; Sheppard & Meyer, 2015).

TABLE 3.26   Gas import sources in China (%)

Turkmenistan	Uzbekistan	Qatar	Australia	Indonesia	Malaysia	Kazakhstan
47.1	5.6	17.1	9.3	6.4	7	0.1

SOURCE: BP STATISTICAL REVIEW OF WORLD ENERGY 2020

Most studies of China's energy security treat the institutional dimension as a major factor in the divergence between its ambitious plans for a low-emission economy and its fossil fuel-based energy system (Nahm, 2019, pp. 1–29; Kostka & Nahm, 2017, pp. 567–582; Lieberthal, 1992, pp. 1–32; Mertha, 2005, pp. 791–810). Although formally it is a unitary, authoritarian state (governed by the Communist Party), China is not a monolith (Heilmann & Perry, 2011, pp. 1–29; Heilmann et al., 2013, pp. 580–628; Baum, 1996; Baogang, 1996, pp. 287–305). Researchers argue that the understanding of the decision-making process in China is the so-called post-institutionalization (Ang, 2015). S. Heilman argues that the decision-making process relating to China's energy sector is an adaptive system based on experiments (Heilmann, 2018; Hongbin & Treisman, 2006, pp. 505–535).

The Five-Year Plans have been the cornerstone of decision-making in China. Since the 1980s and 1990s, as a result of the move away from the economic planning system towards decentralization, the Five-Year Plans ceased to be regarded as directives in the decision-making process, but remained in force as general directions for national development, created by the central government. These plans defined the main priorities of state policy and goals for central government action, but at the same time incorporated autonomy and flexibility in decision-making within government agencies and local administrations (Heilmann & Melton, 2013, pp. 580–628; Andrews-Speed, 2012; Ling, 2010, pp. 69–95; Xuanli, 2015, pp. 44–59; Weingast et al., 2005, pp. 1719–1742).

The Thirteenth Five-Year Plan, covering the period 2016–2020, was accompanied by 18 plans for the energy sector: "Medium and Long-Term Renewable Energy Plan" or the "Thirteenth Five-Year Plan to Control Greenhouse Gas Emissions" (Nahm, 2019, pp. 1–29). The agencies responsible for implementing these plans are the State Council, the National Energy Administration (NEA), the Ministry of Finance, and the Ministry of Industry and Information Technology (Koleski, 2017).

Of the 25 major goals specified under the Thirteenth Five-Year Plan, 10 were related to energy and the environment. The plan was to introduce an emissions trading scheme and increase the share of renewable sources in the energy mix from 9.5% to 15%, as well as reduce energy intensity from 18% to 15%. The plan's assumptions also included reducing the consumption of energy. China is the largest importer of oil and the seventh largest oil producer in the world. After two decades of institutional reforms and experimenting in the oil and gas sector, the sector was dominated by large state-owned energy companies responsible for sourcing and refining, pipeline building, foreign investments, and maintaining strategic national energy reserves (Andrews-Speed & Dannreuther, 2011).

The significance of particular determinants and motives of corporations in the implementation of the national energy security policy has changed in different periods. It also depends on the specific market in which corporations operate. Between 1994 and 1998, in parallel with the development of its geoeconomic strategy in Central Asia, China focused on the acquisition of energy infrastructure by the following corporations: China National Petroleum Corporation (CNPC), China National Offshore Oil Corporation (CNOOC), and China Petroleum and Chemical Corporation (Sinopec). This was related to the "Going Out" strategy, which promoted the involvement of Chinese corporations on an international scale.

The area of Central Asia and the Caspian region has close ties with China and is linked to the historic Silk Road. China's focus in the region is on geopolitical goals and energy needs. The significant increase in demand for energy resources has therefore added to the importance of the Caspian region for the energy security of the country (Xuanli Liao, 2006, pp. 39–51). China's influence in the area challenges the interests of Russia and the West. The PRC's involvement in the area is conditioned by energy and diplomatic issues. China has clearly strengthened its international position in line with the "paradox of emerging international coherence" (Cutter, 2004, p. 23). This involved empowering national corporations within China's state structures.

The PRC's interests in the Caspian region are reflected in its efforts to strengthen bilateral relations with individual countries that are key to the priorities of the superpower's energy security policy. China's activities in Kazakhstan is particularly significant, as the country is one of the world's leading oil producers. During the last few years, the PRC's involvement in Kazakhstan has been highly effective because of two key initiatives: first, the joint pipeline project, and second, the acquisition of the Petro-Kazakhstan company by China (Cutter, 2004). After the collapse of the Soviet Union, Kazakhstan became an attractive partner for the PRC, both strategically and in the field of energy. During this early period, both countries focused on strengthening strategic ties. In 1992, China established diplomatic relations with Kazakhstan. In 1997, China and Kazakhstan signed an agreement to build an oil pipeline connecting Atyrau in Kazakhstan and the Altaw Pass in China. It was one of the most significant overseas investments made by China in the oil industry.

China resumed its involvement in Kazakhstan's oil industry in 2003. At the time, the China National Petroleum Corporation (CNPC) oil corporation launched its operations in the country. In May 2003, China National Oil & Gas Exploration & Development Corp. (CNODC) acquired a 25.12% stake in AktobeMunaiGas Corp. (CNPC Aktobe), which increased CNODC's stake to 85.42%, provided this corporation with the opportunity to make fundamental decisions, and increased oil production to over 1.2 million tonnes per year (Cutter, 2004, p.12). China's key objective was to build a pipeline from Kazakhstan. On June 3, 2003, CNPC and KazMunaiGaz (KMG) signed an agreement on this matter. Moreover, CNPC signed an agreement with the Commission for State Property and Privatisation under the Ministry of Finance of Kazakhstan regarding investments in the oil and gas sector. In accordance with these agreements, CNPC and KMG completed the construction of the western part of the pipeline, running from Atyrau to Kenkiyak in Kazakhstan, in March 2003; it became operational in March 2004. On May 17, 2004, during Kazakh President Nazarbayev's four-day official visit to China, CNPC and KMG signed an agreement to build the eastern part of the oil pipeline, between Atasu and Alashankou. The initiative to build this strategic infrastructure belonged to China, not only due to economic but also to geopolitical considerations. According to L. Ruseckas, "China will prioritise oil from Kazakhstan, as it would be more expensive to transport it from the East" (Cutter, 2004, p. 13).

To quote Yin Juntai, one of CNOOC's top executives, "the construction of the trans-national pipeline indicates that energy cooperation between Kazakhstan and China has entered a new phase" (ibid, p. 14). The pipeline was also seen as a fulfilment of Kazakhstan's aspirations to become a major oil exporter and strengthen cooperation with China.

An example of the intensity of China's activities in Central Asia was its involvement in the consortium exploiting the Kashagan deposits in the Caspian region, especially in light of the policy of nationalization of energy resources in Kazakhstan. Following Nazarbayev's visit to China, Kazakhstan was willing to allow Chinese corporations to participate in this strategic investment. According to the declarations by Kazakhstan's minister of energy, Suat Mynbayev, the decision was made on the basis of commercial criteria (Cutter,

2004; Rosen & Hanemann, 2009). China's energy expansion in Kazakhstan, however, was viewed as a potential threat to Western oil corporations that had operated in the region for a long time. The interests of these actors were competitive in nature.

Turkmenistan is also a significant partner to China in the Caspian region. Turkmenistan's economic dependence on this superpower has been growing rapidly. In 2013, Turkmenistan sold 60% of its gas to China. However, this did not translate into a marked rise in the income from the exports of this resource. China's increased presence in Turkmenistan's market and reduced gas imports to Russia contributed to an imbalance in Turkmenistan's trade. An example of the PRC's expansion in Turkmenistan was the creation of joint infrastructure ventures in the energy sector. President Xi Jinping and President of Turkmenistan Gurbanguly Berdymukhammedov opened a gas refinery in 2013 that purified the crude gas from the large Galkynysh field in eastern Turkmenistan. It covers four major gas fields in the Mary region, 500 km southeast of Turkmenistan's capital city, Ashgabat. The infrastructure was built by the state-owned TurkmenGas in cooperation with the Chinese company CNPC. According to the president of Turkmenistan, "It is the most important complex in the region, with a processing capacity of 30 billion m³ per year" (Jakóbowski & Marszewski, 2018, p. 12). The presidents of both countries participated in the signing of an agreement between CNPC and Turkmen Gas on China's purchase of 25 billion m³ of gas per year. As Berdymuchammedov declared, in the future "it will be possible to ship up to 65 billion m³ of gas per year" (Jakóbowski & Marszewski, 2018, p. 12). According to a representative of the Turkmen gas sector, gas exports to China reached such a level in 2020. The structure of contracts between China and Turkmenistan (that is to say, linking gas prices to oil prices) leads to the draining of Turkmen resources and a markedly reduced inflow of foreign currencies. China may be confronted with the need to stabilize Turkmenistan's economy. As a result of the gas price conflict with Iran (2016), and the reduction and then suspension of imports by Russia's Gazprom after 2009, China is now the only significant buyer of the resource from Turkmenistan. In 2017, it received the delivery of about 94% of Turkmenistan's gas export volume, which accounted for almost 90% of the total value of the country's exports. At the same time, China's market does not compensate for lost revenues from the Russian and Iranian markets, and Turkmenistan's total gas export volume fell from 41.6 to 33.6 billion m³ between 2014 and 2017 (Jakóbowski & Marszewski, 2018). As a result of deep and multilevel economic dependence, the course of the crisis in Turkmenistan has become highly dependent on China's actions. The nature of today's dependency, as well as the current dynamics of the crisis in Turkmenistan, are the results of a long-term policy of the PRC.

The crisis in Turkmenistan also violates the *modus vivendi* of the Sino-Russian cooperation that extends throughout Central Asia and the Caspian region. It involved Russia's acceptance of China's growing economic influence in exchange for concessions in the areas of politics and security. The economic destabilization of the countries in the region, resulting from financial dependence on the PRC, may create an opportunity for Russia to intensify its involvement in the region and to strengthen its influence there.

The success of China's cooperation with the Caspian states is conditioned by the following factors:

1. institutional and normative similarity, which contributes to mutual understanding; and
2. and similarity with respect to decision-making and political culture.

Due to the continual growth of China's economy and its demand for energy resources, the countries of the Caspian region became its key sources of supply. The scale of *upstream* and *downstream* projects is an instrument used by China to achieve its long-term goals related to controlling energy resources in the region.

2.2   *Republic of Turkey*

Turkey is a receptive market for energy resources, and its geographical location enables it to play the role of a transit country for oil and natural gas from Central Asia, the Caucasus, and the Middle East to European markets (Misiągiewicz, 2019b, p. 120, 2012, 2015). It is therefore an important economic partner for countries that possess oil and gas reserves, as well as for countries that do not possess these resources.

The provisions of Turkey's energy security strategy arise from external and internal conditions. The main external factor is the geoeconomic position of the Republic of Turkey. This is a key feature of this state's energy policy (Tekin & Walterova, 2007, p. 123). The country aims to play the role of the main transit corridor for energy resources from Central Asia, the Caucasus, and the Middle East to the European Union. It has been estimated that 15% of gas imports to the European Union would be transported through Turkey (Winrow, 2006, p. 50). The main internal factor is undoubtedly the country's economic transformation, which has resulted in increased demand for energy resources in recent years. The priority of Turkey's economic policy is therefore to intensify its activity in the field of regional energy policy, which would make it an important economic partner for both exporters and importers of energy, and especially for the European Union, which is attaching increasing importance to the issue of energy security (Efegil, 2000, p. 58). Aware of these dependencies, Turkey has used them as a bargaining chip in the EU accession negotiations that have been underway since 2005 (Misiągiewicz, 2011).

In 2017, Turkey consumed 157.7 million tonnes of oil equivalent (BP, 2018). This is estimated to increase to 218 mtoe by 2023 (Winrow, 2014, p. 3). Due to the increasing demand for energy, the country will need to invest about USD 12 billion annually in this sector by 2023.

An analysis of the specificity of the energy commodity consumption in Turkey seems to be essential for this study (Table 3.27). According to the Justice and Development Party's (AKP) plan, by 2023, gas, coal, and renewable sources will each account for 30% of energy consumption in Turkey, while 10% will be covered by nuclear energy.

Gas is a significant energy resource used in Turkey (Table 3.28). It accounts for about 40% of electricity generation. Turkey obtains no more than 0.63 billion m³ of gas from domestic resources. However, estimates of gas consumption until 2020 have varied. The International Energy Agency predicted that this value would reach 59 billion m³, while according to the State Oil Corporation of

TABLE 3.27   Consumption of energy resources in Turkey (million tonnes of oil equivalent - mtoe)

Energy resources	1992	2002	2012	2016	2017
Oil	23.5	30.5	31.5	47.1	48.8
Gas	4.1	15.6	41.7	38.2	44.4
Coal	19	19.3	31.3	38.5	44.6
Nuclear energy	–	–	–	–	–
Hydroelectric power	6	7.6	13.1	15.2	13.2
Other renewable sources	n/a	0.1	1.6	5.4	6.6

TABLE 3.28   Gas Consumption in Turkey (billion m³)

2001	2005	2007	2009	2010	2011	2014	2015	2018	2020
15.9	22.6	36.6	35	38	44.7	48.4	48	53.6	53.6

Turkey, it would amount to 70 billion m³. At the same time, it is expected that the imports of this resource will increase with the development of the country's economy (Table 3.29). Therefore, the government's main goal is to reduce the cost of gas imports by intensifying the exploitation of renewable resources and coal, and by commencing the construction of a nuclear power plant system.

Oil is the main source of energy in the automotive industry as a non-substitutable fuel. It can therefore be concluded that its position in Turkey's energy mix will not change in any significant way (Table 3.30).

About 30% of Turkey's electricity is produced from renewable sources. In February 2014, the Minister of Energy Taner Yıldız announced that Turkey could save over USD 5.5 billion a year in gas imports over the next 49 years if it built new renewable power plants (Winrow, 2014, p. 3).

Turkey's energy security policy strategy emphasizes the fact that the country is a receptive market for hydrocarbon resources. The country is currently experiencing an increase in demand for energy resources due to its dynamic economic development. Over the past decade, Turkey was second only to the People's Republic of China in terms of growth in demand for gas and electricity. This makes the country more and more dependent on imports of energy.

Turkey's energy policy strategy pays special attention to the need to diversify the sources of supply of energy resources, as well as to diversify their consumption. In order to reduce the country's dependence on imports, the strategy takes into account the need to increase efficiency in the state's energy sector (Figure 3.6). An important element of Turkey's policy is to take steps to liberalize the energy market. Three-quarters of the world's oil and gas reserves

TABLE 3.29   Gas imports in Turkey (billion m³)

2001	2004	2007	2009	2010	2011	2014	2015	2018	2020
15.7	21.7	35.8	35.7	38	43.9	48.8	48.4	55.1	55.1

SOURCE: HTTPS://WWW.INDEXMUNDI.COM/G/G.ASPX?V=95&C=KZ&L=EN

TABLE 3.30   Turkey's oil imports (billion barrels per day)

2001	2005	2008	2009	2010	2015	2018	2020
616.500	714.100	734.600	284.400	338.900	503.000	521.500	521.500

SOURCE: HTTPS://WWW.INDEXMUNDI.COM/G/G.ASPX?V=93&C=TU&L=EN

are located in Turkey's vicinity. Given its geographic location between producers and consumers of energy resources, Turkey is not only striving to become a transit country for oil and gas. It also intends to play an active role in the process of their redistribution. The transit and sale of energy carriers are significant sources of revenue for Turkey. They also contribute to the strengthening of its position in Europe and Asia (Misiągiewicz, 2012b). Turkey offers the easiest and safest route to transport hydrocarbons through the eastern part of its territory to the Mediterranean Sea and on to European markets. In this context, the development of the so-called Southern Corridor, which transports hydrocarbons through Turkey, may strengthen the energy security of the European Union and individual member states.

In its 2015–2019 strategy, the Ministry of Energy and Natural Resources has included environmental issues as an indispensable element of the development of the energy market, which was also confirmed in the strategy until 2023 (Ministry of Energy, 2019–2023). The document highlights the fact that Turkey's consumption of energy resources will be increasing in parallel with economic growth (Figure 3.7, Tables 3.31 and 3.32). The strategy of the Ministry of Energy and Natural Resources includes a number of elements:

- transparency and participation—participation of various political and economic actors in the development and implementation of the energy security strategy;
- credibility—conducting activities within credible and recognized state institutions and on an international scale;
- environmental awareness;
- innovation—application of modern technologies in the energy sector;
- efficiency and productivity; and
- consistency and predictability—acting in accordance with the national interest in the long and medium term and taking the international context into account (Ministry of Energy, 2019–2023).

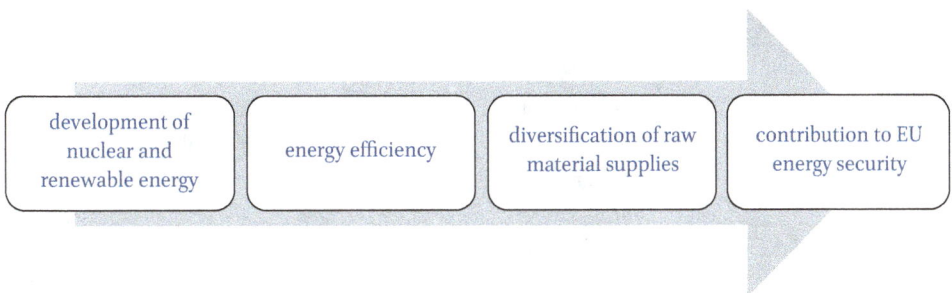

| development of nuclear and renewable energy | energy efficiency | diversification of raw material supplies | contribution to EU energy security |

FIGURE 3.6   Turkey's energy policy priorities
SOURCE: HTTP://WWW.MFA.GOV.TR/TURKEYS-ENERGY-STRATEGY.EN.MFA

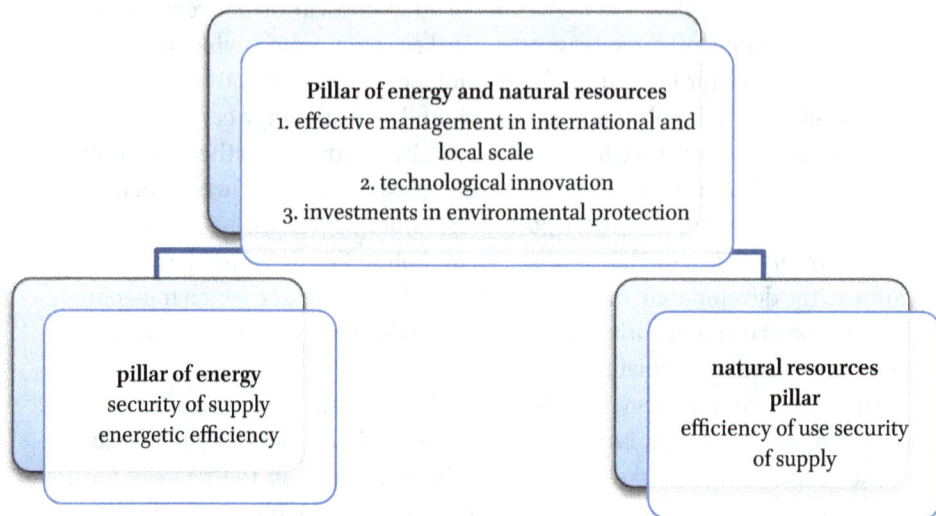

FIGURE 3.7   Strategy of the Ministry of Energy and Natural Resources
              SOURCE: HTTP://WWW.ENERJI.GOV.TR/FILE/?PATH=ROOT%2F1%2FDOCUMENTS%2F
              STRATEGIC+PLAN%2FSTRATEGICPLAN2015-2019.PDF

TABLE 3.31   Turkey's energy policy goals

Security of supplies	Efficiency and economy	Management	Efficiency at the regional and international level	Technological innovation	Investing in the environment
Objective 1. A well-functioning energy infrastructure	Objective 4. Efficiency of energy use	Objective 6. Ministry with the effectiveness of a corporation (the ministry + related state and private institutions)	Objective 9. Integration into the international energy market	Objective 11. Development of domestic technology in the area of energy and natural resources	Objective 13. Conducting market operations in an environment that is transparent, competitive, and encourages investment

TABLE 3.31   Turkey's energy policy goals (*cont.*)

Security of supplies	Efficiency and economy	Management	Efficiency at the regional and international level	Technological innovation	Investing in the environment
Objective 2. Optimized diversification of access to resources (import markets and the national energy mix)	Objective 5. Improving technological capacity to increase energy savings	Objective 7. A ministry making use of information about technologies that improve energy efficiency	Objective 10. Turkey becoming a strong player on the international scene	Objective 12. Research and development activity conducted by research institutes and universities	Objective 14. Increasing foreign investment
Objective 3. Efficient management of demand for energy		Objective 8. Coordinating the activities of the Ministry and related institutions (at the institutional level)			

SOURCE: HTTP://WWW.ENERJI.GOV.TR/FILE/?PATH=ROOT%2F1%2FDOCUMENTS%2FSTRATEGIC+PLA
N%2FSTRAT EGICPLAN2015-2019.PDF

TABLE 3.32   Energy savings in Turkey (in tonnes of oil equivalent—toe)

2009	3.623
2010	6.050
2012	8.478
2013	22.099

SOURCE: HTTP://WWW.ENERJI.GOV.TR/FILE/?PATH=ROOT%2F1%2FDOCUMENTS%2FSTRA
TEGIC+PLAN%2FSTRAT EGICPLAN2015-2019.PDF

One of the elements of the implementation of Turkey's energy policy is the involvement of domestic companies in the extraction of energy resources located outside its borders. The Turkish Petroleum Corporation (Türkiye Petrolleri Anonim Ortaklığı—TPAO) has participated in oil and gas exploration in Central Asian countries and in the Caspian region. Thus, Turkey's energy security strategy is multidimensional, as it must take into account a number of conditions arising from the specifics of the domestic energy sector and the patterns present in the global energy market.

Turkey intends to use its geostrategic position to become an economic power in the gas market (Shulte & Weiser, 2019). The country can strengthen its transit role in the multi-commodity market. At the same time, it intends to expand its capabilities in this area as a European energy hub. The COLUMBUS global gas market model makes it possible to analyze the behaviour of countries such as Turkey in the gas market (Shulte & Weiser, 2019).

It is a dynamic model that demonstrates that demand for investments in gas production and infrastructure depends on economic factors, such as investment costs. This model can explain the strategic behavior of suppliers. Transit states, which are of interest from the point of view of this method, are not tied to a single production region, but may buy gas from different countries. The simulation for 2030 compares Turkey's market power to its transit capacity.

Two scenarios were considered in the analysis of the impact of Turkey's transit power in the EU gas market (Figure 3.8). The first was the scenario of competitive transit through its territory. Producers operating as part of the Southern Gas Corridor have access to Turkey's transit system and pay only transportation costs. The country buys gas from producers participating in the Corridor and resells it to the EU with a certain profit margin. Exporting countries that operate as part of the corridor have access to the EU market only through Turkey (Shulte & Weiser, 2019).

In the second scenario, Turkey plays the role of a transit market force, where gas producers for the Corridor have no access to Turkey's transit system and are forced to sell the raw material to a Turkish exporter. Turkey's re-exports will be lower in this case than under the competitive transit scenario. The implications for the EU are an increase in the price of gas and a drop in demand for the resource. At the same time, some of the gas that will not be imported from Turkey can be replaced with increased imports of LNG or higher imports from Russia (Shulte & Weiser, 2019). In this situation, nearly all of the 13 billion m^3 of gas transports from Turkey to the EU will come from Azerbaijan. This is due to

	Conditions	
Reduction of import from Norway from 115 bcm in 2016 to 65 bcm in 2030	Gas production in the EU is decreasing from 125 bcm in 2016 to 98 bcm in 2030.	Reduction of imports from Russia from 149 bcm in 2016 to 112 bcm in 2030

Import via Turkey				
10 billion m3 reaches the EU market from the Southern Corridor - TAP project	45 billion m3 reaches the EU market in 2030	If Turkey remains competitive and producers from the Corridor will only have to pay for transit through its territory, 23 billion m3 of gas will be transported through Turkey by 2030. Almost 18 billion m3 will come from Azerbaijan, and 5 billion m3 from Iran.	The Southern Corridor covers only 9% of gas consumption in the EU	Turkey and the countries exporting gas to the EU earn more from high gas prices.

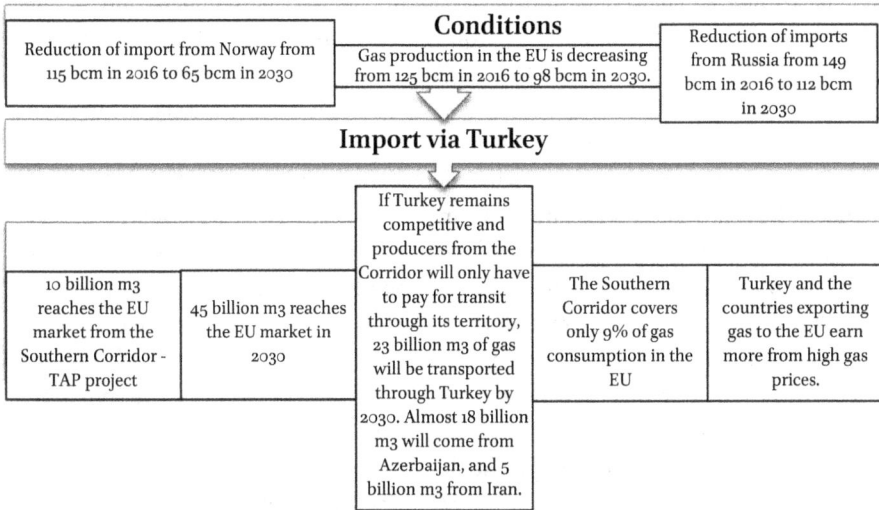

FIGURE 3.8   Scenario of competitive transit through Turkey
SOURCE: AUTHOR'S OWN COMPILATION BASED ON SHULTE & WEISER, 2019

the fact that Azerbaijan is largely dependent on transit through Turkey. However, Turkmenistan and Azerbaijan can supply gas to the EU through Russia. In this situation, Turkey would not act as a transit country for them (Shulte & Weiser, 2019).

Turkey has the potential to exercise market power in the gas sector. According to forecasts for 2030, if the country plays a competitive role, 45 billion m^3 of gas transports from Turkey will reach the EU. In this situation, countries exporting gas through the Corridor will cause market competition to intensify and drive gas prices down. With Turkey playing the role of a transit market force, transport through its territory will fall to 13 billion m^3 in 2030. At the same time, even if we take the competitive scenario into account, gas imports via Turkey and the Gas Corridor will not play an essential role on the European market. Therefore, Turkey's potential is largely limited. Moreover, the EU is increasingly focusing on direct contacts with suppliers of energy, without the involvement of transit countries. A possible solution in this context may be to harmonize Turkey's energy law with EU law in order to obtain non-discriminatory access to transit infrastructure, which would improve relations between producers from the Corridor, Turkey, and the EU (Shulte & Weiser, 2019).

According to Aleksandra Jarosiewicz, for Turkey, the construction of the Trans-Anatolian Gas Pipeline—TANAP is a means of diversifying routes and sources of gas and is expected to contribute to the improvement of its energy security in the context of its reliance on gas supplies from Russia. Turkey has ensured its access to gas supplies from Azerbaijan (transported via the TANAP) and has opened the way for further negotiations on supplies from this producer (Jarosiewicz, 2015). Cooperation with Azerbaijan also enables Turkey to implement the key objectives of its energy policy, that is to say obtaining access to energy deposits (the Turkish concern TPAO has increased its stake in Shah-Deniz from 9% to 19%) and expansion of gas infrastructure on its territory. Turkey's role in the TANAP project is not limited to the role of a transit state. It has greater access to gas sources, it is also a co-owner of the transport infrastructure, can purchase additional gas supplies from Azerbaijan, and, to a limited extent, can participate in the decisions about the transit of gas. TANAP is also a tool used by Turkey to implement its policy towards other countries. In view of this, it has been involved in talks on gas supplies with Turkmenistan (Jarosiewicz, 2015).

The European Union and Turkey are interested in maximizing gas supplies to the European market. Turkey's strategic goal is to transform itself into an energy hub in terms of gas trade, which, in addition to legal changes, ownership transformations, and investments in storage infrastructure requires, above all, an increase in gas supplies to Turkey. This encourages Turkey to be interested in connecting more actors to the Corridor. The actions of this country are thus consistent with the interests of the EU, which is also interested in obtaining the greatest possible amount of the resource from diverse sources. Turkey is becoming a highly desirable partner for both Russia and the EU. It is trying to take advantage of contradictions between these actors in order to maximize the political and financial benefits of its cooperation with each party. According to A. Jarosiewicz, Turkey's actions in the area of energy, especially in relation to the Corridor and the Turkish Stream, "will reflect a reevaluation of its policy towards the EU, Russia, and Azerbaijan" (Jarosiewicz, 2015, p. 12). One of the consequences of the emergence of the Turkish Stream infrastructure project is certainly the reinforcement of Turkey's position in its relations with Azerbaijan.

2.3   *European Union*

The European Union is one of the world's major consumers of energy resources (Figure 3.9). The issue of energy security is thus becoming a key determinant of its operations on the international scene. As one of the most dynamic energy

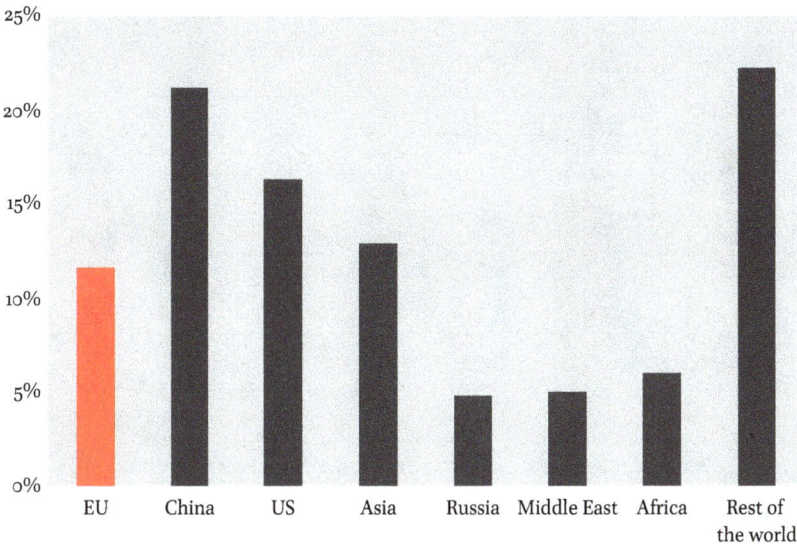

FIGURE 3.9   EU's position in the global energy consumption
SOURCE: AUTHOR'S OWN COMPILATION BASED ON, EU ENERGY IN
FIGURES 2019; INTERNATIONAL ENERGY AGENCY, WORLD ENERGY
BALANCES OVERVIEW 2018

markets on a global scale, the European Union is a key player influencing international energy security (Misiągiewicz, 2019b).

Due to the declining production of oil and gas in the North Sea and the growing consumption of energy, EU member states became interested in the Caspian region as an alternative source of energy resources. The EU has established closer cooperation with most countries in the region, under Partnership and Cooperation Agreements (PCAs). The main supplier of hydrocarbons to the European market was Russia, which treats its resource potential as an instrument of its foreign policy. It changed after the introduction of further packages of sanctions on this country. In this situation, the EU needs to become more active in order to strengthen its economic relations with alternative suppliers of energy resources. EU member states have not yet developed a coherent and solidarity-based policy in this dimension, and their actions are mainly based on the principle of subsidiarity (Duffield & Birchfield, 2011).

When analyzing the determinants of the EU energy security policy, attention should be paid to the structure of consumption of energy resources (Figure 3.10). Fossil fuels play a major role in the EU's energy mix. Oil is the

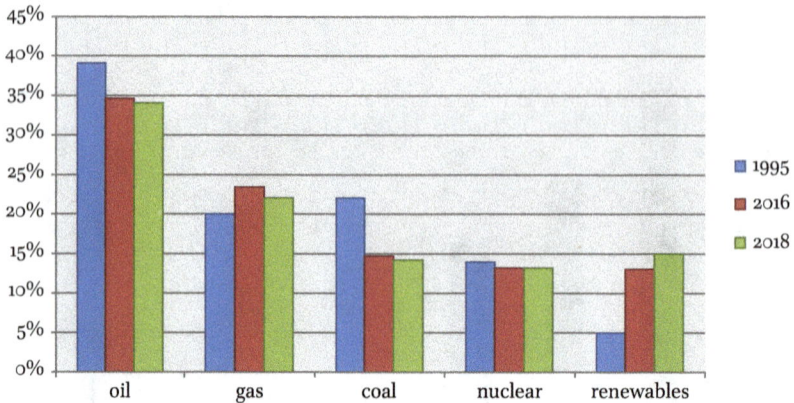

FIGURE 3.10   Consumption of energy resources in the EU
SOURCE: AUTHOR'S OWN ELABORATION EU ENERGY IN FIGURES 2020

main source of energy in the automotive industry (European Commission, 2016, 2020). Demand for oil in EU member states is maintained at around 35%. However, there has been a noticeable drop in demand for this fuel compared with 1995 (39%) due to a decrease in population growth and the growing efficiency of oil consumption. Natural gas is another significant resource in the EU's energy mix. Due to lower carbon dioxide emissions involved in its combustion and lower costs of its exploitation in comparison to renewable sources, it is expected that demand for gas will be on the rise. Comparing 1995 and 2018 data, we can conclude that gas consumption in the EU has remained relatively constant, at the level of 20–25% (European Commission—Directorate-General for Energy, 2020).

For a long time, coal was the main energy resource used to generate electricity in Europe. Although the combustion of coal results in increased carbon dioxide emissions, many countries have significant coal reserves; therefore it will be difficult to eliminate coal from the EU's energy mix. Nevertheless, coal consumption has fallen in recent years from 22% in the 1990s to 17% in 2014 and 15% in 2018 (European Commission—Directorate-General for Energy, 2019). The European Union is the world's largest consumer of nuclear energy (205.3 mtoe) (BP, 2012). Nuclear power is used in 15 EU member states. The exploitation of renewable resources is the greatest challenge for the EU's energy policy. Currently, renewable resources account for about 14% of the energy mix (European Commission—Directorate-General for Energy, 2019).

The EU is "the only major economic actor that produces 50% of its electricity without generating greenhouse gas emissions" (Communication from the Commission, 2013). In the long term, it is essential for the EU's energy security to transition to a competitive low-emission economy, which will reduce its reliance on imports of hydrocarbon resources (Skjærseth et al., 2016).

An important determinant of EU energy security policy is its reliance on the supplies of energy resources. The European Union imports about 60% of the energy it consumes (worth EUR 1 billion per day) (Table 3.33; Figures 3.11–3.13). It relies on imports for almost 90% of its oil supplies and for over 70% of its gas supplies. The main exporter of energy to the EU was Russia, which supplied as much as 40% of its demand for natural gas, 31% of its demand for oil, and 30% of its demand for coal (European Commission—Directorate-General for Energy, 2016, 2020). In terms of gas imports, there has been an increase in imports from Russia and a drop in imports from Norway. As for the oil market, there has been an increase in imports from Russia and from Norway. Coal imports are declining as a result of the European Union's decarbonization policy, which involves limiting the exploitation of the resource (Leal-Arcas et al., 2015, pp. 273–293). The situation in last year's assume a reduction in Russian exports of hydrocarbons. In the near term, this reflects the impact of voluntary and mandatory sanctions on Russian energy exports (BP Energy Outlook, 2023).

Russia exported 71% of its gas to Europe, especially to Germany and Italy before 2022. The strategic goal of EU member states is thus to diversify their sources of energy resource supplies (Rogojanu, 2009, p. 622). EU member states are currently focusing on policies aimed at reducing their reliance not only on specific energy producers, but also on supply routes and fuel consumption in the long term. This issue became crucial in the face of interruptions

TABLE 3.33   EU's reliance on imports of energy (%)

	1995	2000	2005	2010	2012	2014	2015	2016	2017	2018
Overall	43.2	46.7	52.5	52.7	53	53.5	53.9	53.8	55.1	58.2
Coal	21.5	30.5	39.3	39.4	42	45.6	42.4	41.5	43.9	43.6
Oil	74.3	75.7	82.3	84.3	88	87.4	88.8	87.1	86.7	94.6
Gas	43.5	48.9	57.7	62.4	66	67.4	69.0	70.4	74.3	83.2

SOURCE: EU ENERGY IN FIGURES 2020

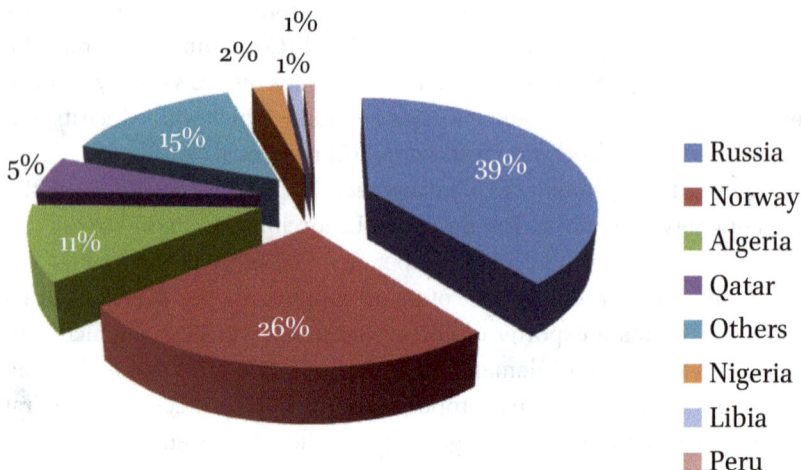

FIGURE 3.11   Main gas importers into the EU, 2017
SOURCE: AUTHOR'S OWN ELABORATION BASED ON EUROPEAN
COMMISSION, EU ENERGY IN FIGURES 2019

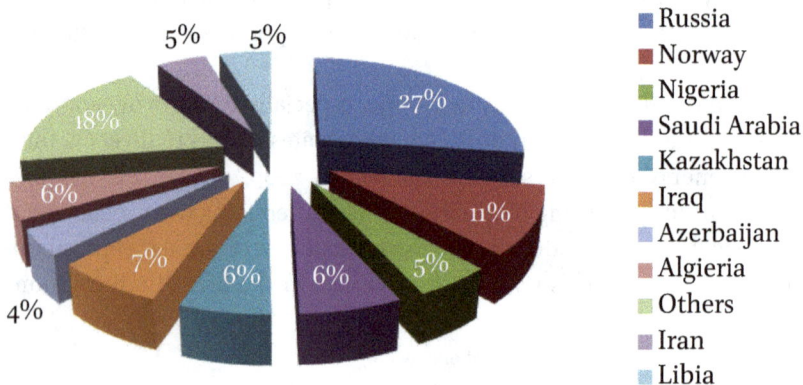

FIGURE 3.12   Main oil importers into the EU, 2017
SOURCE: AUTHOR'S OWN ELABORATION BASED ON EUROPEAN
COMMISSION, EU ENERGY IN FIGURES 2019

in gas supplies from Russia in the winter of 2006. At that time, it restricted
the supply of this resource to Ukraine, which was the main transit country for
Russian hydrocarbons to the European market. This situation had a significant
impact on the energy security in the EU. Another energy crisis between the EU

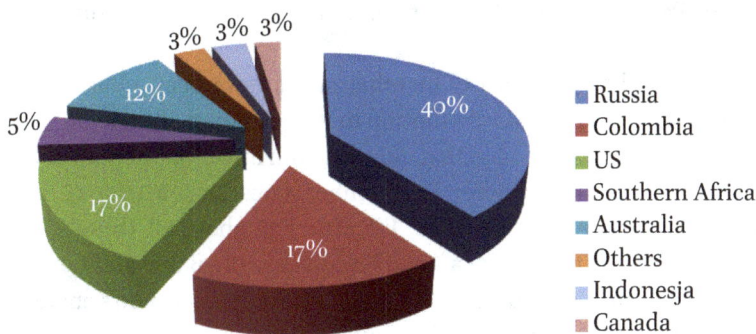

FIGURE 3.13   Main coal importers into the EU, 2017
SOURCE: AUTHOR'S OWN ELABORATION BASED ON, EUROPEAN
COMMISSION, EU ENERGY IN FIGURES 2019

and Russia occurred in January 2009, when the Russian corporation Gazprom suspended gas supplies to Ukraine again.

The current military conflict between Ukraine and Russia lead to another major energy crisis. Turbulence in international energy market become after Russia's invasion of Ukraine on February 24, 2022. In recent months, energy prices have spiked to record highs—most notably in Europe—causing potentially significant economic impacts (IEA, January 13, 2022). These include multiple negative effects on energy companies and consumers—in some cases, resulting in government interventions to limit the damage. The increases in energy prices have also contributed to broader price inflation that is affecting many economies worldwide (IEA, January 13, 2022). "Nobody is under any illusions anymore. Russia's use of its natural gas resources as an economic and political weapon show Europe needs to act quickly to be ready to face considerable uncertainty over Russian gas supplies next winter," said IEA Executive Director Fatih Birol (IEA, March 3, 2022, p. 1). Kadri Simson, European Commissioner for Energy, declared, that: "Reducing our dependence on Russian gas is a strategic imperative for the European Union. [...] But Russia's attack on Ukraine is a watershed moment" (IEA, March 3, 2022, p. 2).

In such situation, depending on a single producer of energy resources is dangerous to importers not only in economic but also in political terms. The energy sector is in fact used by states as an instrument of foreign policy, which has been increasingly common in Russia's case. Since the crises of 2006 and 2009, the EU has enhanced its capacity to cooperate, as well as to avoid and mitigate potential disruptions in gas supplies (Regulation No. 994/2010 of the

European Parliament, 2010). Investments in backup infrastructure are now mandatory.

Since December 3, 2014, EU member states have been obliged to meet demand even when there is a disruption to the operation of their largest infrastructure facility. In addition to that, flows in both directions have to take place on all cross-border links between EU member states. The question of the security of power supply concerns every EU state but, above all, those which are less integrated with the European market, that are the Baltic and Central and Eastern European states. At the same time, the European Union's energy security should be viewed in the broader context of the conditions on the international energy market (Proedrou, 2017, pp. 182–198).

Adopting the "European Energy Security Strategy" on May 28, 2014, the Commission outlined a plan to strengthen the security of energy supplies, meaning in the face of the threat of politicization (European Commission, 2014a). In view of the situation in Ukraine and the resulting threat of disruptions of gas supplies to the EU, this strategy identified the measures that should be put in place immediately to increase the EU's resilience to major gas supply disruptions, particularly during the winter period. As part of these immediate measures, on June 27, 2014, the European Council endorsed the Commission's proposal to carry out "stress tests to assess the resilience of the European gas network to severe disruptions of gas supply to the EU in winter" (Communication from the Commission, 2013). According to the Energy Security Strategy, the Commission and Member States should strengthen their cooperation within the Gas Coordination Group, and, above all, monitor natural gas flows and storage levels, as well as coordinate national risk assessments and emergency response plans at the Community level or regional level (Communication from the Commission, 2013). The EU Energy Security Strategy considers what actions need to be taken in the short, medium, and long term (Tables 3.34 and 3.35). It is based on eight main pillars:
– the ability to act quickly to overcome energy crises;
– strengthening collaborative mechanisms to assess risks, develop contingency plans, and protect strategic infrastructure;
– reducing demand for energy;
– building a well-functioning and fully integrated internal energy market;
– increasing energy production in the European Union;
– developing energy technologies;
– diversifying supplies and energy infrastructure; and
– strengthening the coordination of national energy policies. (European Commission, 2015).

The document "Secure, affordable and sustainable energy" sets out the strategy behind the EU's proposed energy union package. Since energy issues in

TABLE 3.34   EU Energy Security Strategy

Short term	Long term
Solidarity (support for member states particularly vulnerable to disruptions in energy supply) Crisis prevention in case of supply disruptions at the regional level and within the EU mechanisms Increasing energy stocks Possibility of reversing the direction of the flow of resources in the pipelines	Increasing energy efficiency Developing a common energy market Increasing extraction from domestic sources Developing energy technology Diversifying supplies Speaking with one voice on external energy policy

SOURCE: HTTP://EC.EUROPA.EU/ENERGY/SECURITY_OF_SUPPLY_EN.HTM

TABLE 3.35   EU energy objectives

Achieved in 2020	To be achieved by 2030	To be achieved by 2050
Reducing greenhouse gas emissions by at least 20% compared to 1990 levels Increasing the share of energy from renewable sources in the total energy consumption to 20% Improving energy efficiency by 20%	Reducing greenhouse gas emissions by 40% compared to 1990 levels Increasing the share of energy from renewable sources in total energy consumption to 27% Improving energy efficiency by 27–30% Transporting 15% of energy via cross-border interconnections (i.e., 15% of electricity generated in the EU can be transmitted to other EU member states)	Reducing greenhouse gas emissions by 80–95% compared to 1990 levels

SOURCE: HTTP://EUROPA.EU/POL/ENER/INDEX_PL.HTM

the EU are regulated at the national level, the goal of the energy union is to "transform the EU energy system, currently consisting of national frameworks, into a single EU-wide framework" (Energy Union Package, 2015, p. 3) (Table 3.36). The document identifies five main areas that provide the basis for an

TABLE 3.36   Pillars of the energy union strategy

Security of supplies	Reduction of emissions	A fully integrated internal market	Energy efficiency	Research and innovations
Diversifying energy sources, including more efficient use of own sources; close cooperation with the EU's neighbors (including eight non-EU countries which are members of the Energy Community) in the event of energy shortages or crises; establishing a body responsible for joint gas purchases in emergency situations	The EU's objectives for the energy sector until 2030 include the reduction of greenhouse gas emissions by 40% compared to 1990 levels. The activities required to achieve this objective include: revision of the EU Emissions Trading Scheme and the promotion of investment in new technologies and new infrastructure; becoming a world leader in renewable energy, such as solar energy and wind energy	The completion of the development of the internal energy market in the EU will be achieved by way of: creating more interconnections between EU member states, which will facilitate a fast and unobstructed flow of energy; intensifying of the construction and maintenance of the necessary infrastructure elements; increasing competition between suppliers, which should enable price reductions	Reducing energy consumption will reduce the demand for energy imports, result in lower pollution, and help preserve internal energy sources	The EU foresees a breakthrough in low-carbon technologies. It can be achieved by coordinating research and project funding in collaboration with the private sector

SOURCE: EUROPEAN COMMISSION (2015)

energy union strategy, aiming to bring about greater energy security, stability, and competitiveness (Energy Union Package, 2015, p. 4).

On 30 November 2016, the European Commission published the so-called Winter Package, which is a set of recommendations for the EU energy and climate policy in the years 2020–2030. The package contains, among others, proposals for reforming the energy union governance system, amending the Energy Efficiency Directive, the RES (Renewables) Directive, and the plan to complete the development of the European energy market (that is to say, integrate the national and regional markets to enable free trade in electricity). The reform package includes legislative proposals, including plans to reduce coal subsidies and increase energy efficiency to 30%, and to reduce CO_2 emissions by 40% before 2030.

According to the EU Energy Strategy 2020, "energy security is closely related to the priorities of foreign and security policies. Diversification of energy sources, supplies, and transport routes is a cornerstone of security in the EU" (European Commission, 2020). The 2014 EU Energy Security Strategy stated that "prosperity and security depend on sufficient energy supplies" (European Commission, 2013a, p. 2). It also stressed that the EU needs an energy security strategy that would be resilient to external crises and supply disruptions in the short term and would reduce dependence on specific fuels, sources of supply, and export routes in the long term (European Commission, 2013a).

In contrast to the enlargement process, the EU's policy towards the newly formed post-Soviet states was more cautious. Without the prospect of enlargement, the EU had little influence on developments in the Caspian region. Nevertheless, the EU referred to its immediate neighborhood in numerous policy documents. Yet, no coherent policy towards the Caspian region was formulated in this context (Alieva, 2012, pp. 443–453). At the same time, EU member states have shown a lot of interest in accessing energy resources in the region.

An important initiative of the European Union in the Caspian region was the TRACECA (http://traceca-org) project, launched in 1993, and the INOGATE (International Oil and Gas Transport to Europe; http://inogate.org) project, in operation since 1996. The aim of these initiatives was to connect Europe and the Caspian states in terms of transport and energy infrastructure. However, the unstable situation in the region and Russia's domination of the European energy market led to stagnation in EU initiatives in the post-Soviet region in the 1990s. The EU has thus not been active in promoting multilateral policy in the Caspian region due to the fact that it has no member states there. The TRACECA project referred solely to transport issues in the region.

The main objective of the EU's policy since the 1990s has been the construction of oil terminals and transport infrastructure as part of the TRACECA project, with the view to connecting energy resources in the Central Asia region with the European market. However, relying on infrastructure projects only was not enough and in October 2007 the EU published a document titled, "The European Union and Central Asia: A Strategy for a New Partnership." The aim of this strategy was to make the EU a significant political actor in the region. At the same time, it lacked precisely specified goals. The strategy included axiological issues, such as the promotion of democratic values, and pragmatic issues, such as the access to oil and gas resources. However, it is not clear how the EU will behave in the case of conflict between these two dimensions (Kassenova, 2009, pp. 12–22).

Considering the implementation of the EU's energy security policy in the Caspian region, its relations with the states in the region and its involvement in the construction of transport infrastructure should be taken into account. Azerbaijan has the best relations with the EU compared to other Caspian states. Western countries treat it as a partner in the areas of security and energy. It has also been included in the "Broader Black Sea region" project (Alieva, 2012, pp. 443–453). The country has also been included in the European Neighbourhood Policy (ENP) project and then in the Eastern Partnership. At the same time, the EU has not pressed the issue of promoting the democratic system in the country. Even if the ENP Azerbaijan Country Strategy Paper addressed the issue of transformation of the political system, it did not condition cooperation in the area of energy. The conclusion of this document largely reflected the EU's realpolitik towards the Caspian region, which was less focused on the promotion of democracy (Alieva, 2012, pp. 443–453).

During the Baku Energy Summit in November 2008, representatives of European countries signed a declaration aimed at intensifying cooperation in implementing alternative energy export projects and criticizing Russia's policy of "monopolising the energy sector and applying pressure in it" (Alieva, 2012, pp. 443). Thus, the EU needs to develop a common and coherent policy towards partners producing and transporting energy and to create an appropriate institutional framework in this regard.

The goal in this context will be to develop the external dimension of the energy market.

> The EU must demonstrate that it is prepared to engage in the Caspian
> region [...] on a long-term political and economic basis. It must also support major supplier countries like Azerbaijan, Turkmenistan [...] and
> other countries in the region of Central Asia in developing their energy

sectors in an efficient and sustainable manner, in line with EU trade and
investment rules. (Communication from the Commission, 2011)

Thus, relations between the EU and the Caspian states are gaining momentum
in direct proportion to the development of the energy policy in this structure.

The most recent example of closer cooperation between the European Union
and Azerbaijan is the Eighteenth Cooperation Council Meeting held in Brussels
on 19 July 2022. The aim of the meeting was to review the overall EU–Azerbaijan relations and to discuss mutual interest for future cooperation (European
Commission–Council of the European Union, 2022). Energy was therefore a
key issue in the bilateral cooperation between the EU and Azerbaijan. Starting
the new Memorandum of Understanding on a Strategic Partnership in the Field
of Energy is the best example. Moreover, the EU reconfirmed its engagement
in "promoting a secure, stable and prosperous South Caucasus" (Communication from the Commission, 2011). It emphasized its commitment to support the
Azerbaijan and Armenia in progressing towards a comprehensive peace settlement. The Cooperation Council Meeting also "exchanged on the cooperation
within the Eastern Partnership framework, in particular in view of rolling out
the Economic and Investment Plan which will deliver tangible benefits for the
people of Azerbaijan and EU's support to the country's economic diversification, green and digital transition" (Communication from the Commission, 2011).

The construction of pipeline infrastructure from the Caspian region is not
only intended to make the European market independent of Russian export
routes, but also to strengthen the independence of producer countries in the
region. The BTC oil pipeline, an example of key energy infrastructure from
the Caspian region, is a symbol of such a policy, even though it transports no
more than 2–3% of the world's oil supplies. In 2010, the Commission identified infrastructure priorities for the next two decades, including the Southern Gas Corridor among them (European Commission, 2010a, p. 1). "Europe's
energy infrastructure is the key nervous system of our economy. The energy
policy goals, as well as the economic goals of Europe 2020, cannot be achieved
without developing European infrastructure" (European Commission, 2010b).
The Commission's goal with regard to the Corridor is to directly connect the
gas market of the EU with gas resources in the Caspian and Middle Eastern
regions (European Commission, 2010b).

The Commission also stated that "nothing affected EU countries more, at
the time of the 2009 gas crisis between Russia and Ukraine, than poorly developed energy infrastructure" (European Commission, 2010b, p. 2).

It stressed the deepening dependence of Eastern European countries on
a single resource and the need for "diversification of gas supply sources, gas

export routes, as well as a fully integrated and bidirectional gas infrastructure system," which was to be achieved by 2020 (European Commission, 2010b, p. 2). Such a development is to be linked to the EU's strategy towards third countries, mainly suppliers and transit countries. The Commission's goal is to make sure that each EU region has access to at least two sources of gas. The former president of the European Commission, José Manuel Barosso, described the Southern Corridor project as a breakthrough in the process of expanding the EU's energy security, while the Commissioner for Energy Gunther Oettinger described Azerbaijan as a "new partner for gas" (EU Commission Welcomes Decision, 2013, p. 2). Moreover, the president of the Commission commented on the decision to develop the Shah Deniz 2 gas fields, declaring that: "this is a strategic opening of the door to a strong energy security for Europe" (EU Commission Welcomes Decision, 2013, p. 2). And further: "Europe must continue its efforts to diversify supplies and develop the Southern Gas Corridor to supply south-eastern Europe and to achieve the medium-term objective of importing about 10% of European demand from the Caspian region and the Middle East" (Communication from the Commission, 2013). A key element of EU energy policy is to complete the development of the internal energy market and increase the number of energy links between member states. These goals are difficult to implement, as the strategies and preferences of member states in this respect are not coherent.

Energy security is a key element of the EU's engagement in the Caspian region. In this context, Azerbaijan and Turkey are countries of particular interest to the European market due to the routing of gas pipeline infrastructure. The problem, however, is that the possibility of making the Southern Corridor a wide-ranging project, enabling the participation of other countries rich in energy resources, is limited due to political and technological factors. Thus, the potential of the Caspian region has not yet been realized. The EU's main motivation for developing the Corridor project is the need to diversify access to energy sources. Energy infrastructure from the Caspian region to the European market is not only the result of economic calculation, but also a symbol of Western presence in this sensitive region.

3   Conclusion

The above discussion takes into account the specifics of energy security policies of individual participants of the energy market in the Caspian region. It identified their strategies, determinants, and actions in this area. It can be concluded that oil and gas production and transportation in the Caspian region is now the ground of rivalry between state and non-state actors. Thus, the Caspian region plays an increasingly important role in contemporary international relations in the economic, as well as in political and cultural terms.

Analyzing the conditions in which the oil and gas sectors in Azerbaijan operates, we need to consider the main threats to the country's energy security. The first is the risk that the production of energy resources may diminish. The second consists in restricting oil and gas exports. Each of these threats has to be considered and analyzed in the context of the internal and external functioning of the energy market. Azerbaijan, like most countries of its kind, has not taken advantage of the economic boom to implement structural reforms and remains dependent on income from the exports of fossil fuels. If oil and gas prices fall to low levels, the result will be an economic slowdown, an outflow of investments, a drop-in investment activity, an increase in inflation, and a reduction in income, accompanied by a rise in unemployment. Uncertainty about oil prices motivates thinking in terms of a "post-oil period." Azerbaijan continues to be a serious actor on the international stage, whose resources do not so much dictate the rules of the game as they ensure that the country remains an influential regional player. Despite numerous threats and problems, the country is trying to pursue a balanced energy policy based on its geopolitical position and historical legacy. Its aim in this context is to create an atmosphere of cooperation based on equality and mutual benefits in the region. Currently, Azerbaijan is gaining importance not only in the energy dimension, but also in the political and strategic dimension, as evidenced by the tightening of cooperation with the EU in 2022.

As a major exporter of hydrocarbons in the international market, Kazakhstan is interested in expanding the pipeline system. The country aims to diversify its oil and gas export routes. Exploration plans for the Caspian shelf, as well as increased production in the Tengiz and Karachaganak and Kashagan fields, create new opportunities related to increasing the capacity of the pipeline infrastructure. A drastic drop in oil prices on global markets may be a problem for Kazakhstan and its extractive industry, as well as for other rentier states in the Caspian region. In the context of Russia's weakening in the Central Asia region, Kazakhstan's geopolitical position may change. It can become a more assertive and independent player.

The policy of diversifying energy export routes to global markets could not be fully implemented by Turkmenistan due to various systemic problems. The country is dependent on hydrocarbons supplies and, like most post-Soviet states, sells gas below the prevailing price on the European market. Energy-based cooperation dominates Turkmenistan's relations with European countries and China, which treat Turkmen gas as an additional source of supply. In this context, the choice of partners between a booming China and a geographically distant Europe limits Turkmenistan's room for maneuver.

Iran has failed to develop a coherent long-term energy policy in the Caspian region. It limited its role to reactive adaptation to the situation in its immediate environment. Despite references to a "common cultural heritage" associated with Islam and the Persian language, Iran has not achieved the status of a significant actor in the region. From 1991, Iran tried to establish economic relations with the newly established states of the region, especially in trade, transport, and the construction of pipeline infrastructure. At the same time, it tried to strengthen its cultural and scientific ties with these countries, emphasizing the historical "Persian basis" of Central Asian culture. Iran's problematic relations with the West, and especially with the US, were the main obstacle to the realization of the country's ambitions in the region. Moreover, the internal rivalry between political factions in Iran itself was an obstacle to the creation of a coherent and consistent regional policy.

Russia's goal was to take control of the energy sectors in the post-Soviet area and to prevent the former Soviet republics from selling energy resources directly to the West. Analyzing the role of this superpower, not only in the Caspian region but also in the entire area of the so-called "near abroad," Moisés Naím, former Minister of Trade and Industry of Venezuela and editor-in-chief of the journal *Foreign Policy*, wrote that, "Russia's future depends as much on the geology and ideology of its leaders" (Treisman, 2010, p. 85). The "large amounts of oil go hand in hand with public weakness, poverty, inequality and corruption" (ibid, p. 85). It seems that both of them hit the nail on the head when it comes to the specificity of the so-called petro-state, that is to say, countries with an economy based on profits from the fuel sector. The current marginalization of Russia in the international arena due to its aggression against Ukraine should not be forgotten. This issue will have implications for Russia's role in the post-Soviet region.

Kazakhstan and Turkmenistan are strategic states in the transport of fossil fuels to China. The activity of this power in the Caspian region is conditioned not only by economic but also by geopolitical factors. China is a significant regional player, trying to eliminate the influence of the West and Russia. In the last decade, China has made Caspian states dependent on cheap loans and investments in their energy sectors. This superpower treats the Caspian region in terms of the realization of far-reaching economic and political interests. As a result, the energy dimension is dominant in China's relations with its Western neighbors. It can be concluded that the PRC's policy in the region will not change in the near future. Energy market analysts in China suggest a long-term strategy in the Caspian region. It should be based on the complexity of cooperation—taking into account not only price, income, or industrial policy, but also diplomacy. If China moves in this direction, it will be more effective, not only in terms of energy policy but also in terms of achieving its goals in a more transparent manner, inspiring greater trust on an international scale. Finally, China is still a developing country and therefore needs a peaceful environment to implement modernization projects in the economic and energy dimensions.

Turkey is a very receptive market for energy resources. It is located close to 70% of the world's sources of energy resources, mainly located in the Middle East and the Caspian Sea basin. The priority goal of this country is to benefit not only from transit, but also from the re-export of energy resources. Turkey is interested in building as many oil and gas pipelines as possible through its territory, in which energy from Russia, Central Asia and the Middle East would flow in various directions. Turkey also wants to ensure the diversification of supplies in this way and, as a result, to significantly strengthen its own energy security. This country is a challenge to the energy security of the European Union, which it often uses as a bargaining chip during accession negotiations with this organization.

The EU, as one of the most dynamic energy markets on a global scale, is a key player influencing international energy security. The main problem, however, is that the EU is heavily dependent on imported energy resources. The main supplier of hydrocarbons to the European market was Russia. However, in the face of successive packages of sanctions related to aggression against Ukraine, Russia has been eliminated as the main supplier. Thus, the EU is increasingly interested in tightening energy cooperation with the Caspian countries.

According to risk theory, the risk of breaking the energy cooperation of European states with Russia in the face of the war in Ukraine may cause a serious economic crisis (the destructive aspect). Simultaneously, on the other hand, it may affect the emergence of alternative opportunities to economic security through the acceleration of energy transformation towards the development of renewable energy (the constructive aspect). As a consequence, paradoxically, Russia's war in Ukraine may speed up the implementation of the EU's plan to reduce dependence on nonrenewable resources and motivate the member states to pursue a more diversified energy security policy. In such a situation, increased activity of the EU is needed in order to tighten economic relations with alternative suppliers of energy resources.

EU countries have not developed a coherent policy in this respect so far, and their actions are mainly individual. The EU Energy Security Strategy reflects the real problems of the energy market, however, in this context, the declarative sphere should be distinguished from the real interests and needs of individual member states. It is very difficult for 27 countries to speak with one voice, especially considering the fact that participants in the energy market are not only states but also non-state actors, such as transnational corporations, which are also driven by their own interests. A key element of the current EU energy policy is completing the internal energy market and increasing the number of energy connections between member states.

Encouraging economic reforms and transparency in exchange for improving the position on the European market and in the security dimension is an effective strategy of the West towards the newly created states of the Caspian region. It could be implemented not only as a result of direct cooperation between Europe and the countries of the region, but also with the involvement of international corporations. In such a situation, a real diversification of transport routes is needed as a non-zero-sum game. The rivalry between the superpowers, will not stabilize the region, but it may cause further conflicts.

CHAPTER 4

Geopolitical Routes and Policies to Transport Fossil Fuels as a Reflection of Energy Interdependence

The policy of transporting energy resources is a reflection of international energy interdependence. The routes of the pipelines are mapped taking into account economic conditions, but they are also the result of geopolitical actions of states. Pipeline diplomacy is a reflection of thinking about the Caspian region in geopolitical terms. The aim of the research is therefore to analyze the main directions of oil and gas exports, taking into account the projects that are in operation and those that have not yet been implemented (Coburn, 2021, p. 124).

As early as the 19th century, the Caucasus region was an important energy transport corridor, through which oil and gas reached the international market from the Caspian Sea. The subject of energy security policy in the Caspian region since the beginning of the 1990s, has been the issue of how to transport Caspian energy resources to the world market. The development of the transport infrastructure in the Caspian region not only connects the individual states of the region physically, economically and politically, but also strengthens the regionalization process (German, 2018, p. 194). This is because pipelines motivate countries to cross-border cooperation at various levels and lead to closer strategic cooperation.

Modern pipeline infrastructure in the Caspian region began to emerge in the post-Cold War era, when new states appeared in the post-Soviet area. Oil and gas companies and Western powers began to cooperate with the countries of the region. However, in the early 1990s, the Caspian states could only export their energy resources via Russia.

Kazakhstan did not have its own pipeline infrastructure system and had to use Russian pipelines to transport its oil to foreign markets. This country also used road and rail transport, which generated high costs. Thus, the construction of a wide pipeline system was one of the priorities that determined the efficiency of the oil industry in Kazakhstan. The government analyzed various options for the construction of pipelines in consultation with foreign investors (Zonn & Semenov, 2016, pp. 75–84) (Table 4.1).

In Turkmenistan, the gas pipeline system during the Soviet period was also part of the integrated infrastructure of the USSR, which made access to Western markets difficult. The country had enormous energy potential as the second-largest gas producer in the post-Soviet area after Russia, but having no

© JUSTYNA MISIĄGIEWICZ, 2024 | DOI:10.1163/9789004697614_006

TABLE 4.1   States and companies participating in the production and transit of Caspian oil

Exporting country	Transit countries	Oil terminals	Participants in oil consortia	Corporations
Azerbaijan	Iran, Georgia, Russia, Turkey	Iran, Georgia, Russia, Turkey	US, France, Norway, UK, Turkey, Russia, Italy, Iran	Amoco, BP, McDermott, Unocal, SOCAR, LUKoil, Gazprom, Statoil, Exxon, Turkiye Petrolleri, Pennzoil, Itochu, Ramco, Delta, BOTAS, Fluxys, Enagas, Axpo
Kazakhstan	Azerbaijan, Georgia, Russia, Turkmenistan	Turkey, Russia, Georgia, China, Iran	US, Italy, UK, France, Russia, China	Oman Oil Company, Transneft, Chevron, LUKARCO, BG Overseas Holding Limited, ENI International, Lukoil, Rosnieft, CNPC, SINOPEC
Turkmenistan	Azerbaijan, Afghanistan, China	Iran, Pakistan	US, Argentina, Turkey, Russia, Malaysia, UK, Netherlands, Iran	Sofregaz, Chinese Petroleum Engineering& Construction Corporation, CNOC, CNPC, Mitsubishi Corporation, Exxon, Gazprom

SOURCE: AUTHOR'S OWN COMPILATION

connections to the Western market, it incurred high costs of transport through the territories of Uzbekistan, Kazakhstan, and Russia. As a result, gas sales by Turkmenistan dropped many times in the first years of independence. The need to build new pipelines was closely related to the development of oil and

gas fields with high resource potential. Contrary to Kazakhstan and Turkmenistan, Azerbaijan's position in terms of pipeline geopolitics was more favorable.
Pipelines, even those built during the Soviet period, were geographically closer
to the European market. In the post-independence period, Azerbaijan has
become an attractive country for the Western market due to its energy potential and geopolitical position (Zonn & Semenov, 2016).

Russia has focused mainly on pipeline infrastructure projects, operational
and planned, which transported hydrocarbon resources from Kazakhstan,
Azerbaijan and Turkmenistan through its territory. Russia did not have significant resources in the Caspian region, but its undoubted advantage was
its extensive export infrastructure. The competition for routes for the export
of fossil fuels began in the 1990s, and after independence, the Caspian states,
together with oil corporations, started the construction of new pipelines
exporting Caspian hydrocarbons. Discussions on the transit of Caspian fossil
fuels resulted largely from the interests of individual countries and evolved
towards an international political and strategic confrontation.

Thus, the architecture of the regional pipeline network was conditioned by
economic and political issues. Western countries have been actively involved
in the process of transforming the Caspian oil and gas market and developing
pipeline infrastructure projects that reflect their interests. The West's goal
is thus to diversify the routes of energy exports from the Caspian region to
Western markets. The issue of pipelines is also an important foreign policy
problem for Caspian states and a tool of competition for a dominant position
in the region (Voytolovsky & Kosolapov, 1999, pp. 307 323). This resulted in the
emergence of a variety of pipeline projects, some of which could not be implemented for objective economic reasons, but they played a role in the dialogue
process between Western and newly established Caspian states.

John Roberts analyzed the numerous routes of oil transportation from the
Caspian region and distinguished three geographical directions:

1.   Northern—Russian;
2.   Central—Caucasian; and
3.   South—Iran–Pakistan (Roberts, 1996, p. 84).

It would be appropriate in this context to add a fourth direction—eastern,
Asian (Misiągiewicz, 2022, p. 509).

The northern or Euro-Russian direction is mainly associated with the transit of oil from Kazakhstan, especially from the Tengiz field, through the territory of Russia to Novorossiysk and from Azerbaijan to Novorossiysk. Transport
routes pass through Black Sea ports before reaching Western markets. This
poses a number of security risks due to the need for oil tankers to pass through
the Black Sea and the narrow Bosphorus Strait in Istanbul. Over 1.2 million
barrels of oil are transported on this route yearly. The Central, Caucasian, or

Western direction, includes the export of gas from Azerbaijan, via Georgia and Turkey, to the European market. Deliveries from Kazakhstan can also be included here. The southern, or Iranian–Pakistani, direction involves exports from Azerbaijan to Iran and Turkey. Additionally, oil from Kazakhstan can be transported via Turkmenistan to Iran or Pakistan. The Eastern, Asian, or Sino-Japanese direction includes the transport of oil and gas to China and further on, to Japan. If we analyze the geography of pipeline construction in the region, the conclusion is that the above classification is fully valid.

1 The Northern Route of Fossil Fuel Exports from the Caspian Region

From the time the first oil well was drilled in 1846, the development of the oil sector began to shape changes in the energy market in Baku. Thanks to the dynamic technological development, as early as 1894 oil production in Azerbaijan equaled the production of this raw material in the US. In 1901, Baku was the first oil production area on a global scale (Huseynzade & Aliyev, 2016, pp. 169–196). Back then, over 20 million tonnes of oil were produced worldwide, half of it in the territory of today's Azerbaijan. The region's dominance in terms of energy potential resulted mainly from the scale of the production of purified crude oil and the development of the refining industry. In this context, Azerbaijan was technologically highly developed in the energy sector. From 1872, the old mining methods, consisting of excavation to extract underground oil, were replaced by mechanical boreholes, exploring deeper deposits of fossil fuels. In the same year, the first oil company of the Nobel brothers was established in Baku, and foreign capital started flowing into Azerbaijan. From 1877, more and more companies and investors flocked to Azerbaijan. In 1879, more than 126 companies and individual entrepreneurs worked in the oil sector (Huseynzade & Aliyev, 2016). Then, in 1878, the first metal tanks for oil and petroleum products were built on the Apsheronian Peninsula for the company of the Nobel brothers, designed by the Russian engineer W. G. Shukhov. In the same year, the first 9 km pipeline from Baakhana to the Black City was built. The pipe diameter was 7.62 cm and its throughput was 1.280 tonnes per day. It was the first pipeline in Russian history. The following year, a second, more technologically advanced, 12.26 km-long pipeline was built at the request of the entrepreneur G. M. Lioznowa (Huseynzade & Aliyev, 2016). In 1884, there were already five pipelines in the Baku area, and the daily capacity of three of them (Balakhany–Black City, Balakhany–Surakhan, and Surakhan–Zykh) was 3,200 tonnes of oil (Huseynzade & Aliyev, 2016). In 1887, the construction of the longest Baku–Batumi pipeline at 887 km was begun, and was launched in 1907.

The next pipelines in the region were built in the Soviet period. The Novorossiysk–Baku pipeline with a capacity of 22 million tonnes was designed to transport crude oil to the Baku refinery. The source of the oil was the Buzachi field. Later, the pipeline was used for reverse oil transport from the Chirag fields and was called the Northern Export Pipeline Route. The pipeline runs from the Sangachal terminal to the Black Sea. Its length is 1.330 km, of which 231 km runs through Azerbaijan. The pipe diameter is 720 mm, there are 12 pumping stations. The maximum capacity of the pipeline is 6 million tonnes per year (Huseynzade & Aliyev, 2016).

The Mozdok–Kazimagomed gas pipeline, with an annual capacity of 13 billion m³, was designed to supply gas to Azerbaijan. The gas pipeline was commissioned in 1983, and later on, when Azerbaijan became a gas exporter, its direction was changed. The total length of the infrastructure is 680 km (200 km in Azerbaijan). Gas-measuring stations were built as part of the pipeline in 2003 in Shirvanovka (Huseynzade & Aliyev, 2016).

After the collapse of the USSR, Russia's position in terms of pipeline transportation in the Caspian region changed (Bayramov, 2019, pp. 159–181, 2022). The emergence of new, independent states off the Caspian Sea has reduced Russia's dominance in exporting energy resources. The country's pipeline policy has evolved. It had to take into account the presence of corporations and Western organizations in the region that participated in the transport policy (Zhiltsov, 2016, pp. 345–400). Russia's current policy with regard to the transport of Caspian resources was shaped in December 1991, after the formation of the CIS (Zonn & Zhiltsov, 2008, p. 544).

The country sought to maintain its own pipelines and export capacities. Russia's goal was also to continue to control the export of energy resources from the Caspian region. It insisted that the newly created states of the region transport their resources to or through Russia. In a situation where the Caspian states did not have their own extensive pipeline infrastructure, Russia's role in this was fundamental. Thus, the issue of pipeline policy has become a sensitive problem for Russia's foreign policy in the region, especially in the context of geopolitical rivalry with external actors (Zhiltsov & Zonn, 2008, p. 52).

Currently, Caspian oil is transported mainly via routes dominated by Russia and Europe. An important route is the Black Sea, where the main role is played by the terminals in Novorossiysk (680.000 b/d), Tuapse (200.000 b/d), Odessa (200.000 b/d), Supsie (200.000 b/d), and Batumi (70.000 b/d). To get to Western markets, tankers have to pass through the narrow Turkish straits (Mahnovski, 2003).

A new stage in the development of Azerbaijan's oil industry began after the country gained independence and under President Heydar Aliyev. In

September 1994, a contract was signed for the exploitation of the Azeri, Chirag, and Gunashli fields. Due to the exceptional economic and political importance of this event, it was called the "contract of the century." The contract participants were 14 of the world's largest corporations (Amoco, BP, McDermott, Unocal, SOCAR, LUKoil, Statoil, Exxon, Turkiye Petrolleri, Pennzoil, Itochu, Ramco, Delta) from eight countries (Azerbaijan, USA, Great Britain, Russia, Turkey, Norway, Japan, and Saudi Arabia). This was the starting point for the implementation of the Azerbaijani energy strategy (Huseynzade & Aliyev, 2016, pp. 169–196). According to preliminary estimates of the amount of crude oil produced under the famous contract, it was set at 511 million tonnes, but it turned out that these reserves increased to 730 million tonnes (Huseynzade & Aliyev, 2016). In 1995, as part of the Early Oil Project, the Chirag-1 platform was modernized in line with international standards. New drilling equipment was installed and equipment above the sea was modernized. Oil production in this area started in 1997 (Huseynzade & Aliyev, 2016).

The production of hydrocarbons in this period resulted in the intensification of activities in the field of exporting fossil fuels to foreign markets. In October 1995, the Azerbaijan International Operating Company (AIOC) decided to select two oil transport routes: through the territory of Russia and Georgia. Russia strongly opposed the construction of an export infrastructure from Azerbaijan, which bypassed its territory and led to the Mediterranean port of Ceyhan. Thus, the North Road became a priority in the period of the dynamic development of the oil sector in Azerbaijan after the signing of the "contract of the century" (Huseynzade & Aliyev, 2016).

In this context, in January 1996, Russia and Azerbaijan signed an intergovernmental agreement concerning the transportation of Azerbaijani oil over the Baku–Novorossiysk line, 1.500 km long, of which 1.300 km cross the territory of Russia and 235 km go through the territory of Azerbaijan (Zhiltsov, 2016, pp. 345–400).

The implementation of the agreement took place in October 1997, when oil from Azerbaijan flowed northwards. An oil-measurement station was installed on the border of the two countries, in Shirvanovka, in the Gusar region (Huseynzade & Aliyev, 2016, pp. 169–196). It has been equipped with modern appliances and equipment in accordance with international standards. The station was constructed by AIOC in cooperation with the state-owned company SOCAR and the Russian Transneft. It was supposed to control the quantity and quality of crude oil exported to Russia via the Dubendi–Boyuk Shor–Shirvanovka pipeline (Huseynzade & Aliyev, 2016). The pipeline's capacity is 5 million tonnes of crude oil per year. This is the infrastructure that has significantly strengthened Russia's position in the Western Caucasian Sea region. Russia treated the transit of oil through the port in Novorossiysk as the most advantageous export option for Azerbaijan to foreign markets, without the need to build new pipelines.

The Baku–Novorossiysk pipeline required the construction of a terminal on the shores of the Caspian Sea with a capacity of 750.000 m³ barrels, a pumping station with a capacity of 80.000 barrels per day, a 17 km line linking the new terminal with the main pipeline in Grozny, and the rehabilitation of a 31 km line to Guizdak in Azerbaijan and a further 10 km from Guizdak to the main Baku–Grozny pipeline (Huseynzade & Aliyev, 2016). The security of the infrastructure depends on the political situation in Chechnya. In 1996, Russia, Azerbaijan, and Transneft, AIOC, and SOCAR signed interstate and inter-ministerial agreements to transport Azerbaijani oil through the Russian pipeline system. Under the agreement, Azerbaijan had to transport 5 million tonnes of oil each year via this route. Thus, in October 1997, oil from Azerbaijan was already pumped through the Baku–Grozny–Novorossiysk pipeline. The infrastructure was filled mainly with SOCAR, and the oil came from the fields of Azeri, Chirag, and Gunashli. The filling of the Makhachkala–Novorossiysk line, passing through Russia, was dependent on the development of oil fields in the Russian sector of the Caspian Sea (mainly Korchagin, Filanovsky) (Huseynzade & Aliyev, 2016).

In May 2013, Russian Prime Minister D. Medvedev signed an order cancelling, as of February 2014, the Russian–Azerbaijani agreement concerning the transport of oil via the Baku–Novorossiysk pipeline. This decision was made due to the systematic decrease in the capacity of the infrastructure from 2 million tonnes in 2011–2012 to 1.75 million tonnes in 2013 (Huseynzade & Aliyev, 2016). After the contract was canceled, oil from Azerbaijan was diverted west via the Baku–Tbilisi–Ceyhan pipeline. At the same time, Transneft withdrew from operating the pipeline section from the Russian–Azerbaijani border to Makhachkala in Dagestan. This part of the pipeline runs between Makhachkala and Novorossiysk (Huseynzade & Aliyev, 2016). During 2012–2014, the volume of crude oil handled in the port of Makhachkala was approximately 4–5 million tonnes. Half of this was from Kazakhstan and Turkmenistan. The port is able to receive a maximum of 8 million tonnes of crude oil each year. In addition to the transit of oil, Russia is interested in transporting gas from Azerbaijan through its territory. In June 2009, Russia and Azerbaijan signed an agreement to supply 0.5 billion m³ of gas from the Shah Deniz field, starting in 2010. In addition, Russia was interested in obtaining gas from the second phase of the field's expansion. In 2010, Russia and Azerbaijan agreed to increase gas supplies from Azerbaijan to 2 billion m³.

The pipeline system in Kazakhstan is a complex of connections with a total length of 20.238 km, of which gas pipelines are 12.318 km, and oil pipelines are

7.920 km. The infrastructure is equipped with pumping stations, communication lines and telecommunication structures as well as firefighting equipment (Huseynzade & Aliyev, 2016). Currently, Kazakhstan has a pipeline system transporting oil in three directions:

1. A system of oil pipelines in western Kazakhstan, transporting crude oil to the Atyrau refinery and for export. Crude oil is produced by Mangistau-MunaiGaz, KazakhOil Emba, UzenMunayGaz, and KarazhanbasMunai.
2. A system of pipelines transporting crude oil to the Kenkiyak Dispatching Station and for export. Crude oil is produced by JSC AktobeMunaiGas, KMK Munay, and LLP KazakhOil Aktobe.
3. A pipeline system in eastern Kazakhstan and Central Asia transporting crude oil to the Pavlodar and Shymkent refineries and for export (Parkhomchik, 2016, pp. 139–152).

Most of the pipelines in Kazakhstan were built during the Soviet period and require modernization. Gas transport lines are located in the western part of Kazakhstan. KazTransGas is engaged in the modernization of the gas pipeline network in Kazakhstan. In the years 2001–2010, 684 km of new gas pipelines were built. In 2013, a state-owned pipeline operator, KazTransOil, prepared a project to modernize the main Kalamkas–Karajanbas–Aktau and Uzen–Zhetybai–Aktau pipelines (Konaev & Nadir, 2001, pp. 71–81; Andreev et al., 2005, pp. 8–19).

There is also a tendency to develop energy infrastructure in order to export energy. Kazakhstan has rich gas resources, which are exported via the following pipelines: Central-Asia–Center (CAC), Bukhara–Ural, and Bukhara–Tashkent–Bishkek–Almaty. Exports from Kazakhstan are mainly based on the Samara pipeline in Russia (200.000 b/d), then continue to Russia or European markets via Russian terminals or via the Druzhba pipeline. The Caspian Pipeline Consortium (CPC) project from Tengiz to Novorossiysk (Map 4.1) created new export opportunities for Kazakhstan. From the beginning of the 2000s, two export routes were launched: Tengiz–Novorossiysk (part of the Caspian Pipeline Consortium) and Atasu–Alashankou. They transport 28.7 and 11.8 million tonnes of oil, respectively. Kazakhstan produces about 81.8 million tonnes of oil, of which 72 million tonnes is exported (Parkhomchik, 2016, pp. 139–152).

Currently, the main gas transport routes in Kazakhstan are CAC, Orenburg–Novopskov, Soyuz, Bukhara–Ural, and BGR–TBA. All these pipelines transport gas northwards, where they connect with Gazprom's infrastructure. For a long time, Russia was the only way for hydrocarbons from Kazakhstan to exit to Western markets. One of the first transport routes for oil from Kazakhstan to attract Russia's interest was the Tengiz–Novorossiysk pipeline, connecting the Tengiz oil fields with the South Ozereika terminal in the Black Sea. The pipeline exports Kazakh oil to the Western market and strengthens Russia's position in the transit dimension (Fedorov, 1996, pp. 4–17). In July 1992, an agreement was

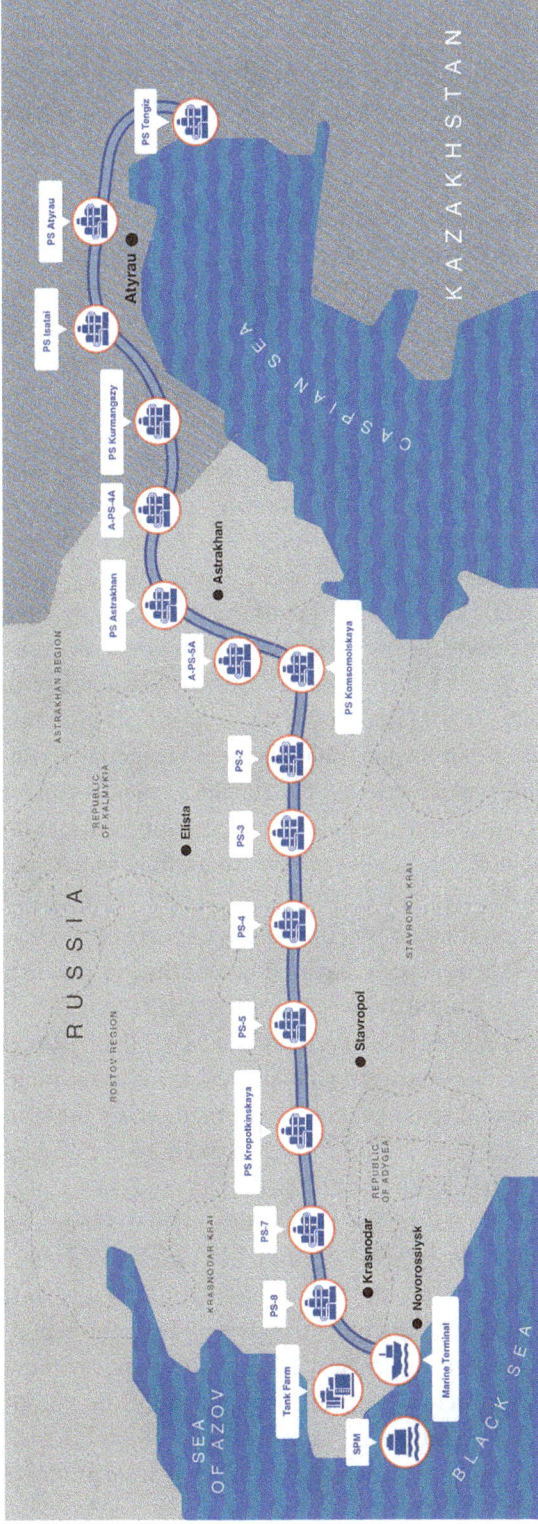

MAP 4.1 Caspian Pipeline Consortium
SOURCE: HTTPS://WWW.CPC.RU/EN/ABOUT/PAGES/MAPS.ASPX

signed between Kazakhstan and Oman regarding the establishment of the CPC (Caspian Pipeline Consortium, 2021; Zhiltsov, 2016, pp. 345–400). In June 1993, the Russian parliament ratified the country's joining the agreement (Caspian Pipeline Consortium, 2021).

It was decided that Russia and Kazakhstan would build a pipeline in their respective territories (Zhiltsov, 2016, pp. 345–400). The cost of the project is USD 215 million. The two countries pledged to provide manpower, materials, equipment, and territory to build the infrastructure. Oman, represented by the Oman Oil Company (OOC), provided project financing, the preparation of the feasibility report, and the development of the investment mechanisms. Kazakhstan was to deliver oil to the pipeline. All CPC project participants were granted equal rights as regards its management and profit sharing (Caspian Pipeline Consortium, 2021). The design was impressive. The length of the pipeline is 1,511 km and its capacity is 67 million tonnes of oil per year (Caspian Pipeline Consortium, 2021). Transneft was the main operator of the infrastructure. It is worth mentioning that 700 km of the pipeline from Tengiz to Russia was built during the Soviet period. The Atyrau–Astrakhan section, on the other hand, is the main part of the Tengiz–Novorossiysk infrastructure (Caspian Pipeline Consortium, 2021). The pipeline transports oil to the export terminal through the Astrakhan region, Kalmykia and Krasnodar Territory, which is the shortest and politically stable option. The infrastructure was significant for Russia, which not only counted on closer cooperation with Kazakhstan in the energy dimension, but also in the political dimension, as part of the integration of the post-Soviet area.

For the first time in Russian practice, the project envisaged loading oil into tankers using the SMP system—single buoy mooring, or an offshore loading anchor, which serves as a link between tankers at sea (Raunek, 2019). The system consisted of a floating platform anchored at a depth of 50 m, and a rubber hose transporting oil and connecting the tankers with the terminal near Novorossiysk. The SMP system was located 5 km from the shoreline, and the storage tanks in the coastal area, 8 km from the sea. It consisted of 18 tanks, with a volume of 90.000 m^3 each (Zhiltsov, 2016, pp. 345–400).

Kazakhstan contributed to the consortium by its energy resources. The connection between Tengiz and Komsomolski and the Atyrau–Samara section were able to transport around 200.000 tonnes of oil per month (for a long time, Kazakhstan has used this route to export oil from the Tengiz fields). The commissioning of the CPC significantly lowered the costs of oil transportation from Kazakhstan and increased its export possibilities. In addition, Western corporations were more interested in investing in oil production in Kazakhstan, as exemplified by Chevron, which started large-scale production from the Tengiz field.

In November 1998, Russia and Kazakhstan approved a project to build an oil pipeline from Tengiz to the port of Novorossiysk. It was planned that Russia's direct and indirect revenues would amount to USD 33 billion over 35 years (Zhiltsov, 2016, pp. 345–400). It is one of the largest pipelines in the Caspian region. In March 2011, the first oil flowed through this pipeline. On the other hand, the first tanker with CPC oil from the South Ozereika terminal in the Black Sea was loaded in October 2011—and thus Kazakhstan began exporting oil to foreign markets. About 28.2 million tonnes of oil could be transported via this infrastructure annually. In 2013, oil exports via the CPC increased to 32.7 million tonnes (Misiągiewicz, 2022, p. 513). The creation of this route was possible as a result of a combination of various factors: the availability of infrastructure in Russia, and the initiation of negotiations on the construction of the pipeline shortly after the collapse of the USSR, while most of the newly established countries in the Caspian region were only just formulating their political and economic priorities. Kazakhstan's actions enabled the country to gain access to foreign markets and increase its revenues from the oil trade. In turn, Russia has achieved its strategic goal by expanding its influence in the Caspian region (Zhiltsov, 2016, pp. 345–400).

The construction of the Tengiz–Novorossiysk oil pipeline is a geopolitical success for Russia in the Caspian region. In addition to the real financial benefits and the development of the Black Sea terminal, the pipeline strengthened Russia's influence in the region, providing an alternative to other directions of hydrocarbon exports from the Caspian region.

The success, in the case of oil exports, was an incentive for Kazakhstan to develop the energy sector, exploit new oil fields, and build new pipelines. In 2003, the first oil flowed through the Kenkiyak–Atyrau pipeline, which allowed for direct transport of this resource from the fields in Aktobe to the CPC system (Kenkiyak–Atyrau Pipeline, 2020). Subsequently, in 2004, Russian oil was also transported through this system. Thanks to the use of a turbulence-reducing agent in the pipes, oil transport has increased to 30 million tonnes per year (Zhiltsov, 2016, pp. 345–400). In 2011, after many years of negotiations, it was decided to increase the pipeline's capacity. Kazakhstan's share in the CPC was to increase from 27 to 52 million tonnes. The CPC capacity expansion was completed in 2015 and reached 67 million tonnes of crude oil per year. In 2014, the SMP-3 system was launched as part of the CPC and increasing the capacity of the Tengiz–Novorossiysk pipeline. This enabled the reloading of more crude oil (67 million tonnes per year) from the CPC terminal (Caspian Pipeline Consortium, 2021). Additionally, the installation of a system reducing turbulence in the pipes led to an increase in throughput of up to 76 million tonnes per year (Misiągiewicz, 2022, p.513; Zhiltsov, 2016, 345–400). Increasing the amount of crude oil transported via the CPC system was possible after the implementation of the first expansion phase of this project in July 2011. This process included the modernization of the existing CPC infrastructure, the replacement of 88 km of the pipeline on the territory of Kazakhstan, and the construction of a third refueling unit and three tanks with a capacity of 100.000 m³ within the terminal of the Novorossiysk Black Sea Port. It should be noted that this extension was planned back in 1998 as part of the CPC system feasibility study. However, in the early 2000s, Russia showed no interest in increasing the efficiency of the system, due to the relatively small amounts of Russian oil transported through it and to debt problems for foreign consortium members. However, as a result of closer cooperation between Kazakhstan and Azerbaijan on the transport of oil, Russia changed its approach and intensified efforts to develop the CPC.

One of the main export routes for oil from Kazakhstan was the Atyrau–Samara pipeline, with a length of 1.000 km. In June 2002, Russia and Kazakhstan signed a long-term international agreement which guaranteed Kazakhstan the transit of no less than 15 million tonnes of oil annually through this pipeline. The infrastructure was designed to transport oil to the Russian ports of Primorsk, Ust-Luga, and Novorossiysk. In 2013, the pipeline transported 15.4 million tonnes of oil.

In total, from 2001 through January 9, 2022, 766.9 million tonnes of crude oil were delivered to world markets via the Tengiz–Novorossiysk pipeline system: 668.967.665 tonnes of that crude came from Kazakhstan and 98.005.466 tonnes of crude was produced in Russia (Caspian Pipeline Consortium, 2021). The number of tankers handled over that period totaled 7.246 (Caspian Pipeline Consortium, 2021).

Based on the estimates of oil production in Kazakhstan and the interest of enterprises in this country in the export direction to Samara, it is expected that the potential of this pipeline will increase to 25 million tonnes of oil annually (Guseinov, 2010, pp. 109–201), and the Uzen—Atyrau section to 40 million tonnes annually (Bystrova, 2009, p. 14).

Under the North Caspian Operating Company, oil supplies from the Kashagan field will be transported northwards to the Russian city of Samara, then to Novorossiysk on the Black Sea, from where exports would be made via the Russian monopoly, Transneft (Assanbayev, 2016, pp. 127–137).

Many consulting agencies under the auspices of the EU Tacis INOGATE program have published a comparison of nine different export options from the Caspian region to the European market. The cheapest route was from Tengiz in Kazakhstan, through the Trans-Caspian Pipeline, to Baku, where, after refilling with oil from Azerbaijan, it will be piped to the port in Supsa, and then, using tankers, will be transported to Trieste through the Turkish Straits.

However, this option was protested by Turkey due to the threats resulting from the increase in tanker traffic in the Bosphorus.

The Caspian Sea region is an important resource and production reservoir, which motivates Russia to increase its activity here in the process of developing a pipeline architecture. The strategic goal of this power was to persuade Azerbaijan and Kazakhstan to transport their resources through the port in Novorossiysk. In the period of over two decades of development of the Caspian region in the energy sector, Russia undoubtedly played a significant role. At the same time, it has not managed to maintain its leading position in oil and gas exports from the Caspian Sea region. As a result, it had to take into account the interests of individual Caspian states when building new pipeline projects.

2   The Western Route of Fossil Fuel Exports from the Caspian Region

The Caspian Basin has no access to the seas and oceans, and the export infrastructure requires an extensive pipeline system (Ebel & Menon, 2000, pp. 1–20). The process of opening the Caspian region and its energy resources to the Western market had a multi-level dimension—local, national, regional, or geopolitical—as it involved various actors. Market expansion in this underdeveloped region, in the form of international financial institutions, international organizations, corporations, or other countries, proves its attractiveness and development prospects (Omarova, 1998, pp. 169–195).

Contrary to Kazakhstan and Turkmenistan, Azerbaijan's position was more favorable as the pipelines, even those built during the Soviet period, were geographically closer to the European market. In the post-independence period, Azerbaijan became an attractive country for the Western market due to its energy potential and geoeconomic position. Azerbaijan's economy is rapidly developing and it is undergoing apolitical transformation. An important element in the functioning of the state was the presidency of the former local KGB leader, Heydar Aliyev, and later his son, Illham, former prime minister and deputy head of the state oil company. The importance of political leadership is also reflected in the naming of the most strategic infrastructure in the country. It is enough to mention the Baku–Tbilisi–Ceyhan pipeline, which was formally called in Azerbaijan "Heydar Aliyev's main export pipeline" (Carroll, 2012, p. 283).

Immediately after independence, the countries of the Caspian region focused on the exploitation of oil resources. This made it possible to gain greater independence from Russia. The pipelines operating in the region so far ran through the territory of this power and were managed by Russian companies. Thus, both Azerbaijan and Kazakhstan were dependent on the Russian Federation for exports. Subsequently, however, the interests of the engaging international corporations were related to the limitation of Russia's role in favor of opening the Caucasian market to the West. Some have described this process as a "Caucasian mania" (Ebel & Menon, 2000, pp. 1–20).

The West also saw in the Caspian region the possibility of diversifying energy supply sources in order to become independent from the resources of the Middle East and Russia (Carroll, 2012, pp. 281–302). After the coup d'état in 1993, Heydar Aliyev became the president of Azerbaijan. He treated the involvement of Western capital in the energy sector as an opportunity to become independent from the Russian infrastructure (Bolukbasi, 1998, pp. 397–414). In September 1994, the so-called "contract of the century" was signed, on the basis of which international corporations gained access to the energy market of Azerbaijan. According to the agreement, the participation of a consortium of Western oil corporations, mainly BP and Amoco, in the production of oil in Azerbaijan was to last 30 years. The agreement concerned in particular the exploitation of the ACG fields, the resources of which were estimated at 4 billion barrels of oil (Carroll, 2012, pp. 281–302).

Georgia is a small country in terms of geography and demographics, but is crucial for the transit of fossil fuels from the Caspian region, which connects this area with the Black Sea and Europe (German, 2018, pp. 181–195). In March 1996, an intergovernmental agreement was signed between Azerbaijan and Georgia for the transport of oil through its territory within the Baku–Supsa pipeline (Map 4.2).

Exports of about 5 million tonnes of oil per year were planned. Part of the operational 788 km line from the Sangachal terminal to Supsa formed the basis of the new pipeline infrastructure. In the rest, 138 km long, a new pipeline, six pumping stations and an oil export registration system were built. Within the overall infrastructure system, 421 km of pipeline across Azerbaijan from the Sangachal terminal to the border with Georgia had to be renewed and the remaining 47 km of lines had to be added. On the other hand, 340 km of the pipeline had to be renewed in the territory of Georgia and 39 km had to be built (Huseynzade & Aliyev, 2016, pp. 169–196). The construction of the pipeline was completed at the end of 1998 and the transport of oil produced under the "contract of the century" began. It took several months fills with oil the pipeline. During this period, the terminal in Supsa was expanded in the maritime area (3 km from the coast). The official opening of the pipeline took place in April 1997 in Supsa. The pipeline was of great importance both for the economic development of Azerbaijan and Georgia. The western

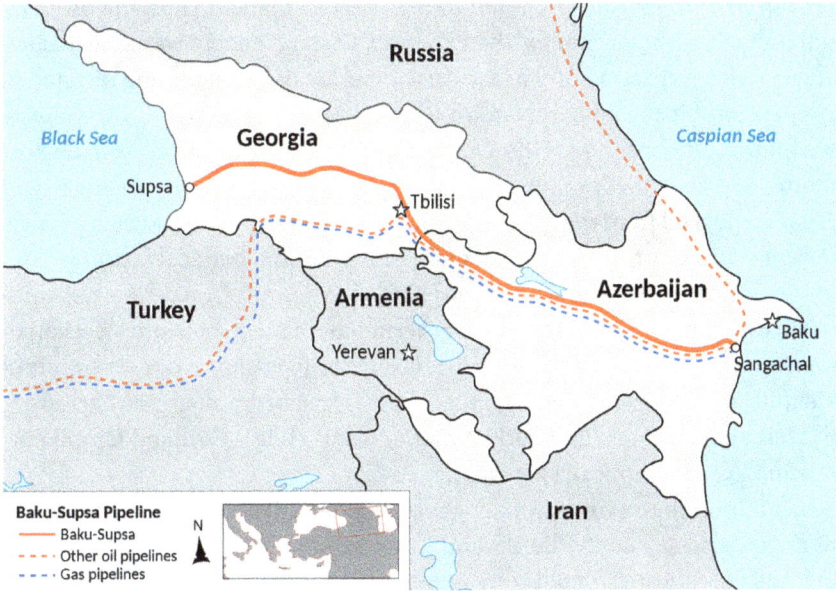

MAP 4.2   Baku–Supsa pipeline
SOURCE: HTTPS://COMMONS.WIKIMEDIA.ORG/WIKI/FILE:BAKU-SUPSA
_PIPELINE.SVG

direction of oil exports also attracted the attention of foreign investors. Of the total number of workers employed in the construction of the pipeline, 70% were Azerbaijani and Georgian nationals. For oil companies, the economic efficiency of the pipeline was mainly due to the low transport costs compared to the northern direction. The launch of the second oil transport route from the Caspian region has also contributed to further international cooperation and the intensification of the exploitation of energy potential. Access to world markets was an incentive for economic development and attracted new investors. The joint Azerbaijani–Georgian initiative has strengthened the geopolitical position of both countries and the entire Caucasian region in the context of the development of relations between Europe and Asia (Huseynzade & Aliyev, 2016).

The president of Azerbaijan described the pipeline as "a spectacular example of friendship and cooperation between Azerbaijan and Georgia" and "an important contribution to strengthening stability and peace in the Caucasus" (Huseynzade & Aliyev, 2016, p. 170). The increase in the production of hydrocarbons in Azerbaijan, as well as the increased demand on world markets, made it necessary to look for new ways of exporting energy. The key issue was the development of oil transportation to the Western market. Thus, the diversity in the pipeline dimension for the export of Caspian energy was a huge challenge for the realization of the interests of market participants and resulted in competition for the construction of a single main export route. The priority was for this pipeline to pass through territory of Russia, the Black Sea, the Bosphorus, and Dardanelles (Bolukbasi, 1998, pp. 397–414). Such a pipeline would also transport oil from the ACG fields and potentially from Kazakhstan. Hence, it was a complex process, dependent on economic and political factors.

The option of building the Baku–Tbilisi–Ceyhan (BTC) pipeline was optimal in this context. The Azerbaijani government made the historic decision to build a mega-pipeline to the west. In November 1999, at the OSCE summit in Istanbul, an agreement was signed on: "Oil Transport through the Territories of Azerbaijan, Georgia and Turkey via the Baku–Tbilisi–Ceyhan Main Export Pipeline" (Carroll, 2012, pp. 281–302).

In addition to the countries directly participating in the project, the agreement was also signed by the US and Kazakhstan. The pipeline was to pass a long and complicated road. The agreement opened up the prospect of building BTC and became the second strategic document after signing the "contract of the century" (Huseynzade & Aliyev, 2016, p. 169). In September 2002, construction of the pipeline began.

The decision on the route of the pipeline was made in 1995 (Armenia and Iran were bypassed). It was mainly conditioned by political issues, which increased the costs of this investment. It was the most expensive and technologically developed transmission infrastructure in the region. The pipeline is not only long, but also rises more than 2.000 m above sea level, which makes it necessary to increase the number of pumping stations. Its length is 1.750 km, 442 km of which runs through Azerbaijan, 248 km through Georgia, and 1.060 km through Turkey (Huseynzade & Aliyev, 2016). Two pumping stations were built for the pipeline in Azerbaijan, two in Georgia, and four in Turkey. The pipeline can transport 1mb/d. Oil flows from one end of the pipe to the other within 10 days. Huge terminals have been built in Sangachal, Azerbaijan, and Ceyhanin Turkey to operate the pipeline (Baku–Tbilisi–Ceyhan Pipeline, 2023).

An important element of the work on the construction of BTC was not only the involvement of the corporation, but also its financing by international institutions, such as the EBRD (European Bank for Reconstruction and Development) and IFC (International Finance Corporation) (Baku–Tbilisi–Ceyhan Pipeline, 2023; Carroll, 2012, pp. 281–302). The only problem was the fluctuation in the price of crude oil, from USD 20 a barrel to USD 10 in the 1990s, the biggest political motivation for building the pipeline was ultimately the increase in the price of this commodity to USD 30 in 2000 (BP Azerbaijan, n.d.). The transnational actor most involved in the construction of the BTC pipeline was BP (BP Azerbaijan, n.d.).

Despite numerous doubts as to the profitability of the project, the prospect of oil transit from Kazakhstan via BTC seemed very promising (Carroll, 2012, pp. 281–302). The pipeline is the most significant transnational infrastructure in recent years. The specificity of this project results from the amount of investments it consumed (around USD 20 billion), its length (17.60 km) or the fact that it runs through three countries that are not free from conflicts (Carroll, 2012).

On a regional and supra-regional scale, the BTC pipeline has contributed to many geopolitical challenges. Its functioning led to an escalation of tensions between Russia and Georgia. Georgia has become one of the participants in the BTC project as a transport corridor, increasing its importance on an international scale. Russia, in turn, opposed the construction of this oil pipeline from the very beginning due to the independence of Azerbaijan and Georgia from its economic influence and export infrastructure. During the Russo-Georgian War in 2008, Russia launched more than 50 missiles in the direction of the pipeline. If this goal was achieved, the Russian Federation would become the only transport route for oil from Azerbaijan (McElroy, 2008). Georgia has tightened its cooperation with Western countries. It condemned the 9/11 attack, even offered the US access to military bases and airspace, and sent its troops to Iraq. Thus, Georgia's relations with the US strengthened, and the construction of the BTC pipeline reflected the influence of this power in the post-Soviet area (Carroll, 2012, pp. 281–302).

On May 25, 2005, the official inauguration of BTC took place and the first oil flowed from the Sangachal terminal. A year later, on May 28, 2006, Azerbaijani oil reached the port of Ceyhan. Another inauguration ceremony was held here on July 13, 2006 (Huseynzade & Aliyev, 2016, pp. 169–196). Currently, the oil pipeline transports over 1% of the world's oil resources, which is 1 mb/d (Misiągiewicz, 2022, p. 527).

The BTC opened up the possibility of an important Baku–Tbilisi–Erzurum export gas pipeline. It was possible thanks to the discovery in 1999 of one of the world's largest fields with gas condensate deposits—Shah Deniz.

In March 2001, during the official visit of the President of Azerbaijan, H. Aliyev to Turkey, the "Agreement between the Republic of Turkey and the Republic of Azerbaijan on gas supplies from Azerbaijan to the Republic of Turkey" was signed (Huseynzade & Aliyev, 2016, pp. 169–196). In February

2003, the first expansion phase of the Shah Deniz field was carried out. A new production platform was built and a pipeline transporting gas to the shores of the Caspian Sea was built. The Baku–Tbilisi–Erzurum gas pipeline was also called the South Caucasus Pipeline (SCP) (BP Georgia, n.d.). It transported gas from the Shah Deniz field to the European market via Turkey. The project's shareholders were: BP, Statoil, SOCAR, Total and TPAO. In the territory of Azerbaijan and Georgia, the gas pipeline ran parallel to BTC. Its maximum capacity was 20 billion m³ of gas per year. The gas pipeline was commissioned in 2006 (Huseynzade & Aliyev, 2016, pp. 169–196).

The number of planned gas transmission lines in 2009–2013 by European countries from Azerbaijan reflected the different interests of individual countries and enterprises in the EU, Azerbaijan and Turkey. In this context, the expansion of the Shah Deniz II (SD2) gas fields was essential (Shah Deniz Stage 2, 2023). First, it was not clear which specific gas pipelines would run and whether Turkey would be a reliable partner in this respect. Second, most of the companies involved in export projects preferred the diversification of the importers of energy and the balance between the Turkish and European markets, as over 70% of exports from Shah Deniz went to Turkey. As a result of the delays in the expansion of Shah Deniz II, Azerbaijan took on the costs of building the gas infrastructure.

In 2021, it is planned to increase Azerbaijan's export capacity to 54 billion m³ of gas annually. The country relies not only on the exploitation of the Shah Deniz fields, but also on the development of smaller gas fields, which could significantly supplement the production. And so, the scenario of such activities includes: export from the Babek field (400 mm3), ACG (300 mm3), Karabakh (20 mm3) and Ashrafi (13 mm3) (SOCAR, 2022).

The crisis in relations between Russia and the European Union in connection with the conflict in Ukraine made the mega energy project—the Southern Gas Corridor implementation (Yorucu & Özay, 2018). The EU sees it as an opportunity for real diversification of gas supplies and a way to strengthen its position vis-à-vis Russia (Misiągiewicz, 2019b). Turkey is a major participant in this project and the main transit state for the pipeline infrastructure (Map 4.3).

There are two conditions that favor the development of the Southern Gas Corridor: changes in the gas market in Europe and the need to diversify gas supply sources. The decline in gas production in the EU resulted in a sustained increase in gas imports. In addition, the limitation of gas production in Algeria and the declining production efficiency in Norway made it necessary to look for new suppliers of gas for the European market (Roberts, 2018, pp. 196–212). In such a situation, Azerbaijan has great export potential, which could transport 25–30 billion m³ of gas in the next 30–35 years. The problem is that the

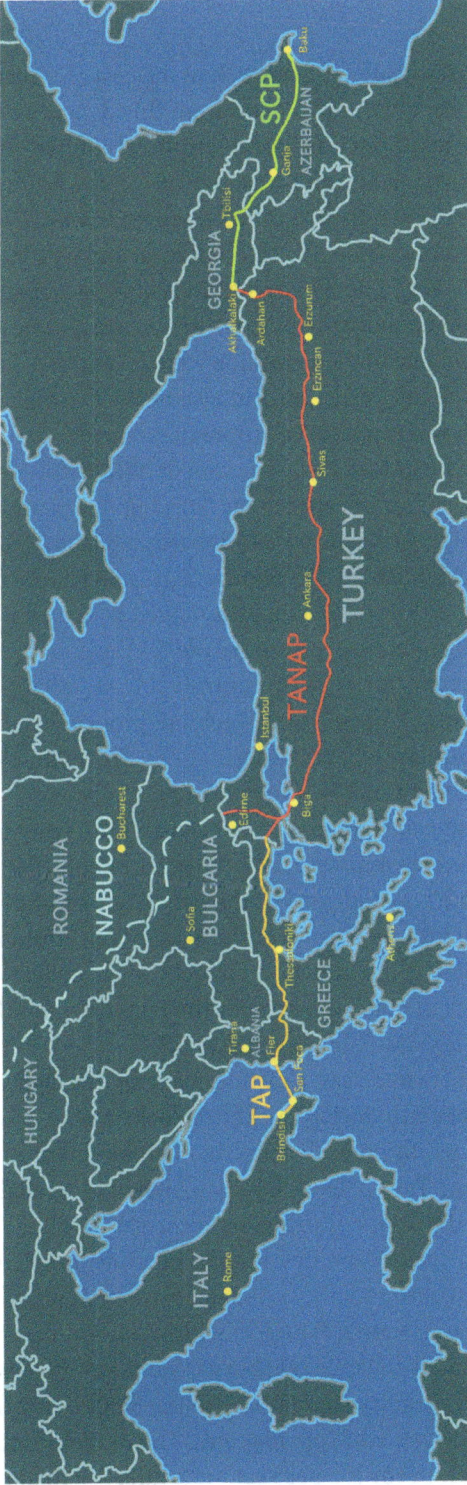

MAP 4.3   Southern Gas Corridor

SOURCE: HTTPS://COMMONS.WIKIMEDIA.ORG/W/INDEX.PHP?SEARCH=SOUTHERN+GAS+CORRIDOR&TITLE=SPECIAL:MEDIASEARCH&GO =GO&TYPE=IMAGE

cost of transporting gas is relatively greater than the cost of transporting crude oil, so there is a question of potential gains from this type of investment. The implementation of the Southern Gas Corridor project required extensive cooperation between its participants, and was also associated with technological and financial challenges. The pipeline infrastructure is crossing the borders of six countries, which is associated with different legal and political specificities (Roberts, 2018, pp. 196–212). Energy corporations also participate in the project, which complicated the implementing comprehensive infrastructure. The very high costs of the project implementation were related not only to the construction of the pipeline infrastructure, but also to the expansion of the Shah Deniz gas fields, which was estimated at approximately USD 22–23 billion. The costs of this expansion include the construction of offshore platforms, production shafts to extract gas from deeper areas with high pressure, and gas processing systems at the Sangachal terminal (Roberts, 2018, pp. 196–212).

The ceremony of establishing the Southern Gas Corridor took place on September 20, 2014, and the gas pipeline was hailed as the "21st-century project" (Southern Gas Corridor, 2023; Huseynzade & Aliyev, 2016, pp. 169–196). The Southern Gas Corridor is currently controlled by Azerbaijan and Turkey as a system of three complementary gas pipeline projects: Trans-Caucasian, Trans-Anatolian (TANAP) and Trans-Adriatic (TAP). The main element of the Southern Corridor concept is the TANAP and TAP gas pipeline.

According to Natural Gas Europe, the total cost of the construction of the Southern Gas Corridor was approximately USD 40 billion (Perzyński, 2018). Most of the expenditure was allocated to the development of the Shah Deniz 2 production infrastructure, expansion of the Sangachal Terminal off the Caspian coast of Azerbaijan, three pipeline projects, a gas collection system in Italy, and the possibility of connections with the regions of Southern, Central and Eastern Europe (Trans Adriatic Pipeline, 2019).

Plans to build the TANAP gas pipeline passing through Turkey were announced in November 2011 during the Third Black Sea Energy and Business Forum. On June 26, 2012, the president of Azerbaijan, Ilham Aliyev, and the prime minister of Turkey, Tayyip Recep Erdoğan, signed an official intergovernmental agreement on the joint construction of the gas pipeline. The TAP project, in turn, envisaged the construction of a gas pipeline from Greece through Albania and the Adriatic Sea to Italy, and the construction of gas reservoirs in Albania. It is the cheapest (shortest) project within the Southern Corridor.

At present, Azerbaijan is the only reliable gas supplier to the Southern Corridor, which used gas from the second phase of the Shah Deniz field development (Huseynzade & Aliyev, 2016, pp. 169–196). The available amounts of the gas amount to 16 billion m³ of gas per year. In future, Azerbaijan is planning production from the Umid and Babek fields, where the Azerbaijani SOCAR is working. It is estimated that gas extraction from these fields may take place within five years, but there are no specific plans for their development, and especially production prospects (Jarosiewicz, 2012). Azerbaijan also has deposits on the Apsheronian Peninsula, where Total is conducting research. According to preliminary information, these resources are estimated at 300 billion m³ of gas (Jarosiewicz, 2012). Deliveries from other potential gas sources to the Southern Corridor are problematic. There is no possibility of deliveries from Iraq, Egypt and Iran (mainly due to the instability in the Middle East) and from Turkmenistan and Kazakhstan (due to the lack of infrastructure for gas exports via the Caspian Sea) (Koukoudakis, 2017, p. 34; Siddi, 2019, pp. 124–144).

The TANAP gas pipeline, known as the Trans-Anatolian Gas Pipeline, is the central transit part of the Southern Corridor. Its shareholders are: SOCAR, 58%; Turkish BOTAS, 30%; and British BP, 12%. The pipeline runs north-east from the border between Georgia and Turkey to the western border between Turkey and Greece. The second phase of the TANAP gas pipeline project was to be completed by June 2019. After the successful completion of the tests, gas transport to Greece began in 2019 (Bojanowicz, 2018; Kublik, 2018).

The TAP gas pipeline is the last element of the Corridor, 800 km (478 km in Greece, 204 km in Albania, 105 km through the Adriatic Sea, and 5 km in Italy) (Trans Adriatic Pipeline, 2017). Its shareholders are: BP, 20%; SOCAR, 20%; Statoil, 20%; Fluxys, 19%; Enagas, 16%; and the Swiss Axpo, 5%. The route's capacity ranges from 10 billion m³ to a maximum of 23 billion m³ of gas per year. Thus, the gas pipeline can meet the energy needs of around 7 million households in Europe. The estimated cost of building the trail was around USD 2 billion (Jarosiewicz, 2014, p. 14; Fandrich, 2013). The construction of the gas pipeline began in 2016.

TAP offers various connection options to a number of existing and proposed pipelines, delivering gas to various European markets:
- *Bulgaria*: connects with the Interconnector Greece—Bulgaria (IGB) pipeline
- *Greece*: connects with the Greek network operated by DESFA
- *Albania*: will provide exit points for the development of the Albanian gas market
- *Italy*: connects to the Italian natural gas grid operated by Snam Rete Gas, from where all Italian gas exit points to European destinations
- *South-East Europe*: TAP provide an exit point to the planned Ionian Adriatic Pipeline (IAP) to link to the markets in Croatia, Albania, Montenegro, and Bosnia and Herzegovina (Southern Gas Corridor, 2023).

From October 2021, Bulgaria received gas via a temporary route through the south-west point of Kułat at the border with Greece, where there is a link between the Greek gas system and TAP. Gas from Azerbaijan started to flow through the Komotini-Stara Zagora interconnector, there is a connection between the TAP gas pipeline (Bulgaria as of January 1, 2021 will start receiving Azeri gas, 2021). The interconnector has an overall length of 182 km and a technical capacity of 3 billion cubic meters (bcm) per year with an option for increasing the transmission capacity to up to 5 bcm per year with the construction of a compressor station on Greek territory that would also allow for reverse flow (ICGB Interconnector, n.d.).

However, it should be noted that an indispensable condition for the effectiveness of the Southern Gas Corridor is the prospect of implementing the Trans-Caspian Gas Pipeline project through the Caspian Sea to Azerbaijan and further onto the European market (Map 4.4). The gas pipeline will run along the bottom of the Caspian Basin and connect the transshipment station in Turkmenbashi with the Sangachal terminal near Baku. The planned capacity of the infrastructure is 30 billion m³ of gas annually (Sikorski, 2011, p. 12). Despite such a prospect, it is not certain how much gas Turkmenistan can possibly contract, given that its main supplies go to China. However, as yet, the pipeline cannot be built due to a dispute between Azerbaijan and Turkmenistan over jurisdiction over the Kapaz/Serdar oil field and the Azeri/Omar and Cirag/Osman fields (Misiągiewicz, 2014a; Pirani, 2018;

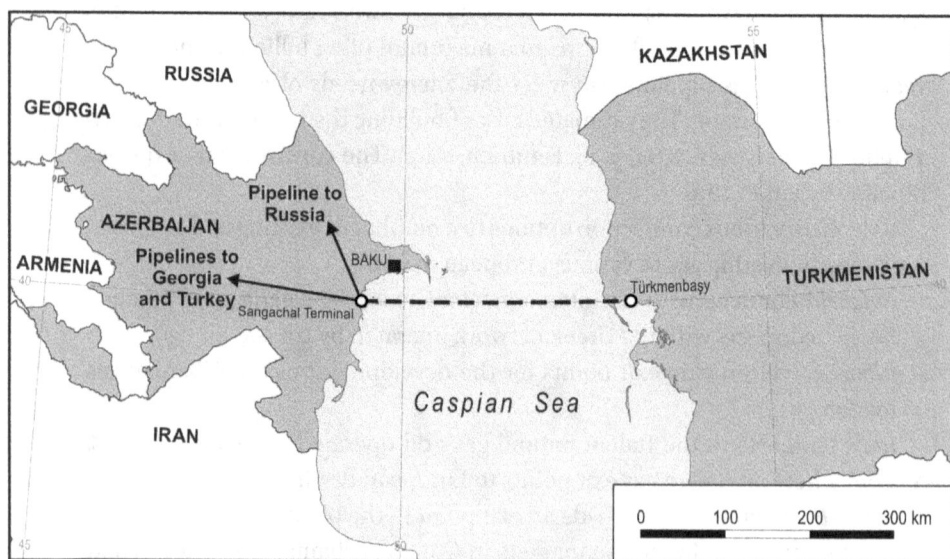

MAP 4.4   Trans-Caspian Pipeline project
SOURCE: MADE BY W. JANICKI IN MISIĄGIEWICZ, 2014

Cutler, 2019). It is also not known what the sources of financing the gas pipeline will be.

There are some problems connected to the issues of security and foreign policy relating to the prospects for the functioning of the Southern Gas Corridor. The first is about the perspective to include additional suppliers, Iran and Turkmenistan. Except that, the corridor runs near territories with regional conflicts (Nagorno-Karabakh and South Ossetia). In view of the tense relations between Armenia and Azerbaijan, the infrastructure is exposed to destruction. In addition, Russian troops stationed in South Ossetia have easy access to part of the infrastructure passing through Georgia, and a real threat to pipelines in this area arose in 2008 (Siddi, 2019, pp. 124–144; Marriott & Minio-Paluello, 2013, pp. 147–157).

The key issue related to gas exports via the Corridor is competition from Russia, which is the gas supplier of Southeastern Europe. Moreover, the Turkish Stream gas pipeline is in direct competition with the Corridor (Gazprom confirms first gas, 2019). Thus, two competing gas infrastructure projects have emerged in the region: the gas pipeline from Azerbaijan via Turkey to the EU and Turkish Stream (Gurbanov, 2017). Both projects run through the territory of Turkey and assume that the point of entry into the EU market is the border between Turkey and Greece or Turkey and Bulgaria. Southern Corridor runs from Azerbaijan via Turkey to EU and Turkish Stream, via Turkey and Bulgaria (Gurbanov, 2018). Russia is trying to maintain the dominant position of a gas supplier to the European market and is not interested in competing with Azerbaijani gas. Turkish Stream is a huge challenge for the energy market in Europe.

3   The Southern Route of Fossil Fuel Exports from the Caspian Region

Due to its attractive geopolitical location, Iran has become an important economic partner for the newly established post-Soviet states. For Caspian countries, Iran was a convenient transport route to the Indian Ocean because of four conditions:

- the operating pipelines run 70–100 km from the Caspian coast, so access to them seems easy and cheap;
- there are large warehouses near the Caspian Sea that can store significant amounts of oil;
- Iranian pipelines can be expanded to transport additional volumes of oil, on a SWAP basis (an agreement between two counterparties to exchange

financial instruments, cash flows, or payments for a certain time), by direct
oil exports via Kharg Island to the Persian Gulf; and
– almost 2 mb/d can be transported by this route (Zonn, 1999, pp. 26–124).
Iran supported existing and planned pipelines:
– the Tabriz–Ankara pipeline from Iran to Turkey;
– the Korpezhe–Kurt-Kui pipeline from Turkmenistan to Iran;
– the Neka–Tehran pipeline (SWAP) in Iran; and
– the Tehran–Kharg pipeline from Tehran to the island of Kharg in Iran (Rakel,
  2005, pp. 235–256).

Despite its convenient geographic location and transit opportunities, Iran's
participation in the construction of strategic pipeline infrastructures was
largely limited due to tensions in its relations with the US. This situation led to
Iran's isolation in the international arena and limited its participation in various infrastructure projects (Zonn & Semenov, 2016).

In the post-Soviet period, various projects appeared for oil transit via the
southern route. Iran was particularly interested in building a pipeline from
Kazakhstan via Turkmenistan to Iran. Already in the early 1990s such a project was prepared but still not realized. Its planned length is 2.500 km, and its
efficiency depends on whether it will be able to transport at least 25 million
tonnes of crude oil annually (Zonn & Semenov, 2016).

It was predicted that the source of the oil would be the Tengiz field, from
where the pipeline would continue to run to Uzen in Kazakhstan, south, to
the border with Turkmenistan, and to the Vyshka pumping station. From
there, oil from the Balkan fields could be transported via a joint export
pipeline to the Iranian border via the Korpedzh pumping station (Zonn &
Semenov, 2016).

Iran has also offered to build a Baku–Tabriz pipeline running south to the
terminal on Kharg Island in the Persian Gulf. The total length of such a pipeline was to be 1,000 km, and its capacity was 40 million tonnes of oil per year
(Zonn & Semenov, 2016).

On the basis of an agreement signed in 1996, Kazakhstan undertook to supply 2–6 million tonnes of oil to Iran over 10 years (Zonn & Semenov, 2016). In
January 1997, oil from the Tengiz field was delivered by Azerbaijani tankers to
northern Iran, under a SWAP agreement. The transaction involved the delivery of oil from Kazakhstan using tankers via the Caspian Sea to the northern
regions of Iran, followed by the transport of the same amount of oil from Iranian ports in the Persian Gulf. Deliveries of crude oil, which began in 1997,
were discontinued due to the situation in the energy market and the quality of
Kazakhstan's crude oil (high level of stickiness and sulphur content). Iranian

refineries were unable to process this type of oil. Deliveries were resumed in 2002, but in limited quantities (Misiągiewicz, 2022, p. 539). In the 1990s, Western experts found that the construction of a pipeline transporting Kazakh oil to Iran involved a number of difficulties. Analysts from British Petroleum stated that the construction of a pipeline from Kazakhstan via Iran to the European market is "rather problematic" as there is no guarantee that Iran will impose lower transit tariffs than Russia (Zonn & Semenov, 2016). In turn, analysts from Chevron stated that they do not want to be dependent on Iran or Iraq and link the future of the Tengiz oil field with the political situation in the Persian Gulf (Zonn & Semenov, 2016).

In addition, the designed capacity of the southern oil pipelines is not large, which means that Kazakhstan is not interested in such investments. Conversely, the reconstruction of existing pipelines to increase their capacity generates high costs (up to USD 10 billion) (Zonn & Semenov, 2016).

Despite numerous political and economic difficulties, the former president of Kazakhstan did not rule out the possibility that Kazakh oil would flow to Iran in the future. With this in mind, N. Nazarbayev asked US Secretary of State Colin Powell to consider the strategic role of Iran in the development of the energy market in the Caspian region. In addition, a special working group was established to prepare an agreement on the construction of the Tengiz–Uzen–Belek (Kazakhstan)–Tehran–Qom–Isfahan–Kharg (Iran) export pipeline, 1.440 km long, of which 500 km were to run through Iranian territory (it is not completed). The cost of the project is approximately USD 1.5 billion (Zonn & Semenov, 2016).

During the meeting of the OECD in Almaty in May 1998, President Nazarbayev discussed with his Iranian counterpart the issue of implementing an oil supply agreement under the SWAP agreement, amounting to 2 million tonnes per year (Zonn & Semenov, 2016). In July 1998, Iran submitted an offer to build a 392 km pipeline from the Caspian port of Neka to Tehran. The cost of the project was estimated at USD 400 million. It was the first step towards the implementation of the "southern route" for oil exports from Azerbaijan, Turkmenistan, and possibly Kazakhstan. It was planned that Iran would be able to pump 380.000 barrels of oil per day. In return for the transport of Caspian oil, it was to supply the world market with oil extracted from the Persian Gulf (Iran to propose oil swap, 2015).

Thus, the territory of Iran was the shortest and cheapest way of transporting Caspian oil to foreign markets. Even US oil companies confirmed the financial attractiveness of a possible pipeline through Iranian territory. The US administration agreed that Chevron would have the exclusive right to sell oil to Iran until a new export route, especially the Tengiz–Novorossiysk oil pipeline, is established (Zonn & Semenov, 2016).

Iran had its own oil resources in the Persian Gulf, but meeting the energy needs of the northern part of the country motivated it to take an interest in Caspian resources. The construction of an oil pipeline through the territory of Iran allowed Azerbaijan to expand southwards and use the Abadan terminals on the island of Kharg (Zonn & Semenov, 2016). However, this export route was blocked by the US, which was the main obstacle to its implementation. The US not only "closed the south gates" to the Caspian states, but also used false arguments for such a move. They declared that the route through Iran was neither the shortest nor advantageous from an economic or strategic point of view.

Thus, the Caspian states, fearing the loss of US support for their infrastructure projects, engaged in the development of projects proposed by the West. Despite the negative attitude of the US to the issue of Iran's participation in Caspian infrastructure projects, Tehran was developing the Caspian Sea Republic's Oil (CROS) SWAP project, which concerned the transport of Caspian oil to terminals in the Persian Gulf (Iran to propose oil swap, 2015).

The idea behind this project was that companies from Russia and other Caspian states supplied oil to the Iranian port of Neka off the coast of the Caspian Sea, and then its equivalent amount was sold through ports in the Persian Gulf. In the first stage, 315.000 barrels of crude oil per day was transported from Kazakhstan from the Tengiz, Kalamkas, and Kumkol fields via the Caspian Sea to the port of Neka, and then to the refineries in Tehran and Tabriz. The same amount of oil was then exported via the southern Iranian ports. Tehran attaches great importance to SWAP transactions, which could increase the capacity of the Neka–Tehran pipeline by up to ten times. This type of solution enables Iran, firstly, to reduce the cost of oil supplies to the northern part of the country, and second, it enables it to participate in the export of Caspian oil, disregarding US sanctions (Zonn & Semenov, 2016).

The second step, in this context, is the construction of a 2.500 km pipeline from Western Kazakhstan to Iran, where it will connect with the Neka–Tehran pipeline via the Turkmenbashi–Okarem section (Zonn & Semenov, 2016). This will allow increasing deliveries to 500.000 barrels a day. The third step will be to increase the infrastructure capacity to 1 mb/d due to the estimated increase in oil production in Kazakhstan and the inclusion of Azerbaijan and Turkmenistan's infrastructure (Zonn & Semenov, 2016). Iran supported the idea of exporting Turkmen gas through its territory to Turkey and further to Europe. In this context, National Iranian Gas Company (NIGC) conducted negotiations with European companies: Gaz de France (France), Ruhrgas (Germany), OMV (Austria), Enagaz (Spain), SSR (Czech Republic), and SPP (Slovakia) on the possibility of transporting Iranian gas to Europe via Turkey. In March 1993, a joint venture was created between Iran and France Gas Co-operation Company (Misiągiewicz, 2022, p. 539).

Iran then opted to link Turkmen gas to a single infrastructure. Thus, an ambitious plan for the construction of the Transcontinental Gas Pipeline was created. In the first stage, a pipeline section was to be built through the cities of Shahrood and Semnan to Tabriz and further onto the border with Turkey. This would provide 15 billion m^3 of gas annually for Turkey. Subsequently, it was planned to increase the pipeline capacity to 28 billion m^3 of gas per year. The estimated cost of this unfinished project is USD 11 billion (Zonn & Semenov, 2016).

Iran was interested in deepening energy cooperation with Turkmenistan. In 1992, Turkmenistan took the first step towards opening up to the world market by cooperating with Iran on the construction of a joint Turkmenistan–Iran gas pipeline. The 2.300 km-long gas pipeline, worth USD 4–5 billion, was to run through Iran, Turkey, and further on to Europe (Zonn et al., 2016, pp. 125–138). However, due to the lack of funds, the gas pipeline was not completed. A year later, the concept of exporting Turkmen gas to Europe via Iran and Turkey was reverted. First, Turkmenistan sought independence from the Russian market. Second, the dynamic development of the gas market in Turkey in the early 1990s showed the need for new sources of this fuel.

In 1992, an agreement was signed between Iran and Turkey regarding the construction of a gas pipeline to Europe. The length of the infrastructure was to be 2.300 km, and the cost of its construction was estimated at USD 4–5 billion (Zonn & Semenov, 2016). However, due to the lack of funds, another route was chosen to connect Western gas resources in Turkmenistan with the distribution system in the industrialized northern part of Iran: Korpezhe (Turkmenistan)–Kurt Kui (Iran). It was the first export line in the region, bypassing the territory of Russia (Zonn & Semenov, 2016).

In 1997, the 200 km-long gas pipeline was put into operation. Gas from Turkmenistan began to flow to Iran. The gas pipeline can transport 30 billion m^3 of gas annually, provided that Iran exports the same amount of gas abroad from the Persian Gulf. Both countries have signed a contract for gas supplies from Turkmenistan for 25 years.

After Turkmenistan initiated the operation of the second-largest gas field in the world, Galkynysh, with reserves ranging from 13.1 to 21.2 tonnes m^3 of gas, there was a need to look for new ways of exporting the fuel (Zonn &

Semenov, 2016). In the second half of the 1990s, Turkmenistan focused on two pipeline projects: through Afghanistan to Pakistan, and to Turkey through Iran, Azerbaijan, Armenia, and Georgia, and further to Europe (Zonn et al., 2016, pp. 125–138). However, the Turkmenistan–Iran–Turkey–Europe pipeline has become a priority of Turkmenistan's policy as an enormous infrastructure that could open the country to an absorbent and prospective gas market. The feasibility report was drawn up by the French Sofregaz. The length of the pipeline was to be 3.219 km. The government of Turkmenistan has guaranteed that within 30 years it will supply about 30 billion m^3 of gas via this pipeline, and the source will be the Yashlar and Dovletabad fields near Serakhsa, in the west of the country, near the border with Iran (Zonn et al., 2016).

In April 1994, Turkmenistan, Iran, and Turkey once again signed an agreement to build the pipeline. In August 1994, the presidents of these countries signed the Final Joint Agreement on the Project for Gas Transportation to Europe. However, due to pressure from the US, the project was not completed again. In 1995, the US adopted the so-called D'Amato Law, on the basis of which sanctions were imposed against foreign companies that invested over USD 20 million annually in the energy sector of Libya and Iran. Turkey was not willing to go against US interests. There were two conditions that linked the aspirations of Turkmenistan and Iran. First, the position of Iran, the world's second-largest gas producer, meant that the country treated any system that allows gas transit to the West through it as an opportunity to increase its position on the European market. Second, Turkmenistan's offer for gas transit harms US interests and strengthens Iran's position in the region (Syroezhkin, 2010, p. 117).

In January 2010, the second gas pipeline from Turkmenistan to Iran, Dovletabad–Serahs–Khangeran, was launched. Its capacity was 6–12 billion m^3 of gas. Thus, gas supplies from Turkmenistan to Iran amounted to 20 billion m^3 annually (Zonn et al., 2016, pp. 125–138).

Iranian Oil Minister Javad Owji told reporters after meeting with newly appointed Deputy Prime Minister of Turkmenistan Batyr Amanov in Tehran on May 2023, that:

> Turkmenistan ranks 4th in the world in terms of gas reserves. Iran has the capacity to transport 40–50 million m^3 of gas daily from this country. Based on this, Iran intends to increase its gas imports, swaps and sales. (Baghishov, 2023, n.p.)

The volume of gas being transited between Turkmenistan, Iran, and Azerbaijan under a three-way swap agreement signed in late 2021 is expected to grow by 70% in 2023 (Turkmenistan–Iran–Azerbaijan Gas Swaps Surge, 2023). M. Chegeni, the head of Iran's national gas company, NIGC did not mention the volume of gas he expected to be transited to Turkmenistan in 2023, but the original agreement allowed for 1.5–2 billion m³ a year, a volume which numerous subsequent reports said would quickly be increased. In mid-2022, Owji announced the "three partners had reached an agreement to double the volume of gas swaps" (Turkmenistan–Iran–Azerbaijan Gas Swaps Surge, 2023).

In the first decade of the 21st century, Iran focused mainly on deepening trade and economic relations with the Caspian states, and especially on participation in the export of hydrocarbons to world markets. It aims to play the role of the main transit country for Caspian hydrocarbons. In this respect, it has tightened relations with Kazakhstan and Turkmenistan as the main suppliers of hydrocarbons in the region. However, Iran's activity in the Caspian region is largely conditioned by restrictions resulting from US sanctions, which prevented the development of pipeline infrastructure to the south (Syroezhkin, 2010, p. 456).

4 The Eastern Route of Fossil Fuel Exports from the Caspian Region

The Caspian region, especially Kazakhstan, is a huge reservoir of oil located near the borders of China. The international activity of the Chinese energy sector was largely conditioned by geopolitical priorities. This area has therefore become an important element of China's new energy strategy—guaranteeing liquid oil supplies at a fixed price (Sharipov, 2008, pp. 392–413). Thus, the availability of energy resources motivated China to build export pipelines. The first supplier of energy to the PRC in the Caspian region was Kazakhstan. It began delivering crude oil to the Middle Kingdom in the 1990s (Zhiltsov & Grishicheva, 2016, pp. 105–116). China was engaged in expansion into the Kazakhstan market, especially its energy sector (Mikhamedzhanova, 2012, pp. 74–82). The implementation of the Kazakhstan–China oil pipeline project reflected China's energy security policy in the Caspian region (Zhiltsov & Grishicheva, 2016, pp. 105–116). The genesis of the project goes back to 1996, when an offer to sell shares of JSC "Uzenmunaigaz" was announced. Shareholders included Amoco (US), Petronas Carigali (Malaysia), Unocal (US), and China National Oil Company (CNOC). In June 1997, the CNOC acquired the majority of shares in Aktobemunaigaz (Zhiltsov & Grishicheva, 2016). Then, in August of the same year, China National Oil and Gas Exploration and Development Corporation, dependent on CNOC, became the second investor. The corporation acquired a 55% stake in Uzenmunaigaz. Over two decades, China has invested approximately USD 4 billion in oil-field equipment and operations. In this way, Chinese companies obtained control packages in two companies involved in oil exploration and transportation: Aktobemunaigaz and Uzenmunaigaz (Zhiltsov & Grishicheva, 2016).

In 1997, Prime Minister Li Peng paid an official visit to Kazakhstan, during which the issues of oil exports to China were discussed. Two intergovernmental agreements were signed on cooperation between the oil and gas industries and on the construction of two pipelines from Kazakhstan to Western China. The Chinese side undertook to design and build an oil pipeline with a length of 3.000 km and to invest USD 3 billion in a project for transporting oil from the Uzen and Aktobe (Aktyubinsk) fields. In this way, Kazakhstan, supported by China, started the process of implementing its policy, aimed at geographically expanding the routes for exporting energy to world markets. Under the contract, China's total investments in Kazakhstan's energy sector were to amount to USD 11 billion. They were to be allocated to the development of oil fields and the construction of a pipeline to the western part of China and Iran (Zhiltsov & Grishicheva, 2016). Chinese enterprises were treated as strategic partners, guaranteeing not only the implementation of pipeline projects, but also the opening of Kazakhstan to the world market (Imangaliev, 2008, pp. 108–109). The report on the feasibility of the pipeline from Kazakhstan to China assumed that no less than 20 million tonnes of oil would be transported on this route annually (Syroezhkin, 2010, p. 160).

The implementation of agreements on cooperation between the energy sectors of both countries and the construction of a common pipeline has encountered certain limitations. First, there was the problem of internal political changes in Kazakhstan, and second, the fall in oil prices on the world market. Such a situation meant that the construction of an expensive and extensive pipeline infrastructure could be ineffective. In addition to the objective economic problems associated with the construction of the pipeline, political considerations also have a role. The development of cooperation between Kazakhstan and the USA in the late 1990s called into question the feasibility of implementing the agreement between Kazakhstan and the PRC. There were declarations and critical opinions in Kazakhstan regarding the prospects for the construction of an oil pipeline to China due to low oil prices. There have been many consultations and talks between Kazakhstan and China regarding the construction of the pipeline.

They were completed in July 2000, when presidents Nazarbayev and Hu Jintao finally confirmed the feasibility of implementing the pipeline infrastructure project between the two countries. However, even the support at the highest level did not result in any actions towards the implementation of the project. The result of three years of negotiations between China and Kazakhstan (1998–2001) was disappointing, especially as there were no additional sources of oil to fill the pipeline. The Chinese company produced only about 5 million tonnes of oil per year, and the planned pipeline infrastructure project needed to transport no less than 20 million tonnes of oil to be economically viable. The only chance in this context would have been to connect at least two additional oil producers to the infrastructure. Furthermore, in 2001, the CPC infrastructure was commissioned, and the Atyrau–Samara pipeline restructuring project and the plan to increase its capacity additionally raised CNOC's doubts as to whether Kazakhstan would be able to fill the pipeline to China (Zhiltsov & Grishicheva, 2016, pp. 105–116).

The expectations regarding the prospects for the exploitation of the Caspian shelf were high, but there were also numerous problems regarding this matter. First, most of the oil companies operating in the region are private actors and negotiations with them would be based on strictly economic, not geopolitical, issues. Second, there were numerous difficulties in the construction of pipelines, such as: long distances, lack of infrastructure, mountainous territories, seismic instability, climatic diversity, or low quality of oil from Kazakhstan (Zhiltsov & Grishicheva, 2016). All this meant that the cost of the pipeline to China was increasing. According to the feasibility report, in the territory of Kazakhstan alone, pipes cross rivers in 22 places and in many cases they pass across roads and railways. It is also significant that the transit tariff was set at USD 9.5 per barrel of oil, which made the project unprofitable. Third, the oil pipeline was designed to complement the energy infrastructure of the Tarim Basin in the Uighur Autonomous Region. In this context, it should be noted that the political situation in the Xinjiang region, as well as in Central Asia, is not stable, and the energy infrastructure, in order to function efficiently and without disruptions, requires a safe international environment (Zhiltsov & Grishicheva, 2016).

Thus, pipeline infrastructure projects in the Caspian region face many problems, both politically and economically. Nevertheless, during his official visit to Beijing in December 2002, President Nazarbayev declared that the key issues of cooperation between Kazakhstan and China were energy, oil, and gas, as well as the construction of a common oil and gas pipeline. Despite numerous problems, China decided to implement the pipeline project from Kazakhstan.

In spring 2003, the Kenkiyak–Atyrau line in western Kazakhstan went into operation, with an initial capacity of 6 million tonnes (European Bank for

Reconstruction and Development, n.d.; Interfax, 2023). It was the first joint Kazakh–Chinese project. Its length was 448 km, and the throughput was increased to 12 million tonnes of oil per year. The pipeline was supplied with the resources of the Kenkiyak, Zhanazhol, Alibekmola, and Kozhasai fields and other resources located in the Aktiubinsk region (Zhiltsov & Grishicheva, 2016, pp. 105–116).

Then, in October 2003, China and Kazakhstan returned to the issue of building international infrastructure. The goal was to ensure oil supplies to China in the amount of 20–50 million tonnes. The eastern direction of oil transport from Kazakhstan was implemented under an agreement signed in 2004 with China. The intergovernmental agreement concerned the development of mutual cooperation within the oil and gas sector and the implementation of the second phase of the Kazakhstan–China pipeline (KCP) by China National Petroleum Corporation (CNPC) and KazMunayGas in 2006 (Parkhomchik, 2016, pp. 139–152). Under the agreement, the Atasu–Alashankou and Kenkiyak–Kumkol pipelines were built, and their operation began in 2006 and 2009, respectively. The pipeline infrastructure route ran through the regions of Karaganda, East Kazakhstan, and Almaty to finally reach Alashankou in China. The Kazakhstan–China Pipeline joint venture was established, consisting of JSC Kaztrans Oil and Chinese National Corporation on Oil and Gas Exploration and Development. The international agreement on the development of cooperation in the energy field formalized joint activities in the field of exploitation, production, processing, and transport of energy resources.

The pipeline project consisted of two phases. In the first phase, the construction of the Atasu–Alashankou line with a capacity of 10 million tonnes of crude oil per year, with the possibility of doubling it, took place. In the second phase, the Kenkiyak–Kumkol–Atasu line was built, with the capacity to transport 20–50 million tonnes of oil per year (Zhiltsov & Grishicheva, 2016, pp. 105–116).

China pushed for the implementation of the infrastructure project due to its aspirations to expand its influence in the Central Asian region in the energy sector. Beijing intended to become an intermediary in the process of Kazakhstan's integration into the global energy market. As a result, construction of the Atasu–Alashankou line began in September 2004 and was completed in December 2005. The cost of the construction was approximately USD 800 milion. The infrastructure was launched in July 2006. China planned to implement the project by 2004 but was prompted to delay it because of low oil prices. The initial capacity of the pipeline was 10 million tonnes of oil per year.

The source of supply was the Kumkol deposits (Zhiltsov & Grishicheva, 2016). Project members began implementing the second stage of the second phase of pipeline infrastructure expansion. The main goal was to expand the Kumkol–Atasu line, connecting the western and eastern parts of the Kazakhstan–China pipeline. As part of the reconstruction, the capacity of the Atyrau to Alashankou pipeline was to be increased to 20 million tonnes. In the medium term, Kazakhstan was not able to fill the KCP system. Kazakhstan signed an agreement with Russia under which Russian oil was to be delivered to China via Kazakhstan. This resulted in 7 million tonnes per year being pumped through the KCP pipeline (from Ommsk in Russia, to Priirtyshska and Atasu in Kazakhstan, to China) (Parkhomchik, 2016, pp. 139–152). China's Export–Import Bank agreed to finance the USD 1 billion construction of the Atyrau refinery as the major hub for the Kashagan field. This represented a significant contribution to the modernization of three refineries in Kazakhstan, which required capital expenditures of USD 4 billion (Zhiltsov & Grishicheva, 2016, pp. 105–116). The entire pipeline was built by the Sino-Kazakh Pipeline Company (a joint venture between CNPC and KMG).

In December 2007, construction began on the Kenkiyak–Kumkol pipeline, the third and final section of infrastructure from Kazakhstan to China. However, system capacity caused some controversy. In the first six months of operation, the Kenkiyak–Kumkol line transported only 1.3 million tonnes of oil but after the test period ended, the volumes of fuel gradually increased. The initial capacity of the line was 10 million tonnes of oil per year with the prospect of doubling (Bogaturov, 2011, p. 549). In the first half of 2023, 10.9 million tonnes of oil were transported through the Atasu–Alashankou pipeline, and 6.7 through the Kenkiyak–Kumkol pipeline.

The project cost about USD 1 billion and the 793 km line was completed in July 2009. Thus, the great infrastructure project from Kazakhstan to China was completed. However, the PRC intended to gain even greater access to Caspian resources, seeing a number of benefits in the launch of an export connection with Kazakhstan (Kuzmina, 2007, pp. 90–98). These were: favorable transport conditions; the possibility of direct contact with the recipient; and no transit through third states, which eliminated additional political and economic risk. At the end of 2012, the pipeline was already transporting 52.1 million tonnes. It was the first oil pipeline from Kazakhstan to bypass Russian territory.

The end of the first decade of the 21st century saw changes in China's energy policy. First, Sino-Kazakh relations strengthened and displayed characteristics of a strategic partnership. Second, Kazakhstan complemented the Chinese economy in terms of resources. Third, China became an active geopolitical actor in the Caspian region and a desirable investor for the post-Soviet states. Since the 1990s, the PRC was also interested in the possibility of building gas pipelines (Zhiltsov & Grishicheva, 2016, pp. 105–116). In this context, Kazakhstan and Turkmenistan were considered potential sources of gas. After the collapse of the USSR, the only way to export gas from Turkmenistan was through Russian territory. This was due to the geographic position of Russia and the fact that the only pipeline infrastructure available on its territory was the post-Soviet one. Turkmenistan therefore joined the talks on building new pipelines to export the resources independently.

In 1993, during the conference on Perspectives of Eurasia as Space for Global Communication held in Berlin, the National Pipeline Research Society of Japan presented a proposal for the Trans-Asian Gas Pipeline project. It represented one of the many options for transporting gas from Northeast Asia to the North Pacific. The Turkmenistan–Western China–Japan international gas pipeline was to be part of this route. The project envisaged the construction of a gas pipeline through the Tarim Basin in western China to transport Turkmen gas to Shanghai and other coastal Chinese areas. From there, some of the fuel would be exported to Japan via a submarine pipeline. At the time, the Chinese government showed interest in the project. The option of the Turkmenistan–Uzbekistan–China–Korean Peninsula gas pipeline was also discussed. It was planned to cost USD 10 billion and have a capacity of 18 billion m^3 per year. However, due to the low price of gas and the high cost of construction, any gas pipeline option in that period seemed ineffective, hence eastern export route projects were suspended (Zhiltsov et al., 2016).

In 1995, Russia changed its energy policy towards the post-Soviet region. In order to enhance gas exports to foreign markets and obtain greater revenues, the state refused to allow Turkmenistan to transit gas through its territory. As a result, Turkmen gas was isolated from foreign markets as it ceased to be competitive due to high transport costs. Uzbekistan and Kazakhstan charged Turkmenistan transit fees that were higher than those in other parts of the world. Due to this, Turkmenistan's gas production fell almost sevenfold between 1991 and 1998 (Zhiltsov et al., 2016). Pipeline insulation motivated Turkmenistan to implement a new strategy for the development of the energy sector and look for additional opportunities to export hydrocarbons (Zhiltsov et al., 2016). The country began making efforts to attract foreign investments, mainly by introducing a legislative framework to facilitate the operation of foreign enterprises. Turkmenistan entered the "game" and has attracted the attention of the West by overestimating its energy resources and their production prospects.

The idea of building a gas pipeline between Turkmenistan and China was mooted as early as 1993, when Western companies were investigating the opportunities of energy development in Central Asia after the fall of the USSR. At the same time, the infrastructure construction plan was delayed due to Turkmenistan's policy of isolationism under President Saparmurat Niyazov.

The issue of Turkmen gas supplies to China was raised in 1996 as part of the Turkmen–China–Japan large-scale pipeline infrastructure project known as the "Energy Silk Road." The pipeline was to be 8.000 km long and deliver 30 billion m^3 gas per year. It was designed by the Chinese Petroleum Engineering & Construction Corporation. Subsequently, Mitsubishi Corporation (Japan) and Exxon (US) joined the project and anticipated greater profits from transporting gas from Turkmenistan than from Siberia (Zhiltsov & Grishicheva, 2016, pp. 105–116). The project was part of a branched infrastructure linking Turkmenistan, Uzbekistan, and Kazakhstan with recipients in China, South Korea, and Japan.

In August 1998, Turkmenistan and China discussed the feasibility of the project. Construction costs of about USD 8–12 billion were considered. China declared that "the dynamically developing energy market in this state needs Turkmen gas" (Zhiltsov & Grishicheva, 2016, p. 105). In October that year, a feasibility report for the project was prepared. Between 2003 and 2005, Chinese enterprises conducted research in the Amu Darya River coastal area in Turkmenistan in search of gas resources (Syroezhkin, 2010, p. 117).

Simultaneously, due to the price rise of this gas in the global market, the pipeline project became more attractive. Consequently, discussions resumed on an infrastructure project to China. The corporations also completed research on the right bank of the Amu Darya River in Turkmenistan, which found great energy potential of the area (Syroezhkin, 2010). It was estimated that gas production would soar as a result of the exploitation both of the existing and newly discovered deposits in Zunguz Karakums and Amu Darya.

The "Chinese option" thus became the dominant direction in gas exports from Turkmenistan (Misiągiewicz, 2022, p. 549). Relations between China and Turkmenistan gained new momentum after the president of Turkmenistan, S. Niyazov, paid an official to visit Beijing in April 2006. At the time, a contract worth USD 1.5 billion was signed for gas exploitation in Turkmenistan. Under the agreement, the CNOC was to carry out 12 exploratory drillings in the southeastern Turkmenistan. It agreed that the Turkmenistan–China infrastructure have a capacity of 30 billion m^3 of gas per year (Central Asia–China Gas Pipeline, 2023). The total length of the world's longest gas pipeline is 7.000 km, of which 200 km operated in Turkmenistan, 550 km in Uzbekistan, 1304 km in Kazakhstan, and over 4.860 km in China (Zhiltsov & Grishicheva, 2016, pp. 105–116). The source of gas for the pipeline were gas fields on the right bank of the Amu Darya River (Galkynysh, Iolatan–Osman, and Dovletabad), and were exploited under production participation contracts.

In 2007, CNPC signed an agreement with Niyazov's successor, Gurbanguly Berdimuhamedov. On this basis, Chinese experts began geological explorations and development of the Bagtiyarlyk gas fields. In July 2007, China signed a contract with Turkmenistan regarding shares in gas production from this field on the right bank of the Amu Darya River. It was planned to produce 13 billion m^3 of gas per year. The remaining 17 billion m^3 was to be extracted from other fields. The states agreed to conduct joint research and exploitation works. Construction of the gas pipeline began in 2007. In August 2008, in Beijing, President Bedimuhamedov of Turkmenistan held talks with CNOC heads, which resulted in an agreement that the pipeline would be built by 2009 with a capacity of 40 billion m^3 of gas, which was more than previously forecast (Central Asia–China Gas Pipeline, 2023). In June 2009, Turkmenistan and China reached an agreement under which Beijing was to grant a loan of USD 3 billion for the expansion of the Galkynysh gas field, viewed as a resource base for the future export pipeline.

In the first phase, the gas pipeline had a capacity of up to 10 billion m^3 per year, from the Samantepe and Altyn Asyr fields. In the second phase, an additional 17 billion m^3 was transported. The volumes of gas transported soared rapidly to 30, 45, and 60 billion m^3 annually. Three phases of infrastructure have been completed and opened. The agreement also provides for the transport of 80 billion m^3 of gas in the future. The first two lines of the gas pipeline from Turkmenistan to China were commissioned in 2009, and the third one in 2014 (Cutter, 2014, pp. 673–698).

In December 2009, in the Samandepe field, where gas supplied to China was extracted, a ceremony was held to launch the Turkmenistan–China line, attended by representatives of Kazakhstan and Uzbekistan (Zhiltsov & Grishicheva, 2016, pp. 105–116). The gas pipeline from Turkmenistan was built in 2010 and its further expansion was planned. China also established close cooperation in the energy sector with Uzbekistan, a transit state for Turkmen gas.

In 2010, gas exports via this pipeline amounted to 10 billion m^3, and in 2014 it transported 30 billion m^3 of gas from Turkmenistan and 10 billion m^3 from Kazakhstan (Zonn et al., 2016, pp. 125–138). In 2014, a fourth gas pipeline line was built through the territory of Uzbekistan. The total capacity of the infrastructure is about 80 billion m^3 of gas (Central Asia–China Gas Pipeline, 2023).

China is accelerating the building of a long-delayed Central Asian pipeline to source gas from Turkmenistan even as Russia pushes its own new Siberian connection, as Beijing juggles its energy security needs with diplomatic priorities (China Prioritizing Turkmenistan, 2023).

By building a gas pipeline in Central Asia, China broke Russia's monopoly on gas exports. It also took control of the greatest resources of Turkmenistan in South Iolotan (Motyashov, 2011, pp. 188–189). The launch of the so-called "gas pipeline of the century" between Turkmenistan and China met the growing demand of the Chinese economy for hydrocarbon resources. The location of the pipeline in the area of the historic Silk Road is also symbolic (Zhiltsov & Grishicheva, 2016, pp. 105–116). In 2022, China imported 35 bcm gas worth USD 10.3 billion via pipelines from Turkmenistan, compared with 16 bcm via a single pipeline from Russia at about USD 4 billion (China Prioritizing Turkmenistan over Russia in Next Big Pipeline Project, 2023).

CNPC also negotiated with KazMunaiGaz to import gas from Kazakhstan. In March 2006, both companies signed an agreement to build a 1.304 km gas pipeline as part of the Turkmenistan–China infrastructure. Kazakhstan signed an agreement for gas supplies to China in August 2007. This project operated within the Central Asia–China transcontinental system (Parkhomchik, 2016, pp. 139–152). In March 2008, KazTransGaz and Trans-Asia Gas Pipeline Company Limited (dependent on CNOC) formed a joint venture, Asian Gas Pipeline, to implement the Kazakhstan–China gas pipeline.

In July 2008, the construction of the pipeline was officially launched, and in July 2009, the first line of the Kazakhstan–China gas pipeline was completed. In this way, Kazakhstan developed a new pipeline infrastructure to export both oil and gas to the foreign market.

The gas pipeline consists of two parallel lines. The first section of the pipeline has a capacity of 40 billion m³ of gas annually and starts at the border between Uzbekistan and Kazakhstan and ends at the Chinese border. The second section, with a capacity of 10 billion m³ of gas annually, runs along the Bainau–Bozoy–Kyzylorda–Shimken route (Zhiltsov & Grishicheva, 2016, pp. 105–116). The first phase of the project included a supply of 10 billion m³ of gas annually to China, the second phase supplied 30 billion m³ of gas from the Karachaganak and Kashagan fields. The pipeline runs from Chelkar in the Aktobe region in western Kazakhstan, where CNPC has been active for a long time. The Kazakh part of the gas pipeline begins at the Uzbek–Kazakhstan border, it then runs through Shimken all the way to Khorgos, 650 km east through Kazakhstan, and ends at the border with China, not far from the Khorgos border post. In 2010, the two states launched the construction of a 1.164 km pipeline from Bozoi to Shimken to supply southern Kazakhstan with gas (Cutter, 2014, pp. 673–698). It was then extended by 310 km to Bainau, where it connects with the Turkmenista–China gas pipeline (ibid). The infrastructure is designed to support the gasification of the southern part of Kazakhstan.

The decision to implement a joint pipeline between Kazakhstan and China was a logical consequence of the energy policies pursued by both states. Chinese energy companies sought to enhance their shares in Kazakhstan's fuel sector. When investing in this industry, they also took into consideration the prospect of a declining hydrocarbon production in the country. Nevertheless, the largest Chinese companies, such as CNPC and SINOPEC, became leaders in oil production in Kazakhstan (Izimov, 2014).

The Chinese operated mainly in the oil fields in the Kyzylorda and Atyrau regions. They gradually took over the Caspian resources. CNPC bought Conoco Phillips' shares in the project to exploit the North Caspian Sea (8.3%). The company became a participant in the Kashagan project. The share of Chinese businesses in Kazakhstan's energy sector is approximately 24% (Parkhomchik, 2016, pp. 139–152).

It is noteworthy that strengthening the line of action of Kazakhstan's Chinese energy policy is connected with the lack of opportunities for the implementation of projects to diversify hydrocarbons export routes (Parkhomchik, 2016). The Turkmen–Chinese gas pipeline, together with the Sino-Caucasian infrastructure, represent the entire structure of pipelines from Central Asia to China.

According to Martin Clark, an analyst at the London-based Petroleum Economist, the operation of the pipeline between Kazakhstan and China is a triumph for both states, as it demonstrates "Beijing's growing influence" over Central Asia, and Moscow's weak control over oil flows from Kazakhstan, which has so far been transported through Russia (Clark, 2005, pp. 2–3). Following the Xinhua news agency: "the development and deepening of cooperation in oil and gas is a strategic economic interest for both states" (Xuanli Liao, 2006, p. 40). William Engdahl, the author of the book *A Century of War: Anglo-American Oil Politics and the New World Order*, stated that close cooperation between China and Kazakhstan will not only strengthen the superpower in terms of energy security but will also limit the influence and possibilities of the US in Eurasia (Engdahl, 2005).

5   Conclusion

After the collapse of the USSR, new independent states emerged in the Caspian Sea region. They had rich deposits of oil and gas. Since then, the exploitation of resources has become their main goal (Yergin, 2011, p. 43; Kruse, 2014, pp. 17–22). The Caspian Sea is a closed reservoir, so the only way to transport fossil fuels is through pipelines.

The development of oil and gas fields in Azerbaijan and Kazakhstan motivated the projects of new pipelines. The newly established states needed modern export infrastructure because the post-Soviet one proved insufficient. New routes were considered not only by fossil fuel producers but also by states that aspired to the role of transit areas. First of all, Georgia and Turkey should be mentioned here because of their location, which is convenient for the transport of oil and gas from Azerbaijan. Simultaneously, various regional actors emerge when significant energy resources appear. In addition to coastal states, external actors such as the US, EU, and China are also involved. Many options for exporting oil from the Caspian region existed but the most significant, though the most expensive, was the route from Azerbaijan, through Georgia, to Turkey and to the Mediterranean port of Ceyhan. The pipeline was constructed after strong pressure from the West, despite Russia's opposition. The emergence of fossil fuels transport routes in the Caspian region made it possible to export hydrocarbons to the international market. The new situation has completely changed the pipeline geography in this region of the world. This process progressed in proportion to the development of the energy potential of the analyzed area. Thus, the competition over the oil and gas export infrastructure intensified.

It evolved into a rivalry in the political, geostrategic, and geoeconomic fields. The states of the region, corporations, and external powers seek to maximize profits from the exploitation of the new mining and transport infrastructure in the region. The Caspian region became an area of international interest. This transformation was termed the "New Great Game," related to access to energy resources and export routes. However, the region is exposed to various types of ethnic and political instability, which affects the security and investment environment. Pipeline diplomacy in the Caspian region is conditioned primarily by relations between the EU and Russia, especially in the context of packages of sanctions related to the energy sector.

Competition between external actors may, on the one hand, be stimulating (in the case of the construction of new pipelines), and, on the other, paradoxically, may lead to blocking individual infrastructure projects.

Although the issue of hydrocarbon export routes in the Caspian region is problematic from a geographical and economic point of view, "flagship" energy infrastructure projects have been developed. An example is the operation and extension of the Southern Gas Corridor, and the expansion of the transport infrastructure from Kazakhstan and Turkmenistan to China. In addition, the littoral states of the region, despite the fact that their economic interests are

not always consistent, show cooperation, as exemplified by increased oil transportation and gas swap between Azerbaijan, Kazakhstan, and Turkmenistan.
It seems that the most promising project, the implementation of which will
definitely strengthen the security of gas supplies in Europe, is the Trans–
Caspian Pipeline. However, the new international order in the post-Soviet area
of Central Asia and the Caucasus, which we expect, given the weakening role
of Russia, may also contribute to changing the pipeline architecture in the
Caspian region.

CHAPTER 5

Perspectives for Energy Security Policies in the Caspian Region

Energy security analyses include long-term development trends as well as unpredictable events related to the functioning of energy infrastructure and technology. Thus, unexpected and sudden events resulting from the dynamics of the international environment gain in importance. New energy systems and new technologies can lead the world towards new dependencies and threats.

The transformations on the energy market, related to the shale gas revolution in the US and the intensified exploitation of renewable resources, caused transformations both in oil prices and revenues for oil-exporting states. Investments in the energy sector of the Caspian region states diminished as a result of this situation. Due to the withdrawal of Western investors, these states are largely targeting Asian markets, where fossil fuels are used more intensively. Thus, Azerbaijan is the most vulnerable to changes in the global market, as it exports to the Western market and became dependent on Western investments.

In the 1990s, following great optimism about the energy potential of the newly established Caspian states, many ambitious pipeline infrastructure projects were developed, which were not completed or have only recently been launched, and the prospect of their exploitation depends on various international energy market conditions. Some are still valid but their implementation is conditioned by the possibilities of exploiting new raw energy sources.

Analyses of oil production prospects in the Caspian states indicate that in 2030s, infrastructure projects that had not been implemented can be implemented. During this period, these states will be able to exploit new hydrocarbon resources, whose export will require new pipelines (Gadzhiev, 2010, pp. 488–509). Moreover, the changing current geopolitical situation, connected with the escalation of the Russian war in Ukraine, will probably increase the role of the Caspian producers as the alternative source for oil and gas to Europe.

The last part of the monograph therefore presents the predictive dimension of energy security policy research in the Caspian region.

1   New Challenges of the International Energy Market

Energy security as security of supply is analyzed in terms of geopolitics, foreign affairs, and energy policy. Energy security analyzes also take into account the future changes in the energy mix, especially in the use of renewable sources and transformation in the social dimension (Heinonen et al., 2017, pp. 2–13). The literature often views energy transformation as an important factor of social development. Energy is a sector under constant change and pressure. The energy sector is not only an economic or technological phenomenon but also a cultural and social as well (Heinonen et al., 2017).

Risk is an inevitable part of the energy sector due to economic conditions and geopolitical or environmental issues. Changes in energy prices can have serious social repercussions in the country. The risk may also arise from possible unrelated factors, such as tsunamis, earthquakes, or other natural disasters (Heinonen et al., 2017). Energy security analyses include unpredictable events related to the functioning of energy infrastructure and technology. Thus, unexpected, sudden events, referred to in the literature as "wild cards" and "black swans," gain importance.

Recently, businesses, governments, and international organizations have paid more attention to the risk and vulnerability of energy systems. Problems and distortions in this dimension inform thinking about innovation and economic and social change. We currently live in times of permanent change caused by the development of technology, the requirements of sustainable development, and unpredictable political and social processes (Heinonen et al., 2017). Concepts such as "megatrends" or "great transformations" were created to describe these phenomena, considering their specific nature. However, far-fetched interpretations are often formulated.

From the theoretical point of view, the dynamic complexity, "dynamite," causes rapid, progressive processes and sudden turning points in which the system undergoes fundamental changes. The indicators of these changes differ in the spheres of finance, mobility, and the way of life.

Following M. Pietraś, we are currently moving from the Westphalian to the post-Westphalian order. A new international environment, created by globalization processes, coexist with the old, Westphalian ones (Pietraś, 2008, pp. 123–134). The technological factor is essential here, as it causes a historical acceleration, social changes, the reorganization of the world economy, the evolution of political processes, and the possibility of communication and movement. This confirms the hypothesis that today we live in the era of acceleration, which means innovation, enormous economic and social changes, and an acceleration of the political decision-making process.

In addition, the international environment is no longer state-centric, and is distinguished by the heterogeneity of actors. Thus, a sector of transnational actors is emerging, which operates across state borders (Pietraś, 2008). Another feature of the so-called late-Westphalian international system is the simultaneous occurrence of opposing tendencies—processes of decentralization, fragmentation, and disintegration, as well as centralization and integration. Fragmegration means simultaneous fragmentation and integration; glocalization, in turn, is the interpenetration and conditioning of that which is global and that which is local. Local decisions and events thus have global repercussions and vice versa (Pietraś, 2008). Hence, the importance of random, nonlinear phenomena increases, and decision-making processes must take into account a greater number of variables, thus increasing the instability of the international environment (Pietraś, 2008).

Some researchers even speculate that in the next three decades, technological transformations will be so dynamic that they will change the structure of the history of mankind (Heinonen et al., 2017, pp. 2–13). One thing is certain: the future will be different from the present but it will not resemble the future we imagine.

In this context, the concept of VUCA was created: an acronym for four phenomena: *volatility, uncertainty, complexity,* and *ambiguity* (Heinonen et al., 2017). The concept is about the relationship between energy transition and societal transformation:

1.   *Volatility*: describes the growth rate in many areas, characterized by the "variability of the directions of change" and a high frequency of "ups and downs" through disruptions of trends. In the energy dimension, volatility manifests itself in new technologies and lifestyle changes in societies. This makes it possible to create radical energy scenarios related to the energy transformation towards renewables (Heinonen et al., 2017).

2.   *Uncertainty*: indicates the conditions under which decisions are made in different eras. Unpredictability has become the norm in recent decades due to the impact of technological innovations. In this context, the multiplicity of actors, and the variety of their interests, influences, and theories about changes in the contemporary world cause uncertainty. Even the most advanced research tools for predicting the future have their limitations mainly due to social conditions (Heinonen et al., 2017). Most of the future civilizational challenges cannot be predicted.

3.   *Complexity*: indicates that many different conditions and elements interact in different ways. This creates specific systems with different dynamics and structures. Regarding the great energy transformations, various actors, structures, and organizations, both centralized and community-based,

play a pivotal role. In recent decades, in the globalization age, the development of social media, and the digitization of the economy, these connections are becoming even closer and more dynamic.

4. *Ambiguity*: identifies difficulties in understanding meaning, forming conclusions, and interpreting new, unusual phenomena. Epistemologically, incompatibility between the processes of prediction and explanation can be seen. Understanding the specificity of the system and interpreting how it functions requires simple models, as opposed to the predictive dimension, which is usually based on complex models that include a variety of conditions. "It is possible to simultaneously make sense of something *ex post* but impossible to foresee it *ex ante*, and predictable but not impossible to interpret" (Heinonen et al., 2017).

Research on VUCA indicators also addresses the probability of disturbances resulting from extreme events. In this context, the concept of the "black swan" and "wild card" or "event X" appears. They inform about the possibility of sudden, unexpected changes that have profound and radical consequences (Mack et al., 2015, pp. 3–41).

The "black swan" concept refers to events that are difficult or even impossible to predict, and when they do occur, their consequences may be global. Such events may be negative or positive. Although "black swans" are unpredictable, a combination of different markers can be indicative of the occurrence of such events.

"Wild cards' are phenomena or solutions with a very low probability of occurrence, but once they occur, they have a huge impact on the system in which they occur. This impact can be negative or positive. These phenomena appear as a "strategic surprise" and often provoke inadequate, delayed or wrong decisions (Heinonen et al., 2017, pp. 2–13).

While "black swans" are unnamed and unimaginable, "wild cards" can be imagined and even identified. We can thus create a "set" of "wild cards" as potential scenarios. Both "black swans" and "wild cards" have varying risks of occurrence as they are difficult to predict due to the lack of precedent. Thus, it is important to be prepared for such "surprises" by creating action scenarios.

Extreme events, the "X events," are viewed as negative and problematic in the short term. In the long term, they may represent opportunities of changing an ineffective system. In this context, such events contribute to civilizational progress. This concept stems from a critique of focusing on an analysis of trends which result from continuity and linearity.

Ariel Colonomos points out that if we want to predict the future, it is important to tell continuation from suddenness of events (Colonomos, 2016).

"X events," "black swans," and "wild cards" largely reflect the researcher's world-view, knowledge, or faith. All of these events are hard to predict but they can be imagined and described according to the observer's vision. In this context, the technological, infrastructural, or economic transformations may induce dramatic changes in the material and mental dimensions. "Black swans" in energy transformation will also manifest themselves in the political and social fields (Heinonen et al., 2017, pp. 2–13).

Energy security, economic development, and the challenges of climate change are interrelated, as the production of energy based on hydrocarbon fuels and the growing consumption of energy resources increase greenhouse gas emissions and environmental pollution (Emmons et al., 2021, p. 3; Młynarski, 2017, p. 11). Therefore, the importance of the ecological aspect of security is growing (Pietraś, 2000). Defining security in terms of energy and climate security makes it necessary to extend the concept of energy security to include the issues of sustainable development (Neag et al., 2017, pp. 24–30), that is to say, one where "the civilisation needs of the present generation are met without compromising the development opportunities of future generations" (Młynarski, 2017, p. 11).

Sustainable development has three pillars: environmental, economic, and social (Konisky, 2020). It is development that ensures that the current needs are met and does not restrict future generations from meeting their needs. The growth of the world population over the past decades is increasing energy demand, especially in developing countries, which, in turn, is increasing CO_2 emissions (Konisky, 2020). At the same time, economically developed and industrialized countries are trying to convince the less affluent ones of the necessity to protect the climate and reduce dependence on fossil fuels. It is difficult, given the prospect of having to invest more in environmental protection. Thus, the international climate change regime has become one of the main determinants of the energy security policy since the 1990s (Pietraś, 2011). Climate change requires the transformation of the energy production structure towards renewable sources. Energy transformation is also linked to reduction in energy consumption. Current energy demand is roughly 110.000 TWh (Heinonen et al., pp. 2–13). It is also estimated that this value will increase to 130.000 TWh, despite a significant increase in energy efficiency.

Reducing access to energy may become a cause of sociopolitical destabilization. Conversely, an increase in energy supply can also cause destabilization of the global market. Greater amounts of cheaper energy along with the technological progress make the VUCA factors increasingly important. Such a situation deepens the changes and leads to a revaluation of power and strength in international relations (Heinonen et al.).

The policy of energy security and climate change is the subject of a game of interests and international negotiations (Neag et al., 2017, pp. 24–30). Neorealist and neoliberal theories are therefore useful as they help identify the level at which cooperation is possible and to determine what kind of benefits actors can produce. Research using these paradigms will provide insight into the interests of actors, both at the international and domestic political levels, as well as the role of international institutions and organizations in creating norms to support the international energy and climate regime (Młynarski, 2017, p. 19; Cannavo, 2011).

The realistic concept in the theory of international relations does not address global warming because it deals with the so-called traditional security threats. The realists dealt more with the geostrategic matters concerning the competition between states for resources. According to John Mearsheimer, environmental degradation and global warming cause for concern but do not threaten the survival of a superpower (Mearsheimer, 2001).

Contemporary realism has expanded the category of security to include aspects of economic policy, recognizing that military power lost its importance, and states seek to establish principles of cooperation that will provide them with effective economic influence, weakening the domination of other states. For neorealists, not only security, strength, and power are important but also independence and ability to influence. According to Robert Gilpin, the economic and technological potential is the driving force behind the activity of states on an international scale, as technological development creates favorable conditions for economic development. He also emphasized the importance of demographic, ecological, and economic determinants as factors of change in the international environment (Gilpin, 1981, p. 56).

Neoliberal institutionalism addresses the role of international organizations in preventing climate change. It provides for the establishment and protection of strong institutions, standards, and procedures for the global management of energy and climate security (Młynarski, 2017, p. 24). Regimes focus on the relationship between state interests and norm systems. According to liberals, regimes are important in the process of influencing the mechanisms of international cooperation and politics, and have become a tool for shaping international interactions. Being the driving force of global politics, international organizations create unified state-level effects (Młynarski, 2017, p. 25).

Liberals stress the analysis of states' intentions for cooperation, while realists point to difficulties in achieving and maintaining the cooperation. Realists believe that states are focused on achieving benefits that are "relative" (affecting their position relative to others). Liberals, in turn, assume that "absolute" benefits in the negotiation process are the most important (maximizing own gains, regardless of what other states receive) (Młynarski, 2017, p. 26; Czaputowicz, 2006).

The link between energy and environmental policy stems from the fact that the energy sector has the greatest impact on the environment. The relationship of climate policy and the energy sector has its consequences for the energy security of states, in particular of those that rely heavily on fossil fuels. Until now, the main issues shaping energy security have been access to energy resources, continuity of supply, and stable prices. Currently, in the face of the necessity to counteract global warming, the assumptions of the energy policy of states are increasingly influenced by environmental aspects, that is to say, climate policy, which increasingly conditions their energy mixes (Młynarski, 2017, p. 30).

States increasingly attach importance to the need to increase investment in green technologies. Thus, the importance of the environmental dimension of energy security is growing. It includes the reduction of negative environmental impacts at all levels of energy management: from extraction, through processing, transportation, and consumption. Energy production is one of the most environmentally damaging industries. It accounts for 80% of global greenhouse gas emissions (Młynarski, 2017, p. 31).

Climate change is therefore undermining the traditional understanding of energy security, which has so far been associated with resource scarcity. The concept of energy security must be redefined and expanded to include climate security. The objectives of the climate policy must be reflected in the energy policies of states and in international law. Traditional concepts of energy security must be re-evaluated, especially in terms of the tendency to prefer cheap energy sources, preventing the effective reduction of greenhouse gas emissions. Energy security, based on a diversified energy mix and in line with the concept of sustainable development, requires raising the importance of the so-called alternative energy sources, that is to say RES and nuclear energy (Bahr et al., 2021, p. 125) (Table 5.1).

With growing demand for energy, reducing emissions from the energy sector will be key to mitigating the effects of global warming. The energy intensity of the global economy, despite economic growth, fell by 3% in 2014. Global emissions related to the energy sector are rising but at a slower rate. This is related to the commitments made by the different states (Młynarski, 2017, p. 38). The relationship between economic growth and environmental care should be shaped in a way that balances economic, social, and environmental needs. The need to reduce emissions stimulates the demand for low-emission technologies on a global scale and influences the development of domestic sources of its production (Młynarski, 2017, p. 38).

TABLE 5.1   Environmental impact of individual energy sources

Source	CO_2/KWh emissions	Environmental impact
Oil	0.80	High CO_2 sulfur oxide, nitrogen emissions Environmental disaster risk in the transportation and extraction process
Coal	0.96	Very high emissions of GHGs (greenhouse gases) and fluids that amplify the greenhouse effect Negative impact of dust emissions on human health Land deformation, lowering of the groundwater level, drinking water contamination as a result of the exploitation of resources
Natural gas	0.4	GHG emissions from gas flaring and methane escape at drill holes Wastes from gas desulfurization processes (sulfur). Degradation of areas by drilling and transport infrastructure
Nuclear energy	0.0	The risk of radioactive contamination in the event of an accident or in the transport of radioactive materials or as a result of improper disposal of waste. Emission of pollutants to air and water in the enrichment of uranium ore Thermal pollution of rivers and lakes caused by power plant cooling water
RES	0.0	Landscape transformation Disturbance of aquatic ecosystems by noise and vibration. The risk of birds colliding with wind turbines Generation of hazardous waste from batteries

SOURCE: MŁYNARSKI, 2017

There is a fundamental contradiction between energy security and environmental security (Collins, 2022, p. 6). Energy is essential for the functioning of modern industrial and post-industrial societies (Hughes, 2019, p. 343). Security of energy supply and energy production is a guarantee of the prosperity and development of societies. Environmental safety, in turn, is associated with threats that are mainly of a forward-looking nature. Its energy dimension is based on the use of hydrocarbon fuels. However, their use has dire consequences for the environment (Młynarski, 2017, p. 38).

Richard Ullman, in the article, "Redefining Security," declared the need to redefine threats to national security. According to him, it includes: wars, rebellions, boycotts, shortages of energy, natural disasters, and epidemics. He defined threats to national security as "actions or sequences of events" that:

1. threaten drastically and can degrade the quality of life of a community in a short time; and
2. threaten the discretion of governments to shape state policy (Ulman, 1983, p. 133).

Norman Myers pointed out that national security is not just about the military dimension, but it increasingly relates to access to water resources, arable land, forests, biodiversity, climate, and other factors (Myers, 1993, p. 21). At the turn of the 20th and 21st centuries, environmental protection became one of the main challenges in international cooperation and scientific research (Hughes, 2019, p. 348). The catalogue of threats in security research has been expanded. Thus, the so-called Copenhagen School has incorporated environmental concerns into its broader definition of safety (Młynarski, 2017, p. 38).

Energy and climate security is a non-military dimension of state security. On the other hand, environmental challenges were recognized as sources of threats in strategic documents of many security organizations and institutions, for example in the 2010 NATO Strategic Concept (Młynarski, 2017, p. 65).

Energy transformation means a change in the way energy is generated and the transition from the current energy system (using nonrenewable energy sources) to a system based on renewable sources. This means a wider use of alternative energy sources and the development of new industries based on long-term strategies implementing innovative technologies (RES, ensuring the storage of surplus energy from RES, smart transmission and distribution networks, synthetic fuels, electromobility) (Bahr et al., 2021, p. 125). Energy transformation is a process that includes not only the replacement of fossil fuels with renewable energy but also socioeconomic changes, such as: development of innovation, increasing energy efficiency, waste management, and changing consumer approaches to energy use. The effect of this process is the reduction of the negative impact of the energy sector on climate, and in particular the reduction in greenhouse gas emissions from energy production. Energy transformation means building sustainable economies with the use of low-emission energy sources, as well as the so-called clean coal technologies and rational use of energy (Młynarski, 2017, p. 75). This process includes: energy efficiency, application of more efficient technologies in the production process (energy efficiency), heat and energy cogeneration, energy recovery in industrial processes, the creation of a decentralized and ecological energy supply system based on local production and distribution of energy from renewable sources (prosumer energy), and consumer habits (Młynarski, 2017, p. 76). The effectiveness of the energy transformation depends on the structural reconstruction of the economy and changes in many sectors—from the production of energy from renewable sources, to the improvement of energy efficiency, waste recycling, ecological reclamation, energy-saving technologies, transport modernization, to increasing the awareness of societies in energy saving and consumption. Industrial processes need to be cleaner and more resource efficient.

Energy transformation is a challenge of the 21st century and also creates great opportunities for the development of the energy sector. Increasing the share of RES in the overall energy balance of states helps improve energy security through diversification of energy sources, and is also associated with economic benefits (Hughes, 2019, p. 370). Energy security is no longer just a question of ensuring the supply of resources but is related to political and economic issues, which should be considered in the context of social and economic transformations that take place at the international level and reflect the civilizational progress (Młynarski, 2017, p. 76). Therefore, the 21st century will be a test for the development of the global, sustainable energy security system.

Anthony Giddens argued that energy security should be achieved not by spreading concerns about the depletion of fossil fuels, but by emphasizing the environmental advantages and financial benefits of owning energy-efficient homes (Młynarski, 2017, p. 76). Such a concept of energy security leads to the transformation of the energy generation sector towards innovation and energy efficiency. Energy transformation has three goals: improving energy security (stability of supplies), enhancing energy efficiency (reducing costs), and technological modernization (improving the competitiveness of the economy). It is a process related to the development of civilization from the Industrial Revolution to sustainable development societies. Energy transformation assumes the modernization of the economy based on the reconstruction of energy sectors, which means:

1. building a competitive low-carbon economy;
2. environmental protection;
3. new, environmentally friendly technologies and methods of energy production;
4. smart energy networks; and
5. consumer education.

According to the declaration of the International Energy Agency, the world needs a green energy revolution to become independent from fossil fuels (International Energy Agency, n.d). Such a revolution would increase global energy security, ensure sustainable economic growth, and foster solutions to environmental problems (International Energy Agency, n.d.a).

The process of energy transformation will take various forms, depending on the state's energy potential, the degree of access to low-carbon technologies, and social expectations. Energy transformation also strengthens economic competitiveness. Reducing greenhouse gas emissions is driving the demand for low-carbon energy generation technologies. Energy modernization creates a context for the development of new industries. It is an opportunity to build an innovative economy and achieve benefits by gaining a competitive advantage of low-emission economies on the global market. The policy of green energy transformation implements economic objectives (Gryz, 2018, p. 80). In this context, the complexity, which refers to the differentiation of the social structure and the change in its organization and behaviour, is gaining importance. The increase in energy supply boosts the possibilities of the operation of various actors in the technological and social dimensions (Heinonen et al., 2017, pp. 2–13). Energy transformation towards renewable sources has multidimensional and complex consequences.

In the article, "'Geotechnical Ensembles': How New Technologies Change Geopolitical Factors and Contexts in Economy, Energy and Security," David Criekemans pointed out that:

> As a result of new technologies in communication, transportation or production, some places in the world become more important compared to others. New economic relations may be forged between resource rich areas and consumer regions. For example, the evolution towards a world increasingly run on renewable energy will also mean that the needs of many countries will shift; from conventional oil over natural gas towards the critical materials that will power a renewable energy future. (Criekemans, 2022, p. 61)

This could lead to scarcity, supply problems, and geopolitical competition. The interaction between technologies and geopolitical factors may also have consequences for the foreign policy of states. "Patterns of conflict and cooperation may be affected. At the same time, the introduction of new technologies may also have far-reaching geostrategic consequences and implications for whether and how nations have to be protected" (Criekemans, 2022, p. 61). To answer the question, how do new technologies change geopolitical factors and contexts in economic, energy, and security relations, the thesis of Criekemans must be taken into account. He derives from the analysis that:

> territorial entities (states, regions or cities) which invest in ground-breaking technological know-how, both fundamental and applied innovation, as well as in the industrial base that comes with it, will in many ways be able to shape tomorrow's world in its geoeconomic, geopolitical and geostrategic. Technologies come in many different shapes and forms. Nevertheless they act as force multipliers. (Criekemans, 2022, p. 62)

Finally, the author develops some concluding thoughts on how today's technological trends could affect tomorrow's world politics from a geoeconomic, geopolitical, and geostrategic point of view: "If power constitutes the 'currency' of global geopolitics, then technology could be seen as its 'conductor' and 'facilitator'" (Criekemans, 2022, p. 63).

Lack of continuity is a feature of complex systems. A system is complex if it is connected to many other systems and if the effects of these relations are not linear (Heinonen et al., 2017, pp. 2–13). The global economy is an example of such a system. Each phenomenon in international relations affects the world economic system. In a situation where the world becomes more and more complex (due to more interdependencies between states), we will observe an increase in discontinuity, and, thus, instability (Heinonen et al., 2017, pp. 2–13). Therefore, more attention should be paid to "black swans," "wild cards," and "weak signals" rather than to trends. "Weak signals" are events, new technologies, and practices that indicate that specific events will occur. They are the first symptoms of significant discontinuities. These may be threatening signals or signals indicative of new opportunities.

An example of unpredictable events, which have a significant impact on the future functioning of the energy market, are the consequences of the Covid-19 pandemic of 2019. With the pandemic and the associated economic slowdown, oil demand declined and its price plummeted. This was a consequence of the breakdown of the OPEC+ agreement, which was to stabilize the market, and the rivalry between Saudi Arabia and Russia for shares in this market. As a result, oil prices dropped to "record low levels, which – apart from the over-supply of oil and the economic crisis—will be a serious challenge for the largest producers and states dependent on oil exports" (Bieliszczuk, 2020, p. 2). The first factor behind the oil price drop was the decline in economic activity related to the threat of a pandemic (Bieliszczuk, 2020). Another problem was the "price war" between the Saudi Arabia (KAS) and Russia.

Falling oil prices, lower demand, and the fight for the market are serious challenges for other producers. This particularly concerned states dependent on export revenues that already had internal challenges (including the Caspian states). A decline in budget revenues may be a serious economic shock for states and "place the international community in a position of having to deal with destabilisation or humanitarian crises, which will be difficult to address due to the pandemic" (Heinonen et al., 2017, p. 10). These factors would challenge the stability of the authoritarian regimes of oil-producing states, which might make them more oppressive.

According to Bartosz Bieliszczuk, "reducing oil prices does not currently boost demand—its decline is a result of economic slowdown, and in view of the oversupply, the storage of surplus oil may become a challenge in the coming months" (2020, p. 2). Concerns would cut investments, and exporters would fight for the oil market, for which demand fell by 20% in 2020 compared to 2019.

Currently, because of the geopolitical transformations caused by the war in Ukraine, we find ourselves at the "heart of an international energy storm driven by turmoil in natural gas markets" (Birol, 2022, n.p.). According to Fatih Birol, "Understanding the causes of this crisis – which is having serious repercussions for governments, businesses and households – and drawing the right lessons from it is essential for the transition to more sustainable, secure and affordable energy supplies in the future" (Birol, 2022, n.p.). In 2022, energy prices have spiked to record highs, causing potentially significant multiple negative effects on companies, state industrial sectors, and consumers. The increases in energy prices have also contributed to broader price inflation that is affecting many economies worldwide (Birol, 2022, n.p.).

It is logical that the future is always based on change, and therefore in this context the importance of "weak signals" and "black swans" increases. They mark future potential changes in the economic or energy systems. Thus, technological development, growing consumption of renewable resources, and fluctuations in energy prices are indicators that may herald an unknown future (Heinonen et al., 2017, pp. 2–13). If we assume that the modern world will depend on VUCA determinants, "weak signals" and "black swans" will become more and more significant in the analysis of international interdependencies. As a method of anticipation, however, these indicators are impractical. Single issues and events that are difficult to predict are not credible when predicting the future. In this context, trends are more useful as they address issues that are familiar. If we view unpredictable events as "normality," this has implications for energy security, and especially for renewable energy.

Through successive historical periods, humanity developed at different rates. Until the 17th century, energy needs were met using wood-burning energy and wind and water power. The first Industrial Revolution in the 19th century was based on a coal- and steam-powered economy. The second one, in the 20th century, was the result of the popularization of the combustion engine, the third will be based on renewable sources, energy saving, and energy efficiency. In the 21st century, new sources and methods of energy production are gradually reducing the dominant share of fossil fuels. Hydrocarbons will not be eliminated from state energy mixes but their share will decline substantially.

2   The Importance of the Caspian Region in the Context of Future Challenges to the Global Energy Market

The shale gas revolution and energy transition towards the expansion of renewable sources initiated a new era in the functioning of the energy market. Traditional fuel producers became victims of these market changes (Guliyev, 2019, pp. 2–8). According to the "volatility" category, we are witnesses to the "variability of the directions of change" and a high frequency of "ups and downs" through disruptions in energy market trends.

The global energy order is changing rapidly. Technological progress in the mining industry make it possible to exploit unconventional and previously inaccessible energy reserves. In addition, Western states are focusing more and more on renewable sources as part of their energy mix (Guliyev, 2019). Market analysts more and more often talk about the "new energy order," in which the potential of traditional fuel producers, such as Iran, Russia, or Venezuela will decline due to the development of renewable energy and uncertain oil prices (Van de Graaf & Bradshaw, 2018, pp. 1309–1328). Thus, geopolitical changes constitute an important condition for the functioning of the international energy market. In addition, the shale gas revolution shifted the US position from a consumer to a major producer of oil and liquefied natural gas (LNG). This drastically changed the geopolitical energy map (Guliyev, 2019, pp. 2–8).

Given those conditions, the global oil price has been steadily dropping, reaching USD 65 per barrel in 2019, and even around USD 43 in the second quarter of 2020. Comparing this data to that of March 2022, when the price per barrel was USD 130, it is safe to say that we are currently at a turning point in the development of the global energy market.

The previous global energy system during the Cold War was based on the demand for fossil fuels, and Western states were dependent on their imports from the Middle East, North Africa, Russia, and Venezuela. Since then, it was impossible to imagine an industrialized world without access to hydrocarbons (Mitchell, 2011; Verrastro & Ladislaw, 2007).

The new unstable energy order also has an impact on the West's demand for hydrocarbons from the Caspian region. International oil corporations were reluctant to invest in the region's resources to the same extent as they did at the beginning of the 21st century (Guliyev, 2019, pp. 2–8). Ambitious infrastructure plans, such as the Trans-Caspian Pipeline, which is to connect Central Asia and Azerbaijan, function only in theory.

In this context, the Caspian states that depend on hydrocarbon exports, were losing revenues from this sector of the economy. For Azerbaijan, Kazakhstan, and Turkmenistan, changes in the energy market have far-reaching consequences. As for Western industrialized countries reducing their dependence on conventional energy sources, in the long and even medium term, the Caspian region may lose its geopolitical and economic importance for them. This process is confirmed by the deficit of large-scale investments of international corporations since 2014, when the oil price fell globally. Simultaneously, nowadays, it is not certain how this situation will change in the context of the geopolitical changes caused by the war in Ukraine. The importance of hydrocarbon resources from the Caspian region for Western countries can be expected to increase as the alternative for the Russian oil and gas. However, it will not be a revolutionary change.

In view of the declining interest of the US, the EU, and Western corporations in investing in the region after 2014, the Caspian states, except Azerbaijan, are focusing on the Asian markets (Guliyev, 2019, pp. 2–8). Kazakhstan and Turkmenistan have targeted the Chinese and Indian markets, where the economies continue to rely on fossil fuels. Turkmenistan completely directed its gas exports to the PRC. Kazakhstan also directs its energy to the East, even planning to enhance exports in connection with the estimated development of hydrocarbon production. Azerbaijan, on the other hand, focuses on implementing a very expensive gas pipeline infrastructure system to Europe. It finances it using loans from international banks and its own resources (Guliyev, 2019). At the same time, the filling of the gigantic infrastructure will be a challenge, as Azerbaijan's resources are insufficient, and so far it is not possible to add gas from Central Asia or Iran to it. Some corporations, such as Statoil, ExxonMobil, and Chevron, have withdrawn from major energy projects in this state.

From the 1990s until 2014, the energy resources of the Caspian Sea region were attractive both to the industrialized West and energy-hungry China. From the 2000s until mid-2014, the demand for energy coincided with high oil prices (Guliyev, 2019). Thus, both corporations and energy-producing countries benefited from the energy system. Investors' incomes grew as they treated the construction of strategic energy infrastructure as an investment for the future. The largest project of that period was the BTC oil pipeline. It came into being largely due to diplomatic support from the US. It was not only a reflection of economic thinking, but also a of the US strategy to limit the role of Russia and the Middle East in the energy market.

The energy industry requires the implementation of modern mining technologies. The technology of hydraulic fracturing and that of directed horizontal drilling allowed the US to access and exploit unconventional oil and gas reserves (Guliyev, 2019). In 2015, the US Congress lifted the oil export ban, and the sudden surge in shale gas energy production from 2007 turned the US into a major energy producer. In addition, starting in 2016, during the presidency of Donald Trump, the US announced a new energy policy of "America first," which sought to make the state independent from the import of energy resources and make the US much more skeptical in supporting infrastructure building in the Caspian region. In fact, the goal of the US is to export gas as LNG directly to Europe (Andrew, 2018; Alcindor, 2018, pp. 23–45). With regard to producers from the Caspian region, although the US President Joe Biden, declared his support for the idea of building a Trans-Caspian Gas Pipeline connecting Turkmenistan with Azerbaijan and transporting gas to Europe without Russia's participation after Russian invasion in Ukraine, this project is still not a priority for this superpower. As long as the US does not offer specific investments to implement this project, declarations are of no measurable value in this respect. This is not a good prospect for the Caspian states. After earning huge sums of money on energy exports until 2014, they are facing many challenges related to fluctuations in energy prices, poor infrastructure efficiency, less corporate activity in their energy sector, and a reduction in the geopolitical importance of the region to the US administration (Arezki & Matsumoto, 2017).

In this context, it is worth answering the questions of whether and how the Caspian region states are adapting to the contemporary conditions of the energy market. The late-Westphalian international system—heterogeneous in the subjective dimension and including the modern trends of decentralization, centralization, integration, and fragmentation—definitely influenced the change of the perception of its role in the international energy market by the Caspian region states.

Opening to foreign investments and enabling transnational corporations to operate within the *upstream* and *downstream* sectors is simultaneous with central power consolidation following rising revenues from hydrocarbon exports. This phenomenon is particularly evident in the case of the energy security policies of Azerbaijan and Kazakhstan. Therefore, market trends associated with international corporation's activity coexist with regional, local, and state conditions. This increases instability and unpredictability in the process of creating energy security policy.

Therefore, volatility, uncertainty, complexity, and ambiguity—the components of the VUCA concept—gain importance. However, the analysis of the energy security policies of the Caspian region states leads to the conclusion that they do not adapt sufficiently to the conditions of the contemporary energy market. Elusiveness, or "volatility of the directions of change" (Heinonen et al., 2017, pp. 2–13), requiring modern energy technologies and transformation towards increased exploitation of renewable sources, presents a major challenge for the Caspian states. Analyzing the structure of their consumption and production of energy resources, and the strategies of the energy security policy, a clear focus on nonrenewable energy sources can be seen. All the states in this region base their economies on revenues from exports of mainly oil and gas. The lack of a diversification policy in this dimension causes uncertainty as to their future role in the international energy market. Transformation in the energy dimension also requires changes in the social dimension. However, the authoritarian and repressive political systems of the Caspian states do include complexity in energy security strategies, requiring intensified interactions between various actors, structures, and organizations, and the centralized state. Difficulties in the process of determining the future role of the Caspian states in the international energy market are caused by the unclear interpretation of new phenomena, and the potential of sudden and unexpected changes that bring far-reaching consequences. The specificity of the Caspian states in the political, social, and economic dimensions, hampers the process of adaptation to the unstable and turbulent international environment.

Thus, their current energy security policies need to be re-evaluated towards energy transformation and the need to expand the understanding of the concept of energy security to include sustainable development. The current challenge for hydrocarbon producers is the necessity to include the perspective of functioning in the "post-petroleum era" into their energy security strategies. Thus, the Caspian rentier states do not employ a proactive adaptation strategy but only a retroactive one, which in the future may lead to a serious crisis as a result of the loss of revenues from oil and gas exports (Pietraś, 1989).

In this context, it is necessary to pay attention to the activities of the Caspian states. Once a pioneer in the development of the energy sector in the Caspian region, Azerbaijan is greatly affected by the changes in the international energy market. Its aim now is to fill the Southern Gas Corridor, a huge gas pipeline infrastructure from the Caspian region to Europe, a project comparable to the

BTC mega-pipeline (Guliyev, 2019, pp. 2–8). However, its financing is a challenge. Azerbaijan obtained most of the financing through loans from international institutions and through its own national SOFAZ fund. In contrast, the BTC project was politically supported by the US and financed by international corporations (Boersma & Johnson, 2018). The concept of the Corridor is a project by Azerbaijan and Turkey that does not enjoy US support (Guliyev, 2019, pp. 2–8). So, for Azerbaijan, it is a significant challenge to fill a huge new pipeline in a new era of energy market development with negligible US and EU participation. Furthermore, there is the problem that Azerbaijan's energy reserves are not impressive. The state is currently focusing on gas exports and views this resource as a key, especially because it has not transformed its energy sector towards the exploitation of renewable resources. Since 2019, Azerbaijan has increased its gas exports as part of the second phase of the development of its largest gas field, Shah Deniz (Guliyev, 2019). Most of its gas goes to Turkey, and following the extension of the Southern Corridor to Italy, its gas has also been going to recipients in Southern Europe. According to Azerbaijan's estimates, revenues from operating the gas pipeline amount to an average of USD 2–3 billion per year since 2019 (Istrate, 2019), that is to say, much less than from oil exports (USD 140 billion) (Azerbaijan may earn billions, 2019). The total cost of construction of the Corridor is estimated at USD 40 billion. In the case of BTC, 70% of the financing came from loans and the pipeline was built by Baku–Tbilisi–Ceyhan Pipeline Company (BTC Co.), with BP representing the largest shareholder. The consortium owns and operates the pipeline. The Trans-Anatolian gas pipeline has a different ownership structure. Initially, there were only two shareholders: the Azerbaijani oil company SOCAR (80%) and Turkey (20%). International energy corporations have also shown little interest in the project (O'Byrne, 2018). At the same time, gas from Azerbaijan is not enough to make the corridor project commercially viable in the long term. Total gas reserves in the state amount to approximately 1.2 tonnes m^3 (nearly 1.1% of total global reserves) (Guliyev, 2019, pp. 2–8). Without gas supplies from Turkmenistan, the Corridor will not be able to cover even the costs of its construction and operation.

Kazakhstan has huge oil reserves (30 billion barrels), exports the fuel under binding long-term commitments. It has a pipeline infrastructure targeting Western markets via the CPC pipeline, to Russia and China. Oil from the largest oil field, Tengiz (operated by Tengizchevroil, a joint venture between Chevron, ExxonMobil, KazMunaiGaz, and LUKoil), is transported via the CPC pipeline to Novorossiysk (O'Byrne, 2018). Smaller quantities of oil are transported by tankers across the Caspian Sea. Kazakhstan is expanding its port in Kuryk, 60 km south of Aktau, to prepare for the transport of more oil from the Kashagan field across the Caspian Sea (O'Byrne, 2018). The new reality on the energy market makes foreign investments riskier. Kazakhstan was reluctant to invest in the Trans-Caspian Pipeline project (O'Byrne, 2018). On the other hand, additional oil, coming from the huge Kashagan field, will be exported to China or other Asian countries. In 2019, Kazakhstan declared that it would direct some of its exports from the west towards the PRC market (Afanasyeva, 2019, p. 12). The flow of oil on the Kenkiyak–Atyrau pipeline, which until now has been dedicated to oil exports to the West, will therefore be reversed. Nevertheless, in 2018, Kazakhstan's oil exports to China fell to a record low of 1.3 million tonnes. This was due to the decline in the productivity of oil fields exploited by Chinese corporations (Bisenov, 2018).

Turkmenistan has huge gas reserves, estimated at 50.4 tonnes m³. This state is completely economically dependent on gas exports revenues. The fall in energy prices thus triggered a serious crisis, which was also caused by the country's ineffective energy policy. Its agreement with China resulted in Chinese companies investing in the construction of refineries and pipelines in Turkmenistan (Guliyev, 2019, pp. 2–8). In addition, the Chinese have invested around USD 20 billion in the development of gas fields in the country. In March 2019, US President Trump communicated to Turkmen President Berdimuhamedov that he "hopes Turkmenistan will take advantage of new possibilities of exporting gas to the West in connection with the recent determination of the legal status of the Caspian Sea" (Cutler, 2019, p. 12). He later sent a similar declaration to Azerbaijan President Aliyev, with assurances of support for the Trans-Caspian Gas Pipeline (Letter from President Trump to President Aliyev, 2019). However, these were not assurances about specific investments in this project. As for the policy of diversification of gas export routes, Turkmenistan is interested in strengthening cooperation in the joint pipeline with Afghanistan, Pakistan, and India within the TAPI structure, with a planned capacity of 33 billion m³ of gas annually. Thus, it is unlikely that Turkmenistan will become involved in a project to transport gas to the West.

Paradoxically, the energy resources in the Caspian region may become both a cause for conflict and a motive for international cooperation. For security in the region and beyond, it is important to create a regime of cooperation. Such possible regional cooperation would contribute to the economic development of individual states. Otherwise, the rivalry between them will deepen, which may turn into conflict in the future. The production and trade of energy resources depend on the short-term interests of political elites and transnational corporations. The possibility of cooperation in technology transfer is limited in such a situation. However, it would increase investors' confidence in the region. Possible collaboration required that each interested party would agree to a common system of rules and norms that would sanction the practice related to the expectations of other actors (Guliyev, 2019, pp. 2–8).

Currently, energy business activities in the Caspian region are mainly competitive. Such a situation may lead to a monopolistic position of one of the corporations, eliminating smaller businesses from the market and limiting local production possibilities.

A possible cooperation regime could utilize a liberal-institutional idea, not based on hegemony but on principles accepted by all system participants (Molchanov & Yevdokimov, 2004). Neoliberal institutionalism claims that "international organisations facilitate cooperation by reducing transaction costs, access to information, and create rules for decision-making" (Keohane, 1984, p. 35). In the absence of a hegemon, collaboration does not require either side to play the role of a "policy-maker" and allows various interests to coexist among participants. All that is necessary is a system of rules and norms that apply equally to participants. The idea of cooperation creates a good practice, even for participants who benefit from the current system, in which the winner takes all as a result of bilateral agreements with authoritarian states in the region. It should be noted that even strong rivals in the geoeconomic game in the Caspian region lose some of their profits that they could have obtained in a more competitive regime as a result of reduced risk and uncertainty.

The development of international cooperation regimes could be accepted in the Caspian region on the grounds that such systems ensure equal access to key resources and reduce the likelihood of disruptions in the distribution of power or economic growth. Such a system further boosts the possibility to implement and operate modern technology (Bresnahan & Trajtenberg, 1995, pp. 83–108). When member states of such a potential organization adopt new rules and possibilities, they begin to think about the region as a common resource which they share with other participants (Molchanov & Yevdokimov, 2004). In such a situation, energy resources would more easily reach foreign markets, and workforce productivity would rise significantly in a competitive environment and contribute towards higher living standards.

Analyzing various international regimes, one can see that many of them take into account the accumulation of technological innovations (Gilpin, 2001; Keohane & Nye, 2001). The assumption is that the creation of a cooperation system in energy in the Caspian region would contribute towards technological and diplomatic progress. This can raise productivity and lead to technology transfers, which, in turn, can stimulate the development of the least developed countries.

The regime of political and economic cooperation in the region will also increase foreign direct investment, bringing fundamental changes in the organization of the production process in the energy sector in Azerbaijan, Turkmenistan, and Kazakhstan. Since energy is a key industry in the region, the development of this field may result in the effectiveness of other sectors of the economy. This condition is the so-called "spillover effect."

The above scenario may affect the economy and development in the energy sector in the Caspian region, and provides an example of the implementation of a technology that is open to new production possibilities, work organization, and innovation (General Purpose Technology, GPT) (Helpman, 1998). Such a system is characterized by multidimensionality, high technological development potential, and complementarity in terms of innovation, resulting in an economy of scale. The consequence is economic development in a holistic and comprehensive dimension. The idea behind GPT is that one sector becomes a leader in technological advancement, having a multilevel impact on the entire economy (Grossman & Helpman, 1991). What determines development in the energy sector is "knowledge and politics" (Molchanov & Yevdokimov, 2004). Both phenomena influence, direct, and mobilize each other. A cooperative regime in the Caspian energy sector could therefore promote knowledge exchange and technological transfer between the oil and gas industries of the states in the region, and the "domestication" of progressive approaches from foreign investors.

In economic terms, such a regime would reduce transaction costs and initiate an economy of scale in the economic dimension, leading to lower production costs per energy unit. It may also cause a self-propelling effect in other sectors, such as agriculture and manufacturing, which are underdeveloped in the countries of the region. Moreover, this kind of cooperation would have implications for security and regional stability. Such as situation would also increase the activity and profits of transnational corporations (Molchanov & Yevdokimov, 2004).

Experts on international regimes of political rivalry have considered at least three basic types of such regimes (Molchanov & Yevdokimov, 2004):

1. anarchy;
2. harmonization; and
3. political coordination.

Anarchy in this case refers to the activity of nation-states that act only in their own interest. Harmonization favors a more or less uniform international political regime applying international law applicable within an international organization. An example is the World Trade Organization. Political coordination means a regime of multilateral cooperation in the form of mutual consent on the code of conduct of all participants in the absence of a central structure or hegemon. Such a situation can be seen as a free path of minimum standards, negotiations, and multilateral agreements on the functioning of the energy market (Molchanov & Yevdokimov, 2004).

The regime of energy cooperation in the Caspian region could lead to technological progress, both inside and outside the energy industry, and would be in line with the "spillover" principle, and help overcome the so-called "Dutch disease"—which, according to the observations of many researchers, affects many post-Soviet states, such as Azerbaijan and Turkmenistan. Introducing the cooperative regime of energy production and distribution would result in the spread of political and economic solutions in the region, which may enable structural reforms. The international cooperation regime in the event of the development of Caspian oil and gas deposits will reduce investment risk, but also fosters the development of innovation and the organizational efficiency of regional markets (Molchanov & Yevdokimov, 2004).

The introduction of the cooperative regime brings about positive changes in the organization of the industry (Shumpeter, 1934). It shapes the socioeconomic system of cooperating elements, which determines the new form of industrial organization on a wider regional scale. The snow ball effect in various sectors of the economy in connection with the development of regional cooperation leads to modernization in the technological dimension, increasing productivity in the energy and related industries. As a consequence, the GDP may increase and the standard of living in the countries of the region may rise. In this case, international cooperation would be the main driver of technological advancement (Molchanov & Yevdokimov, 2004).

An international regime must have different rules of collective behaviour among all participants. Such a system requires a change in the organization of economic and political activities in the extraction, production, and distribution of energy resources in the region. This will not only lead to changes understood as progress in production methods. First, such a system must take into account new forms of organizing international relations, international trade, capital, labor, and technology movements. Second, the new system of cooperation should open up new paths for innovative processes, mainly related to research and development activities. Third, to be beneficial to all participants, the regime must take into account the integration of technological, economic, and intellectual systems, which will have positive effects in sectors other than energy. A coherent system of cooperating elements within the regional energy sector will result in increasing the potential and innovation of the countries of the Caspian region (Wasserman & Faust, 1994). Technological changes may be reflected in the increase in productivity in the countries of the region, manifested in the form of the activities of the labor force and/or in the form of the

Total Factor Productivity (TFP), also referred to as Multi-factor Productivity (MFP) (Molchanov & Yevdokimov, 2004).

Workforce productivity is measured by the productivity of an employee per hour worked. In contrast, TFP is measured as efficiency converted into total cost of production. In addition, according to the neoclassical theory of growth, labor productivity consists of an increase in the amount of capital per employee as well as an improvement in the quality of work and an increase in TFP (Molchanov & Yevdokimov, 2004). Under specific conditions, the system of cooperation between states leads to an increase in productivity and an improvement in the quality of life of individual members of the system. Moreover, according to economic theory, national and international welfare is closely related.

3   Conclusion

Energy security policy has so far been narrowly defined, and thus the issue of thinking in terms of the various development opportunities in the energy industry is often overlooked. The dilemma associated with "non-linear" thinking often ignores a variety of solutions that together can cause a radical turnaround in the energy market and its evolution. In the context of the VUCA method analyzed in this book, predicting the future in the energy dimension is currently gaining importance. Discontinuities are not so much sudden events or isolated phenomena, these are long-term processes consisting of trends, weak signals, or "black swans." When new energy technologies provide more energy than before, it can have a transformational effect on the social dimension. This is especially the case with the increased use of renewables. In the face of the transformation and turbulence of the energy market on a global scale, a system of cooperation between actors can increase productivity in the Caspian energy sector, as well as accelerate development in the technological sector in various areas, on the basis of a self-reinforcing effect. The creation of such a system would take into account the states and transnational corporations involved in the extraction, exploitation, and transportation of energy resources. Cooperation between these actors would improve the economic situation and increase the competitiveness of the Caspian states in global energy markets.

The implementation of pipeline projects from the Caspian region is currently a huge challenge, both economically and geopolitically. Growing competition for export routes for fossil fuels from the Caspian region under conditions of uncertainty about the sufficiency of supplies means that not all ambitious infrastructure projects can be implemented. The only chance for their implementation is to increase hydrocarbon production in the region and favorable geopolitical circumstances.

One thing is certain, the prospects for the development of energy security policies in the Caspian region are conditioned by many factors. Among them, the energy transition towards renewable sources is gaining importance. Thus, a proactive approach and effective adaptation to the challenges of the modern energy market are crucial nowadays.

Conclusions

The analysis of geopolitics and energy security policies in the Caspian region indicates that interdependence in this area determines the dynamics of international relations. The capacity for extraction and transmission of hydrocarbons affects not only the economic position of the Caspian countries but also economic relations on a global scale, as energy market participants include states as well as numerous international businesses, which are getting increasingly involved in the production and distribution of hydrocarbons. The oil and gas transport policy is a determinant of interdependence on the international energy market. Pipeline routes are mapped taking into account economic conditions, but are also the result of geopolitical actions taken by Caspian states and the global players.

The purpose of the study was to answer the following research question: how and as a result of what conditions does the evolution of energy security policies in the Caspian region occur? The answer to this question was not obvious, due to the specificity of the region that was analyzed—the Caspian region—its complexity, and the dynamics resulting not only from internal but also from international conditions related to changes in the international energy market. The Caspian region is presented as an area of great geopolitical and geoeconomic importance, facing numerous problems of a political, economic, and social nature. The security environment in the Caspian region is largely determined by the relationship between the major sovereign and non-sovereign players. The energy security in the region is a system of pipeline infrastructures pointing in different directions. The northern, western, southern, and eastern directions were all covered in the analysis. As a closed reservoir, the Caspian Sea cannot be exploited for energy resources if there is no possibility of exporting hydrocarbons to the international market. Thus, both the relationship between the actors of energy security policy in the region and its object are subject to dynamic changes and largely based on rivalry. However, these relationships often take the form of a non-zero-sum game, as evidenced by multidimensionality when it comes to the activity of actors and directions of oil and gas exports.

The cognitive purpose of the research presented was to carry out the research tasks. First, the energy security policies of the actors in the Caspian region were analyzed. The energy security policies of regional states (Azerbaijan, Kazakhstan, Turkmenistan, Russia, and Iran) and extra-regional participants (China, Turkey, and the EU) were taken into account in this context. Second, the energy potential of countries in the Caspian region was analyzed. The

variety of available data, and especially the discrepancy between official government sources and those produced by international actors, has made this
task difficult. An important element of the analysis was also the characterization of the geological peculiarities of the Caspian Sea and the main threats
and challenges associated with the exploitation of energy deposits. Third, the
Caspian region has been defined as a geopolitical space, within which a "game"
is played between different actors, whose activity is motivated both by issues
related to energy and by political interests. Fourth, the prospects for the implementation of energy infrastructure projects in the Caspian region in the context of changes in the international energy market were identified. Fifth, the
interdependencies between the actors defining the shape and future functioning of the energy market in the Caspian region were analyzed. Thus, in order to
address the research problem undertaken, answers to the research questions
posed in the Introduction of this study have been provided:

1. What is the specific character of the security environment in the Caspian
   region?

   The essence and specificity of the Caspian region and its dynamics in the international security system is conditioned by interactions
   between state, sub-state, transnational, regional, and international levels
   of analysis. The analysis indicates that the Caspian region is vulnerable to
   many potential security threats. We can include the conflict in Nagorno-
   Karabakh, which has not been definitively ended, or the conflict over fossil fuel resources in the Caspian Basin. Moreover, a halt in the economic
   development in the newly formed states of the Caspian region may also
   cause an escalation in social discontent and, as a result, become the
   cause of a possible conflict in this area. We also cannot rule out potential geopolitical turbulence in the region related to the consequences of
   Russia's war in Ukraine. It seems that the geopolitical situation in the
   post-Soviet area is evolving, which will imply the situation in the Caspian
   region is evolving, too. Thus, we can conclude that there will be "black
   swans" in the near future, which may turn into "strategic surprises" for
   the countries of the region. One thing is certain, the unstable geostrategic
   situation causes investment risk. Hence, within the interdependence of
   interests, the countries of the region should create a specific regime of
   cooperation.

2. What are the interdependencies of energy security policy in the Caspian
   region?

   According to the theory of complex interdependence (transnational
   approach) developed by Robert Keohane and Joseph Nye, energy security
   policy is shaped by growing interdependence, transnational processes,

and the emergence of new phenomena of a global character. The modern energy market is conditioned by VUCA indicators: volatility, uncertainty, complexity, and ambiguity. They are a huge challenge for rentier states in the post-Soviet area, which are not prepared for the energy transformation in the technological and climate dimension. Summing up the above discussion, we need to pay attention to the fact that the policy of oil and gas transportation is a determinant of international interdependence on the energy market in the Caspian region. The essence of energy interdependence in the Caspian region stems from the complexity of relationships between the various actors involved in the implementation of energy infrastructure projects.

3. What are the prospects for developing energy security policies in the Caspian region?

Modern transformations of the international energy market have resulted in a fluctuation in the price of oil. Investments in the energy sector of the Caspian region states diminished as a result of this situation. The implementation of pipeline projects from the Caspian region is currently a huge challenge, both in economic and geopolitical terms. Paradoxically, in the face of volatility of the energy market on a global scale, the system of cooperation between its participants in the Caspian region can increase productivity in their energy sector, as well as accelerate technological development in various areas, on the basis of a self-reinforcing effect. It is also important to transform the energy sector in the region to promote the development of renewable sources, which so far seems unrealistic. The post-Soviet countries are not yet prepared for the post-oil period.

4. What determines the evolution of energy security policies in the Caspian region?

The evolution of energy security policies in the Caspian region is conditioned by the challenges affecting the global energy market, the ability to implement major infrastructure projects, and relations between producers and consumers of energy resources. Undoubtedly, the current geopolitical changes in the world related to Russia's ongoing war in Ukraine will change the balance of power in the whole of Eurasia. It is unclear how and when this conflict will end. However, the signs of change in the Caspian region are already becoming visible: Russia has weakened in the region, and the prospect of China increasing its power and involvement is more likely. In this context, we should expect increased interest in the Caspian region by the European Union. Further packages of sanctions on hydrocarbon supplies from Russia and the creation of the Cooperation

Council between the EU and the Republic of Azerbaijan herald a change in energy security policy in the Caspian region. All of these changes will motivate the Caspian countries to adapt to the new geoenergetic reality. The research hypotheses outlined in the Introduction were positively verified in the monograph. First, it has specified the significance of the Caspian region on the international energy market and outlined its evolution determined by numerous geopolitical and economic factors. The research results of my study enabled the verification of this hypothesis, as Chapter 2 addressed the geopolitical and geoeconomic position of the Caspian region and its energy potential. The Caspian region was presented as a space for energy security policies. In addition to this, the analysis in the last chapter made it possible to answer the question concerning the future role of the Caspian region in the international energy market. Thus, the prospects for the evolving importance of the region in the face of future challenges on the global energy market were analyzed.

Second, it has been shown that the specific nature of the Caspian region, conditioned by political, economic, and social instability, makes it highly susceptible to the influence of external players. The hypothesis was verified in Chapter 2 of the study. It outlines the main threats to energy security in the Caspian region. It also addresses the problem of political, economic, and social instability, related mainly to the transformation processes taking place in newly formed states in the Caspian region. Particularly significant was the analysis of the international conflicts occurring in the Caspian region, and especially the Nagorno-Karabakh conflict, and their implications for energy security.

Third, the evolution of energy security policies in the Caspian region and the prospect of its development, largely driven by relations in the global energy market, was presented. The analysis featured in Chapter 5 of the study identifies new challenges on the international energy market and their implications for the evolution of energy security policies in the Caspian region. The analysis also took into account the possible prospect of cooperation between the countries of the region, in the context of the interdependence of interests in the energy dimension.

Fourth, it has been proven that the implementation of pipeline projects extending from the Caspian region is currently a huge challenge both in economic and geopolitical terms. The intensifying rivalry over the routes for exporting oil and gas from the Caspian region in conditions of uncertainty regarding the sufficiency of supplies and turbulence in the geopolitical situation, results in a situation in which not all ambitious infrastructure projects can be implemented. The analysis in the second part of the monograph defines the subject of energy security policies in the Caspian region. It includes both hydrocarbon export routes that are already in operation and those that are prospective and still await implementation. The main challenges related to the implementation of new energy infrastructure projects in the Caspian region were also identified.

The research presented here provides a comprehensive analysis of geopolitics and energy security policies in the Caspian region, taking into account their determinants, subjects, and objects. The combination of geopolitics and energy security, creates a new quality for the social sciences. An important element of the study was the determination of the essence and specificity of energy security in contemporary international relations, with particular emphasis on the Caspian region as a case study. The aim of the analysis given in the monograph was to show that the energy security policy is influenced not only by market and economic conditions, but also by geopolitical conditions related to the location of the region on the world map. Thus, the geopolitical and geoeconomic position of the Caspian region was a very inspiring research field, due to its geographical location in the center of Eurasia and geological abundance.

This study tried to identify the main threats to security in the Caspian region, which significantly restrict its position on the global energy market. It was found that issues related to border demarcation, navigation, or contradictions over strategic aspects of export infrastructures affect energy security in the Caspian region, in Europe, and even in Eurasia as a whole. Various scenarios for the development of energy security policies in the Caspian region can be put forward. From the perspective of the increase in demand for energy resources on a global scale, the so-called "Great Game" in the Caspian region might gain momentum. In this context, the consequences of Russia's war in Ukraine should be taken into account: limiting the export of oil and gas from Russia will increase the interest of Western countries in the resources of the Caspian states. However, with the prospect of the transformation of the structure of energy consumption towards the exploitation of renewable sources, the geopolitical importance of the region may decrease.

The analysis also referred to the actors of energy security policies in the Caspian region, taking into account the littoral states in the Caspian Basin and external participants. It has been proved that the decision-making process of creating energy security policies in the Caspian states is a result of multiple factors, such as: the specifics of the regime formed after the collapse of the USSR, the issue of national identity, the influence of social groups, the geopolitical location of the state, the interests and influence of external actors, and investments made by foreign corporations. The Caspian region has become an area of interest for external players, who are not only looking for an opportunity to obtain energy resources, but are also influential in the geopolitical dimension.

The main directions of energy transport from the Caspian region to the global market were also considered. The architecture of the regional pipeline network was conditioned by economic and geopolitical issues. It has also been demonstrated that pipeline diplomacy in the Caspian region is primarily conditioned by the relationship between external geopolitical players. On the one hand, competition between them can stimulate the construction of new pipelines but, on the other hand, it can lead to the obstruction of specific infrastructure projects.

The final part of the study was predictive in nature. It analyzes the perspectives for energy security policies in the Caspian region, considering the changes in the international energy market. It has been shown that energy security policy has so far been narrowly defined and, consequently, the thinking in terms of various development opportunities and new threats in the energy sector has often been overlooked. Thus, it was taken into account, that unpredictable phenomena appear on the contemporary energy market that will affect the future architecture of energy security in the Caspian region.

There is no single theory that would explain the specific nature of the Caspian region and its security environment in a comprehensive manner. However, the theoretical approach facilitated the understanding of certain regularities that are specific to the region in question and that enabled the analysis of the research subject. The most useful theoretical approaches applied in the process of writing the book included the geopolitical approach, securitization theory, interdependence, regional studies and regionalism, and the rentier state theory. With regard to the methodological framework of the study, the most useful research methods were the factor method, comparative method, and predictive analysis.

The Caspian region is a very interesting and controversial research area. First of all, there are numerous controversies in the literature on the subject of whether it is a "region"? Second, the Caspian states were often treated in the scientific and political discourse as the exclusive sphere of influence of Russia. This approach made it difficult to capture and understand their specificity and uniqueness. Using the above theories and methods, the study tried to prove that it is a region composed of various countries representing different interests in an area of interest to external powers. The analysis of the Caspian region, as a case study, shows how the "rentier" states function on the energy market, how they adapt to the processes of energy transformation and geopolitical changes, and how resistant they are to various risks associated with those phenomena. Taking into account a different (wider) perspective, the analysis presented makes it easier to understand the regularities and phenomena that occur on the international energy market. Thus, the case study used in the monograph makes it easier to understand the different levels of analysis of the research subject, which is especially valuable in academic literature.

The analysis of energy security policies in the Caspian region was a huge research challenge and the author is aware of the limitations of the research that was presented. The study may therefore serve as an inspiration for further analysis of energy security policies in this area, as it is a very dynamic issue, given the numerous uncertainties related to the operation of the international energy market.

It is worth emphasizing in this context that the analysis presented opens up further discussion an energy security research field for the future. It seems that we are currently at a critical point in the development of international relations. Some scholars argue that we are dealing with a new Cold/Hot War, that new poles of power are emerging in the security environment, and that a new international order is just taking shape and no one can predict in which direction it will go. Thus, new research questions should be considered, which can be the basis for the analysis of the research problem, taking into account the new geopolitical conditions:

What role will the Caspian region play in the new energy security architecture after the end of Russia's war in Ukraine?

What will be the geopolitical and geoeconomical implications of weakening Russia's influence in the Caspian region?

What will be the geopolitical consequences of the collapse of the modus vivendi of Russia and China in Central Asia?

How are the countries of the Caspian region adapting to the new conditions of the energy market in the context of technological transformation towards renewable sources?

So far, the answers to the above questions would be difficult or even impossible in the face of the uncertainty and complexity of contemporary international relations. International relations become complicated more quickly than they mature, which means that every book on this subject becomes outdated on the day of its publication. Thus, the area of international relations is a huge challenge for a researcher. After all, the research workshop allows you to solve research problems in a creative way. In the context of the analyzed VUCA method, predicting the future in the energy dimension is currently gaining importance. The concept of the Late Westphalian order also seems useful, especially when we concentrate on the "bifurcation" or "fragmegration" of the international system. Based on research findings of the geopolitical dimension of energy security, an analysis of the Caspian region as a geoenergy space will not lose its importance. Undoubtedly, risk category is the conceptual basis of the future analysis of energy security in the Caspian region. On the one hand, risk (connected with uncertainty of the energy market) may cause a threat and, on the other, it may affect economic security through the emergence of alternative opportunities.

To sum up, taking into account the research conducted in the book, it seems that the connection between geopolitics and energy is gaining importance in contemporary international relations. Thus, it is recommended to develop this research area within scientific institutes and within the framework of political discourse in the regional and global dimension.

References

Documents

Asian Development Bank (2014). *Azerbaijan: Country Partnership Strategy (2014–2018)*. https://www.adb.org/documents/azerbaijan-country-partnership-strategy-2014 –2018.

Concept of the Republic of Kazakhstan for Transition to a Green Economy, Astana 2013. https://policy.asiapacificenergy.org/node/133.

Consolidated Version of the Treaty on the Functioning of the European Union (2016) Art. 194. *Official Journal of the European Union* C202/134. https://eur-lex.europa.eu /legal-content/EN/TXT/?uri=CELEX%3A12016E194.

Developing Europe's East (Remarks at conference). U.S. Department of State Archive. 1 November. US Department of State. http://2001-2009.state.gov/p/eur/rls/rm/94553 .htm.

Doing Business in Azerbaijan: A Country Commercial Guide for U.S. Companies (2008), International Trade Administration. https://www.trade.gov/azerbaijan -country-commercial-guide.

Energy Strategy of Russia for the period up to 2030. http://www.energystrategy.ru /projects/docs/ES-2030_(Eng).pdf.

Eurasian Development Bank (2012). *Ukraine and the Customs Union: Comprehensive assessment of the macroeconomic effects of various forms of the deep economic integration of Ukraine with member states of the Customs Union and the Common Economic Space* (Report 1). https://eabr.org/en/analytics/integration-research/cii-reports /a-comprehensive-assessment-of-the-macroeconomic-effects-of-various-forms-of -the-deep-economic-integr/.

European Bank for reconstruction and development (2014). European Commission (2010a). *Energy infrastructure: Commission proposes EU priority corridors for power grids and gas pipelines* (Press release IP/10/1512). https://ec.europa.eu/commission /presscorner/detail/en/IP_10_1512.

European Commission (2010b). *Communication from the Commission to the European Parliament, the Council, the European Economic and Social Committee and the Committee of the Regions: Energy infrastructure priorities for 2020 and beyond – A blueprint for an integrated European Energy Network* (Report COM (2010b) 677 final). https://eur-lex.europa.eu/legal-content/GA/TXT/?uri=CELEX:52010DC0677.

European Commission (2010c). *Communication from the Commission to the European Parliament, the Council, the European Economic and Social Committee and the Committee of the Regions: Energy 2020: A strategy for competitive, sustainable and secure*

energy (Report COM (2010) 639 final). November 10. Brussels. https://eurlex.europa
.eu/LexUriServ/LexUriServ.do?uri=COM:2010:0639:FIN:En:PDF.

European Commission (2011). *Communication from the Commission to the European Parliament, the Council, the European Economic and Social Committee and
the Committee of the Regions: On Security of Energy Supply and International
Cooperation – "The EU Energy Policy: Engaging with Partners beyond Our Borders"* (Report COM (2011) 539 final). https://eur-lex.europa.eu/legalcontent/EN
/TXT/?uri=CELEX%3A52011DC0539.

European Commission (2013a). *Communication from the Commission to the European
Parliament, the Council, the European Economic and Social Committee and the
Committee of the Regions* (Report COM (2013) 711 final). 14 October, Brussels.

European Commission (2013b) *European Commission welcomes decision on gas pipeline: Door opener for direct link to Caspian Sea* (Press release IP/13/623). Brussels:
European Commission.

European Commission (2014). *Communication from the Commission to the European Parliament and the Council: European Energy Security Strategy* (Report COM
(2014) 330 final). https://eur-lex.europa.eu/legal-content/EN/ALL/?uri=CELEX%3
A52014DC0330.

European Commission (2015). *Communication from the Commission to the European
Parliament, the Council, the European Economic and Social Committee, the Committee
of the Regions and the European Investment Bank: A framework strategy for a sustainable energy union based on forward-looking climate policies* (Report COM (2015) 80
final). https://eurlex.europa.eu/legalcontent/EN/TXT/?uri=COM%3A2015%3A80
%3AFIN.

European Commission–Council of the European Union (2022). EU–Azerbaijan
Cooperation Council, 19 July 2022. https://www.consilium.europa.eu/en/meetings
/international-ministerial-meetings/2022/07/19/.

Freedom Support Act, Pub. L. No. 102–511, § 907 (1992).

Iran and Libya Sanctions Act of 1996, H.R.3107 (1996). Retrieved September 13, 2023.
https://www.congress.gov/bill/104th-congress/house-bill/3107.

European Commission (2015). COMMUNICATION FROM THE COMMISSION TO THE
EUROPEAN PARLIAMENT AND THE COUNCIL on the short term resilience of
the European gas system Preparedness for a possible disruption of supplies from
the East during the fall and winter of 2014/2015 (Report COM/2014/0654 final/2).
https://eur-lex.europa.eu/legal-content/EN/TXT/?uri=CELEX:52014DC0654R(01).

Letter from President Trump to President Aliyev on the 26th anniversary of the Caspian
oil and gas show, May 30, 2019.

Ministry of Energy and Natural Resources (2009). The Republic of Turkey Strategic
Plan 2015–2019. https://policy.thinkbluedata.com/sites/default/files/Ministry%20
of%20Energy%20and%20Natural%20Resources%20%28MENR%29%20Strategic
%20Energy%20Plan%202015-2019%20%28EN%29.pdf.

Ministry of Energy of the Russian Federation (2007). National Security Concept of the Republic of Azerbaijan, May 23, 2007. www.azembassy.org.au/uploads/docs /Azerbaijan.pdf.

Ministry of Energy of the Russian Federation (2010a). *Energy strategy of Russia: For the period up to 2030.* http://www.energystrategy.ru/projects/docs/ES-2030_(Eng).pdf.

National Security Concept of the Republic of Azerbaijan (2007, May 23). https://www .files.ethz.ch/isn/154917/Azerbaijan2007.pdf.

North Atlantic Treaty Organization (2014, January 16). *Joint press point with NATO Secretary General Anders Fogh Rasmussen and the President of Azerbaijan, Ilham Heydar oglu Aliyev.* https://www.nato.int/cps/en/natohq/opinions_106145.htm.

North Atlantic Treaty Organization (2019). *Energy security: Operational highlights, vol. 12. https://enseccoe.org/data/public/uploads/2019/01/nato-ensec-coe-operational -highlights-no12.pdf.*

Opening speech by Ilham Aliev of the Cabinet of Ministers. http://ru.president.az /articles/29539.

Pakiet o Unii Energetycznej: bezpieczna, przystępna cenowo i zrównoważona energia. http://eur-lex.europa.eu/legal-content/PL/TXT/HTML/?uri=LEGIS-SUM:1801_7 &from.

Winter Package puts competitive sustainability at the heart of the European Semester. https://ec.europa.eu/commission/presscorner/detail/en/ip_20_320.

President Addresses American Legion, Discusses Global War on Terror, The White House (2006) 24 February. http://2001–2009.state.gov/r/pa/ei/wh/rem/62075 .htm.

President Donald J. Trump is unleashing American energy dominance, White House (2019), May 14.

President of the Republic of Azerbaijan, (n.d.). *Azerbaijan: Oil and gas projects.* https:// president.az/en/pages/view/azerbaijan/contract.

Republic of Azerbaijan, Ministry of Defense (2010). https://mod.gov.az/en/news -archive-141/

Republic of Azerbaijan, Ministry of Foreign Affairs (n.d.). https://www.mfa.gov.az/en.

Republic of Turkey Strategic Plan 2010–2014, Ministry of Energy and Natural Resources. http://www.enerji.gov.tr/yayinlar_raporlar_EN/ETKB_2010_2014_Stratejik_Plani _EN.pdf.

Republic of Turkey Strategic Plan 2015–2019, Ministry of Energy and Natural Resources. http://www.enerji.gov.tr/File/?path=ROOT%2fi%2fDocu- ments%2fStrategic+Plan %2fStrategicPlan2015–2019.pdf.

Republic of Turkey Strategic Plan 2019–2023, Ministry of Energy and Natural Resources. file:///C:/Users/admin/AppData/Local/Temp/2019–2023_Strate-jik_Plan%C4 %B1–1.pdf.

Strategy for Turkmenistan. https://www.ebrd.com/downloads/country/strategy/turk menistan.pdf.

Turkey's Energy Profile and Strategy. https://www.mfa.gov.tr/turkeys-energy-strategy
.en.mfa

United Nations Environment Programme (n.d.). *The Caspian Sea: The Tehran Convention*.
https://www.unep.org/explore-topics/oceans-seas/what-we-do/working-regional
-seas/regional-seas-programmes/caspian-sea.

World Bank (2015, November 23). *Social snapshot and poverty in Armenia – Main outcomes
of 2014 household integrated living conditions survey* (Press release). https://www
.worldbank.org/en/news/press-release/2015/11/23/social-snapshot-and-poverty
-in-armenia-main-outcomes-of-2014-household-integrated-living-conditions
-survey.

World Bank for Reconstruction and Development (2008). *Doing Business 2009:
Comparing regulation in 181 economies*. https://www.doingbusiness.org/content
/dam/doingBusiness/media/Annual-Reports/English/DB09-FullReport.pdf.

World Development Indicators: Energy Dependency, Efficiency and Carbon Dioxide
Emissions, Washington, DC, World Bank. 2017. https://wdi.worldbank.org/table/3.8.

Articles, Books, and Internet References

Abolhosseini, S., Hashmati, A., & Rashidghalam, M. (2017). Energy security and competition over energy resources in Iran and Caucasus region. *AIMS Energy, 5* (2),
224–238.

Abrams, M. A., & Narimanov, A. A. (1997). Geochemical evaluation of hydrocarbons
and their potential sources in the western South Caspian depression, Republic of
Azerbaijan. *Marine and Petroleum Geology, 14* (4), 451–468.

Acharya, A. (2007). The emerging regional architecture of world politics. *World Politics,
59* (4), 123–130.

Afanasyeva, A. (2019). *Kazakhstan to divert some oil flows from Europe to China*. Reuters, July 13, https://www.reuters.com/article/us-kazakhstan-china-oil-idUSKCN1
TY1W6/.

Agnew, J. (1986). *Western geopolitical thought in the twentieth century*. Routledge.

Akdoğan, Y. (2019). *Political leadership and Erdoğan*. Cambridge University Press.

Alcindor, Y. (2018). At NATO, Trump says Germany is "totally controlled by Russia."
PBS news Hour, July 11, https://www.pbs.org/newshour/politics/at-nato-trump-says
-germany-is-totally-controlled-by-russia#:~:text=%E2%80%9CGermany%20is%20
totally%20controlled%20by,its%20energy%20from%20the%20pipeline.

Alieva, L. (2012). Globalization, regionalization and society in the Caspian Sea Basin:
Overcoming geography restrictions and calamities of oil dependent economies.
Southeast European and Black Sea Studies, 12 (3), 443–453.

Aliyev, I. (2013, May 29). Opening speech by at the Azerbaijan–USA Forum Future
Vision. https://president.az/en/articles/view/8311.

Almaz, A. (2015). Testing the rentier state theory: The case of Azerbaijan. *Journal of Global Analysis*, 5 (1), 60–72.

Altunisik, M. B., & Tanrisever, F. O. (Eds.) (2018). *The South Caucasus: Security, energy and Europeanization*. Routledge.

Amineh, M. P., & Houweling, H. (2005). *Central Eurasia in global politics conflict, security, and development*. Brill.

Anceschi, L. (2017). Turkmenistan and the virtual politics of Eurasian energy: The case of the TAPI pipeline project. *Central Asian Survey*, 36 (4), 409–429.

Anceschi, L. (2019). Caspian energy in the aftermath of the 2018 Convention: The view from Kazakhstan and Turkmenistan, *Russian Analytical Digest*, 235, 6–8.

Andreev, F. A., Chirikov, A. B., & Timraliyev, Z. G. (2005). Economic problems of oil and gas resources development in the Republic of Kazakhstan. *Oil & Gas*, 4, 8–19.

Andrew, A. (2018, July 12). Kremlin accuses Trump of trying to bully Europe into buying U.S. LNG. *Reuters*. https://www.reuters.com/article/us-nato-summit-trump-kremlin-idUSKBN1K21A8/#:~:text=MOSCOW%20(Reuters)%20%2D%20The%20Kremlin,into%20buying%20American%20energy%20supplies.

Andrews-Speed P. (2012). *The governance of energy in China: Transition to a low-carbon economy*. Palgrave Macmillan.

Andrews-Speed, P., & Dannreuther, R. (2011). *China, oil and global politics*. Routledge.

Ang, B. W. (2015). LMDI decomposition approach: A guide for implementation. *Energy Policy*, 86, 23–25.

Arezki, R., & Matsumoto, A. (2017). *Shifting commodity markets in a globalized world*. International Monetary Fund.

Åslund, A. (2017). The three regions of the Old Soviet Bloc. *Journal of Democracy*, 28 (1), 89–101.

Assanbayev, M. B. (2016). Kazakhstan's energy policy on the eve of Kashagan oil field production. *Caucasus International*, 6 (2), 127–137.

Ataman, M. (2018). Editor's note. *Insight Turkey*, 20 (4), 89–101.

Auty, R. (1993). *Sustaining development in mineral economies: The resource curse thesis*. Routledge.

Auty, R. (2004). *Natural resources, governance and transition in Azerbaijan, Kazakhstan*. Routledge.

Babayeva, F. (2016, April 6). Legal status of Caspian Sea back on agenda. *Azernews*, https://www.azernews.az/nation/94732.html.

Baev, P. (1997). *Russia's policies in the Caucasus*. Royal Institute of International Affairs.

Baghishov, E. (2023, June 2). *Iran eyes to sign contract on gas import with Turkmenistan in coming days*. Trend News agency. https://en.trend.az/business/energy/3756509.html.

Bagirov, S. (2001). Azerbaijan's strategic choice in the Caspian region. In G. Chufrin, (Ed.) *The security of the Caspian Sea region* (389–400). Oxford University Press.

Bahgat, G. (2005). Energy security: The Caspian Sea. *Minerals & Energy*, 20 (2), 3–10.

Bahgat, G. (2006). Central Asia and energy security, *Asian Affairs*, 37 (1), 1–16.

Bahgat, G. (2010). Russia's oil and gas policy. *OPEC Energy Review, 3,* 162–183.

Bahr, K., Szarka, N., & Boeing, E. (2021). Renewable energy: A technical overview. In J. Emmons, A. Hanckock, & K. J. Hanckock (Eds.), The *Oxford handbook of energy politics* (125 - 150). Oxford University Press.

Bajrektarevic, A. H., & Posega, P. (2016). The Caspian Basin: Status related disputes, energy transit corridors and their implications for the EU energy security. *International Journal of Asia–Europe Relations, 1,* 237–264.

Bal, I. (2000). *Turkey's relations with the West and the Turkic Republics: The rise and fall of the "Turkish Model."* Routledge.

Balci, B., & Liles, T. (2018). Turkey's comeback to Central Asia. *Insight Turkey, 20* (4), 11–26.

Ball, J., Reicher, D., Sun, X., & Pollock, C. (2017). *The new solar system: China's evolving solar industry and its implications for competitive solar power in the United States and the world.* Stanford University Press.

Balmaceda, M., & Heinrich, A. (2019). The energy politics of Russia and Eurasia. In K. J. Hancock, & Allison, J. E. (Eds.), *The Oxford handbook of energy politics* (465–505). Oxford University Press.

Baogang, H. (1996). Dilemmas of pluralist development and democratization in China. *Democratization, 3* (3), 287–305.

Batyrov, A. B. (1994). Desertification control in Turkmenistan on the national and local level. *Problems of Desert Development, 4* (5), 102–106.

Baum, R. (1996). *Burying Mao: Chinese politics in the age of Deng Xiaoping.* Princeton University Press.

Bayramov, A. (2019). Great game visions and the reality of cooperation around post-Soviet transnational infrastructure projects in the Caspian Sea region. *East European Politics, 35* (2), 15–20.

Bayramov, A. (2022). *Constructive competition in the Caspian Sea region.* Routledge.

Beblawi, H. (1990). The rentier state in the Arab world. In G. Luciani (Ed.), *The Arab state* (23–34). Routledge.

Belopolsky, A., Talwani, M., & Berry, D. L. (1998). *Geology and petroleum potential of the Caspian region.* The Center for Political Economy and the James A. Baker III Institute for Public Policy, Rice University.

Bielecki, J. (2002). Energy security: Is the wolf at the door? *The Quarterly Review of Economic and Finance, 42* (2), 235–250.

Bieliszczuk, B. (2020). Załamanie cen ropy naftowej—konsekwencje gospodarcze i polityczne. *Biuletyn PISM, 71,* 1–2.

Bihun, U. (2018). Conceptualization of economic security in the context of energy markets' integration. *CES Working Papers, 10* (2), 161–181.

Birol, F. (2022, January 13). *Europe and the world need to draw the right lessons from today's natural gas crisis.* International Energy Agency https://www.iea.org/commentaries

/europe-and-the-world-need-to-draw-the-right-lessons-from-today-s-natural-gas-crisis.

Bisenov, N. (2018, October 28). Kazakhstan to double gas exports to China in 2019. *Nikkei Asian Review*. https://asia.nikkei.com/Business/Markets/Commodities/Kazakhstan -to-double-gas-exports-to-China-in-2019.

Blanche, E. (2008). Pipeline politics: Washington seems determined to wreck Iran's plan to build gas link to India and Pakistan. *Middle East, 393*, 22–25.

Blank, S. (2013). Russian defence policy in the Caucasus. *Caucasus Survey, 1 (1)*, 7–10.

Blank, S. (2014). Azerbaijan's expanding strategic perspective. *Central Asia–Caucasus Analyst*. https://www.cacianalyst.org/publications/analytical-articles/item/12930 -azerbaijans-expanding-strategic-perspective.html.

Błoński, M. (2013). Bezpieczeństwo energetyczne jako element systemu bezpieczeństwa zbiorowego Unii Europejskiej In Z. Lach (Ed.), *Bezpieczeństwo energetyczne wyzwaniem XXI wieku* (15 - 20). AON.

Boban, D., & Loncar, K. (2016). Geopolitical consequences of resolving the legal status of the Caspian Sea: Security and energy aspects. *Hrvatski Geografski Glasnik, 78* (2), 77–100.

Bodio, M. (2009). *Polityka energetyczna w stosunkach między Unią Europejską a Federacją Rosyjską w latach 2000–2008* [*Energy policy in relations between the European Union and the Russian Federation in 2000–2008*]. ASPRA.

Boersma, T., & Johnson, C. (2018). *US energy diplomacy*. Columbia Center on Global Energy Policy.

Bogaturov, A. D. (2011). *International relations in Central Asia: Events and documents*. University of California Press.

Bojanowicz, R. (2018, July 6). *Południowy Korytarz Gazowy z dofinansowaniem EBOR*. Biznes Alert. http://biznesalert.pl/oliticspoludniowy-korytarz-gazowy-z-dofinanso waniem-ebor/.

Bolukbasi, S. (1998). The controversy over the Caspian Sea mineral resources: Conflicting perceptions, clashing interests. *Europe–Asia Studies, 50* (3) 397–414.

BP (2012). *BP statistical world review of world energy June 2012*. https://www.laohamutuk .org/DVD/docs/BPWER2012report.pdf.

BP (2017). *BP statistical review of world energy, June 2017*. https://www.bp.com/content /dam/bp/business-sites/en/global/corporate/pdfs/energy-economics/statistical -review/bp-statistical-review-of-world-energy-2017-full-report.pdf.

BP (2018). *BP statistical review of world energy 2018*. https://www.bp.com/content/dam /bp/business-sites/en/global/corporate/pdfs/energy-economics/statistical-review /bp-stats-review-2018-full-report.pdf.

BP (2020) *Statistical review of world energy 2020*. https://www.bp.com/content/dam /bp/business-sites/en/global/corporate/pdfs/energy-economics/statistical-review /bp-stats-review-2020-full-report.pdf.

BP (2023). *BP energy outlook.* https://www.bp.com/content/dam/bp/business-sites /en/global/corporate/pdfs/energy-economics/energy-outlook/bp-energy-outlook -2023.pdf.

BP Azerbaijan (n.d.) *Baku–Tbilisi–Ceyhan Caspian Pipeline.* https://www.bp.com/en _az/azerbaijan/home/who-we-are/operationsprojects/pipelines/btc.html.

BP Azerbaijan (n.d.). Shah Deniz Stage 2. https://www.bp.com/en_az/azerbaijan /home/who-we-are/operationsprojects/shahdeniz/shah-deniz-stage-2.html.

BP Georgia (n.d.). *South Caucasus Pipeline Project.* https://www.bp.com/en_ge/georgia /home/who-we-are/scp.html.

Bresnahan, T., & Trajtenberg, M. (1995). General purpose technologies: "Engines of Growth"? *Journal of Econometrics, 65,* 83–108.

Bridge, G. (2015). Energy (in)security: World-making in an age of scarcity. *The Geographical Journal, 181 (4),* 328 - 339.

Brzeziński, Z. (1999). *Wielka szachownica.* Politeja.

Buchta, W. (2000). *Who rules Iran?* The Washington Institute.

Bulgaria as of January 1st, 2021 will start receiving Azeri gas (2021). https://www.cire .pl/artykuly/serwis-informacyjny-cire-24/178542-bulgaria-od-1-stycznia-2021-r -zacznie-otrzymywac-azerski-gaz.

Bun, D. A. (1999). Second advent. *Oil Gas Vertical, 1,* 12–24.

Butyrina E. G. (2013). Billions in Investment Basket. *Kazenergy, 6 (61),* 20–24.

Buzan, B. (1991). *People, States and Fear.* ECPR Press.

Buzan, B. (1997). Rethinking security after the Cold War. *Cooperation and Conflict, 32 (1),* 5–28.

Buzan, B., & Wæver, O. (2003). *Regions and powers: The structure of international security.* Cambridge University Press.

Buzan, B., Wæver O., & de Wilde J. (1998). *Security: A new framework for analysis.* Lynne Rienner.

Bystrova, A. K. (2009). *Problems of transport infrastructure and ecology in the Caspian Region.* IMEMO.

Calabrese, J. (2009). The Consolidation of Gulf-Asia Relations: Washington Tuned In or Out of Touch? *Policy brief: Middle East Institute, 25,* 1–12.

Campbell, C. J. (2001). Peak oil: A Turning for mankind. *Hubbert Center Newsletter, 2 (1).* 21–22.

Cannavo, P. F. (2011). Political theory and environmental ethics. In J. P. Tomain (Ed.), *Ending dirty energy policy: Prelude to climate change* (23–40). Cambridge University Press.

Carroll, T. (2012). The cutting edge of accumulation: Neoliberal risk mitigation, the Baku–Tbilisi–Ceyhan Pipeline and its impact. *Antipode, 44 (2),* 281–302.

Caspian oil and gas. Retrieved September 12, 2022, IEA. https://www.iea.org/reports /caspian-oil-and-gas.

Caspian Pipeline Consortium, (2021). Retrieved September 12, 2022, https://www.cpc.ru/EN/Pages/default.aspx.

Charlick-Paley, T., Williams, P., & Oliker, O. (2003). The evolution of Central Asia and South Caucasus: Implications for regional security. In O. Oliker & T. Szayna (Eds.), *Faultlines of conflict in Central Asia and the south Caucasus: Implications for the U.S. Army* (7–39). RAND.

Cherp, A., & Jewell, J. (2011). *Measuring energy security: From universal indicators to contextualized framework.* Routledge.

Chufrin, G. I. (2001). *The security of the Caspian Sea Region.* Oxford University Press.

Ciuta, F. (2010). Conceptual notes on energy security: Total or banal security?. *Security Dialogue, 41* (2), 123–144.

Clark, M. (2005, December 21). Beijing triumphs with inauguration of Kazakhstani crude pipe. *FUS Oil & Gas Monitor,* 120–136.

Coburn, T. C. (2021). Oil and gas infrastructure: A technical overview. In J. Emmons, A. Hanckock, & K. J. Hanckock (Eds.), *The Oxford handbook of energy politics* (99–124). Oxford University Press.

Cohen, S. B. (2003). *Geopolitics of the world system.* Rowman & Littlefield.

Collins, A. (2022). *Contemporary security studies.* Oxford University Press.

Colonomos, A. (2016). *Selling the future: The perils of predicting global politics.* Oxford University Press.

Committee of Statistics of the Republic of Kazakhstan, Fuel energy balance of Kazakhstan Statistical Publication, Astana, 2016. https://stat.gov.kz/en/industries/business-statistics/stat-energy/publications/75978/.ctrlstate%3Dghl9nvtkq8.

Contessi, N. (2017). European energy security and the governance of the Caspian Sea: An overview of dynamics and trends. In J. Novogrockiene & E. Siaulyte (Eds.), *Addressing emerging security risks for energy networks in South Caucasus* (25–40). IOS Press.

Correlje, A., & van der Linde, C. (2006). Energy supply security and geopolitics: A European perspective. *Energy Policy, 34* (5), 532–534.

Criekemans, D. (2017). Where geoeconomics and geostrategy meet: The troubled relations between the European Union and Russian Federation. In J. M. Munoz (Ed.), *Advances in geoeconomics* (113–120). Routledge.

Criekemans, D. (2018). Geopolitics of the renewable energy game and its potential impact upon global power relations. In D. Scholten (Ed.), *The geopolitics of renewables* (37 - 74). Springer.

Criekemans, D. (2022). "Geotechnical ensembles": How new technologies change geopolitical factors and contexts in economy, energy and security. In D. Criekemans (Ed.), *Geopolitics and international relations* (61–93). Brill.

Csurgai, G. (2022). The main components of geopolitical analysis. In D. Criekemans (Ed.), *Geopolitics and international relations* (13–61). Brill.

Cullen, R. (1999). The Caspian Sea. *National Geographic, 195* (5), 2–35.

Cullingworth, J. B. (1990). *Energy, land, and public policy.* Routledge.

Cutter, R. M. (2004, January 15). *Emerging triangles: Russia–Kazakhstan–China.* Oilgaseuropeasia. https://oilgaseuropeasia.com/energy-geopolitics/greater-central-asia/2004/01/emerging-triangle-russia-kazakhstan-china/.

Cutter, R. M. (2014). Chinese energy companies' relations with Russia and Kazakhstan. *Perspectives on Global Development and Technology, 13,* 673–698.

Cutler, R. M. (2019). The Trans-Caspian Gas Pipeline and its international Significance. *Geopolitics of Energy, 1,* 1–56.

Czaputowicz, J. (2006). Bezpieczeństwo w teoriach stosunków międzynarodowych. In K. Żukrowska, & M. Grącik (Eds.), *International security. Teoria i praktyka* (13–24). PWN.

Czarny, R. M. (2009). *Dylematy energetyczne państw regionu nordyckiego.* Scandinavium.

Dabelko, G. (2022). Environmental security. In A. Collins (Ed.), *Contemporary security studies* (100–248). Oxford University Press.

Dalby, S. (2001). *Environmental security.* University of Minnesota Press.

Daniloff, R. (1998). Waiting for the oil boom. *Smithsonian, 28* (10), 24–35.

Dannreuther, R. (2003). Bridging the Gulf? Iran, Central Asia and the Persian Gulf. *Review of International Affairs, 2* (4), 32–46.

Dannreuther, R. (2017). *Energy security.* Cambridge University Press.

Deitchman, B. H. (2016). *Climate and clean energy policy: State institutions and economic implications.* Routledge.

Dekmejian, R. H., & Simonian, H. H. (2003). *Troubled waters: The geopolitics of the Caspian region.* Routledge.

DeLuca, M. (1998). Caspian mobile rig clubs pick up slack in availability. *Offshore, 58,* 12–20.

Demirbas, A. (2008). Energy issues and energy priorities. *Energy Sources, Part B: Economics, Planning, and Policy, 3,* 41–49.

Dincer, I. (2001). Environmental issues: I-energy utilization. *Energy Sources, 23,* 69–81.

Dublaga, M. (2013). Bezpieczeństwo naftowe współczesnego świata—katalog zagrożeń. In Z. Lach (Eds.), *Bezpieczeństwo energetyczne wyzwaniem XXI wieku* (61- 70). PWN.

Duffield, J., & Birchfield, V. (2011). *Toward a common European Union energy policy. problems, progress, and prospects.* Palgrave Macmillan.

Duncan, P. J. S. (2018). Russia and the South Caucasus. In M. B. Altunisik & O. F. Tanrisever (Eds.), *The South Caucasus: Security, energy and Europeanization* (235–252). Routledge.

Dyczka, J. (2013). Terroryzm morski. In Z. Lach (Ed.), *Bezpieczeństwo energetyczne wyzwaniem XXI wieku* (pp. 73 - 80). PWN.

Ebel, R., & Menon, R. (2000). *Energy and conflict in Central Asia and the Caucasus.* Rowman & Littlefield.

Edinger, R., & Kaul, S. (2000). Humankind's detour toward sustainability: Past, present and future of renewable energies and electric power generation. *Renewable Sustainable Energy Review, 4,* 295–313.

Efegil, E. (2000). In the 21st century new world order and Turkey. In M. Tahiroglu & T. Y. Ismael (Eds.), *Turkey in the 21st century: Changing role in world politics?* (40–58). Routledge.

Emmons, J., Hanckock, A., & Hanckock, K. J. (2021). The politics of energy in a changing climate: An introduction. In J. Emmons, A. Hanckock, & K. J. Hanckock (Eds.), *The Oxford handbook of energy politics* (3 - 23). Oxford University Press.

Emmons, J., Parinandi, A., & Parinandi, S. (2021). The energy politics of the United States. In J. Emmons, A. Hanckock, & K. J. Hanckock (Eds.), *The Oxford Handbook of Energy Politics* (273- 407). Oxford University Press.

Engdahl, E. W. (2005, December 20). *China lays down the Gaguntlet in energy war.* http://www.engdahl.oilgeopoitics.net/Geopolitics/geopalitics.html.

European Bank for Reconstruction and Development (n.d.). *Kenkiyak–Atyrau Pipeline.* https://www.ebrd.com/work-with-us/projects/psd/kenkiyakatyrau-oil-pipeline.html.

European Commission (2012) *EU energy in figures 2012, EU energy in figures statistical pocketbook.* https://op.europa.eu/en/publication-detail/-/publication/4fbba65f -6690-4c3f-878a-e4ce0bc3515c/language-en/format-PDF/source-297192355.

European Commission—Directorate-General for Energy (2016). *EU energy in figures: Statistical pocketbook 2016.* https://data.europa.eu/doi/10.2833/670359.

European Commission—Directorate-General for Energy (2019). *EU energy in figures: Statistical pocketbook 2019.* https://data.europa.eu/doi/10.2833/197947.

European Commission—Directorate-General for Energy (2020). *EU energy in figures: Statistical pocketbook 2020.* https://data.europa.eu/doi/10.2833/29877.

Fairgrieve, J. (1915). *Geography and the world power.* University of London Press.

Fandrich, D. (2013). Nabucco Project "over" after Trans-Adriatic Pipeline (TAP) wins Azeri Gas bid. http://www.pipeline-conference.com/news/nabucco-project-over -after-trans-adriatic-pipeline-tap-wins-azeri-gas-bid.

Fedorov, Y. E. (1996) *Caspian oil and international security.* Cambridge University Press.

Feldpausch-Parker, A. M. (2022). Energy democracy: An introduction. In A. M. Feldpausch-Parker, D. Endres, S. L. Gomez, & T. Rai Peterson (Eds.), *Routledge handbook of energy democracy* (222–227). Routledge.

Fettweis, C. J. (2009). *No blood for oil: Why resource wars are obsolete.* In G. Luft & A. Korin (Eds.), *Energy security challenges for the 21st century* (67–80). RAND.

Firoozfar, A., Broomhead, E., & Dykes, A. (2012). Caspian sea level change impacts regional seismicity. *Journal of Great Lakes Research, 38,* 667–672.

Fitzpatrick, C. A. (2011, October 30). Turkmenistan beefs up Caspian presence, irritating Russia. *Eurasianet*, https://eurasianet.org/turkmenistan-beefs-up-caspian-presence-irritating-russia.

Flaherty, C., & Filho, W. (2013). Energy security as a subset of national security. In W. Filho & V. Voudouris (Eds.), *Global energy policy and security* (11–27). Springer.

Flint, C. (2017). *Introduction to geopolitics*. Routledge.

Frappi, C., & Garibov, A. (2014) *The Caspian Sea chessboard geo-political, geo-strategic and geo-economic analysis*. Egea.

Fredholm, M. (2011). Globalization and Eurasia's energy sector. *The Journal of Central Asian Studies*, *20*, 2–18.

Fridleifsson, I. B. (2001). Geothermal energy for the benefit of the people. *Renewable Sustainable Energy Review*, *5*, 99–312.

Froggatt, A., & Levi, M. A. (2009). Climate and energy security policies and measures: synergies and conflicts. *International Affairs*, *6*, 1129–1141.

Gadzhiev, K. S. (2010). *Caucasian knot in the geopolitical priorities of Russia*. Logos.

Garibov, A. (2018). Legal status of the Caspian Sea is finally defined what is next?. *Caucasus International*, *8* (2), 179–195.

Gartzke, E., Quan, L., & Boehmer, C. (2001). Investing in the peace: Economic interdependence and international conflict. *International Organization*, *55* (2), 391–438.

Gasparyan, A. (2019). Understanding the Nagorno-Karabakh conflict: Domestic politics and twenty-five years of fruitless negotiations, 1994–2018. *Caucasus Survey*, *7* (3), 235–250.

Gawlikowska-Fyk, A., & Terlikowski, M. (2018). *Energia i obronność w regionie nordycko-bałtyckim*, Polski Instytut Spraw Międzynarodowych, Norweski Instytut Spraw Międzynarodowych. PISM.

Gazprom confirms first gas via new TurkStream route to Turkey by Dec 31. (2019, May 14). *SP Global*. https://www.spglobal.com/commodityinsights/en/market-insights/latest-news/natural-gas/051419-gazprom-confirms-first-gas-via-new-turkstream-route-to-turkey-by-dec-31.

Geri, L. R., & McNabb, D. E. (2019). *Energy policy in the U.S. politics, challenges, and prospects for change*. Routledge.

German, T. (2018). The South Caucasus and European energy security. In M. B. Altunisik, & O. F. Tanrisever (Eds.), *The South Caucasus: Security, energy and Europeanization* (181–195). Routledge.

Gilpin, R. (1981). *War and change in world politics*. Cambridge University Press.

Gilpin, R. (2001). *Global political economy: Understanding the international economic order*. Princeton University Press.

Gils, E. (2020). *Azerbaijan and the European Union*. Routledge.

Glaser, C. (1997). The security dilemma revisited. *World Politics*, *50* (1), 171 - 201.

Goble, P. (2009). Azerbaijan's balanced foreign policy and the Muslim world. *Azerbaijan in the World*, *2* (12), 3–20.

Goldberg, J. (1998, October 4). Getting crude in Baku: The crude face of global capitalism. *The New York Times Magazine.* https://www.nytimes.com/1998/10/04/magazine/the-crude-face-of-global-capitalism.html.

Górecki, W. (2020a). Górski Karabach: kapitulacja Armenii, sukces Rosji. *Analizy OSW,* 1–12.

Górecki, W. (2020b). Kaukaski węzeł gordyjski. Konflikt o Górski Karabach. *Raport OSW.*

Górecki, W. (2022), Tension escalates in Nagorno-Karabakh. *OSW Analyses,* 1–13.

Gotev, G. (2018, May 8). Turkmenistan to tap into Southern Gas Corridor. *Euractiv.* https://www.euractiv.com/section/energy/news/turkmenistan-to-tap-into-southern-gas-corridor/.

Gradziuk, A., Lach, W., Posel-Częścik, E., & Sochacka, K. (2003). Co to jest bezpieczeństwo energetyczne państwa? In S. Dębski, & B. Górka-Winter (Eds.), *Kryteria bezpieczeństwa międzynarodowego państwa* (76–80). PWN.

Grison, N. R. (2013). NATO's energy security policy put to the Caspian test. *The Quarterly Journal, 1,* 83–94.

Grossman, G. M., & Helpman, E. (1991). *Innovation and growth in the global economy.* Cambridge University Press.

Gryz, J. (2018). Bezpieczeństwo energetyczne—związki między nauką, polityką a rzeczywistością. In J. Gryz, A. Podraza, & M. Ruszel (Eds.), *Bezpieczeństwo energetyczne. Koncepcje, wyzwania, interesy* (27–80). PWN.

Guliyev, F. (2019). Caspian energy producers in the "New Oil Order": Neglected by the West, *Looking East. Caucasus Analytical Digest, 112,* 2–8.

Gungormus, G. (2006). The social, political and economic problems Central Asian republics face and the role of Turkey in the Central Asian region. *Turkish Review of Eurasian Studies, 6,* 188–230.

Gurbanov, I. (2017, January 21). *Perspective for "Turkish Stream" Project: Possible scenarios and challenges.* Natural gas world. https://www.naturalgasworld.com/perspective-for-turkish-stream-project-possible-scenarios-and-challenges-35401.

Gurbanov, I. (2018). Caspian convention and perspective of Turkmenistan's gas export to Europe. *Caucasus International, 8* (2), 159–179.

Guseinov, V. A. (2010). *Central Asia: geopolitics and economics of the region.* Routledge.

Gyorgy, A. (1944). *Geopolitics.* University of Michigan Press.

Haas, M. (2007). The Shanghai Cooperation and the OSCE: Two of a kind? *Helsinki Monitor, 18*(3), 246–259.

Hajizada, M., & Marciacq, F. (2013). New regionalism in Europe's Black Sea region: The EU, BSEC and changing practices of regionalism. *East European Politics, 29* (3), 305–327.

Hall, G., & Grant, T. (2009). Russia, China and the Energy—Security politics of the Caspian Sea region after the Cold War. *Mediterranean Quarterly, 2,* 12–24.

Hall, S., & Sturrock, V. (2001). The tectonic control on the creation of supergiant fields in the Central and South Caspian area. *Bulletin of the Houston Geological Society, 43* (5), 12–15.

Hanckock, K. J., Palestini, S. & Szulecki, K. (2021). The politics of energy regionalism. In J. Emmons, A. Hanckock, & K. J. Hanckock (Eds.), *The Oxford handbook of energy politics* (173–197). Oxford University Press.

Harris, M. (2003). Energy and security. In M. Brown (Ed.), *Grave new world: Security challenges in the twenty-first century* (158–170). Georgetown University Press.

Hartshorne, R. (1939). *The nature of geography*. Oxford University Press.

Haydar Aliyev Foundation (2005). *The Khojaly Genocide*, Vol. 3: *True Facts about Garabagh*. Haydar Aliyev Foundation.

Heilmann, S. (2018). *Red Swan: How unorthodox policy-making facilitated China's rise*. The Chinese University of Hong Kong.

Heilmann, S., & Melton, O. (2013). The reinvention of development planning in China, 1993–2012. *Modern China, 39* (6), 580–628.

Heilmann, S., & Perry, J. (2011). Embracing uncertainty: Guerrilla policy style and adaptive governance in China. In S. Heilmann & E. J. Perry (Eds.), *Mao's invisible hand* (1–29). Cambridge University Press.

Heilmann, S., Shih, L., & Hofem, A. (2013) National planning and local technology zones: Experimental governance in China's torch programme. *The China Quarterly*, *21*, 896–919.

Heinonen, S., Karjalaien, J., Routsalainen, J., & Steinmuller, K. (2017). Surprise as the normal implications for energy security. *European Journal of Futures Research, 5* (12), 2–13.

Helpman, E. (1998). *General purpose technologies and economic growth*. Cambridge University Press.

Herzig, E. (2004). Regionalism, Iran and Central Asia. *International Affairs, 80* (3), 503–517.

Herzog, M., & Robins, P. (2014). *The role, position and agency of Caspian States in International Relations*. Routledge.

Hill, F., & Spector, R. (2001). The Caspian Basin and Asian energy markets. The Brookings Institution, Global Economics. https://www.brookings.edu/wp-content/uploads /2016/06/cro8.pdf.

Hilterman, J. R. (2005, January 18). Iran's nuclear posture and the scars of war. *MERIP: Middle East Research and Information Project*. https://merip.org/2005/01/irans -nuclear-posture-and-the-scars-of-war/.

Hoffmann, T., & Magierek, D. (2015). Polityka energetyczna Unii Europejskiej w wybranych teoriach badawczych. In J. Maj, P. Kwiatkiewicz, & R. Szczerbowski (Eds.), *Między ewolucją a rewolucją—w poszukiwaniu strategii energetycznej* (181–202). Fundacja na rzecz Czystej Energii.

Hongbin, C., & Treisman, D. (2006). Did government decentralization cause China's economic miracle?. *World Politics, 58* (4), 505–535.

Hornby, L. (2017, April 5). China's emergence as top US oil buyer highlights economic ties. *Financial Times.* https://www.ft.com/content/8a144f2e-19c8-11e7-a53d -df09f373be87.

Howell, S. (2009). Jia You! (Add Oil!): Chinese energy security strategy. In G. Luft & A. Korin (Eds.), *Energy security challenges for the 21st century* (191–219). RAND.

Hoyos, C. (2007). The new Seven Sisters: Oil and gas giants dwarf Western rivals. *Financial Times.* https://www.ft.com/content/471ae1b8-d001-11db-94cb-000b5df10621.

Hughes, L. (2019). The politics of energy and climate change. In K. J. Hancock & J. E. Allison (Eds.), *The Oxford handbook of energy politics* (343–370). Oxford University Press.

Hunter, S. (2003). Iran's pragmatic regional policy. *Journal of International Affairs, 56* (2), 133–147.

Huntington, S. P. (1997). *The clash of civilization and the remaking of world order.* Simon & Schuster.

Hurrell, A. (1995). Explaining the resurgence of regionalism in world politics. *Review of International Studies, 21* (4), 38–53.

Hurrell, A. (2005). The regional dimension in international relations Theory. In M. Farrell, B. Hettne, & L. Van Langenhove (Eds.), *Global politics of regionalism: Theory and practice* (331–358). Pluto Press.

Huseynzade, R., & Aliyev, A. (2016). Experience of Azerbaijan in construction of main oil and gas pipelines in the Caspian Sea region: Environmental aspects. In I. S. Zonn & A. G. Kostianoy (Eds.), *Oil and gas pipelines in the Black–Caspian Seas region* (169– 196). Springer.

ICGB Interconnector (n.d.) *IGB project.* https://www.icgb.eu/about/igb-project/.

Imangaliev, R. N. (2008). *Kazakhstan in the labyrinth of the world politics.* Institute of history of academy of Sciences of the Republic of Tajikistan.

Interfax (2023, May 29). *KazMunayGas, CNPC discuss expansion of Kenkiyak–Atyrau, Kenkiyak–Kumkol oil pipelines.* https://interfax.com/newsroom/top-stories/90922/.

International Energy Agency (n.d.a). *Low-emission fuels.* https://www.iea.org/energy -system/low-emission-fuels.

International Energy Agency(n.d.b). Oil market and Russian supply. https://www.iea .org/reports/russian-supplies-to-global-energy-markets/oil-market-and-russian -supply-2.

International Energy Agency (n.d.c). Azerbaijan energy profile: overview. https://www .iea.org/reports/azerbaijan-energy-profile/overview.

International Energy Agency (2008, November). *World energy outlook 2008.* https:// www.iea.org/reports/world-energy-outlook-2008.

International Energy Agency (2010). *World energy outlook 2010.* https://www.iea.org /reports/world-energy-outlook-2010.

International Energy Agency (2017). *Statistics energy balances*. https://doi.org/10.1787/world_energy_bal-2017-en.

International Energy Agency (2019, November). *World energy outlook 2019*. https://www.iea.org/reports/world-energy-outlook-2019.

International Energy Agency (2020). *Global Energy Review 2020: The impacts of the Covid-19 crisis on global energy demand and CO2 emissions*. https://www.iea.org/reports/global-energy-review-2020.

International Energy Agency (2022). *How Europe can cut natural gas imports from Russia significantly within a year*. https://www.iea.org/news/how-europe-can-cut-natural-gas-imports-from-russia-significantly-within-a-year.

International Energy Agency (2023, July). Oil market report – July 2023. https://www.iea.org/reports/oil-market-report-july-2023.

Ipek, P. (2009). Azerbaijan's foreign policy and challenges for energy security. *Middle East Journal, 63* (2), 228–239.

Iran to propose oil swap resumption to Kazakhstan (2015, July 13). *Financial Tribune*. https://financialtribune.com/articles/energy/21178/iran-to-pro-pose-oil-swap-resumption-to-kazakhstan.

Işeri, E. (2009). The US grand strategy and the Eurasian heartland in the twenty-first century. *Geopolitics, 14*, 26 — 46.

Islamova, P. (2015). Negotiations about the legal status of the Caspian Sea and impact of this process on local and regional energy security. *Turkish Studies, 10* (2), 483–490.

Ismayilov, M. (2019). Azerbaijan and Russia: Towards a renewed alliance, for a new era. *Caucasus Analytical Digest, 109*, 5–10.

Istrate, D. (2019, July 2). New Azeri pipeline ready to supply Europe with natural gas. *Emerging Europe*. https://emerging-europe.com/news/new-azeri-pipeline-ready-to-supply-europe-with-natural-gas/.

Ivanovich, D. (1998). Politics will draw route for oil pipeline out of Azerbaijan. *Houston Chronicle, 23*, 8–16.

Izimov R. Y. (2014, June 21). *Chinese TNC in Kazakhstan oil industry*. http://sayasat.org/arti-cles/962-kitajskie-tnk-v-kazahstanskoj-neftjanke.

Jafarova, E. (2017). The role of Azerbaijan in shaping regional cooperation for energy security. In J. Novogrockiene & E. Siaulyte (Eds.), *Addressing emerging security risks for energy networks in South Caucasus* (30–44). IOS Press.

Jakóbowski, J., & Marszewski, M. (2018). Kryzys w Turkmenistanie. Test dla polityki Chin w regionie. *OSW Komentarz, 08 (31)*, 1–13.

Jakubik, W. (2017, May 29). *Turkmenistan ma jedną dziesiątą gazu świata. Europa chce z niego skorzystać*. Biznes Alert. http://biznesalert.pl/turkmenistan-jedna-dziesiata-gazu-swiata-europa-chce-niego-skorzystac/.

Jarosiewicz, A. (2012). Południowy Korytarz Gazowy Azerbejdżanu i Turcji. *Komentarze OSW, 07 (18)*, 12–14.

Jarosiewicz, A. (2014). Start zmodyfikowanego Południowego Korytarza Gazowego. *Analizy OSW, 09 (24),* 14.

Jarosiewicz, A. (2015). Południowy Korytarz Gazowy. Azersko-turecki projekt w rozgrywce Rosji i UE. *Punkt Widzenia,* 54 (11), 12–16.

Jarosiewicz, A., & Lang, J. (2015). Turkmenistan patrzy na Zachód. *Analizy OSW, 04 (01),* 10–13.

Jewell, J. (2011). *The IEA Model of Short-term Energy Security (MOSES): Primary energy sources and secondary fuels OECD/IEA.* Working Paper, *2011 (17,)* 13–41.

Jewell, J., & Brutschin, E. (2021). The politics of energy security. In J. Emmons, A. Hanckock, & K. J. Hanckock (Eds.), *The Oxford handbook of energy politics* (249–275). Oxford University Press.

Kahneman, D., & Tversky, A. (1979). Prospect theory: An analysis of decision under risk. *Econometrica, 47* (2), 263–292.

Kalehsar, O. S. (2016). Iran–Azerbaijan energy relations in the post-sanctions era. *Middle East Policy, 23* (1), 136–142.

Kamenopoulos, S. N., & Tsoutsos, T. (2019). Assessment of renewable energy projects using a decision support system. In A. Flamos, H. Doukas, & J. Lieu (Eds.), *Understanding risks and Uncertainties in energy and climate policy* (223- 239). Springer.

Kandiyoti, R. (2008). What price access to the open seas? The geopolitics of oil and gas transmission from the trans-Caspian republics. *Central Asian Survey, 27* (1), 75–93.

Karagiannis, E. (2003). The Caspian oil market after regime change in Iraq, European Rim Policy and Investment Council. *Perihelion, 11,* 12–23.

Karatayev, M., Hall, S., Kalyuzhnova, Y., & Clarke, M. (2016). Renewable energy technology uptake in Kazakhstan: Policy drivers and barriers in a transitional economy. *Renewable and Sustainable Energy Reviews, 66,* 120–136.

Kassenova, N. (2009). Beyond enlargement and neighborhood policies: EU's Central Asia strategy. *EU 4 Seas Papers: Politics and Society,* 12–22.

Kaveshnikov, N. (2010). The issue of energy security In relations between Russia and the European Union. *European security, 19* (4), 585–605.

Keohane, R. O. (2002). *Power and governance in a partially globalized world.* Routledge.

Keohane, R. O. (1984). *After hegemony: Cooperation and discord in the world political economy.* Princeton University Press.

Keohane, R. O., & Nye, J. S. (2001). *Power and interdependence.* Taylor & Francis.

Kerimray, A., Baigarin, K., Bakdolotov, A., De Miglio, R., & Tosato, G. C. (2015). *Improving efficiency in Kazakhstan's energy system: Informing energy and climate policies using energy systems models insights from scenario analysis increasing the evidence base.* Springer.

Kerimray, A., Kolyagin, I., Suleimenov, B. (2018). Analysis of the energy intensity of Kazakhstan: From data compilation to decomposition analysis. *Energy Efficiency, 11,* 315–335.

Khan, M. H. (2020). Kazakhstan's energy policy, development, transformation and diversification. *Defence Journal*, *2*, 13–22.

Kissinger, H. (1982). *Years of upheaval*. Routledge.

Klare, M. T. (2008). *Energy security*. In P. D. Williams (Ed.), *Security studies: An introduction* (483–496). Routledge.

Klare, M. T. (2009). There will be blood: Political violence, regional warfare, and the risk of great-power conflict over contested energy sources. In G. Luft & A. Korin. *Energy security challenges for the 21st century* (44–66). RAND.

Kocon, M. (2013). Wpływ kultury energetycznej na bezpieczeństwo energetyczne kraju. Rynki energetyczne Litwy, Francji i Niemiec. In Z. Lach (Ed.) *Bezpieczeństwo energetyczne wyzwaniem XXI wieku* (120–138). PWN.

Koknar, A. M. (2009). The epidemic of energy terrorism. In G. Luft & A. Korin (Eds.), *Energy security challenges for the 21st century: A reference handbook* (18–26). RAND.

Kolchin, S. V. (1998). The Caspian oil and gas: The strategic interests of Russia. *World Economy and International Relations*, *3*, 97–103.

Koleski, K. (2017). *The 13th Five-Year Plan*. U.S.–China Economic and Security Review Commission.

Kolundzić, S. (2009). *Eurasia, energy cooperation or conflict? Part 2: Caspian Region, Oil and Geopolitics*, *2* (*23*), 203–212.

Konaev, E. N., & Nadir, N. K. (2001). Pipeline transport of Kazakhstan and the prospects for its development. *Oil & Gas*, *2*, 71–81.

Konisky, D. M. (2020). *Handbook of U.S. environmental policy*. Elgar.

Kosarev, A. N. (2005). Physico-geographical conditions of the Caspian Sea. In A. G. Kostianoy & A. N. Kosarev (Eds.), *The Caspian Sea environment* (5–31) Springer.

Kosarev, A. N., & Yablonskaya, E. A. (1994). *The Caspian Sea*. Pemberley.

Kosowska, K., Czarnota, R., Stopa, J., Wojnarowski, P., & Janiga, D. (2018). Azerbaijan facing new challenges on the energy market after the collapse of Soviet Union. *Section Oil and Gas Exploration*, 18 International Multidisciplinary Scientific Geo Conference SGEM, 267–274.

Kostka, G., & Nahm, J. (2017). Central–local relations: Recentralization and environmental governance in China. *The China Quarterly*, *231*, 567–582.

Koter, M., & Heffner, K. (1998). *Borderlands or Transborder regions: Geographical, social and political problems*. Silesian Institute.

Koukoudakis, G. (2017). EU energy security and Turkey's contribution to the Southern Energy Corridor. *Mediterranean Quarterly*, *28* (2), 34–39.

Kretov, P. (2013). Caspian Transport Consortium: Diary expansion. *Truboprovodnyi transportnefti*, *7*, 18–23.

Krüger, H. (2010). *The Nagorno-Karabakh conflict: A legal analysis*. Springer.

Kruse, F. (2014). *Oil politics: The West and its desire for energy security since 1950*. Anchor.

Kubicek, P. (2013). Energy politics and the geopolitical competition in the Caspian Basin. *Journal of Eurasian Studies, 4* (2), 171–180.

Kublik, A. (2018, June 13). *Kaspijski gaz u granic Europy. Nadchodzi konkurencja dla Gazpromu.* https://wyborcza.biz/biznes/7,179190,23531503,kaspijski-gaz-u-granic-europy-nadchodzi-konkurencja-dla-gazpromu.html

Kucera, J. (2006, April 13). Iran expanding ties with Central Asian states to counterbalance US geopolitical pressure. *Eurasia Insight.* https://eurasianet.org/iran-expanding-ties-with-central-asian-states-to-counterbalance-us-geopolitical-pressure.

Kucera, J. (2014, October 14). In Azerbaijan, Russian DefMin proposes "collective security"' on Caspian. *Eurasianet.* https://eurasianet.org/in-azerbaijan-russian-defmin-proposes-collective-security-on-caspian.

Kuchukova, N., Sadvokasova, K., Salykov, O., & Muhiyaeva, D. (2016). The improvement of the innovation development funding in the Republic of Kazakhstan with regard to international experience. *International Journal of Economic Perspectives, 10 (4),* 244–255.

Kupchan, C. (2005). Iranian beliefs and realities. *National Interest, 81,* 106–110.

Kurecić, P. (2015). The New Great Game: Rivalry of geostrategies and geoeconomies in Central Asia. *Hrvatski Geografski Glasnik, 72* (1), 21–46.

Kuzmina, E. M. (2007). *Geopolitics of Central Asia.* RAND.

Kyzym, M., & Rudyka, V. (2018). Analysis of the theoretical and methodological support of the study of energy security of the country. *Makroekonomika, 4 (5),* 18–23.

Labban, M. (2009). The struggle for the heartland: Hybrid geopolitics in the Transcaspian. *Geopolitics, 14,* 1–25.

LaCasse, C., & Plourde, A. (1995). On the renewal of concern for the security of oil supply. *The Energy Journal, 16*(2), 1–24.

Lakoff, A., & Collier, P. (2008). *Biosecurity interventions: Global health and security in question.* Columbia University Press.

Laruelle, M., & Peyrouse, S. (2009). The militarisation of the Caspian Sea: Great Games and Small Games over the Caspian fleets. *China and Eurasia Forum Quarterly, 7* (2), 17–35.

Leal-Arcas, R., Elemany Rios, J., & Grasso, C. (2015). The European Union and its energy security challenges: Engagement through and with networks. *Contemporary Politics, 21* (3), 273–293.

Legieć, A. (2019). Perspektywy rozwiązania konfliktu o Górski Karabach. *Biuletyn PISM, 168,* 2–12.

Legieć, A. (2020). Rozejm w Górskim Karabachu. *Komentarz PISM, 83,* 1–12.

Legucka, A. (2018). Uregulowanie statusu Morza Kaspijskiego. *Biuletyn PISM, 116* (1689), 1–3.

Leizerovich, E. E. (1968). *Economic-geographical issues of desert development.* MYSL.

Lerche, I., Bagiro, E., Nadiro, F., Tagiyev, M., & Guliyev, I. (1997). *Evolution of the South Caspian Basin: Geologic risks and probable hazards.* Springer.

Lesser, I. O. (1992). *Mediterranean security: New perspectives and implications for U.S. policy.* RAND.

Levit, D. (2016, June 29). Kazakhstan's Parliament approved changes into joint North Caspian Sea usage with Russia. *Economic Calendar,* 34–44.

Levy, J., & Jack, S. (2003). Applications of prospect theory to political science. *Synthese, 135* (2), 215–241.

Li, Y. (2018). *Governing environmental conflicts in China.* Routledge.

Lieberthal, K. (1992). Introduction: The "Fragmented Authoritarianism" model and its limitations. In K. Lieberthal & D. M. Lampton (Eds.), *Bureaucracy, politics, and decision making in post-Mao China* (1–32). Berkeley.

Lieberthal, K., & Oksenberg, M. (1988). *Policy making in China: Leaders, structures, and processes.* Princeton University Press.

Ling, C. (2010). Playing the market reform card: The changing patterns of political struggle in China's electric power sector. *The China Journal, 64,* 69–95.

Lixia, Y. (2021). *Energy security in times of economic transition: Lessons from China.* Emerald.

Loschel, A., & Rubbelke, U. (2010). Indicators of energy security in industrialized countries. *Energy Policy, 38,* 1665–1671.

Luft, G., & Korin, A. (2009). *Energy security challenges for the 21st century.* RAND.

Łukaszewski, J. (2020, December 17). Jest porozumienie w Górskim Karabachu. Gwarantem pokoju ma być Rosja. Ormianie są wściekli. *Gazeta Wyborcza.* https://wyborcza.pl/7,75399,26497098,erewan-i-baku-podpisaly-porozumienie -gwarantem-pokoju-w-gorskim.html.

Lynch, D. (2000). *Russian peacekeeping strategies in the CIS: The cases of Moldova, Georgia and Tajikistan.* Routledge.

MacFarlane, N. (2018). Regional powers and security in the Caucasus. In M. B. Altunisik & O. F. Tanrisever (Eds.), *The South Caucasus: Security, energy and Europeanization* (143–160). Routledge.

MacFarlane, S. N., & Weiss, T. (1992). Regional organizations and regional security. *Security Studies, 2* (1), 277–295.

Mack, O., Khare, A., Krämer, A., & Burgartz, T. (2015). *Managing in a VUCA world.* Routledge.

Mackenzie, R. (1993). The United States and the Taliban. In W. Maley (Ed.), *Fundamentalism reborn? Afghanistan and the Taliban* (13–34). Routledge.

Mackinder, H. (1919). *Democratic ideas and reality.* National Defense University.

Mahnovski, S. (2003). Natural resources and potential conflict in the Caspian Sea region. In O. Oliker & T. S. Szayna (Eds.), *Faultlines of conflict in Central Asia and the South Caucasus: Implications for the U.S. Army* (109–143). RAND.

Malek-Ahmadi, F., (2015). *Democracy and constitutional politics in Iran.* Springer.

Mammadov, F. (2017). Azerbaijan's geopolitical identity in the context of the 21st century challenges and prospects. V*aldai Discussion Club, 1,* https://eng.globalaffairs
.ru/articles/azerbaijans-geopolitical-identity-in-the-context-of-the-21st-century
-challenges-and-prospects/.

Mantel, R. (2016). Energy security strategy in Kazakhstan: Environmental security and renewable energy sources. *Caucasus International, 6* (2), 139–143.

Marketos, T. (2009). Eastern Caspian Sea energy geopolitics: A litmus test for the US–China–Russia struggle for the geostrategic control of Eurasia. *Caucasian Review of International Affairs, 3* (1), 2–4.

Marriott, J., & Minio-Paluello, M. (2013). *The oil road: Journeys from the Caspian sea to the city of London.* Springer.

Marszewski, M. (2018). Spóźniony podział Morza Kaspijskiego. *Analizy, 08* (22), 1–2.

Mcarthy, J. (2000). The geopolitics of Caspian oil. *Jane's Intelligence Review, 7,* 21–29.

McElroy, D. (2008, August 10). Georgia: Russia targets key oil pipeline with over 50 missiles. *The Telegraph.* http://www.telegraph.co.uk/news/worldnews/europe/georgia
/2534767/Georgia-Russia-targets-key-oil-pipeline-with-over-50-missiles.html.

Mcutcheon, H., & Osborn, R. (2001). Discoveries alter Caspian region energy potential. *Oil & Gas Journal, 99,* 18–25.

Mearsheimer, J. (2001). *The tragedy of Great Power politics.* Norton & Company.

Mehdiyoun, K. (2000). International law and the dispute over ownership of oil and gas resources in the Caspian Sea. *The American Journal of International Law, 94* (1), 179–189.

Menga, F. (2015). Building a nation through a dam: The case of Rogun in Tajikistan. *Nationalities Papers, 43* (3), 479–494.

Mertha, A. C. (2005). China's "soft" centralization: Shifting Tiao/Kuai authority relations. *The China Quarterly, 184,* 791–810.

Mesbahi, M. (1997). Iran and Tajikistan. *Europe–Asia Studies, 49* (4), 109–139.

Mikhamedzhanova, D. S. (2012). Influence of China on the economics of Central Asia. *Analytic, 2,* 74–82.

Miller, B. (2007). *States, nations, and the Great Powers.* Cambridge University Press.

Misiągiewicz, J. (2011). Działania Turcji wobec państw Azji Centralnej. Implikacje dla Unii Europejskiej. In A. Szymański (Ed.), *Turcja i Europa—wyzwania i szanse* (234–335). PWN.

Misiągiewicz, J. (2012a). Geopolitics and energy security in the Caspian region. *TEKA Komisji Politologii i Stosunków Międzynarodowych, 7,* 719–745.

Misiągiewicz, J. (2014b). The Caspian region and its significance for the energy security policy of China. *The Journal of China and the World* (in Chinese), 23–34.

Misiągiewicz, J. (2014a). Boundaries and energy security under dispute in the Caspian region. In *Border Conflicts in the Contemporary World* (234–335). UMCS.

Misiągiewicz, J. (2015). Teoria sekurytyzacji w analizie energetycznego wymiaru bezpieczeństwa międzynarodowego. In *Normy, wartości i instytucje we współczesnych stosunkach międzynarodowych* (393–448). PTSM.

Misiągiewicz, J. (2016). China's "One Belt, One Road" initiative: The perspective of the European Union. *Annales UMCS sec. Politologia, 23* (1), 34–45.

Misiągiewicz, J. (2017a). Bilans światowych zasobów surowcowych—główne wyzwania dla międzynarodowego bezpieczeństwa energetycznego. In M. Pietraś & J. Misiągiewicz (Eds.), *Bezpieczeństwo energetyczne we współczesnych stosunkach międzynarodowych. Wyzwania, zagrożenia, perspektywy [Energy security in the contemporary international relations: Challenges, threats, perspectives]* (261–281). UMCS.

Misiągiewicz, J. (2017b). The Caspian states perception of the conflict between the Ukraine and Russia. In K. Stokłosa & G. Besier (Eds.), *Neighbourhood Perceptions of the Ukraine Crisis* (345–358). Routledge.

Misiągiewicz, J. (2018). Strategia bezpieczeństwa energetycznego Unii Europejskiej. In J. Gryz, A. Podraza, & M. Ruszel s. (Eds.), *Bezpieczeństwo energetyczne. Koncepcje, wyzwania, interesy* (56–66). PWN.

Misiągiewicz, J. (2019a). Kazakhstan in the People's Republic of China's energy security policy. *Annales UMCS sec. Politologia, 26* (2), 34–45.

Misiągiewicz, J. (2019b). The Southern Gas Corridor infrastructure project—implications for the energy security of the European Union. *Rocznik Instytutu Europy Środkowo-Wschodniej, 17* (4), 44–56.

Misiągiewicz, J. (2022). *Polityki bezpieczeństwa energetycznego w regionie kaspijskim.* UMCS.

Misiągiewicz, J. (2012b). Turkey as an energy transit state between Asia and the European Union. In M. Pietraś, J. Misiągiewicz, & K. Stachurska-Szczesiak (Eds.), *Europejska Polityka Sąsiedztwa Unii Europejskiej* (234–250). UMCS.

Mitchell, T. (2011). *Carbon democracy: Political power in the age of oil.* Verso.

Młynarski, T. (2011). *Bezpieczeństwo energetyczne w pierwszej dekadzie XXI wieku. Mozajka interesów i geostrategii.* Wydawnictwo Uniwersytetu Jagiellońskiego.

Młynarski, T. (2017). *Bezpieczeństwo energetyczne i ochrona klimatu w drugiej dekadzie XXI wieku.* Wydawnictwo Uniwersytetu Jagiellońskiego.

Molchanov, M. A., & Yevdokimov, Y. (2004). Regime building as a prime mover of Technological progress: The energy sector in the Central Asia–Caspian region. *Perspectives on Global Development and Technology, 3* (4), 417–435.

Molo, B. (2008). Polityka bezpieczeństwa energetycznego Federacji Rosyjskiej. In E. Cziomer (Ed.), *Międzynarodowe bezpieczeństwo energetyczne w XXI wieku* (74–80). AFM.

Mori, A. (2019). Climate–energy policy: Domestic policy process, outcome and impacts. In A. Mori (Eds.), *China's climate-energy policy: Domestic and international impacts* (23–45). Routledge.

Motyashov, V. P. (2011). *Gas and geopolitics: Chance of Russia*. IOP Press.

Mouraviev, N., & Koulouri, A. (2019). *Security policy challenges and solutions for resource efficiency*. Springer.

Muñoz, G. (2008). Iran, a geopolitical player in the Middle East. *Mediterranean Yearbook, 3* (2), 22–23. https://www.iemed.org/publication/iran-a-geopolitical-player -in-the-middle-east/.

Myers, N. (1993). *Ultimate security: The environmental basis of political stability*. Routledge.

Nadirov, R. S., Bagirov, E., Tagiyev, M., & Lerche, I. (1997). Flexural plate subsidence, sedimentation rates, and structural development of the super-deep South Caspian Basin. *Marine and Petroleum Geology, 14* (4), 389–400.

Nahm, J. (2019). The energy politics of China. In K. J. Hancock & J. E. Allison (Eds.), *The Oxford handbook of energy politics* (507–533). Oxford University Press.

Nahm, J. (2021). The energy politics of China. In J. Emmons, A. Hanckock, & K. J. Hanckock (Eds.), The *Oxford handbook of energy politics* (506–534). Oxford University Press.

Nanay, J., & Smith Stegen, K. (2012). Russia and the Caspian region: challenges for transatlantic energy security?. *Journal of Transatlantic Studies, 10* (4), 343–357.

Narimanov, A., & Palaz, A. I. (1995). Oil history, potential converge in Azerbaijan. *Oil & Gas Journal, 93*, 32–39.

NATO in the Caucasus: The case of Azerbaijan (2014). https://www.atlanticcouncil.org /commentary/event-recap/nato-in-the-caucasus-the-case-of-azerbaijan-recap/.

NATO's role in energy security (2020). https://enseccoe.org/data/public/uploads/2017 /02/esoh-201302.pdf.

Neag, M. M., Halmaghi, E. E., & Cucuiet, P. (2017). Contributions on the determination of the relationship among globalization, sustainable development and energy security. *Scientific Bulletin, 22* (43), 24–29.

Neumann, I. (1994). A region-building approach to Northern Europe. *Review of International Studies, 20*, 53–74.

Nevolin, N. V., & Fedorov, D. L. (1995). Paleozoic pre-salt sediments in the Pre-Caspian petroliferous province. *Journal of Petroleum Geology, 18* (4), 453–470.

Newman, S. (2008). *The final energy crisis*. Pluto Press.

Nichol, J. (2014). Armenia, Azerbaijan, and Georgia: Political developments and implications for U.S. interests. *Current Politics and Economics of Russia, Eastern and Central Europe, 29* (2), 193–279.

Nincic, D. J. (2009). Troubled waters: Energy security as maritime security. In G. Luft & A. Korin (Eds.), *Energy security challenges for the 21st century* (31–44). RAND.

Nixey, J. (2012). The long goodbye: Waning Russian influence in the South Caucasus and Central Asia. Chatham House, Russia and Eurasia Programme. *Briefing Paper*, London.

Nuriyev, E. (2015, September 27). Russia, the EU and the Caspian Pipeline gambit. *Journal of Energy Security*. http://www.ensec.org/index.php?option=com_content&view =article&id=584:russia-the-eu-and-the-caspian-pipeline-gambit&catid=131:esupda tes&Itemid=414.

O'Byrne, D. (2018, March 16). European Investment Bank approves $1 billion funding for TANAP gas pipeline. *Eurasianet*. https://eurasianet.org/european-investment -bank-approves-1-billion-funding-for-tanap-gas-pipeline.

O'Byrne, D. (2023, June 20). Turkmenistan–Iran–Azerbaijan gas swaps surge. *Eurasi- anet*. https://eurasianet.org/turkmenistan-iran-azerbaijan-gas-swaps-surge.

O'Sullivan, S. (1996). *Gazprom: A strategic assessment*. MC Securities.

Okolo, J. E. (1985). Integrative and cooperative regionalism: The Economic Community of West African States. *International Organization, 39* (1), 121–153.

Oliker, O., & Shayna, T. S. (2003). Sources of conflict and paths to US involvement. In O. Oliker & T. Szayna (Eds.), *Faultlines of conflict in Central Asia and the south Caucasus: implications for the US Army* (307–352). RAND.

Omarova, S. (1998). Oil, pipelines, and the "scramble for the Caspian": Contextualizing the politics of oil in post-Soviet Kazakhstan and Azerbaijan. In P. Ciccantell & S. Bunker (Eds.), *Space and transport in the world system* (169–195). Routledge.

Organization for the Petroleum Exporting Countries (2021). *2021: World oil outlook* 2045. https://www.opec.org/opec_web/static_files_project/media/downloads/WOO _2021.pdf.

Organization for Security and Co-operation in Europe (n.d.). OSCE Minsk Group. http://www.osce.org/mg.

Pahlavi, P., & Hojati, A. (2010). Iran and Central Asia: The smart politics of prudent pragmatism. In E. Kavalski (Ed.), *The new Central Asia: The regional impact of international actors* (215–238). World Scientific Publishing Company.

Parker, G. (1998). *Military revolution: Military innovation and the rise of the West, 1500– 1800*. Cambridge University Press.

Parkhomchik, A. L. (2016). Kazakhstan Pipeline policy in the Caspian region. In I. S. Zonn & A. G. Kostianoy (Eds.), *Oil and gas pipelines in the Black–Caspian Seas region* (139–152). Springer.

Paul, T. V. (2012). *International relations and regional transformation*. Cambridge University Press.

Penerliev, M. (2012). Asian "energy players" and their role in the Balkan energy strategy. *Journal of Settlements and Spatial Planning, 3* (2), 2–4.

Perzyński, M. (2020). TANAP *oficjalnie otwarty w Baku*. Biznes Alert. https://biznesalert .pl/poludniowy-korytarz-gazowy-oficjalnie-otwarty-w-baku/.

Peyrouse, S. (2015). *Turkmenistan strategies of power, dilemmas of development*. Routledge.

Pietraś, M. (2000). *Bezpieczeństwo ekologiczne w Europie: studium politologiczne*. UMCS.

Pietraś, M. (2003). Bezpieczeństwo państwa w późnowestfalskim środowisku międzynarodowym. In P. Dębskis. & B. Górka-Winter (Eds.), *Kryteria bezpieczeństwa międzynarodowego państwa* (161–177) PISM.

Pietraś, M. (2006). Bezpieczeństwo międzynarodowe. In M. Pietraś (Ed.), *Międzynarodowe stosunki polityczne* (431- 450). UMCS.

Pietraś, M. (2008). Hybrydowość późnowestfalskiego ładu międzynarodowego. In M. Pietraś & K. Marzęda (Eds.), *Późnowestfalski ład międzynarodowy* (123–134). UMCS.

Pietraś, M. (2011). *Międzynarodowy reżim zmian klimatu.* Adam Marszałek.

Pietraś, M. (2017). Autonomiczność bezpieczeństwa energetycznego w stosunkach międzynarodowych. In M. Pietraś & J. Misiągiewicz (Eds.), *Bezpieczeństwo energetyczne we współczesnych stosunkach międzynarodowych. Wyzwania, zagrożenia, perspektywy. [Energy security in the contemporary international relations: Challenges, threats, perspectives]* (23–40). UMCS.

Pietraś, M. (2021). Bezpieczeństwo międzynarodowe. In M. Pietraś (Ed.), *Międzynarodowe stosunki polityczne* (437–450) UMCS.

Pietraś, Z. J. (1989). *Procesy adaptacji politycznej.* UMCS.

Piórko, K. (2008). Korporacje transnarodowe w globalnym sterowaniu ekologicznym. In M. Pietraś & K. Marzęda (Eds.), *Późnowestfalski ład międzynarodowy* (462- 470). UMCS.

Pirani, S. (2018). Let's not exaggerate: Southern Gas Corridor prospects to 2030. *OIES Paper*, Oxford Institute for Energy Studies. https://www.oxfordenergy.org/wpcms/wp-content/uploads/2018/07/Lets-not-exaggerate-Southern-Gas-Corridor-prospects to-2030-NG-135.pdf.

Polachek, S., Seiglie, C., & Xiang, J. (2012). Globalization and international conflict: Can foreign direct investment increase cooperation among nations? In M. R. Garfinkel & S. Skaperdas (Eds.), *The economics of peace and conflict* (736–755). Oxford University Press.

Pomfret, R. (2006). Resource abundance, governance and Economic performance in Turkmenistan and Uzbekistan. In R. Auty & I. de Soysa (Eds.), *Energy, wealth and governance in the Caucasus and Central Asia: Lessons not learned* (657–668). Routledge.

Poussenkova, N. (2010). The global expansion of Russia's energy giants. *Journal of International Affairs, 63* (2), 103–124.

Proedrou, F. (2017). A Framework for EU energy security: putting sustainability first. *European Politics and Society, 18* (2), 182–198.

Pronińska, K. (2006). Bezpieczeństwo energetyczne w stosunkach międzynarodowych— aspekty strategiczne. In E. Haliżak, R. Kuźniar, G. Michałowska, S. Parzymies, J. Symonides, & R. Zięba (Eds.), *Stosunki międzynarodowe w XXI wieku. Księga jubileuszowa z okazji 30-lecia Instytutu Stosunków Międzynarodowych Uniwersytetu Warszawskiego* (406- 422). Scholar.

Pronińska, K. (2011). Geopolityka surowców energetycznych—trendy globalne i regionalne po kryzysie finansowym. *Rocznik Strategiczny 2010–2011*, 262–270.

Pronińska, K. (2012). Nowe problemy bezpieczeństwa międzynarodowego: bezpieczeństwo energetyczne i ekologiczne. In R. Kuźniar, A. Bieńczyk-Missala, & R. Balcerowicz (Eds.), *Bezpieczeństwo Międzynarodowe* (306–320). PWN.

Rabinowitz, P. D., Yusifov, M. Z., Arnoldi, J., & Hakim, E. (2004). Geology, oil and gas potential, pipelines, and the geopolitics of the Caspian Sea region. *Development & International Law, 35*, 19–40.

Rakel, E. (2005). Paradigms of Iranian policy in Central Eurasia and beyond. In M. P. Amineh & H. Houweling (Eds.), *Central Eurasia in global politics conflict, security, and development* (235–256). Brill.

Raphael, S., & Stokes, D. (2022). Energy security. In A. Collins (Ed.), *Contemporary Security Studies* (340–368). Oxford University Press.

Raunek (2019, June 17). *How single point mooring (SPM) offshore operation works?*. Marine Insight. https://www.marineinsight.com/offshore/how-single-point-mooring -spm-offshore-operation-works/.

Razavi, H. (2007). *Financing energy projects in developing countries*. Pennwell Books.

Recknagel, C. (2002, April 25). Iran: Khatami tours Central Asia to press for Iran energy routes, lower US presence. *RFE/RL Weekday Magazine*, 22–27.

Riedel, R. (2010). Bezpieczeństwo energetyczne we współczesnej securitologii. In P. Mickiewicz & P. Sokołowska (Eds.), *Bezpieczeństwo energetyczne Europy Środkowej* (19–30). Adam Marszałek.

Rioran, S. (2019). *The geopolitics of cyberspace: A diplomatic perspective*. Brill.

Roberts, J. (1996). *Caspian pipelines*. The Royal Institute of International Affairs.

Roberts, J. (2018). Regional energy cooperation along Europe's Southern Energy Corridor. In M. B. Altunisik & O. F. Tanrisever (Eds.), *The South Caucasus—Security, energy and Europeanization* (84–90). Routledge.

Robins, P. (2014). A double gravity state: Turkish foreign policy reconsidered. *British Journal of Middle Eastern Studies, 33*(2), 199–211.

Rodionov, S. N. (1994). *Global and regional climate interaction: The Caspian Sea experience*. Springer.

Rogojanu, D. (2009). The role of Turkey in the energy security environment of the European Union. *Philobiblon, 14*, 622–640.

Ronek, G. (2017). Polityka bezpieczeństwa energetycznego Rosji. In M. Pietraś & J. Misiągiewics.z (Eds.), *Bezpieczeństwo energetyczne we współczesnych stosunkach międzynarodowych. Wyzwania, zagrożenia, perspektywy.* [*Energy security in the contemporary international relations: Challenges, threats, perspectives*] (161–185). UMCS.

Rosen, D., & Hanemann, T. (2009). *China's changing outbound foreign direct investment profile*. Policy Brief 9–14, Institute for International Economics. https://www.piie

.com/publications/policy-briefs/chinas-changing-outbound-foreign-direct-invest
ment-profile-drivers-and

Ross, M. L. (2008, May/June). Blood barrels: Why oil health fuels conflict. *Foreign Affairs*. 2–8.

Ross, M. L. (2012). *The oil course: How petroleum wealth shapes development of nations.* Princeton University Press.

Sachs, J. D., & Warner, M. (1995). Natural resource abundance and economic growth. *National Bureau of Economic Research Working Paper* 6398. Cambridge University Press.

Sadri, H. (1999). An Islamic perspective on non-alignment: Iranian foreign policy in theory and practice. *Journal of Third World Studies, 16* (2), 29–46.

Sagers, M. J., & Matzko, J. R. (1993). The oil resources of Azerbaijan: Survey and current developments. *International Geology Review, 35*, 1093–1103.

Sallis, D. (2003). Azerbaijan: Gateway to the newly independent states. *Euroinvest, 2*, 50–52.

Saramak, B. (2014). Bezpieczeństwo teleinformatyczne infrastruktury energetycznej państwa. In Z. Lach (Ed.), *Bezpieczeństwo energetyczne wyzwaniem XXI wieku* (147–160). PWN.

Schroeder, P. (1994). Historical reality versus neo-realist theory. *International Security, 19* (1), 108–148.

Schulz, M., Soderbaum, F., & Ojendal, J. (2001). *Regionalization in a globalizing world.* Bloomsbury.

Schwab, K. (2014). The global competitiveness report, 2014–2015. *World Economic Forum*, 22–34.

Schweller, R. (1994). Bandwagoning for profit: Bringing the revisionist state back. *International Security, 19* (1), 72–107.

Schweller, R. (1996). Neorealism's status quo bias: What security dilemma? *Security Studies, 5*(3), 90–121.

Seiple, C. (2004). Heartland geopolitics and the case of Uzbekistan. *Foreign Policy Research Institute, 3*, 22–30.

Sen, S., Khazanov, G., & Kishimoto, Y. (2011). Environment, renewable energy and reduced carbon emissions. *Radiation Effects & Defects in Solids, 166* (10), 834–842.

Senderov, S. M. (2019). Geopolitical features of energy security in the Caspian regions of Russia and Azerbaijan. *Geopolitics of Energy, 5*–11.

Sharipov, E. U. (2008). *Energy resources of the Caspian region and foreign relations of Kazakhstan and Turkmenistan in hydrocarbons.* CIS countries in the System of International Relations. Springer.

Sheppard, D., & Meyer, G. (2015, May 10). China oil imports surpass those of US. *Financial Times*. https://www.ft.com/content/342b3a2e-f5a7-11e4-bc6d-00144feab7de.

Shlapentokh, D. (2014). Dugin, Azerbaijan, and Russian energy strategy. *Central Asia, Caucasus Analyst*, 7–10.

Shneider, J., & Peeples, J. (2022). Energy dominance. In A. M. Feldpausch-Parker, D. Endres, S. L. Gomez, & T. Rai Peterson (Eds.), *Routledge handbook of energy democracy* (124–140). Routledge.

Shorokhov, V. V. (1997). Oil and policy of Azerbaijan. *Investigations of CCN MGIMO*, 9, 65–70.

Shulte, S., & Weiser, F. (2019). Natural gas transits and m Market power: The case of Turkey. *The Energy Journal*, 40 (2), 77–100.

Shumpeter, J. (1934). *The theory of economic development*. Cambridge University Press.

Siddi, M. (2019). The EU's botched geopolitical approach to external energy policy: The case of the Southern Gas Corridor. *Geopolitics*, 24 (1), 124–144.

Sikorski, T. (2011). Perspektywy realizacji gazociągu trans kaspijskiego. *Biuletyn PISM*, 50, 12–15.

Sil, R., & Katzenstein, P. (2010). Analytic eclecticism in the study of world politics: Reconfiguring problems in and mechanisms across research Traditions. *Perspectives on Politics*, 8 (2) 411 - 431.

Skinner, R. (2005). Energy security and producer–consumer dialogue: avoiding a Maginot mentality. http://www.oxfordenergy.org/wpcms/wp-content/up-loads/2011/02/Presentation31-Energy-Security-and-Producer-Consumer-DialogueAvoidinga MaginotMentality-RSkinner-2005.pdf.

Skjærseth, J.B., Eikeland, P. O., Gulbrandsen, L.H., & Jevnaker, T. (2016). *Linking EU climate and energy policies: Decision-making, implementation and reform*. Edward Elgar.

Sloan, G. (1999). Sir Halford J. Mackinder: The heartland theory then and now. *Journal of Strategic Studies*, 22, (15–38).

Snyder, J. (2000). *From voting to violence: Democratization and nationalist conflict*. Routledge.

SOCAR., https://www.socar.az/socar/en/home.

Socor, V. (2007). Gas discussions in Turkmenistan, Azerbaijan after the Budapest Nabucco Conference. *Eurasia Daily Monitor*, 4 (176), 24–30.

Sovacool, B. K., Scott Brown, M. A., & Valentine, S. V. (2016). *Fact and fiction in global energy policy: Fifteen contentious questions*. Johns Hopkins University Press.

Speight, J. G. (1996). *Environmental technology handbook*. Routledge.

Stachowiak, Z. (2006). Ekonomiczny wymiar bezpieczeństwa narodowego. In *Bezpieczeństwo narodowe Polski w XXI wieku* (386–400). Bellona.

State Statistical Committee of the Republic of Azerbaijan (2016). https://www.stat.gov.az/source/others/Entrepreneur.pdf.

Stern, J. (2002). *Security of European gas supplies*. Kluwer.

Stokes, D., & Raphael, S. (2010). *Global energy security and American hegemony*. Johns Hopkins University Press.

Strakes, J. (2015). Azerbaijan and the non-aligned movement: Institutionalizing the "Balanced Foreign Policy" doctrine. *IAI Working Papers*. http://www.iai.it/sites/default/files/iaiwp1511.pdf.

Suny, R. G. (2007). Living in the hood: Russia, empire, and old and new neighbors. In R. Legvold (Ed.), *Russian foreign policy in the twenty-first Century and the shadow of the past* (35–76). Routledge.

Svyatets, E. (2016). *Energy security and cooperation in Eurasia: Power, profits and politics.* Routledge.

Syroezhkin, K. L. (2010). *Kazakhstan–China: From border trade to strategic partnership.* Institute of Strategic Research by President of the Republic Kazakhstan.

Tanrisever, F. O. (2014). Ukraine as a cusp state: Politics of reform in the borderlands between the EU and Russia. In M. Herzog & P. Robins (Eds.), *The role, position and agency of cusp states in international relations* (60–79). Routledge.

Tekin, A., & Walterova, I. (2007). Turkey's geopolitical role: The energy angle. *Middle East Policy, 14* (1), 123–134.

Ter-Petrossian, L. (2018). *Armenia's future, relations with Turkey, and the Karabagh Conflict.* Springer.

Terterov, M. (2018). The energy charter as a framework for intergovernmental cooperation in the energy markets of the South Caucasus states. In M. B. Altunisik, & O. F. Tanrisever (Eds.), *The South Caucasus: Security, energy and Europeanization* (213–230). Routledge.

Tordo, S., Tracy, B. S., & Arfaa, N. (2018). National oil companies and value creation. *World Bank Working Paper 218.*

Tosun, J., Schulze, K., Biesenbender, S. (2015). *Energy policy making in the EU: Building the agenda.* Springer.

Trans Adriatic Pipeline (TAP), Italy, Greece. http://www.hydrocarbons-technology.com/projects/trans-adriatic-pipeline-italy-greece/.

Treisman, D. (2010). Is Russia cursed by oil?. *Journal of International Affairs, 63* (2), 85–102.

Tuathail, O. G., & Dalby, S. (1998). *The geopolitics reader.* Routledge.

Ulatowski, R. (2017). Rola Narodowych Koncernów Naftowych we współczesnym reżimie rynku ropy naftowej. In M. Pietraś & J. Misiągiewicz (Eds.), *Bezpieczeństwo energetyczne we współczesnych stosunkach międzynarodowych. Wyzwania, zagrożenia, perspektywy. [Energy security in the contemporary international relations: Challenges, threats, perspectives]* (67–87). UMCS.

Ulman, R. H. (1983). Redefining security. *International Security, 8* (1), 129–153.

United Nations Conference on Trade and Development (2005). *World Investment Report 2005: Transnational Corporations and the Internationalization of R&D.* United Nations. https://unctad.org/system/files/official-document/wir2005_en.pdf.

US Energy Information Administration (2015). https://www.eia.gov/conference/2015/.

Van de Graaf, T., & Bradshaw, M. (2018). Stranded wealth: Rethinking the politics of oil in an age of abundance. *International Affairs, 94* (6), 1309–1328.

Verrastro, F., & Ladislaw, S. (2007). Providing energy security in an interdependent world. *The Washington Quarterly.* https://relooney.com/NS4053-Energy/0-Energy -Security_22.pdf.

Vostokov, E. N. (1997). Destabilization of the natural environment of the Caspian region in connection with development of the fuel-power resources. RF Ministry of Natural Resources. *Geoinformmerk, 3,* 76 -88.

Voytolovsky, G. K., & Kosolapov, N. A. (1999). *Peculiarities of the geopolitical situation in the Caspian region. Europe and Russia: Problems of the Southern Direction. Mediterranean–Black Sea–Caspian.* Springer.

Walt, S. (1987). *Origins of alliances.* Cornell University Press.

Walt, S. (2005). *Taming American power.* Routledge.

Waltz, K. (1979). *Theory of international politics.* Addison-Wesley.

Wasserman, S., & Faust, K. (1994). *Social network analysis: Methods and applications.* Cambridge University Press.

Weigert, H. (1942). *Generals and geographers.* SAGE.

Weingast, B., Jin, H., & Qian, Y. (2005). Regional decentralization and fiscal incentives: Federalism, Chinese style. *Journal of Public Economics, 89,* 1719–1742.

Where India's and China's energy consumption is heading. (2016, November 24). *The Economist.* https://www.economist.com/special-report/2016/11/24/where-indias -and-chinas-energy-consumption-is-heading.

Whittlesey, D. (1939). *The earth and the state.* SAGE.

Winrow, G. (2006). Possible consequences of a new geopolitical game in Eurasia on Turkey as an emerging energy transport hub. *Turkish Policy Quarterly, 5* (2). https:// www.esiweb.org/pdf/esi_turkey_tpq_id_62.pdf.

Winrow, G. (2014). Realization of Turkey's energy aspirations. *Turkey Project Policy Paper, 4* (3). https://www.brookings.edu/wp-content/uploads/2016/06/Turkeys -Energy-Aspirations.pdf.

World Bank (n.d.a). The World Bank in Kazakhstan https://www.worldbank.org/en /country/kazakhstan/overview#3.

World Bank (n.d.b). The World Bank in Turkmenistan. https://www.worldbank.org/en /country/turkmenistan/overview.

World Bank (2015). Turkmenistan Partnership Program snapshot. http://documents .worldbank.org/curated/en/904321485161087742/World-Bank-Group-Turkmenistan -partnership-program-snapshot.

World Bank (2021). Russia economic report 46. https://www.worldbank.org/en/country /russia/publication/rer.

World Bank (2022a). Islamic Republic of Iran. https://www.worldbank.org/en/country /iran/overview.

World Bank (2022b). China Economic Update – June 2022. https://www.worldbank .org/en/country/china/publication/china-economic-update-june-2022.

World Bank (2023b). Priority reforms key for sustaining growth and achieving China's long-term goals. https://www.worldbank.org/en/news/press-release/2023/06/14 /priority-reforms-key-for-sustaining-growth-and-achieving-china-s-long-term -goals-world-bank-report.

World Economic Forum (2013) Energy vision–Energy transitions: Past and future (Report REF 070113). http:// www3.weforum.org/docs/WEF_EN_IndustryVision.pdf.

Wyciszkiewicz, E. (2008). *Geopolityka rurociągów. Współzależność energetyczna a stosunki międzypaństwowe na obszarze postsowieckim.* PISM.

Xuanli Liao, J. (2006). A Silk Road for oil: Sino-Kazakh energy diplomacy. *Brown Journal of World Affairs*, 12 (2), 44–59.

Xuanli, J. (2015). The Chinese government and the National Oil Companies (NOCs): Who is the principal? *Asia Pacific Business Review*, 21 (1), 44–59.

Xuetang, G. (2006). The energy security in Central Eurasia: The geopolitical implications to China's energy strategy. *China and Eurasia Forum Quarterly*, 4 (4), 117–131.

Yergin, D. (2006). Ensuring energy security. *Foreign Affairs*, 85 (2), 69–82.

Yergin, D. (2011). *The quest: Energy, security, and the remaking of the modern world.* Penguin.

Yorucu, V., & Özay, M. (2018). *The Southern Energy Corridor: Turkey's role in European energy security.* Springer.

Zamnitskaya, H., & von Geldern, J. (2011). Is the Caspian Sea a sea: And why does it matter? *Journal of Eurasian Studies*, 2 (1), 1–14.

Zeinolabedin, Y., Yahyapour, M. S., & Shirzad, Z. (2009). Geopolitics and environmen tal issues in the Caspian Sea. *Caspian Journal of Environmental Science*, 7 (2), 113–121.

Zhiltsov, S. S. (2009). *Rivalry in energy resource export and regional security in Central Asia/Central Asia in conditions of geopolitical transformation and global economic crisis.* Institute of Strategic Research of Kazakhstan.

Zhiltsov, S. S. (2016). *Russia's policy toward the pipeline transport in the Caspian region: Results and prospects.* In I. S. Zonn & A. G. Kostianoy (Eds.), *Oil and gas pipelines in the Black–Caspian Seas region* (345–400). Springer.

Zhiltsov, S. S., & Grishicheva, O. G. (2016). Chinese pipeline projects in the Caspian region. In I. S. Zonn & A. G. Kostianoy (Eds.), *Oil and gas pipelines in the Black– Caspian Seas region* (105–117). Springer.

Zhiltsov, S. S., Kostianoy, A. G., Zonn, I. S., & Kostianaia, E. A. (2016). Geographic characteristics of the Black–Caspian Seas region. In I. S. Zonn & A. G. Kostianoy (Eds.), *Oil and gas pipelines in the Black–Caspian Seas region* (23–45). Springer.

Zhiltsov, S. S., Zonn I. S., Semenov A. V. (2016). Hydrocarbon potential of the Caspian Region. In I. S. Zonn, A. G. Kostianoy (Eds.), *Oil and gas pipelines in the Black– Caspian Seas Region.* (7–37). Springer.

Zonenshain, L. P., Kuzmin, M., & Natapov, K. (1990). Summary of the tectonic development of the USSR territory. In B. M. Page (Eds.), *Geology of the USSR* (Chapter XIV) (206–224). American Geophysical Union.

Zonenshain, L. P., & LePichon, X. (1986). Deep basins of the Black Sea and Caspian Sea as remnants of Mesozoic back-arc basins. *Tectonophysics, 123*, 181–211.

Zonn, I. S. (1999). *Caspian: illusions and reality.* Springer.

Zonn, I. S., & Kostianoy, A. G. (2016). Environmental risks in production and transportation of hydrocarbons in the Caspian–Black Sea region. In I. S. Zonn & A. G. Kostianoy (Eds.), *Oil and gas pipelines in the Black–Caspian Seas region* (211–225). Springer.

Zonn, I. S., & Semenov, A. V. (2016). Iranian direction of hydrocarbon transport: Present state and difficulties. In I. S. Zonn & A. G. Kostianoy (Eds.), *Oil and gas pipelines in the Black–Caspian Seas region* (23–45). Springer.

Zonn, I. S., & Zhiltsov, S. S. (2008). *New Caspian: Geography, economics, politics.* Delta.

Zonn, I. S., Zhiltsov, S. S., & Semenov, A. V. (2016). Hydrocarbon potential of the Caspian region. In I. S. Zonn & A. G. Kostianoy (Eds.), *Oil and gas pipelines in the Black–Caspian Seas region* (123–140). Springer.

Index

Absheron Peninsula   83
Aktobe   150, 182, 216, 219, 238, 245
Alan Collins   29, 31
Alashankou   182, 216, 240, 241
Alborz/Alov field   83
Aliyev   107, 108, 119, 126, 127, 135, 136, 140, 141,
    143, 161, 162, 212–216, 221–225, 228, 267,
    282–284, 294, 295
Amoco   26, 27, 113, 141, 171, 210, 214, 222, 237
Amu-Darya   106
André Plourde   48
Andrew Warner   11
Anthony Giddens   258
Apsheronian Peninsula   135, 155, 212, 229
Araz–Alov–Sarq fields   115
Ariel Colonomos   252
Armenia   77, 115, 118–127, 129, 130, 140, 162,
    203, 224, 231, 236, 284, 303, 309
Asia Pacific Energy Research Centre   48
Astrakhan   82, 83, 88, 92, 165, 167, 218
Astrakhan Summit   82
Azerbaijan   2, 3, 26–28, 39, 75, 77–81, 83, 84,
    86, 88–90, 93–95, 101, 103–105, 107, 108,
    110, 111, 113–127, 129–145, 151, 159, 161,
    162, 171, 174, 190, 192, 202–205, 210–215,
    220–226, 228, 230, 231, 233, 234, 236,
    247–249, 263–265, 267, 269, 270, 273,
    276, 281–285, 287, 288, 292, 295–299,
    301, 303, 304, 307–309

Baku   2, 77, 82, 83, 88, 89, 94, 107, 108, 115,
    117, 129, 135, 136, 139, 141, 142, 163, 202,
    212–215, 220–226, 230, 232, 266, 288,
    293, 304
Baku Summit   82
Baku–Tbilisi–Ceyhan   94, 141, 215, 221, 224,
    266, 288
Barry Buzan   10, 30
Benjamin Miller   10, 130
Berdymuhamedov   158
Black Sea   4, 79, 92, 94, 112–114, 134, 202, 211,
    213, 216, 219, 220, 222, 224, 228, 284, 293,
    310, 312
black swan   252
Blue Stream   161

Bosphorus   61, 211, 221, 224
bottlenecks   61
BP   3, 12, 25, 27, 28, 90, 92, 109, 110, 115, 137,
    141, 142, 168, 171, 174, 178, 180, 185, 194,
    195, 210, 214, 222, 225, 226, 229, 266,
    287, 288
British Petroleum   2, 27, 28, 109, 115, 233
Bugrinsky   165

Caspian Basin   12, 13, 26, 70, 77–82, 84, 90,
    92, 95, 99, 106, 107, 111–113, 115–117, 138,
    149, 150, 154, 161, 169, 171, 221, 230, 274,
    277, 286, 294, 299, 300, 303
Caspian energy   4, 11, 42, 111, 112, 209, 224,
    269, 271, 285, 293
Caspian Pipeline Consortium   216–220, 289
Caspian region   1–7, 10–13, 15, 16, 26–28, 33,
    35, 36, 38, 39, 42, 43, 45, 46, 50, 57–59,
    69, 70, 72–77, 80, 81, 83, 86, 87, 90,
    92–118, 124, 129–136, 138–141, 146, 152,
    153, 160–162, 169–176, 181–184, 190, 193,
    201–206, 208, 209, 211, 213, 219–223, 230,
    233, 237, 239, 242, 247, 249, 263–265,
    267–279, 285, 286, 290, 301–304, 307,
    310, 311, 312
Caspian Sea   3, 44, 70, 77–79, 81–96, 101,
    106–108, 111–115, 138–140, 154, 155, 157,
    165, 167, 169, 171, 174, 207, 209, 213, 215,
    221, 226, 229–232, 234, 246, 263, 266,
    267, 273, 274, 282, 284–287, 289, 290,
    292, 293, 295, 296, 298–301, 306, 311, 312
Caucasus   2–4, 13, 64, 73, 88, 92, 93, 97,
    98, 100, 103, 105, 106, 112, 113, 118, 120,
    122–124, 127, 129, 139, 150, 160, 169,
    184, 203, 209, 223, 226, 248, 284, 285,
    287–293, 296, 300, 301, 303–306,
    308, 309
Central Asia   2–4, 13, 17, 27, 54, 73, 93,
    96–98, 100, 101, 103–106, 112, 113, 139,
    141, 146, 152, 169, 175, 181, 182, 184, 202,
    205, 207, 216, 239, 243–246, 248, 263,
    279, 285–287, 289–291, 293, 294, 297,
    299–306, 308, 311
Central Caspian   107, 155
Chantale LaCasse   48

Cheleken   154, 155

Chevron   25–27, 113, 142, 150, 210, 218, 233, 263, 266

China   3, 4, 6, 12, 13, 22, 25, 26, 55, 57, 58, 70, 75, 93–95, 97–101, 103, 104, 111, 130–133, 151, 152, 156, 158, 159, 169, 170, 176–184, 186, 205, 206, 210, 212, 230, 237–247, 263, 266, 267, 273, 275, 279, 284–287, 290, 291, 293–295, 298–303, 306, 307, 309, 310, 311

China National Oil Company   237

Chirag fields   82, 116, 213

CO2 emission   35, 36

Cold War   2, 5, 8, 9, 32, 49, 71, 93, 97, 99, 100, 102, 133, 134, 160, 161, 209, 262, 288, 293

Commonwealth of Independent States   95, 134, 162

contract of the century   27, 39, 141, 161, 214, 222, 224

Convention on the Law of the Sea   62, 79, 84

Copenhagen Peace Research Institute   7, 30

Covid-19   52, 53, 55, 65, 66, 68, 178, 260, 296

Daniel Yergin   47, 49, 51

David Criekemans   6, 38, 259

Deniz   108, 138, 139, 142, 192, 204, 215, 225, 226, 228, 266, 288

Diversification   17, 34, 35, 151, 201

Donald J. Trump   60, 283

downstream   33, 94, 134, 184, 264

Economic Research Institute   33

Energy corporations   26, 228

Energy culture   19

energy demand   29, 30, 48, 52, 53, 57, 66, 68, 178, 253, 296

energy infrastructure   1, 4, 7, 11, 17, 22, 25, 29, 48–50, 62, 77, 96, 98, 100, 101, 103, 104, 105, 117, 133, 161, 167, 168, 173, 181, 188, 198, 201, 203, 216, 239, 247, 249, 250, 263, 274, 275, 277

energy market   2, 4–9, 11, 13, 15, 17, 18, 20–22, 25, 26, 29, 30, 32, 33, 37–43, 46, 47, 49–52, 54–56, 58, 60, 64–66, 68–70, 94, 97, 102, 106, 111, 114, 130–133, 137, 141, 143, 145, 157, 167–169, 175, 186–188, 190, 197–202, 204, 205, 207, 212, 222, 231–233, 240, 243, 249, 260, 262–265, 267, 270–280, 298

energy markets   2, 21, 40, 42, 49, 54, 65, 143, 177, 193, 207, 271, 286, 294, 309

energy resources   1–5, 7–10, 12, 13, 15–17, 19, 22, 25, 26, 29, 32, 35, 37–41, 43, 45, 47, 48, 50–52, 54–58, 61, 62, 64–67, 69, 70, 76–78, 80, 94, 96–98, 100, 101, 103–106, 108, 112–115, 124, 130, 133, 135–141, 143, 145, 150, 154, 157, 158, 161, 163, 168, 169, 174–176, 181, 182, 184–187, 190, 192–195, 197, 201, 202, 204–207, 209, 213, 218, 221, 237, 240, 242, 247, 253, 255, 263–265, 267, 268, 270, 271, 273, 275, 277, 284

energy sector   7, 10, 17, 20, 24, 26, 28, 29, 39, 40, 42, 45, 48, 49, 51, 53, 58, 65, 68, 94, 102, 103, 108, 113, 132, 135, 141, 144, 150, 157, 158, 167–169, 177, 180, 183, 186, 187, 190, 197, 200, 202, 212, 219, 221, 222, 236–238, 240, 242, 244, 246, 247, 249, 250, 255, 257, 258, 264, 265, 269–271, 275, 278, 292, 302

energy security   1–8, 11–13, 15–22, 25, 26, 28–36, 38–51, 53, 55, 57, 60, 61, 64, 66, 68–70, 77, 81, 87, 99, 100, 103, 115, 130–133, 135, 138, 141, 143–146, 149–151, 153, 156–158, 160, 163, 167–169, 171, 174–177, 180, 181, 184, 186, 187, 190, 192, 193, 195, 196, 198, 201, 202, 204, 205, 207, 209, 230, 237, 245, 246, 249, 250, 253–256, 258, 259, 261, 264, 265, 271–279, 283–286, 289–303, 305–311

Energy transformation   253, 257–259

Eurasia   2, 7, 93, 96–98, 100, 103, 104, 106, 130, 139, 145, 176, 242, 246, 275, 277, 285, 286, 292, 298, 299, 301, 303, 306, 308, 309, 310, 311

European Commission   21, 105, 134, 194–198, 200, 201, 203, 204, 281, 282, 291

European Energy Security Strategy   198, 282

European integration   21

European Union   4, 13, 21, 105, 131, 133, 134, 159, 184, 187, 192, 194, 195, 197, 198, 201–203, 207, 226, 275, 281, 282, 287, 289, 290, 292, 297, 299, 302, 306

Exclusive Economic Zone   79

ExxonMobil   25, 26, 27, 113, 142, 263, 266

Fatih Birol   197, 261

flat peak   56

gas   2, 4–6, 9, 16–19, 26, 27, 32, 34–36, 39–41,
        43, 46, 51, 53, 59–61, 64–67, 78, 83, 84,
        86, 90, 92–96, 99, 103, 105, 106, 108–110,
        113, 123, 124, 130, 133, 135, 137–146,
        148–163, 165, 167, 171, 173–178, 181–186,
        190–200, 202–205, 207, 209, 211–213,
        215, 216, 221, 225, 226, 228–231, 234–236,
        238–240, 242–249, 253, 255–257, 259,
        261–265, 267, 269, 270, 273, 275–277,
        281–283, 285–289, 291–293, 295–298,
        301, 304, 306, 308, 311, 312
Gazprom   26, 158, 159, 162, 167, 183, 197, 210,
        216, 231, 292, 304
Geoeconomics   37
geo-energetic   4, 5, 36, 37
geo-energy   7
Geopolitical   6, 37, 38, 51, 91, 101, 209, 259,
        287, 307
Geopolitics   6, 36, 37, 40, 91, 289, 290, 291,
        293, 296, 298, 299, 301, 307, 308, 311
Georgia   64, 77, 111, 114, 118, 124, 130, 140, 144,
        160–162, 210, 212, 214, 222–226, 229, 231,
        236, 247, 288, 300, 301, 303
Globalisation   7
Great Game   4, 74, 93, 96, 98, 99, 104, 130, 131,
        169, 247, 277, 299
great transaction   9, 39
greenhouse   8, 19, 32, 46, 66, 67, 195, 199, 200,
        253, 255, 256, 257, 259
Greg Mattson   28
Gunashli   108, 138, 139, 141, 214, 215
Gunther Oettinger   204
Gyula Csurgai   36

Halford J. Mackinder   96, 308
Heartland   96, 97, 103, 176, 307
Henry Kissinger   16, 42

idealists   9, 39
India   3, 22, 57, 159, 175, 178, 267, 287, 310
International Energy Agency   12, 16, 22,
        52–55, 57–59, 64, 65, 109, 137, 138, 145,
        146, 165, 177, 179, 185, 193, 259, 286,
        295, 296
International Oil Companies   25
international organizations   8, 12, 15, 16, 21,
        25, 28, 38, 74, 162, 173, 221, 250, 254
international security   11, 12, 15, 21, 28, 37, 47,
        69, 127, 274, 288, 291

Iran   2, 3, 6, 12, 18, 23, 59, 64, 70, 75–84, 86,
        87, 90–95, 98, 100–102, 105, 109, 111,
        113, 115–117, 123, 130, 132, 135, 140, 144,
        151, 158, 159, 161, 169–175, 179, 183, 206,
        210–212, 224, 229, 231–238, 262, 263, 273,
        282, 284, 285, 287, 288, 290, 294–297,
        299, 301, 303, 304, 306, 310
Israeli–Arab War   23
Iver Neumann   73

James R. Schlesinger   68
Janusz Bielecki   48
Jarosław Gryz   19
Jeffrey Sachs   11
Joe Biden   60, 264
John Agnew   92
John Mearsheimer   74, 254
José Manuel Barosso   204
Joseph Nye   7, 42, 274

Karabakh   70, 76, 77, 114, 115, 118–129, 135, 139,
        140, 226, 231, 274, 276, 292,
        293, 298
Karachaganak   107, 149, 150, 205, 245
Karl Haushofer   92
Karpinsky Belt   107
Kashagan   107, 109, 149–151, 182, 205, 220,
        241, 245, 246, 266, 285
Kazakhstan   3, 26, 59, 78 81, 83, 84, 86, 88,
        93–95, 101, 103, 107, 109–111, 113, 116–118,
        132, 133, 137, 140, 145–153, 173, 176, 177,
        179, 181, 182, 205, 206, 209–211, 215,
        216, 218–222, 224, 225, 229, 232–234,
        237–247, 263, 264, 266, 269, 273, 281,
        284, 285, 287, 289, 290, 295–300, 302,
        304, 307, 309–311
Kazakhstan–China pipeline   240, 241
KazMunaiGaz   151, 182, 245, 266
KazTransGas   216
Kenkiyak–Atyrau   219, 239, 267, 291, 295
Khojaly   119, 294

late-Westphalian   251, 264
liberal theory   9

Mahoud Ahmadinejad   172
Mangyshlak   106, 148
Marek Pietraś   14, 21, 28, 47
Marion King Hubbert   55

Maritime Transportation Security Act   61
Michael T. Klare   9
Middle East   2, 26, 35, 55, 92, 98, 102, 104, 124,
    184, 204, 207, 222, 229, 262, 264, 287,
    288, 294, 296, 297, 303, 309
Model of Short-Term Energy Security   33
Moscow Protocol   90
Muhammad Khatami   171

National Oil Fund   142
NATO   3, 22, 70, 98, 103, 104, 134, 161, 163, 257,
    283, 284, 293, 303
Neka–Tehran pipeline   232, 234
Nobel   2, 136, 154, 212
Norman Myers   257
North Caspian   88, 106, 111, 150, 151, 167, 220,
    246, 300
North Sea   55, 70, 109, 114, 193
North Ustyurt   106
Novorossiysk   211, 213–216, 218–221, 234, 266

oil   2, 4–6, 8, 9, 16–20, 22, 23, 25–28, 32, 35,
    36, 39–41, 43, 44, 46, 48, 50–65, 67,
    77, 79, 80, 84, 86, 90, 92–96, 99, 103,
    105–110, 113, 115, 116, 123, 124, 130, 132,
    133, 135–157, 159, 161, 165–167, 169, 171,
    173–179, 181–186, 189, 190, 193–196,
    202–207, 209–216, 218–222, 224, 225,
    228, 230–234, 237–241, 245–249,
    259–264, 265, 266, 269, 270, 273,
    275–277, 282, 284–286, 288, 290,
    291, 295–299, 301, 302, 304, 306, 307,
    309–311
oil shock   16, 22, 64
Ole Wæver   10
Organisation for Economic Co-operation and
    Development   18
Organization of the Petroleum Exporting
    Countries   23

Pakistan   3, 175, 210–212, 236, 267, 287
peak regions   3, 10, 11, 72
Persian Gulf   54, 58, 64, 70, 156, 169, 174,
    232–235, 290
Pipeline geopolitics   132
post-Westphalian   250
Production Sharing Agreements   27
Promyslovskoye   165

Realists   38, 254
regionalism   9, 70–72, 278, 293–295, 304
Richard Armitage   171
Richard Auty   11
Richard Ullman   257
Rimland   97
risk category   42, 279
Robert Ebel   61
Robert Gilpin   254
Robert Keohane   7, 42, 274
Robert Skinner   49
Royal Dutch Shell   2, 25, 27, 115, 136, 150
Rudolph Kjellén   91
Russia   2–4, 6, 12, 17, 18, 58, 60, 64, 66, 70,
    74–84, 86–89, 91, 93–107, 109, 111, 114–
    118, 120–124, 126, 127, 130–133, 135–137,
    140, 141, 143–145, 151, 152, 156, 158–170,
    175, 179, 181, 183, 184, 190, 192, 193, 195,
    197, 201–203, 205–207, 209–211, 213–216,
    218–222, 224–226, 231, 233–235, 241, 242,
    244–248, 260, 262, 264, 266, 273–275,
    277–279, 281, 283–286, 290, 292, 293,
    296–298, 300–305, 307, 309–311

Saparmurat Niyazov   243
Sardar Jangal field   82
Saudi Arabia   18, 23, 25, 59, 165, 179, 214, 260
securitization   7, 8, 11, 30–33, 69, 278
Seven Sisters   26, 295
Shah Deniz   139, 226
South Caspian   106, 111, 155, 284, 293,
    300, 303
Southern Gas Corridor   142, 143, 159, 190,
    203, 204, 226, 228– 231, 247, 265, 293,
    302, 305, 308
Soviet–Iranian Sea   77
Soviet Union   2, 3, 26, 77, 78, 98, 112, 133, 136,
    181, 298
State Oil Corporation of Turkey   186
Statoil   27, 141, 210, 214, 226, 229, 263
Stepanakert   120, 129
Supsa   220, 222, 223
Supsie   213

Tabriz   232, 234, 235
Tehran Agreement   84
Tengiz   107, 149, 150, 205, 211, 216, 218–220,
    232–234, 266

Trans-Caspian Gas Pipeline   83, 86, 89, 91,
      159, 230, 264, 267, 290
Trans-Caspian Pipeline   77, 87, 88, 117, 141,
      163, 220, 230, 263, 267
Transport infrastructure   60
Turkey   3, 6, 13, 27, 72, 76, 77, 94, 95, 98,
      100–102, 105, 111, 113, 117, 118, 123, 124,
      127, 130, 133, 134, 143, 144, 152, 161, 162,
      169, 184–192, 204, 207, 210, 212, 214, 221,
      224–226, 228, 229, 231, 232, 234–236,
      247, 266, 273, 282–286, 291–293, 298,
      302, 306, 308–311
Turkish Oil Corporation   27
Turkish straits   213
Turkish Stream   192, 231, 293
Turkmenistan   3, 26, 75, 77–79, 81–84, 86,
      88–90, 93–95, 102, 110, 111, 113–117, 132,
      133, 142, 151, 153–159, 163, 173, 175–177,
      183, 184, 191, 192, 202, 205, 206, 209–212,
      215, 221, 229–237, 242–245, 247, 263,
      264, 266, 267, 269, 270, 273, 283, 285,
      286, 292, 293, 296, 297, 304, 305, 307,
      308, 310

Ukraine   5, 58, 60, 63, 64, 66, 72, 99, 118, 131,
      135, 145, 161, 163, 168, 196–198, 203, 206,
      207, 226, 249, 261, 263, 264, 274, 275,
      277, 279, 281, 302, 309
United Nations Conference on Trade and
      Development   23, 309
United States   4, 8, 32, 113, 134, 165, 286,
      291, 300
upstream   33, 65, 94, 134, 184, 264
Ural   93, 107, 148, 165, 216
US Department of Energy   53, 108

Volga   79, 92, 93, 114, 117, 150
Volga–Don Canal   79
VUCA   251–253, 261, 265, 271, 275, 279, 300

Washington Energy Conference   16
wealth paradox   10
West   8, 32, 39, 75, 94, 95, 98–100, 103, 114,
      123, 126, 131, 141, 160, 161, 165, 168–172,
      181, 206, 208, 211, 222, 234, 236, 242, 247,
      263, 267, 286, 293, 298, 304
Wild cards   252

Zbigniew Brzeziński   3, 98, 100

www.ingramcontent.com/pod-product-compliance
Lightning Source LLC
Chambersburg PA
CBHW070555270326
41926CB00013B/2320